TAIWAN

Acknowledgement

No travel book could be written without the help of countless friends and fellow travelers. My sincere thanks to Dirk Bennett, Mike Boydell, Andy Brown, Nik Gould, Ben Lim, Ann Mooney, Eileen Mooney, Dirty Roger, Richard Vuylsteke, and Earl Wieman. I would also like to thank the Council for Cultural Planning and Development, the Tourism Bureau, and the editors of *Echo*, the *Free China Review*, *Sinorama*, and *Travel in Taiwan*.

Paul Mooney is an American journalist who has lived and worked in Asia for 12 years, including eight in Taiwan. He first came to Taiwan in 1974 to study Mandarin Chinese at Fu Jen University and returned to Taipei in the mid 1980s to work as special correspondent for a number of international publications. In 1990 he moved to Hong Kong as a freelance journalist.

Nigel Hicks has spent eight years in Asia living in Hong Kong, Japan and Taiwan. Currently based in Hong Kong, he writes and photographs for a number of magazines, is a Fellow of the Royal Geographical Society and a Licentiate of the Royal Photographic Society. He has travelled widely in Taiwan and in 1989 climbed the island's highest peak, Yushan (3997 meters).

The transliteration of Chinese names in this book is normally given in Wade-Giles except when referring to the People's Republic of China when *pinyin* is used. Chinese characters for names and addresses of hotels, restaurants and shops are provided in the listings under 'Practical Information'. Names of all the sights and other places described in the book are also given in Chinese characters in the Index.

TAIWAN

Paul Mooney
Photography by Nigel Hicks

Hong Kong

Distribution in the United Kingdom, Ireland, Europe and certain Commonwealth countries by
Hodder & Stoughton, Mill Road, Dunton Green, Sevenoaks, Kent TW13 2YA

British Library Cataloguing-in-Publication Data
A catalogue record for this book is available from the British Library

Grateful acknowledgement is made to the following authors and publishers for permission granted:

RENDITIONS, a Chinese–English translation magazine (Hong Kong: The Chinese University of
Hong Kong, Research Centre for Translation), No 23 (Spring 1985), pp84–103 for
The Ugly Chinaman by Bo Yang, translated by Don J Cohn

Indiana University Press for
"The Rain from the Sun" by Li Yung-P'ing translated by Candace Pong and Robert Eno
© 1983 by Indiana University Press/Bloomington

M E Sharpe Inc for
"Mountain Road" by Chen Yingzhen translated by Rosemary Haddon
© 1991 by M E Sharpe Inc, Armonk, New York

Editor: Paddy Booz
Series Editor: Anna Claridge
Illustrations Editor: Caroline Robertson
Design: B/W Graphics
Map Design: Bai Yiliang

Photography by Nigel Hicks
Additional photography courtesy of: Department of Kuomintang Party History, Taipei 22, 23, 26, 27, 29, 30, 32, 33, 187; Hanart T Z Gallery 111; Hsiung Shih Art Books Co Ltd 161; the National Palace Museum 139; Outdoor Life Publishing Company 49, 100, 121, 160, 339; Wattis Fine Art 20

Production by Twin Age Limited, Hong Kong
Printed in Hong Kong by Sing Cheong Printing Co Ltd

The National Theater, Taipei

Contents

Maps

Special Topics

Excerpts

Introduction

The Physical Setting

Shaped like a tobacco leaf, Taiwan lies 160 kilometers off the coast of mainland China, separated from Fujian Province by the Taiwan Straits. The northern tip is 1,000 kilometers south of Japan, and the southern tip 350 kilometers north of the Philippines. The total land area is 36,000 square kilometers and the island is 394 kilometers long and 144 kilometers wide at its widest point. Taiwan is bisected by the Tropic of Cancer. Mountains and hills cover two-thirds of its surface.

The island is surrounded by some 20 smaller islands considered to be geologically linked to it. Taiwan also claims jurisdiction over the Pescadores (Penghu) Islands, the islands of Quemoy and Matsu near the mainland, Orchid Island, Green Island and a few islands in the South China Sea. All of the land under Taiwan's jurisdiction is also claimed by the People's Republic of China, which regards Taiwan as one of its provinces.

Some geologists argue that Taiwan was once part of the Asia mainland. More recent geological studies, however, suggest that the island rose from the sea relatively recently, around a million years ago.

Climate

Taiwan's best months are during the brief spring and autumn. The island's subtropical climate has an average annual temperature of 21°C (71.2°F) in the north and 24°C (75.7°F) in the south. Summer months (May–October) are hot and humid, sometimes punctuated by daily flash showers. The winter is short, but January and February are often cold enough to bring snow to the mountains. Summer temperatures hover around 30°C (86°F) and winter temperatures can drop to as low as 5°C (41°F).

The island's average annual rainfall is 100 inches, with marked regional variation. As a result of its proximity to the Asian land mass and its position in the world's largest ocean, Taiwan's winds are monsoonal and seasonal. May to October is typhoon season. These storms can be very severe and frequently cause building and crop damage, and flooding. If a typhoon warning has been announced, it is advisable to avoid travelling to outlying areas, which are sometimes cut off for several days after severe storms.

Flora and Fauna

Taiwan's lowland plains and valleys are rich in alluvial soil. The soil in the uplands and at higher elevations is leached, acid and infertile, and has been seriously eroded. Much of the soil is volcanic, or partly volcanic, and remains fertile despite centuries of farming.

The variations in soil quality, elevation, and climate have given the island a wide diversity of flora. One-third of the more than 190 plant families and nearly 4,000 species are considered indigenous.

No less than 60 different mammals have been found in Taiwan, of which 45 are native species. The largest predatory mammal is the Formosan black bear. Foxes, flying foxes, deer, wild boar, bats and squirrels live in the less populated parts of the island. There are 330 species of birds and more than 65 species of reptiles and amphibians. Snakes are found all over the island and 13 species are said to be poisonous.

The People

Taiwan has a population of slightly over 20 million and is one of the most densely populated areas in the world, with 533 persons per square kilometer. The population can be divided into four ethnic groups: aborigines, Taiwanese, Hakkas and mainland Chinese.

Aborigines
The aborigines, said to be of Indonesian or Malayan origin, are classified into ten tribes, with the Ami, Atayal, and Paiwan accounting for 85 per cent of their population. There are an estimated 300,000 aborigines in Taiwan, accounting for less than 1.5 per cent of the total population. When the first Chinese immigrants arrived on the island some 1,000 years ago, they drove the lowland aborigines into the mountains where many continue to live in inaccessible and less developed mountain areas. While the government has given them special privileges and protection from Chinese buyers and developers, the aborigines have been left behind by Taiwan's economic miracle and are beset by serious social problems which are threatening their survival. With a birthrate that is lower than that of other ethnic groups in Taiwan, and with increasing intermarriage with Chinese, it is not likely that the aborigines will escape assimilation.

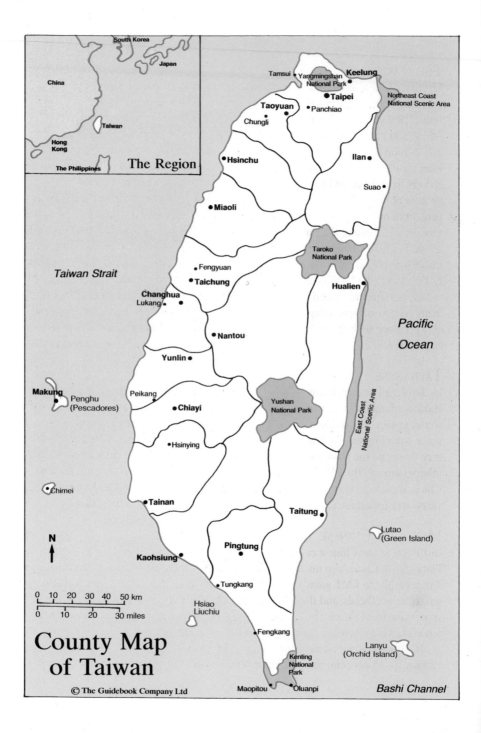

The Region

County Map
of Taiwan

© The Guidebook Company Ltd

THE HAKKAS

The first Chinese to arrive in Taiwan were the Hakkas, or 'guest people'. The Hakkas were originally a persecuted minority in northern China, driven from Henan Province some 1,500 years ago. They gradually moved to southern China, and took part in fishing and trading in the coastal areas. The Hakkas later migrated to the Pescadores, and then on to Taiwan, setting up significant settlements in the southwest part of the island around AD 1000. Due to their long years of persecution on the mainland, the Hakkas have developed a unique self-identity, which they retain in Taiwan today. Because of the constant threat the Hakkas faced, Hakka women, unlike their counterparts from other parts of China, long ago engaged in manual work, mainly agriculture. For this reason, the Hakka women never adopted the habit of foot-binding, and are said to have a quieter temperament than other Chinese women. Because of their inability to obtain decent land, or because they had their land removed by the majority Taiwanese, the Hakkas have tended to enter government service, working for the railway administration and the police, for example, or in small businesses. However, many remain farmers today. The Hakkas see themselves as Taiwanese, but they probably get along with the mainlanders more easily than the Taiwanese do. There are an estimated two million Hakkas on the island. President Lee Teng-hui is a Hakka.

TAIWANESE

In the Ming Dynasty, Chinese from Fujian Province sailed to the island, pushing the Hakkas inland (who in turn pushed back the aborigines) and taking over most of the western plain. The collapse of the Ming Dynasty in 1644 saw a new wave of settlers arrive from Fujian. The Fujian Taiwanese were originally farmers and traders. Today they dominate the business community and enjoy a better socio-economic status than other groups on the island. Although many families can trace their ancestry back to China, there has been little or no contact with the mainland for several hundred years and Taiwanese tend to identify with the island more than with China.

MAINLAND CHINESE

In 1949 after the Chinese communists drove the Kuomingtang (KMT), or Nationalist Party, out of China, two million Chinese from all corners of the mainland retreated to Taiwan with the KMT government of Chiang Kai-shek. The majority were soldiers or government officials, and their dependents. While they represent all parts of China, most come from the southern central region, primarily the coastal provinces. Many top leaders are natives of Zhejiang Province, the home of the Chiang family.

In Taiwan today, Taiwanese account for about 70 per cent of the population, Hakkas 10–15 per cent, mainlanders around 14 per cent, and the aborigines 1.5 per cent. There has been a history of hostility between the various groups, but such differences are disappearing, particularly among younger generations, as intermarriage increases.

Language

Mandarin Chinese, the national language in both Taiwan and China, is a derivative of the Chinese dialect spoken in Beijing. However, Taiwanese, a derivative of the Fujian dialect of Amoy, is spoken by the majority Taiwanese, and several Hakka dialects are spoken in Taiwan. None of these three major dialects are mutually intelligible. Some older Taiwanese do not speak Mandarin at all, but can speak Japanese, owing to the Japanese occupation of 1895–1945. Most mainlanders speak Mandarin, and many also speak the dialect of their home province. The younger generation is more familiar with English, which is taught from junior high school. There are also several aborigine dialects, resembling Malay, but most aborigines speak Mandarin and Taiwanese as well.

History

PREHISTORY AND EARLY HISTORY

Little is known about the early history of Taiwan. Proof of human life goes back 10,000 years, but scholars differ on the origin of the first inhabitants. Artifacts indicate links to the Asian mainland and Southeast Asia. Whether or not the first inhabitants were the ancestors of the present-day aborigines is not clear. Many anthropologists, pointing to similarities in language and culture, believe the aborigines came from Southeast Asia and are related to the contemporary Malays. Other scholars, however, say the aborigines are related to the Miao, a non-Chinese people in southern China. According to this view, the earliest visitors to northern Taiwan were from China, crossing the sea at a very remote time, and northern Taiwan was the first step in the movement from continental China to the Pacific.

All that is known for sure is that the early inhabitants lived throughout the island and that they made their living fishing, hunting and practising shifting agriculture. An early aborigine name for the southern part of the island was *Pekan*, a Malay word that was usually applied to a resting place after a long journey.

Taiwan is mentioned in early Chinese records, but seldom appears in early official dynastic chronicles. In fact, early court records indicate that Taiwan was not considered a part of China. In AD 239, a 10,000-man expeditionary force was sent to explore I Chou, as it was then called, but still no claim was made to the island, which was considered 'outside the pale of Chinese civilization'. From the Sui Dynasty to the Ming Dynasty the island was known as Little Liu Chiu. It was not until the Ming Dynasty that the Chinese discovered Taiwan's exact location and the name Taiwan was used.

Admiral Cheng Ho led several sea expeditions to distant lands, and when returning from Siam (Thailand) in 1430 was forced off course by a typhoon, which drove his fleet as far east as southern Taiwan. Cheng fell ill on the island, but was cured by local doctors using a traditional herbal remedy. On returning to China, a grateful Cheng told the emperor that 'the natives of the magnificent island, though barbarous in character, are of a kind disposition, even providing me with the means of returning to my own land'. Cheng's stories about Taiwan created quite a stir at the Ming court, but the excitement died down almost as quickly as it had risen.

Despite the isolation engendered by dangerous seas, frequent typhoons and sand shoals, formidable mountain ranges, malarial plains and inhospitable aborigines on the west coast, a few brave Chinese traders from Fujian and Guangdong ventured across the Taiwan straits to carry out a profitable trade in deer hides and crushed deer horns, believed to be an aphrodisiac. These traders gradually established small settlements in the southwest corner of the island, where Chinese and Japanese pirates also found shelter along the coast.

For the most part, Taiwan was to remain neglected by official China for more than two centuries after Admiral Cheng's visit, with the mainland only beginning to notice the island again after the arrival of Western powers in the early 1600s.

WESTERN COLONIALISM

Up until the start of the seventeenth century, shipwrecked sailors and missionaries had been the only Western visitors to the island. In 1517 Portuguese vessels on their way to Japan sighted Taiwan, and impressed with the island's beauty, called it Ilha Formosa, 'beautiful island'. The Portuguese did not stay however, but withdrew, determined to keep Macao their main base in East Asia.

It was the Dutch who were to make the first claim to the island. Anxious to establish a foothold from where they could develop trade with China, they occupied the Pescadores Islands (Penghu) in 1622 after repeated requests for permission to set up a trading post somewhere along the China coast were rejected by the imperial court in Beijing. The Chinese were not happy having foreigners in the Pescadores either, and suggested the Dutch set up in Taiwan instead. The Dutch accepted and sailed into a natural harbor on the southwest coast of the island in 1624. At that time, Taiwan was already occupied by aborigine tribes, Chinese settlers and a small number of

First Encounters

As to the frame and stature of the natives, we cannot give any general description, as those vary in different parts of the island. The men are mostly well-bodied and lusty, especially those in the valleys and plain country, those living in the mountain regions being rather smaller and less robust. Their women do not equal the men in size, but are staring beauties for all that, having a full face, great eyes, flat noses, and long ears with breasts hanging down like a flitch of bacon. They would have handsome beards too, if the custom were not followed of pulling out the hair by the roots. The tips of their ears are perforated and pressed flat with a piece of horn made for the purpose, which leaves them very neat-looking, as they suppose. I am uncertain as to the reason why the name Formosa has been given to this island; whether seriously, from the land itself, or, ironically, from the monstrous people who inhabit it.

During the time I was in the island, I often heard that there were men in it who had tails, but to this story I never gave much heed, regarding it as being something quite fabulous. And yet, I can assure the reader, by every lawful asseveration, that I found the rumour to be a truthful one. For during my stay, it happened that a Formosan of the south country was apprehended for an inhuman murder commited upon a clergyman. After the matter was examined and the man pronounced guilty, he received sentence that he should be burned. On the day of execution, the murderer was brought forth and tied to a pale, and so soon as his clothes were stripped off we saw his tail, which was about a foot long, and all grown over with hair. Out of curiosity, some of my acquaintances went to see him, having heard that he had a tail, and he told them that nearly all the people down south were similarly furnished. As to the certainty of this latter statement, I cannot say much; for, being ignorant of the man's dialect, my friends might have been mistaken. I only solemnly aver that I was an eye-witness of the man's own condition, and I would be loth to impose upon the credulity of any one if it were not truly as I have described.

During summer, the natives are attired only in a cotton cloth, wide about the shoulders like a sheet, and tied by two corners across the breast;

it being also girded about the middle, and allowed to hang down to the calf of the leg. Their shoes, which are rarely worn, are made of goat-skins, and are fastened above the foot with thongs. In winter, they wear garments of fur made of the skins of tigers, bears, and apes. The people of Soulang were formerly apparelled as Europeans, but all the others as Chinese. Before the first coming of the Spaniards to Formosa, the natives were all naked, like those who now occupy the hill-country, who wear only a cloth about their middle.

The habit of the women is the same as that of the men, only with this distinction, that their robes are wrapped about their legs and made fast. Sometimes, too, they wear an upper coat which reaches to the knees, while around their heads they tie a black kerchief so as to look like two horns. Every woman has a pig which follows her about everywhere.

The Formosans have neither tradesmen nor mechanics amongst them, every man making what he has occasion for himself. When they lie down to sleep, they use only two deerskins, one on which to repose and the other as a coverlet. They are excellent swimmers, and are also expert with the bow and arrow; but above all other attainments, they surpass any one I have ever seen at running, no horse being able to keep pace with them for a stretch of six or eight leagues together. When they run, they carry in each hand a tinkling instrument, with which they every now and then strike the iron hoop about their arm to encourage them forward.

Those natives are wholly ignorant of the art of navigation, the only craft with which they go fishing being a sort of canoe made out of a hollowed-out tree. This, with hunting, is the sole occupation by which they sustain themselves; for agriculture is but seldom followed, partly because of their slothful habits, and partly from fear of their enemies, they being continually engaged in tribal warfare and averse to everything like peace.

Reverend William Campbell,
Formosa Under the Dutch, 1903

Fighting Words

To Gonsalo Portilio, Governor of the Spanish fortress in the Island of Kelung

Sir,

I have the honor to communicate to you that I have received the command of a considerable naval and military force with the view of making me master by civil means or otherwise of the fortress Santissima Trinidad in the isle of Kelung of which your Excellency is the Governor. If your Excellency is disposed to lend an ear to the terms of capitulation which we offer, your troops will be treated in good faith according to the usages and customs of war, but if your Excellency feigns to be deaf to this command there will be no other remedy than recourse to arms. I hope that your Excellency will give careful consideration to the contents of this letter and avoid the useless effusion of blood.

   May God protect your Excellency many years.
   The Friend of your Excellency,

                                        Paulus Tradenius
                                        6 August 1641

To the Governor of Taiwan, Fort Zelandia

Sir,

I have duly received your communication of August 26th, and in response I have the honor to point out to you that as becomes a good Christian who respects that oath he has made before his king, I cannot and I will not surrender the forts demanded by your Excellency, as I and my garrison have determined to defend them. I am accustomed to find myself before great armies, and I have engaged in numerous battles in Flanders as well as other countries, and so I beg of you not to take the trouble of writing me further letters of like tenor. May each one defend himself as best he can. We are Spanish Christians and God in whom we trust is our protector.

   May the Lord have mercy on you.

                                        Gonsalo Portilis
                                        6 September 1641

Japanese traders. The Dutch built Fort Zeelandia on a piece of land separated from the main island by a strip of water in 1634. A smaller fortress, Fort Provintia, was built on the shore of the main island across the harbor from Zeelandia in 1653.

The Spanish had captured Keelung in the north in 1626, later expanding their control to Tamsui on the northwest coast. Both the Spanish and the Japanese pirates were driven away from the island by the Dutch in the early 1640s, making the Dutch the sole rulers of the island. The Dutch soon enjoyed a lucrative trade between the island, the Dutch East Indies and the merchants and administrators of China's eastern coastal provinces.

In the meantime, the Ming government was being challenged by the Manchus in the north. In an effort to prevent his government from falling, the desperate Ming court made Cheng Chi-lung, a pirate operating from Taiwan, commander of the declining Ming naval force. Cheng defected to the Qing in 1646, two years after the Manchus established their dynasty. However, Cheng's son, Cheng Cheng-kung, refused to give in, and threw his large force of men and ships behind the retreating Ming.

The younger Cheng, better known in the West as Koxinga (the imperial name given him by the Ming was pronounced Kok-seng-ia in the Fujian dialect and was changed by Westerners into Koxinga), was born in 1624 to a Japanese mother. His fleet fought the Manchus all along the east coast of China through the 1650s, and he did not meet with a decisive defeat until he attempted a frontal assault on Nanjing in 1659. When the Qing forces closed in on his main base in Amoy (Xiamen), Koxinga decided to attack Fort Zeelandia, force the Dutch off the island and use it as a base for retaking the mainland from the Manchus.

The Dutch would most likely have remained on the island indefinitely had it not been for Koxinga. The naval warrior arrived on the island in 1661 at Luerhmen (Deer Ears Gate) with 30,000 soldiers in 8,000 warships. He quickly seized Fort Provintia, but Fort Zeelandia proved more of a problem. The Dutch at this fort put up stiff resistance and managed to hold off its attackers for nine months before finally surrendering. Within one year of his arrival Koxinga succeeded in forcing the Dutch colonists from the island. Under the surrender agreement, the Dutch were allowed to retire to Batavia in the Dutch East Indies, taking with them only what they could carry. They left behind some one million ounces' worth of silver in trade goods and cash.

Koxinga soon received news that his father and brothers had been executed in Beijing due to his intransigence. His mother had long before been killed by the Qing government and this new outrage exacerbated his already unstable mental condition. Koxinga began to abuse his subordinates, frequently flying into mad rages. He died at his residence in Zeelandia one year after defeating the Dutch, at the age of 38, his

Aquatint by E Ducan after a painting by W J Huggins, 1843: Loss by Fire of the Honourable East India Company War Steamer Madagascar. *Captain James Minns Dicey and crew were caught in a typhoon, at the entrance of the Formosa Channel, whilst employed in the expedition against the Chinese. Three boats of four were lost and 57 of the crew drowned.*

dream of restoring the Ming unfulfilled. His forces continued their fight against the Manchus under his son, Cheng Ching.

After four fruitless years, Cheng Ching retreated to Taiwan and died shortly later. Following his death, the house of Cheng was troubled by palace intrigue, internal dissension and unrest. The Manchus took advantage of the situation, sending a naval expedition to the Pescadores under the command of Admiral Shih Lang, a former ally of Koxinga's who had surrendered to the Manchus in the 1650s.

The choice of Shih was a wise one. Koxinga had executed Shih's father, brother and son after Shih joined the Manchus, and the excellent naval commander was bent on getting revenge. Shih made methodical plans to defeat his former ally, sailing from Fujian with 300 warships and achieving a crushing victory over Cheng's forces in the Pescadores in July 1683. When Shih's soldiers landed on Taiwan three months later, the remnants of Cheng's forces surrendered, ending more than two decades of Cheng family rule on the island.

Emperor Kanghsi, probably tired of all the bloodshed, dealt with the vanquished House of Cheng and their officers with unexpected leniency and grace. He ennobled some of them, allowing them to settle in Beijing. The majority of the Cheng troops were moved from Taiwan and used to reinforce garrisons against the Russians in northern China.

The future of the island was now hotly debated. Some court officials called for it to be abandoned, but Admiral Shih argued that it should be turned into a strong base to protect China from menacing Dutch warships. Kanghsi decided to incorporate the island into his kingdom and the next year Taiwan was officially made a prefecture of Fujian Province, with its capital at Tainan in the south. This marked the beginning of what was to be more than 200 years of nominal Chinese rule. A Qing garrison of 8,000 soldiers was stationed there permanently, but further Chinese emigration was to be strictly limited. The failure to enforce this rule, however, led to Taiwan's development as a rowdy dependency, a rough frontier society, only marginally bound to the administrative structure of Qing rule.

During most of this period, the Manchu officials assigned to the island were inefficient and corrupt, leading to numerous uprisings and social and political instability. 'Every three years a rebellion, every five a revolution', it was said of Taiwan at the time.

In the mid-19th century the Western powers began to show renewed interest in the island. In 1854, Commodore Oliver Perry called on the United States to establish a presence on the island, and a few years later, Townsend Harris, the US representative in Japan, suggested that Washington negotiate for the purchase of Taiwan. Despite the fact that China disclaimed any responsibility for the island, the United States made no attempt to colonize the territory.

Under the treaties of Tientsin secured by the British and French in 1858, two ports in Taiwan were opened to foreign trade. Western ships soon began arriving at the ports of Keelung and Tamsui and several countries set up trading posts and consulates. Shortly afterwards, Christian missionaries began arriving.

Trouble came in 1871, when a storm forced a group of fishermen from the Ryukyu islands ashore at Hengchun, on the southern tip of Taiwan. On arrival the fishermen were cut down by aborigines. The Japanese government was anxious to put the Ryukyus, then a Chinese protectorate, under their control, and so used the incident as an excuse to invade Taiwan in May of 1874, wringing suzerainty and other major concessions out of the Chinese.

Ten years later Taiwan found itself embroiled in the Sino-French War, which had broken out over a dispute regarding the Yunnan-Indochina border. The seaport of Keelung was bombarded by three French warships and occupied by French marines until peace was restored eight months later.

Liu Ming-chuan, a capable official and a reformer, was sent to administer the island in 1885. One year later Taiwan was made a separate province of China, with Liu as its first governor. Liu transferred the seat of the capital from Tainan in the south to Taipei in the north, and immediately went to work modernizing the island. A year after his arrival, Taipei became the first city in all of China to be electrified. In 1889, China's first train made its maiden voyage from Taipei to Keelung.

JAPANESE OCCUPATION

In the Sino-Japanese War of 1894–95, China suffered a humiliating defeat on sea and land. Under the terms of the Treaty of Shimonoseki, China was forced to hand over Taiwan to the Japanese. The inhabitants of the island objected and declared a republic—the first in Asia—but they were unable to resist the stronger Japanese.

Japan worked hard to improve the island. Agricultural productivity increased sharply and the infrastructure was improved. Prior to the occupation, Taiwan had just 30 miles of railroad, but by 1905 there were 300 miles of track, with another 700 either being laid or planned. New roads and harbors were built, and old ones improved. In 1903, hydro-electric generators were turned on near Taipei, giving birth to small industries. Japan also set up a modern economy, standardizing the monetary system, establishing banks, and promoting uniform commercial practices. The standard of public hygiene was raised significantly, and the educational system was greatly improved.

There was a negative side to all this. Much of Taiwan's impressive growth served its colonial rulers. The island became an important military base and source of foodstuffs and raw materials for the Japanese. The Taiwanese were forced to learn Japanese, and Chinese was not allowed to be taught in the schools. Taiwanese were

Japanese soldiers stand guard over captured aborigines following the Wushe Uprising, 1930

encouraged to take up medicine, engineering and science and technology, but not politics and the social sciences (although Taiwanese who made it to universities in Japan were able to study such subjects there). The Japanese lived in their own areas and their children studied in separate schools. Overall, however, the Japanese ruled Taiwan effectively, but they were stern masters and never treated the Taiwanese as equals.

By World War II the island's ties to China had already blurred, and most

Nationalist troops celebrate the return of Taiwan to Chinese rule, October 25, 1945

Taiwanese either supported Japanese rule, or had accommodated themselves to it. During the war, Taiwanese worked in war-related industries, and hundreds of thousands were forced to serve in the Japanese military. Thousands died fighting for the Japanese emperor in Southeast Asia.

As the final days of the war approached, the US Navy contemplated invading Taiwan, but gave up the plan due to the lack of good maps of the island. Americans were also not very sure that the Taiwanese could be relied upon to rise up against their Japanese rulers, and they feared the Taiwanese might even defend the Japanese-ruled island. Okinawa was chosen instead, and as a result Taiwan suffered little wartime damage, except for the bombing of some military targets.

Mother Love

These were past events of which she often spoke, and spoke without tiring. The year was 1953, exactly thirty years ago today. It was a windy, dry morning of early summer. Hauling a little bundle, the girl by the name of Cai Qianhui took the train alone the one stop from Thotin to Engtin. "Once I walked out of the station, do you think I dared ask the way?" While she was reminiscing, Dasao would ask this of Li Guomu, who would be listening attentively at her side. "Who would dare say how to get to the home of someone who had been taken away and shot?" At this point she would sigh and would always start talking about those dreadful days. "During that time in Thotin, friends would go out every day and roam about incommunicado on the street," she would recall. "Off in the distance you would see someone or other and know that he or she was still unharmed. If several days had passed without seeing so-and-so, you could be sure that person had been taken away."

It was during those terrible days that the young Li Guomu on the doorsill watched Cai Qianhui as she walked over from the distance, treading the ties of the trolley track. Both sides of the track were thick with lush, green groves of acaia trees. A black butterfly, each wing etched with a design of bright blue, danced and flitted in the groves. He remembered, too, that the young girl occasionally raised her head to look at the lonely mud brick cottage that was his home, and while she continued along the ties of the trolley track, she looked at him, just as lonely, where he sat on the cool doorsill. They gazed at each other wordlessly and fearlessly. A flock of gray starlings made a clamor somewhere in the acacia, and now and then the sound of a coal trolley reverberated as it rolled down the hill: "Clack clack clack!" From the distance it gradually drew closer, and from nearby it moved off again. He, the young and sickly Li Guomu, watched her without once turning away his eyes as she jumped away from the trolley tracks and, *selecting a little pathway full of pampas and other grasses, walked toward him.*

"Excuse me, does ... does Mr Li Qishi live here?" she asked.

He would never forget it. He remembered raising his head to look at her, feeling not the slightest curiosity or shyness. Her eyes were swollen, unfamiliar. In that instant he said nothing, only nodded his head lightly, aware of a creeping lethargy he felt whenever he was hungry. The moment he nodded, he discerned a smile that spread over the corners of her thin-lipped mouth, a smile that told of boundless love, and from those puffy, single-lidded eyes that gazed at him so intently, a stream of crystal tears fell.

They heard his mother's voice from inside the house.

"Ah-mu, who's that?"

Silently, he led her inside the dark house. His mother lay on the bed; the bitter smell of herbal medicine, simmering in the kitchen, permeated the entire house. Laboriously propping up the upper half of her body, his mother said, "Who is that? Ah-mu, who is this person you've brought in?"

The young girl, Cai Qianhui, sat down quietly at the edge of the bed. She announced:

"I'm Guokun's ... wife."

At that moment, though little Li Guomu distinctly heard every word she said, he did not fully understand the meaning. After a moment of stunned silence, his mother began to weep: "My son, my beloved son ..." She sobbed, choking back the sounds that swelled like a chant. He looked out the window, realizing only then that the sky had largely darkened. Muted thunder sounded in the distance.

Chen Yingzhen, *Mountain Road*

Sun Yat-sen, the father of modern China, with Chiang Kai-shek on a train in Guangzhou, China

Return To Chinese Rule

With Japan's defeat in 1945, Taiwan was returned to Chinese rule, and apart from a small minority which advocated independence for the island, most Taiwanese welcomed Chiang Kai-shek's troops as liberators, expecting that reunification would give them a greater role in running the island. The euphoria faded fast, with many soon viewing the KMT as even more repressive than the Japanese. The notorious General Chen I was appointed governor of the island. This was an unfortunate choice. Chen I was stubborn and discriminatory and his rule was marked by numerous scandals.

The KMT soldiers who took over the island from the Japanese saw the Taiwanese as tainted by five decades of association with Japan, and treated them as citizens of a defeated nation. The mainlanders, in turn, were perceived by the Taiwanese as carpetbaggers, uneducated, undisciplined, dirty and dishonest to boot. Mainland officials and their relatives soon took over property and key positions in the government and industry, in many cases forcing out Taiwanese, who were disappointed that they had no voice in decision-making.

Taiwan's well-being began to suffer as the economy, health standards and public order deteriorated under KMT misrule. Public and private buildings were stripped clean, and pickings were shipped to the mainland. Food was appropriated for the KMT armies fighting on the mainland, leading to unprecedented shortages in Taiwan. Epidemics of cholera and bubonic plague broke out, public works fell into disrepair and the education system deteriorated. Nationalist leaders in China, busy fighting for their survival against the communists at home, had little time for Taiwan's problems.

Public indignation suddenly broke out unexpectedly in February 1947. On the evening of February 27, monopoly bureau officers tried to confiscate black market cigarettes being sold by a 40-year-old widow on a street in Taipei. The woman was wounded on the head with a gun. A crowd of Taiwanese came to her defense and the retreating officers opened fire, killing one man. The incident led to demonstrations in the city the next day, and several people were killed after soldiers fired into a crowd of demonstrators. A violent uprising quickly spread throughout the island, and mainlanders became easy prey for angry Taiwanese crowds.

Governor Chen I called for military reinforcements from the mainland. A large contingent of heavily armed nationalist troops landed in Keelung on March 8, launching an island-wide ruthless and calculated massacre of unarmed Taiwanese. Thousands of Taiwanese disappeared, dragged from their homes, while others were cut down on the streets when soldiers arbitrarily opened fire. According to a government report released in 1992, between 18,000 and 28,000 people—a whole generation of Taiwanese intellectuals, doctors, lawyers, teachers and artists—were wiped out in the spring of 1947 in what is now known as the February 28th Incident.

The incident forced Chiang Kai-shek to briefly turn his attention back to the island to try and rectify the situation. Chen I was promoted to another position on the mainland and Taiwanese were appointed to official positions. But the damage had already been done. Chen I's misrule seriously hurt the KMT cause and embittered the Taiwanese against the government and the party. The memory of 2-28, as it is known in Taiwan, has been the driving force behind the Taiwan independence movement, and lies at the heart of the many political and social problems that plague Taiwan today, engendering

Generalissimo and Madame Chiang Kai-shek, 1948

continued Taiwanese bitterness toward mainlanders. Ironically, Chen I reportedly attempted to jump to the communist side when their victory appeared imminent. Unfortunately, his plan was uncovered by the once-admiring Generalissimo, who had him arrested and returned to Taiwan in 1949. A military tribunal found him guilty of consorting with the communists, and on June 18, 1950 he was executed by a firing squad in Taipei.

With the rapid deterioration of the KMT's military situation in China at the end of 1948, and the communists' fast approaching victory, Chiang was left with the same options that the Ming Court had faced after the Manchus seized Beijing and the northern plain 300 years earlier. He could try to regroup in central or southern China, attempt to consolidate in the southwest, or establish a coastal base in Amoy or in Guangdong. Chiang chose to follow Koxinga's steps: he would retreat to Taiwan and use the island as the base for the recovery of the mainland.

To prepare for this, Chiang named General Chen Cheng, a confidant, governor of Taiwan in December, and on January 21, 1949, resigned as president. He then retired to his native home in Ningbo, near Shanghai, to draw up contingency plans for his retreat to the island, using his retained position as director-general of the KMT. With the fall of Nanjing in April 1949, Chiang saw that his government was in imminent danger and he began ordering the evacuation of military troops and equipment, as well as US$300 million in gold reserves and foreign currencies to Taiwan, where he assumed *de facto* leadership, despite the fact that Li Tsung-jen, his former vice-president, remained the official head of state on the mainland.

In October 1949, Mao Zedong established the People's Republic of China in Beijing, and two months later the beleaguered KMT government retreated to Taiwan with two million supporters. On March 1, 1950, Chiang resumed the post of president of China in Taipei, vowing to use the small island as a base for the eventual recovery of the mainland.

Chiang moved fast to assert his leadership over the island and the more than one million soldiers who had retreated there with him. The commanders of the Peoples' Liberation Army (PLA) realized that ousting the nationalists from Taiwan to win the final victory would not be so easy.

In the summer of 1950, a large force of veteran PLA troops was moved to the coast of Fujian, just opposite Taiwan, to prepare for the last offensive. No action was taken, however. One explanation is that the communists were hoping for the Taiwanese to mount an insurrection against the hated KMT. Another reason given is that the PLA was brought down by an epidemic that raged through their forces that summer, making most of their soldiers unfit for combat.

US President Harry Truman, no admirer of Chiang and his government, had announced in January 1950 a policy of non-involvement in China's affairs, saying the

United States would not supply military aid or advice to KMT forces on Taiwan. With the nationalists' fate apparently sealed, the State Department proceeded to draft the statement they would make once Taiwan had been overrun by the People's Republic of China (PRC). But as Taiwan waited nervously, history stepped in to save the KMT, and the island.

On June 25, 1950, a massive force of North Korean troops crossed the 38th Parallel and invaded South Korea. Worried that Beijing might take advantage of the situation to attack Taiwan, Truman ordered the Seventh Fleet to patrol the Taiwan Strait. At the same time, he urged the KMT to refrain from attacking the mainland. Taiwan thus acquired a new strategic importance in US defense strategy, leading General Douglas MacArthur, commander of United Nations forces in Korea, to express his support for Chiang's regime, stating that Taiwan had become a part of America's 'island chain' of air-power bases.

Fortunately, the flight to refuge on Taiwan had purged the Nationalist Party, government and military of large numbers of corrupt and incompetent officials, who opted for the safety of Hong Kong and other places. Those who stuck by Chiang were either very loyal to him, or had no other place to go. Chiang and his followers realized that they shouldered a significant responsibility for the turn of events on the mainland. They knew Taiwan was their last chance and that major changes would have to be made in their administration.

President Chiang speaks to Chinese POWs held in North Korea in 1953 as son Chiang Ching-kuo looks on

Chiang Kai-shek shakes hands with US President Dwight Eisenhower in Taipei, 1958

Although it claimed to be a constitutional democracy, the government did not grant full democratic freedoms on the grounds that restrictions were necessary during the period of the 'communist insurgency'. The media was tightly controlled by the KMT, and anyone who criticized or appeared to pose a threat to the party or the government faced possible arrest, and sometimes even torture at the hands of the island's security apparatus.

The highly respected Sun Li-jen, the commander-in-chief of the army who was very popular with the US military, was removed from his position in 1955 and charged with having communists under his command. He remained under house arrest up until the 1980s. In 1960 Lei Chen, a mainland intellectual who published *Free China*, a political journal, attempted to form an opposition party. He was charged with harboring a communist on his staff, and was given a 10-year prison sentence.

The constitutional stipulation limiting the number of terms of office for the president was suspended in 1960 so that President Chiang could serve five terms, three more than the Constitution permitted. The KMT further cemented its position by refusing to hold national elections for Parliament or the National Assembly, thereby freezing into office indefinitely KMT members elected to these bodies in the late 1940s. Although elections were held to fill Taiwan seats and over the years supplemental seats were added and filled by candidates from the island, mainland deputies monopolized these bodies and worked as a rubber stamp for the KMT.

While the refusal to hold full elections was justified by the argument that new elections could not be held until the mainland was recovered by the KMT government, the KMT actually began to play down its plans of recovering the mainland as early as the late 1950s. In his New Year's speech in 1959, Chiang Kai-shek said that recovery was 70 per cent political, and only 30 per cent military. The decision was based on the practical realization that Washington would not support the nationalist dream of recovering the mainland. However, this was never openly stated, as abandoning its one-China policy would have undermined the justification for the KMT's one-party rule by mainlanders.

Taiwan was hit hard in 1971 with Taipei's forced withdrawal from the United Nations following the admission of Beijing. Another blow came when President Richard Nixon visited China in February 1972, signing the Shanghai Communiqué, which laid the groundwork for the eventual normalization of Sino-American relations. The two incidents led to further popular discontent with the unrepresentative Chiang regime and its continued restrictions on individual freedom. The government feared growing discontent and the small Taiwan independence movement, which it was able to suppress through strict police and political control, backed up by an overwhelming military force.

It was under such circumstances that Chiang Kai-shek passed away on April 5, 1975, his goal of recovering the mainland unfulfilled. The death of Chiang, the last surviving major allied leader of World War II, and the death of Chinese communist leader Mao Zedong a year later, marked the end of an era in Chinese politics.

Vice-president C K Yen succeeded to the presidency to complete the term, serving as titular head while Premier Chiang Ching-kuo, the late president's son, exercised the real power from behind the scene. In 1978, Chiang Ching-kuo was elected president. Chiang differed from his father in outlook, temperament and lifestyle. While the elder Chiang was formal, stern, distant and military oriented, his son was personable, approachable and economically oriented. He portrayed himself as a man of the people, and was constantly seen visiting farmers, workers and soldiers, or mixing with intellectuals, artists and baseball players. While his father often wore the traditional *chang pao*, or long gown, the younger Chiang seemed more comfortable in a Western suit or baseball cap and simple windbreaker.

Chiang saw a need to bring the majority Taiwanese into the KMT, and as early as the mid-1970s began to cultivate promising young native sons, promoting them into the government. At the same time, however, he refused to abandon the KMT's claim to sovereignty over all of China, and defended the government's *san bu zheng ce*, or Three Nos Policy—no contact, no compromise and no negotiation—toward Beijing. He also remained adamantly opposed to the Taiwan independence movement.

The most serious setback came in December 1978 when President Jimmy Carter announced that the United States would switch recognition to the Beijing government on January 1, 1979 and that the 1954 mutual defence treaty with Taiwan would be allowed to lapse at the end of that year, with all US troops to be withdrawn from the island.

The loss of its only superpower ally was a severe, but short-lived blow. In April, the US Congress passed the *Taiwan Relations Act*, which restored relations to an almost normal level. The American Institute in Taiwan was established to replace the embassy (staffed by professional foreign service officers who temporarily retire from the foreign service during their tour in Taiwan) and assurances were given that

Washington remained deeply concerned about the security of the island, and would continue to sell defensive arms to Taiwan. The economy was not adversely affected, and lucrative trade between the two countries continued to boom.

President and Madame Chiang review National Day parade in Taipei

Chiang was re-elected president in 1984, with Lee Teng-hui, a Taiwan-born agricultural economist educated in Japan and the United States, serving as vice-president. Chiang continued to focus on infrastructure projects, but looked around him and saw a changing world. The tide of democracy that swung across the Philippines, leading to the overthrow of President Ferdinand Marcos, the violent protests in South Korea that toppled President Chun Doo-Hwan, and the mass student protests in mainland China in 1985–86, most certainly influenced his thinking.

Taiwan was also changing. The rapid pace of industrialization created an equally fast-rising professional middle class, which was more sophisticated and politically conscious and by 1985 accounted for half the population. For the first time people began to participate in politics, and were no longer afraid of speaking out publicly on major issues, such as human rights, freedom of speech, freedom of the press, political pluralism, and the environment. For the first time since coming to the island four decades earlier, KMT rule came under close scrutiny and increasing criticism.

Chiang Ching-kuo realized that only through continued political liberalization and a stronger law could Taiwan avoid the pains experienced by other countries, and the KMT continue its dominant role in politics. Chiang, who was bothered by diabetes, heart disease, and other problems, knew that his time was limited and that he was the only person in the KMT with the power and influence to initiate such reforms.

In September 1986, a loose group of opposition politicians known as the Tangwai (literally 'outside the party', a reference to the Kuomintang's one party control), defied a ban on the formation of political parties to set up the Democratic Progressive Party (DPP). Despite pressure from the old guard to smash the new illegal party, Chiang wisely ruled out a crackdown and allowed the DPP to participate in the forthcoming December national elections. Although it only managed to garner about 30 per cent in elections over the coming years, the fledgling DPP became a major force in the island's politics, exerting an influence on the KMT that far outstripped its small size and forcing the KMT to quicken its march on the road to democratization.

In July 1987, the president announced the lifting of martial law, which his father had imposed nearly four decades earlier, and the removal of foreign exchange controls. In November of that same year he also allowed local residents to visit relatives on the mainland for the first time since the KMT retreated to Taiwan in 1949.

Following New Year's Day 1988, Chiang's health began to deteriorate rapidly, and he passed away on January 13, 1988, bringing to a close six decades of 'Chiang-dynasty' rule, which extended from China to Taiwan.

Lee Teng-hui smoothly succeeded to the presidency, becoming the first native Taiwanese president of the Republic of China. However, Lee had no ties with the mainland-dominated military bureaucracy or the security apparatus, leading to fears that he would be nothing more than a puppet, manipulated by behind-the-scenes hardliners. With help from moderates within the party, Lee managed to overcome right guard opposition—including that of Madame Chiang Kai-shek—to become the first Taiwanese chairman of the KMT in July 1988, when many other Taiwan-born members rose to leadership positions in the party.

Lee continued to mouth Chiang's 'one China' rhetoric, making it clear that he was not sympathetic to the Taiwan independence movement. Much to the surprise of political analysts, he accelerated Chiang's liberalization program and the policy of gradual opening up to the communist-ruled mainland.

President Chiang Kai-shek and son Chiang Ching-kuo

Lee Teng-hui was elected to a six-year term as president in 1990, despite a last-ditch attempt by the KMT's old guard to promote Chiang Wei-kuo, a mainlander, and the generalissimo's only living son.

As the country headed into the last decade of the 20th century, it appeared to be being pulled in two directions, leading one presidential adviser to say frankly that 'creative ambiguity' was needed in policy-making.

In May, 1991 Lee lifted the 'Period of Communist Rebellion' and the 'Temporary Provisions', under which the presidency enjoyed extra-constitutional powers. In July, the Planning Commission for the Recovery of Mainland China was disbanded, a further step toward reducing tensions with the mainland. At the end of the year hundreds of senior deputies in the National Assembly, Parliament and Control Yuan who had held office since being elected on the mainland in the late 1940s, stepped down, making way for full elections in Taiwan.

During the elections, which were held at the end of 1991, the DPP began to vig-orously advocate independence for the island under the name Republic of Taiwan. Opponents argued that few countries would dare to offend Beijing by recognizing an independent Taiwan, and that there was nothing to be gained by provoking China.

The movement drew sharp condemnations from Beijing, which has refused to rule out the use of military force to retake the island if it cannot be reunified peacefully. 'Those who play with fire perish by fire,' warned China's President Yang Shangkun, reaffirming Beijing's threat to 'wash the island in blood' if it moved toward legal separation.

Several people in Taiwan were arrested for advocating independence, which seemed almost like a nod to Beijing that Taipei was not softening. Yet the commu-nists, and even some of the more conservative members of Lee's own party, appear to distrust the island's first native-born president, who they regard as actually working harder to protect the status quo than to move toward reunification. They fear that Lee's realistic policies may be aimed at subtly achieving independence by delaying unification, rather than openly seeking to break away.

The independence movement received a setback in the year-end elections for the National Assembly when KMT candidates garnered a large majority of the votes cast. However, this loss was not seen as a rejection of independence, but more as a vote for the status quo—which many say is thinly-veiled *de facto* independence—in the face of a serious threat from an unpredictable China.

With the economic gap as wide as the political chasm, and with deep mistrust on both sides, conditions for reunification do not seem promising at the present. How-ever, barring any unforseen tensions, the two Chinas can be expected to grow closer in the 1990s as the restrictions and obstructions imposed by both sides continue to fall away.

Chronology

AD 239
A 10,000-man expeditionary force is sent to explore I Chou, as the island was then known.

1430
Admiral Cheng Ho returning from Siam is forced off course by a typhoon, which drives his fleet as far east as southern Taiwan. Cheng's tales of his visit to Taiwan create a stir at the Ming court, but the euphoria soon dies down, and the island sinks back into oblivion for the next two centuries.

1517
Portuguese sailors on their way to Japan sight Taiwan and name it Ilha Formosa, 'beautiful island'.

1624
The Dutch East India Company begins to establish bases in Taiwan, setting up a fortified capital in the area of present-day Tainan.

1626
The Spanish set up a stronghold in northern Taiwan.

1641
The Spanish are driven out of Taiwan by the Dutch.

1661
Koxinga, the Ming-dynasty loyalist, arrives in Taiwan.

1662
Koxinga defeats the Dutch, forcing them from the island.

1683
The Manchus, who overthrew the Ming Dynasty in China in 1644, defeat Ming loyalists in Taiwan and bring the island under their control.

1684
Taiwan is made a prefecture of Fujian Province.

1737
Mangka (present-day Wanhua) becomes a prosperous center of trade in the Taipei basin.

1860
As a result of the Treaty of Tientsin, which ended the First Opium War, several of Taiwan's ports are opened to foreign trade and Christian missionaries. Over the next decade trade with the outside world begins to take off.

1884
French forces seize the Pescadores, a group of small offshore islands, blockade

Taiwan and occupy Keelung, but leave the island eight months later.
1885
Liu Ming-chuan is sent to Taiwan and begins a series of far-reaching reforms.
1886
Taiwan becomes a province of China and Governor Liu makes Taipei the capital.
1887
Governor Liu turns on the first light bulb in Taipei, making it the first city in China
to be electrified. Liu introduces modern mines, improves harbor works and
establishes overseas cable connections. Under his rule, Taiwan becomes the most
progressive province in China.
1889
China's first train makes a trip from Taipei to the port city of Keelung.
1895
Taiwan is ceded to Japan following China's defeat in the Sino-Japanese War and
Taipei is made the seat of the Japanese governor's office. The Japanese prohibit foot-
binding, opium smoking and the wearing of queues. For the next decade, Taiwanese
guerilla groups keep pressure on Japanese military forces.
1919
The Japanese build the President's Office, which serves as the Governor-General's
Office during the occupation.
1943
Franklin D Roosevelt, Winston Churchill and Chiang Kai-shek meet in Cairo and
declare that when World War II ends, Japan will be stripped of all its occupied territories, including Taiwan, which will be restored to the Republic of China.
1944
American planes bomb major cities in Taiwan. Thousands of people move from the
city to the hills or country homes. Some 18,000 Taipei residents are made homeless
when the Japanese cut wide fire lanes between crowded Twatutia and the heart of the
city. Winds blowing from the west spare Mangka and Twatutia as repeated US air
raids spark big fires in the city's administrative district.
1945
Japan's surrender ends World War II and closes the book on 50 years of Japanese rule
as Taiwan is returned to Chinese control.
1947
An estimated 18,000–28,000 Taiwanese are massacred by KMT soldiers following
anti-government rioting.
1949
The KMT government, overpowered by Chinese communists on the mainland,
retreats to Taiwan and makes Taipei the temporary capital of the Republic of China.

1950

Chiang Kai-shek resumes the presidency in Taipei in March. In June, US President Harry Truman orders the US Seventh Fleet to prevent a communist attack against Taiwan and at the same time asks the KMT government to cease air and sea operations against the mainland.

1954

The Sino-American Mutual Defense Treaty is signed in Washington.

1955

More than 700 defenders are killed in battle as Chinese communist forces take over Ikiangshan, the northernmost islet of the Tachen Islands, on January 20. Six days later the US House of Representatives approves a resolution authorizing President Dwight Eisenhower to employ US forces to defend Taiwan, the Pescadores, and 'related positions and territories'.

1958

The battle of the Taiwan Straits begins on August 23 with the Chinese communists firing a two-hour, 41,000-round barrage at Quemoy.

1971

The UN General Assembly votes to expel Taipei and seat Beijing.

1975

President Chiang Kai-shek, the long-time leader of the Republic of China, passes away in Taipei at the age of 88, his dream of recovering the mainland unfulfilled. Vice-president Yen Chia-kan assumes the presidency to complete the remaining term of office.

1978

Chiang Ching-kuo is elected president. Protesters demonstrate outside the US Embassy in Taipei in December after Washington announces it will establish diplomatic relations with the communist People's Republic of China, cutting ties with Taipei.

1979

The US Embassy in Taipei is closed as the United States inaugurates diplomatic ties with Beijing on January 1. The 28-year-old US military presence in Taiwan also comes to a close as Rear Admiral James Linder, commander of the US Taiwan Defense Command, leaves Taipei.

1982

On August 17, Washington and Beijing sign the second Shanghai Communiqué, in which the US promises to reduce sales of arms to Taiwan.

1986

Tangwai politicians defy the government ban on the formation of new political parties to establish the Democratic Progressive Party at the Grand Hotel in Taipei.

1987

Chiang Ching-kuo continues to move toward political and economic liberalization, lifting the 39-year-old martial law rule and foreign exchange controls. In November, Taiwan residents are allowed legally to return to the mainland to visit relatives, ending the ban on travel that had been in place since 1949.

1988

President Chiang Ching-kuo, son of the late Generalissimo Chiang Kai-shek, dies in Taipei on January 13. Chiang's death brings to an end more than five decades of Chiang family leadership of the Republic of China (ROC). Hundreds of thousands of citizens wait in line for hours at the Martyr's Shrine in Taipei to pay their last respects. Vice-president Lee Teng-hui assumes office, becoming the first native Taiwanese president of the ROC and chairman of the KMT.

1990

Lee Teng-hui is elected the eighth president of the ROC, despite a last ditch attempt by the KMT's old guard to promote Chiang Wei-kuo, the generalissimo's only living son, for the post.

1991

In May, President Lee Teng-hui lifts the 'Period of Communist Rebellion' and the 'Temporary Provisions' under which the presidency enjoyed extra-constitutional powers. This move opens the way for full elections to Taiwan's legislative bodies. In December, aging parliamentarians elected on the mainland more than four decades earlier, and frozen in office since, are forced to step down from office, leading to the first full national elections in Taiwan.

CHINESE DYNASTIES

Xia	c. 2205–1766 BC
Shang	c. 1766–1027 BC
Zhou	1027–221 BC
Qin	221–206 BC
Han	206 BC–AD 220
Three Kingdoms Period	220–265
Jin	265–316
Northern and Southern Dynasties	317–581
Sui	581–618
Tang	618–907
Five Dynasties	907–960
Song	960–1279
Yuan (Mongol)	1279–1368
Ming	1368–1644
Qing (Manchu)	1644–1911
Republic of China	1912–1949
People's Republic of China	1949–

Economy

Before the Japanese occupation, Taiwan's economic structure closely resembled that of southern China, with a wide gap between the rich and the poor majority. Most of the Chinese on the island made their living from agriculture, while the aborigines relied on hunting, fishing and gathering fruit.

Taiwan had some advantages over the mainland. It had not suffered frequent famines caused by flooding and crop failures. Fish was an important source of food. The island's rich volcanic soil and more even rainfall provided better crop yields. The island's economy was more oriented toward trade, including foreign trade. Capitalism, introduced by European colonialists, took root much earlier here. The Dutch, for example, introduced agriculture as a capitalist enterprise and the spread of internal commerce and trade resulted in more economic specialization than was found in China at that time.

China's rule of the island actually slowed down its economic development, and the economic reforms instituted in the final years of Chinese control of Taiwan were short-lived.

The modern development of Taiwan's economy actually began with the arrival of the Japanese. Emphasis was given to the economic structure, including the building of roads, railroads, harbors and an electrification system; the establishment of local industries and an export-oriented economy; and the organization of the labor force.

The Japanese contributed capital investment, technology and management to build up the agricultural sector, and improved output through the introduction of new farming techniques, irrigation and fertilizers. And even before the start of World War II, small factories were established, launching Taiwan's industrial revolution. The war stimulated this process, and Taiwan soon became a major contributor of supplies to the Japanese war machine.

The first four years of KMT rule were marked by several economic shocks. The first was the sudden departure of Japanese administrators and businesses. Second, corrupt officials sent from the mainland to administer the island soon pushed the economy to the brink of ruin. The KMT, occupied with fighting the Chinese communists on the mainland, failed to deal with this problem and economic growth began to decline with many consumer goods no longer readily available. Prices soared as food rose 700 per cent and fertilizers skyrocketed an amazing 25,000 per cent. The problem was exacerbated in 1949 when some two million immigrants arrived from the mainland, straining an already failing economy.

Their bitter defeat on the mainland taught the KMT that they could no longer ignore social and economic problems. Taiwan's economic planners gave emphasis to agriculture and light and heavy industry in that order. From 1949, when the KMT

government retreated to the small island, until 1960, the thrust was aimed at the development of agriculture and light industry.

With help from the United States, the government instituted a highly successful land reform program, which in the first stage in 1949 reduced annual land rent from the current 50 to 70 per cent to 37.5 per cent of the main crop. In the second stage in 1951 the sale of 430,000 acres of public land enabled close to 140,000 farmers to become landowners. The third stage in 1953 allowed farmers to sell land to the government, which in turn resold it at the same price. As a result of the land reform program, tenancy was cut from 39 to 15 per cent, a total of some 400,000 families became landowners, and agricultural production increased substantially.

Washington's decision to assign the US Seventh Fleet to patrol the Taiwan Strait and US military guarantees and economic aid engendered public confidence and allowed the KMT government the time it needed to carry out economic and political changes. The island also benefited from the new available pool of trained personnel from the mainland, many of whom were US educated, and who enjoyed more influence in decision-making because of the heavy US involvement.

In the early 1950s, the government encouraged the development of the agricultural sector and import substitution manufacturing, mainly in the cement, paper and fertilizer industries. This policy laid a strong economic base for the island, and resulted in an average growth rate of 7.7 per cent in the 1950s.

Being a small island with no real resources to speak of, the government realized it would have to depend on trade, and so in the 1960s, the import substitution strategy was replaced gradually by an emphasis on light industrial manufacturing and exporting, with textiles and electrical appliances, which were labor-intensive and export-oriented, becoming the island's key industries. Using its low labor costs and high quality control, Taiwan was able to compete in international markets.

The suspension of US aid to Taiwan in 1964 forced Taiwan to rely more on itself. Foreign investment from overseas Chinese, the United States, Japan and Western Europe helped introduce modern labor-intensive technology in the 1960s. The island's economy began to take off, paving the way for what was to be one of the fastest growing economies in the world over the next two decades.

In the 1970s, the focus shifted to the development of sophisticated and heavy industry, and government spending on infrastructure projects. The Ten Major Projects got under way in 1973, and included the building of the North–South Freeway, the Chiang Kai-shek International Airport, the northern coastal railway, Taichung Harbor and the expansion of Suao Harbor, a nuclear power plant at Chinshan and several industrial projects. With the completion of these projects six years later, Taiwan was on the road to becoming a rich developing nation. The Ten Major

Fruit orchards, Lishan

New Wealth

According to an old saying, the money in Taiwan rises to your ankles. By the late 1980s, however, people appeared to be up to their necks in the stuff, and almost in danger of drowning in a sea of cash. The stock market skyrocketed (the Taiwan Stock Exchange was the second most active in the world in terms of transactions in 1989), real estate prices were spiralling out of control (rising 400 per cent between 1986 and 1989) and foreign exchange reserves jumped to a record high of more than US$75 billion, giving the small island the second largest reserves in the world just behind Japan.

The dizzying pace by which large numbers of people became millionaires almost overnight had adverse effects on society, leading more than one commentator to refer to Taiwan as the 'Island of Greed'.

Factory workers, taxi drivers and other working class people got so caught up in the stock market that they stopped working altogether to devote their time to studying the market, which could bring them more money in a week than they could earn in a month. According to one estimate, 25 per cent of the island's 20 million people were playing the stock market virtually full-time. One government official said that 60,000 badly needed workers could be returned to the labor market if the stock market cooled down. And in rural areas monitors were color-coded to indicate which shares were rising or falling, so illiterate farmers could more conveniently make their choices. Soon, analysts were calling the island a 'floating casino'.

Those too poor to invest in real estate or the stock market turned to illegal lotteries. Workers could not be found on drawing days, forcing factories to miss production schedules, and telephone lines were tied up by gamblers checking the winning numbers, making it almost impossible to call around the island. Twenty-four hour *pachinko* (pinball) parlours opened in hundreds of store fronts around the island, and in the southern city of Tainan thousands of dollars were changing hands every night on street-side cricket-fighting contests.

The instant wealth led to lavish spending, as the island's *baofa hu*, or *nouveau riche*, turned to conspicuous consumption, purchasing expensive exotic pets, or patronizing restaurants which garnished their dishes with real gold shavings, in order to keep up with the Wangs.

The situation began to return to normal at the beginning of the 1990s as the island's stock and real estate markets returned to earth, and as illegal lotteries and underground investment houses began to fold, leaving people a bit more wary of getting rich too quick.

Projects pumped huge amounts of capital into the economy, and lessened the effects of the 1974–75 recession. More important, the economic planners, engineers, technicians and laborers who worked on these projects gained a great deal of experience, and the confidence to make further strides.

When the United States announced in late 1978 that it would switch recognition to Beijing on January 1, 1979, there were widespread fears that this would hurt the economy. The change had little impact on the island, however, as foreign trade and investment increased even more rapidly.

By the 1980s, Taiwan began to face serious problems. Wages, real estate and other production costs ate away at the island's developing nation competitive advantage. As Taiwan's labor intensive industries began losing out to other countries in the region with lower costs, many industries, such as toys, footwear and textiles, began to move abroad to Southeast Asian countries and mainland China. Others, realizing that they could only survive at home by climbing the high-tech ladder, attempted to produce higher value-added goods.

With almost 50 per cent of the island's exports going to the US, and enjoying a record 16.9 million dollar surplus in 1987, Taiwan came under increasing pressure from Washington to open its doors wider to US goods by removing non-tariff barriers and allowing its under-valued currency to appreciate. Taiwan responded by reducing and eliminating many tariffs, and allowing the currency to rise a staggering 40 per cent over a two-year period. The island also began to diversify its export-driven economy away from dependence on the US market, and the surplus with the United States fell to US$8 billion by 1991, less than one third of total exports.

While direct trade with mainland China was banned, indirect trade via third countries, mainly Hong Kong, was approved and commerce with the mainland began to increase rapidly. Two-way trade soared to US$5.5 billion by 1991.

The government's ambitious six-year infrastructure development plan, expected to cost US$310 billion, was announced in late 1990 and is now the centerpiece of national economic policy .

The government also made moves to liberalize its antiquated financial system in 1991, allowing the licensing of new private banks, breaking the oligopoly of the state-run commercial banks and opening the local stock market to foreign institutional investors.

Religion

The two dominant religions in Taiwan are Buddhism and Taoism. However, as one expert on Taiwan has noted, it might be more correct to say religion in Taiwan is a combination of many beliefs: Confucianism serves as a code of ethics and propriety, Buddhism provides a framework for incorporating other religious concepts, and Taoism provides a philosophical foundation. The majority of people in Taiwan seem unaware of the different origins of their religious beliefs and see no conflict. This is characteristic of the tolerance toward religion. Buddhists and Taoists also claim some of the same gods, such as Kuanyin and Lu Tung-pin. Elements of Taoism, Buddhism and folk religion exist side by side. In many temples, one can find all three elements grouped together, a main altar maintained by a *sai kong*, or Taoist priest, who reads from Taoist canons; a side altar devoted to Kuanyin and cared for by Buddhist monks and nuns, and a proliferation of local patrons in between.

While Buddhism is the most popular institutionalized religion in Taiwan, folk religion is still embraced by two thirds of the adult population. The aborigines originally practiced nature worship, but since the 1960s many have converted to Christianity, and Protestantism and Catholicism are now the dominant religions in aborigine society.

The Taiwanese believe that upon death a person becomes a spirit, but that he or she still has the same needs as on earth: a place to live, clothing, food and money to spend. For this, the spirits depend on their family members. Therefore when a member of the family passes away they will burn paper money and miniature paper houses. In modern times, luxury items such as expensive automobiles have been added to the list. Numerous stores still carry on a lucrative business producing these elaborate paper offerings which, it is believed, prevent the unhappy spirit from wandering around causing harm to people.

In the main room of most Taiwanese homes you will find a family altar where the household gods and ancestors are worshipped, an ancient tradition that has changed little over the ages. The family altar is set in a central position against the wall and on it are placed statues of the household god. To the left are the ancestral tablets, which contain family records, including the names and dates of ancestors as far back as 17 or 18 generations, long before the family migrated to the island. Offerings of food are placed on the family altar on special days. Family altars vary in shape and size depending on the status of the family. A modest family may have a simple shelf hanging on the wall, while wealthier families will have rather large, intricately carved altars.

Burning incense at Tien Hou (Matsu) temple, Lukang

BUDDHISM

Sakyamuni Buddha was born in the 6th century BC, the son of a king in northern India. A Hindu, he was upset by the misery in the world and dismayed by the failure of Hinduism to overcome it. He decided to abandon his palace and his family for a life of suffering. It is believed that after meditating for a long time under a Bodhi tree, he attained spiritual enlightenment and became a Buddha. The classics of Buddhism, recorded by his disciples, propose that all living creatures are endowed with the Buddha nature and that everyone can become a Buddha through self-discipline.

Buddhism was first introduced to China about AD 65 but did not achieve great popularity until the Sui and Tang dynasties, more than 500 years later. As Buddhism proliferated it took on many local attributes, and evolved a truly Chinese style. Hsuan Tsang, a famous Chinese Buddhist monk, made a major contribution to the spread of Buddhism by travelling to India and returning with more than a thousand Buddhist scriptures, many of which he translated upon his return.

Buddhism was probably first firmly established in Taiwan during the end of the Ming Dynasty, when increasing numbers of Chinese migrated here from Fujian and Guangdong provinces. By the time Cheng Cheng-kung (Koxinga) drove the Dutch out in 1662, Buddhist monks were coming to the island and building temples with the help of the Cheng family. In the Qing Dynasty several temples were built on the island by officials, gentry and local believers. Buddhist missionary work was still limited at this time.

The Japanese occupation at first had little effect on Buddhism, but the middle period of the occupation introduced Japanese Buddhism to the island, and by 1925 more and more Japanese monks were becoming influential in Taiwan temples. In accordance with Buddhist tradition on the mainland, monks and nuns did not live in the same temple. In Taiwan today, however, nuns often live in the same complex, as is the case in Japan.

In 1949, after the KMT moved to the island, a large number of Chinese monks came to Taiwan, taking many Taiwanese monks and nuns as their disciples, and worked for the re-establishment of Chinese Mahayana Buddhism. In recent years Taiwanese Buddhism has attempted to meet the challenges of modernization, with monks and nuns frequently leaving the confines of their temples to meet with the faithful in their homes and on the streets. They are also getting more involved in social work, building hospitals, schools and other institutions for the public good.

There are now an estimated two million Buddhists in Taiwan.

TAOISM

Taoism is viewed as the original Chinese religion, since unlike Buddhism, Christianity and Islam, it does not have foreign roots. When speaking of Taoism, it is important to distinguish between the philosophical and religious aspects. The Taoist religion bears little resemblance to the teachings of its founding philosophers. Its system derived chiefly from the *Tao Te Ching*, a 5,000-character classic attributed to Lao Tzu, a contemporary of Confucius, and written in the third century BC. This book describes man's ideal state of freedom from desire and of effortless simplicity obtained by following the *Tao* (The Way). Subsequently, Taoism began to stress the search for effects, such as immortality, which was believed to flow from the Tao, and encouraged the study of alchemy. By the fifth century AD Taoism had absorbed many features of Mahayana Buddhism, and evolved into a developed religious system.

Taoism first came to Taiwan toward the end of the Ming Dynasty and is closely linked to folk religion. During the Japanese occupation, Taoism was vigorously suppressed and the latter years saw many Taoist images burned and its followers persecuted. After retrocession in 1945, Taoist temples, which had registered as Buddhist temples to escape Japanese persecution, came out into the open again and Taoist priests began arriving from the mainland in increasing numbers. Today, Taoist priests are still commonly employed for funerals and in the exorcizing of evil spirits.

FOLK RELIGION

The early immigrants to Taiwan carried their religious beliefs with them, beliefs which were very much intertwined with the rigors of the rugged pioneer life. Folk religion has since played an important role among the people of Taiwan, and still remains the most popular religion. Despite strong influences from Buddhism and Taoism, it differs considerably and has some gods of its own.

Over the last four decades Taiwan society has changed rapidly from a rural agricultural society to an urban industrial one, and standards of living have risen sharply. While one would expect the folk religion tradition to fade in popularity, this has not been the case. The rapid social change in Taiwan over the past decade has brought with it psychological tensions, encouraging many people to seek comfort in the familiarity of traditional folk religions. Furthermore, just as the early immigrants adapted their religious tradition to meet the needs of pioneer society, modern-day believers have done the same. A good example of this is the *hsiang pao*, which is made with ashes from temple incense wrapped in yellow paper, on which mysterious characters are written. The yellow paper is then wrapped again in red cloth forming a small amulet. This is the same *hsiang pao* as worn by the ancestors of the present-day Taiwanese when they crossed the dangerous Taiwan Strait more than 300 years ago. Today, however, it is hung on rear-view mirrors to protect drivers from the dangers of the road.

I KUAN TAO

The I Kuan Tao religion, which dates back to folk religions founded during the Qing Dynasty, entered Taiwan from different areas of the mainland shortly after World War II.

Controversy surrounding the religion led to its being banned soon after the government moved here from the mainland. The prohibition resulted from rumors that adherents worshipped in the nude. Furthermore, since the religion stresses a synthesis of the three main belief systems in China—Confucianism, Buddhism and Taoism—I Kuan Tao aroused the ire of orthodox Buddhist leaders who saw it as heretical. The ban drove the religion underground, but it still remained highly popular with temples throughout the island. The ban was lifted in February 1987. The number of followers is estimated at between 200,000 and 400,000, but the I Kuan Tao claim 800,000 faithful.

OTHER LOCAL RELIGIONS

Several new religions grew out of existing religions. Representative of this group is the Ju Tsung Shen Chiao, or Confucian Spirit Religion, which attracts crowds of people to its ritual 'spirit writing' in the religion's 'phoenix halls'. Also popular is Hsuan Yuan Chiao, which combines Confucian, Taoist and Mohist philosophies, emphasizes respect for heaven and ancestors, and worships China's ancient Yellow Emperor. The religion was founded in 1957 by Wang Han-sheng, a former legislator from mainland China, who was haunted by the fall of the mainland to the Chinese communists, which he attributed to the loss of national spirit. Wang felt that this national spirit could only be restored through a Chinese cultural renaissance, which he hopes his religion can achieve. While critics say this is more of a club for the study of Chinese classics than a religion, Hsuan Yuan Chiao now has more than 100,000 followers worshipping in over 20 temples around the island.

ISLAM

The Ming Dynasty was a golden age for Islam in China, and many of the soldiers serving under Koxinga in Taiwan were Chinese Moslems from the mainland. Some eventually made Taiwan their permanent home, building mosques as their numbers increased. During the Japanese occupation, the imams were stamped out and Islamic rituals and teachings disappeared with them. By modern times the descendants of these Moslems no longer embraced the religion, except in isolated pockets in Lukang, Tamsui and a few other places where Moslems were known to settle. The religion got a new lease on life in 1949 when some 20,000 Moslems retreated to Taiwan with the nationalist government, the majority soldiers, civil servants, and food service workers. However, the religion has not flourished, with growth mainly due to natural population growth. There are around 50,000 Moslems in Taiwan today, worshipping at five mosques in Taipei, Taoyuan, Taichung and Kaohsiung.

CHRISTIANITY
■ PROTESTANTISM

The Dutch occupiers of Taiwan in the 1600s brought Protestantism to the island when George Candidius, a minister of the Reformed Church of Holland, converted members of six Pingpu tribes near present-day Tainan. His work was continued by other missionaries, with 6,000 aboriginal converts by the year 1643. After that conversions tapered off. The defeat of the Dutch at the hands of Koxinga ended the spread of Christianity on the island until English and Canadian missionaries arrived in Taiwan more than 200 years later, laying the foundation for the modern development of Christianity. Like other religions, Christianity was affected by the return of the island to Chinese rule in 1945, and the retreat of the nationalist government to the island four years later. Thousands of Protestant clergy and lay people fled the advancing communists, swelling the numbers of Christians in Taiwan. The ensuing economic and social hardship in the 1950s gave people a need for religion, and the

Canadian missionary Reverend George Mackay pulling teeth, late 1800s

Protestant churches benefited, with tens of thousands of Taiwanese being baptized. In recent years, however, most Christian groups have faced slower growth rates. Protestants now number about 400,000.

■ CATHOLICISM

The history of Catholicism in Taiwan closely follows the experience of Protestantism. In 1626 a Spanish Catholic priest called Father Martinez, accompanied by Spanish troops from the Philippines, arrived in Taiwan with four Dominican missionaries. For the next 16 years the missionaries worked in Spanish-occupied northern Taiwan winning 4,000 aborigines over to Catholicism. This proselytizing came to an end in 1642 when Dutch forces routed the Spanish and drove them off the island. Nothing is known of what happened to these first Catholics since no traces have been found. Like Protestantism, it was another 200 years before the religion was to make a comeback. In 1859, Dominican missionaries came to Taiwan to lay a foundation for the spread of Catholicism around the island.

After retrocession large numbers of Catholics moved to Taiwan with the retreating nationalist government, giving new strength and vigor to the small local Catholic establishment. The number of Catholics, which stood at 1,000 in 1945, climbed to 80,000 by 1957 when the church experienced its peak growth. Analysts attribute the rise in numbers to the influx of believers from the mainland. Some of these newcomers were Catholic, or suffering the trauma of being uprooted from their homes during the war, were willing converts. Economic and social instability in Taiwan caused by the sudden arrival of refugees also encouraged conversions and newly arrived missionaries brought about mass conversions of aborigines. Catholics now number about 300,000 but, like the Protestants, growth is sluggish.

Other foreign religions popular in Taiwan include Baha'i, Jehovah's Witnesses, Tenrikyo and the Unification Church.

Taiwan Gods

Agricultural societies are marked by their polytheistic view of god. The spirit world is very similar to the ancient feudal world, with a spirit official fulfilling almost every post of a ruler in ancient China.

The Taiwanese pantheon of gods originates mainly from the southern Chinese provinces of Fujian and Guangdong, and was brought to Taiwan by the early Chinese immigrants. In transplanting their gods to Taiwan's soil, these immigrants adapted their religion functionally to their new society, in some cases even creating new gods and rituals to meet their need for security and survival. Originally, people worshipped gods particular to the geographic area where they came from. For example, Hakka immigrants worshipped Sanshan Kuowang, a local god from Guangdong Province. Others worshipped gods who were patrons of certain professions. Carpenters worshipped Lu Pan, a famous carpenter in ancient China. For the most part, this practice has declined since the 1950s, as more universal gods such as Kuanyin and Matsu have become popular. The reason is likely due to migration and rapid social mobility, as well as the impact of technological developments on traditional occupations.

The Buddhists are rather conservative, however. Chinese have long believed that exceptionally virtuous mortals could become gods or goddesses after dying, and so Buddhist temples have been dedicated to deceased monks believed to have reached enlightenment. Many of the deities found in Taoism and folk religions, however, come from famous characters in history, literature and folk tales, such as Kuankung (*The Romance of the Three Kingdoms*), a historical figure, and the Monkey King (*Travels to the West*), a fictional character. During the Japanese occupation it is reported that a brothel was raided and it was discovered that the prostitutes there worshipped Chupachieh, or Pigsy, the most debauched character in *Travels to the West*. They prayed to him as Siu-siu-ia, his divine name: 'Siu-siu-ia, Siu-siu-ia, feet bent up, wrinkled face, we beseech you to bring us rich guests, foolish as they come in, witless as they leave, may we completely fleece them.' In fact, prostitutes have been known to be quite generous to temples, sometimes organizing annual group trips to worship at religious sites around the island.

The Taiwanese are very utilitarian when it comes to religion. They go to temples looking for security and help, and when this is not forthcoming from one god, they will immediately turn to another. Meanwhile, gods with a reputation for responding to prayers are marked by the billowing clouds of incense smoke at their temples.

At large temples you can frequently see people seeking answers to their questions with divining blocks, small pieces of crescent-shaped wood or bamboo, flat on one side, convex on the other. After a question is asked of the gods, a pair of divining blocks are held in both hands, waved before the god and then thrown on the floor. If they land with the flat side up on one block, and the convex side up on the other, they are called holy blocks and the answer to one's question is yes. If they both land with the same side up, they are called laughing blocks, meaning that the god is laughing at the questioner. Another method is *chien shih*, or numbered fortune sticks. Usually, once holy blocks are cast by throwing the divining blocks, one can pick a numbered fortune stick from a bamboo cup. The number on the stick corresponds with numbered poems that are hung on a rack. An expert at the temple usually interprets the poem for the worshipper, who may be seeking advice on whether to start a certain type of business, or the suitability of a proposed marriage partner. People who do not get the answer they are hoping for will often keep going to different temples until they finally do.

In their search for prosperity and security, Taiwanese appear willing to worship whatever has the power to help or harm them. One Taiwanese theologian tells of a young girl who died in the 1970s during a flood. The villagers were afraid that the girl's spirit would harm them because of her unnatural death, and so they began to worship her as a goddess.

Jesus, Mohammed, Sun Yat-sen, Koxinga and Chiang Kai-shek have all been adopted as gods in local folk beliefs, but the best example of the *laissez-faire* nature of folk religion in Taiwan is the belief that strange looking boulders or old trees have a special spirit within them, and have their own god. Although these gods are usually worshipped *in situ*, and not at a temple, there are several temples around the island dedicated to tree and boulder gods. Animals and their bones can also be worshipped. In Ilan there is a temple where the god of wild cats is worshipped, and in another nearby temple there is an idol to a cat god. In Chiayi County there is a temple dedicated to the dog god and one where the shin bones of cattle are worshipped. Another example is the Temple of the Eighteen Princes, dedicated to 17 sailors and a dog who died at sea in a storm 100 years ago (see Taipei, page 129). Here the dog is the main object of worship.

The adaptability to meet needs arising from a changing society can still be seen in Taiwan. When an illegal lottery craze swept across the island in the 1980s, the utilitarian orientation of some folk religions attracted followers to temples to ask the gods for winning numbers, a practice that would have been considered sacrilegious in Buddhist temples. Superstitious gamblers opened new temples around the island, dedicated to long-forgotten folk gods. When the gods gave a correct number they were rewarded with a striptease show while those gods that failed to come up with the right numbers were often smashed. Bodyguards had to be hired to protect them. Traditional magical calculations used in geomancy and physiognomy were also employed by investors in hopes of striking it rich in the booming stock market of the 1980s.

Pantheonic society mirrors human society, and like humans, Taiwan gods require food, clothing and money for daily expenses. Huge quantities of food are prepared on religious days and during festivals, to be eaten later by the worshippers. With modernization, canned foods and packaged cookies are now commonly put on altars as offerings. Large amounts of paper money are also burned for the use of the gods, and even new clothes are sometimes offered. The gods also have spouses and children in heaven, and some, like the City God, have several wives.

Over 250 gods are worshipped by the Taiwanese. A few of the most important ones are introduced below. The names in brackets are other names by which these gods are known.

WANGYEH (CHIENSUIYEH, FUCHIENSUI)

There are several legends about the origins of Wangyeh and of his temples in Taiwan. Wangyeh was first regarded as a god of plagues, for it was thought that the place his ship drifted to was destined to suffer a plague. Therefore, the people would immediately sacrifice and worship the god out of fear, hoping to turn aside the punishment from heaven. Subsequently, due to the influence of Taoist priests, the image of Wangyeh was changed from a god of plagues to a god of healing. Wangyeh is still the most important god of healing among the Taiwanese, though he is by no means restricted to this, and is considered powerful enough to bestow wealth and happiness or to relieve calamities. In these capacities Wangyeh has become a god of joy.

Temples to Wangyeh are most prevalent in the Pescadores and the seacoast along Tainan, Kaohsiung and Pingtung. Northern Taiwan and the east coast have very few. Hualien has none. In all of Taiwan there are almost 700 temples to Wangyeh, more than to any other god on the island. The largest are Tainan's Nankunshen and Tungkang's Tungnungkung.

MATSU

According to legend, Matsu was born in AD 960. Using mystical powers in her dreams, young Matsu tried to save her father and brothers after a typhoon sank their ship. Upon waking she learned that her brothers had been miraculously saved, but her father had drowned. At the age of 28, Matsu is said to have ascended into heaven.

Her spirit is believed to have often appeared upon the sea, and many sailors have told of how she saved them in storms, during which a red fire, called the 'fire of Matsu', was reportedly seen. After the Song Dynasty an emperor had her deified by calling her the 'Holy Mother of Heaven'.

The Taiwan Straits are known for being treacherous and difficult to navigate. Many of the early immigrants from the mainland carried statues of Matsu or the incense ash from one of her temples with them on their rough sea journey to Taiwan. It is said that if a ship is in danger and it petitions Matsu for help she will save it. Matsu has been credited with the safe passage of numerous ships across the Taiwan Strait. A lamp on the bow of a ship to guide it at night is known as the lamp of Matsu. A large club kept on boats to beat the side if it encounters any large fish or strange sea creature is called the club of Matsu, and if St. Elmos' fire is spotted on the mast of a ship it is called the fire of Matsu, and is considered a bad omen. Matsu is no longer just considered a sea goddess, for she may be petitioned for any possible need.

The earliest temple to Matsu, Matsu Kung, was built in the Pescadores in 1573.

Makung, the name of the main island of the Pescadores, is a corruption of this. In Taiwan now there are close to 383 temples to Matsu, the most famous being Chao-tien Kung of Peikang. On the festival of Matsu's birthday (23rd day of the third lunar month) hundreds of thousands of people go to Peikang to worship at this temple.

KUANYIN

Kuanyin, or the Goddess of Mercy, is a Buddhist deity considered to be a bodhisattva, thus having the power to bring all creatures to Nirvana. She is not just one personality, but may change into 38 different forms, all of which coalesce into one. Some consider her a disciple of Amida-buddha and others an incarnation of him. Her names are many.

The Taiwanese believe her to be a very merciful bodhisattva who saves men from pain and adversity. Images usually portray Kuanyin seated or standing on a lotus, holding a vase. The vase symbolizes harmony, and Kuanyin's hands are said to contain the Dew of Compassion. The lotus symbolizes purity because it grows out of the mud but is not soiled by it.

Sacrifices to Kuanyin consist of only fruit and vegetables, as it would be blasphemy to offer her meat or wine. In Taiwan there are more than 440 temples in which Kuanyin is the main god. The most famous of these is the Lungshan Temple in Taipei's Wanhua district.

KUANTI (KUANKUNG)

Kuanti is a historical person who was born in Shanxi Province. At a young age he became a close friend of the emperor, and supported him in establishing his dynasty. However he was later seized by their enemy Tsao-tsao, a famous general during the wars of the Three Kingdoms. Kuanti was faithful to his oath to the emperor and would not surrender to Tsao-tsao. He was eventually released, and at the age of 68 was killed in battle. Because he was a faithful, loyal and brave man succeeding generations have built temples to him. His adventures have been retold in *The Romance of the Three Kingdoms*, one of China's most famous novels. Kuanti is the patron deity of soldiers, martial arts experts and policemen.

Kuanti has become one of the 'Five Gods of Literature', and scholars revere him as a complete man, possessing the five constant virtues of benevolence, righteousness, propriety, wisdom and sincerity. He is famous for the careful account he kept of all his expenses while imprisoned by Tsao-tsao, returning Tsao-tsao the exact amount he had been given when he was released. Kuanti is also said to have developed a system of accounting, and this is why he is worshipped by merchants and businessmen.

Matsu, the Goddess of the Sea, Matsu Temple, Lukang

Above the family altar in a businessman's home you may see his picture, red-faced, flanked by two men, one with whiskers bristling out and holding a long Chinese fighting knife and the other a handsome looking scholar. The fierce one is Chouchang, Kuanti's right-hand man, while the handsome one is his adopted son, Kuanping.

There are some 200 temples dedicated to Kuanti in Taiwan, concentrated in the Ilan, Tainan and Miaoli areas. However, the most famous temple to this god is the Hsing Tien Temple, located in Taipei on Minchuan East Road.

CHENGHUANG (CITY GOD)

Worship of the City God dates back to the legendary Emperor Yao. Needless to say the City God is in charge of the city, basically working in heaven in the same capacity as the local magistrate, or Yamen, in the world of mortals.

The worship of Chenghuang is quite unique because it illustrates the deification of a man-made object. Chenghuang actually means 'city moat'. The ancient Chinese would worship the wall and moat of their city for they depended on these things for protection. Consequently, the city moat was eventually deified and called Chenghuangyeh. It was not until the period of the Three Kingdoms that temples were built to this god, and they were not common until the Tang Dynasty. During the Qing Dynasty the worship of Chenghuangyeh received official support. Mandarins were required to worship the god at the proper times, and new officials arriving in a town to assume positions were required to report in at the local Chenghuang temple before reporting for work. The worship of Chenghuang was thus supported by the Manchus in order to encourage the common people to virtue and obedience.

In Taiwan, the concept of Chenghuang has been altered quite radically by the people. It is assumed now that any truly good person, after death, can become Chenghuangyeh. This is a very typical theme of Taiwanese puppet shows. The Taiwanese also consider Chenghuang to be the god who judges men.

It is still common today for a person accused of a crime to sacrifice a chicken and swear an oath declaring his innocence in the Chenghuang Temple. On his birthday (the 13th day of the fifth lunar month) Chenghuang leaves his temple to patrol the surrounding area. His two assistants, Generals Hsieh and Fan, clear the way for him. In Taiwan Chenghuangyeh is noted for his many underlings and a great number of wives. Some of the wives were gifts to him.

Taiwan has 44 temples dedicated to Chenghuangyeh. The most famous, Hsiahai Chenghuang Temple, is in Taipei on Tihua Street. The birthday celebration of the City God, fifth lunar month (usually in June), is one of the biggest festivals held annually in Taipei, and has been held at the Hsiahai Chenghuang Temple for over 100 years.

YUHUANG SHANGTI (THE JADE EMPEROR)

The Jade emperor is the main deity in Taoism, and is considered equal to an emperor. His birthday falls on the ninth day of the first lunar month, when offerings of pork, chicken and duck are placed before his image.

PAOSHENGTATI (TATAOKUNG, HUACHIAOKUNG)

This god was formerly a renowned herb doctor who lived during the Song Dynasty, residing in Tongan county, Quanzhou, in Fujian Province. Legends tell of his fame and his ability to heal men and animals of all types of ailments. Paoshengtati is most popular in Tongan county, where he lived. When the people of Tongan began emigrating to Taiwan, they naturally brought their gods and Taiwan now has 160 temples dedicated to the God of Medicine, most of them in Tainan and Chiayi counties. Paoshengtati's birthday is on the 15th day of the third lunar month.

TUTIKUNG (THE EARTH GOD)

Tutikung's formal name is Futechengshen, which means 'the god who brings joy to men'. The worship of this god stems from the early Chinese worship of the soil and the grains it produced. The earth, producer of all food and hence sustainer of man's life, was deified. Folk legend added to the gradual change from worshipping the earth, a natural element, to the worship of an idol. On the mainland a distinction was made between Houtukung and Tutikung, the former being a god of cemeteries while the latter is god of the earth. In Taiwan they are not distinguished but considered one.

The Taiwanese regard the worship of Tutikung as extremely important, with his birthday falling on the second day of the second lunar month. It is a big festival, and includes the sacrifice of chickens and pigs. Temples to Tutikung are small and innumerable. There are probably over a thousand distributed throughout the island.

LU TUNG-PIN

Lu Tung-pin, probably the best known of the Eight Immortals, has been adopted by both Buddhists and Taoists. He was a magistrate, but disappointed went with his wife to live on a mountain as a recluse. His adopted personal name, Tung-pin, literally means 'cave guest'. After his wife died Lu trained himself in the way of the Tao, and finally gained immortality. He is usually represented holding a sabre in one hand and a whisk in the other. The weapon represents his fame for slaying devils, and the whisk his ability to fly and walk on the clouds. He is the patron saint of barbers, and his image is often found on the altars of barbershops. According to legend, an emperor had killed scores of barbers for wounding his ulcerated head. Lu transformed himself into a barber and used his magic to cure the emperor of his sores, and from then on he has been the patron saint of barbers. Lu, who was once spurned in love, is said to be terribly jealous, and capable of breaking up lovers. Even today, young lovers hesitate to visit Taipei's Chihnan Temple, which is dedicated to Lu. During World War II it is said that Lu, Kuankung and Matsu teamed up to divert planes from their targets and defuse falling bombs in mid-flight, safe-guarding the lives and property of the residents of Taipei. Unlike most gods, Lu has a reputation of being a bit of a clown and a play-boy, with numerous stories told of his pranks and amorous adventures. While there seems little in his life that would warrant deifica-tion, those who worship him swear by him.

Door incense holder, Penghu

GENERAL HSIEH AND GENERAL FAN

These are the City God's bodyguards. According to local lore, the two men were close friends who lived in Fujian Province. One day, they were caught in a heavy rain-storm. Hsieh, the tall one, volunteered to get an umbrella to shield the two from the rain. However, when a flood rose, Fan, who was waiting beside a stream, drowned. When Hsieh returned and found his friend dead he was so sad he hung himself. Since General Fan drowned he is painted black, while General Hsieh is in white garments with his tongue hanging out a foot long, a sardonic reminder of his method of suicide. When the statues of these deities are carried in processions, Hsieh is seen carrying a large, folded umbrella over his shoulder. In Taiwan, these two are more commonly called Chiyeh and Payeh.

Temples

The Chinese temple can be traced back to the introduction of Buddhism from India to China in the 4th century AD when Buddhists gathered together in the capital in small groups. These early devotees were mainly intellectuals and aristocrats, as the common people were too uneducated to understand the profound philosophical principles of the religion. The Buddhist monks of that period had no places to establish themselves, and so a few of the nobles generously offered them the use of their houses. The monks soon converted the donated houses into temples, one reason why Chinese temples bear a resemblance to Chinese palaces, traditional official buildings and the homes of high-ranking officials. As Buddhism became more popular and attracted a wider following, temples were erected all over China in the style of these earlier architectural designs. In time, Buddhism began to exert an influence on Taoism, which evolved into a religion with its own temples, similar to Buddhist ones.

When the pioneers arrived in Taiwan from the mainland more than 300 years ago they brought with them deities worshipped in their native areas. Soon after settling down they would invite skilled architects and craftsmen from the mainland to design and construct temples for these homeless gods. In those days, all the major construction materials were also brought from the mainland, including hard granite and durable, insect resistant fir planks from Fujian Province. It was not until many years later that Alishan was discovered to have suitable camphor wood, and Mt Kuanyin high quality stone. In wealthy areas pious Buddhists donated large sums of money to build lavish temples, sparing no cost. Craftsmen carved almost every piece of stone and wood, making each piece an object of art.

Chinese temples can be divided into three categories according to the gods worshipped: orthodox Buddhist temples where deities of Indian origin are enshrined; popular Buddhist temples where people worship virtuous monks who have been elevated to the rank of god; and Taoist and folk temples where homage is paid to deified historical figures and literary characters. The architectural style and structure in all three types of temple are similar. Visitors pass into the temple complex through an arched gate behind which stand three halls, and a drum tower and bell tower on each side of the courtyard. The bell is rung twice a day, once in the morning and once in the evening, to summon monks and nuns to devotions. The bell can also help to release the souls of the dead from hell and can stop material desires and evil thoughts of humans. The drum is for assembling monks and nuns and represents the Buddha and his power.

In Buddhist temples, the first hall is the Heavenly King Hall, which houses the statues of the four guardian gods. In the second hall, the Ta Hsiung Pao Hall, is the major god or goddess of the temple. The third hall is known as the Ta Shih Hall, which is used as a classroom.

In a Taoist temple, the first hall is known as the front hall. It is flanked with door gods from Chinese folklore. In the center of the second and main hall sits the major deity of the temple, surrounded by lesser gods. The third, or rear, hall is home to 'guest gods', the gods of other temples who have been invited for a stay in the temple. If there are no guest gods, the rear hall enshrines the parents of the major deity of the temple, and so is referred to as the Parents' Hall. Buildings flanking the halls are used for offices, meeting rooms and other similar purposes.

In addition to their religious function, temples soon developed into centers of neighborhood, village and city life. In areas where the local administration was not firmly in place, monks would act as mediators in disputes. The temple also served as the site for community meetings, with the front courtyard used for recreational and social events. This is still the case in Taiwan today. Visit a popular temple and you will see the elders of the area sitting around the temple chatting, playing chess, drinking tea or playing traditional Chinese music. Prior to the arrival of television and cinemas, temples provided public entertainment as well, with Taiwanese operas, puppet shows and other folk arts frequently performed in temple squares. It is still common to see such happenings, and even modern films. During elections the more popular temples are major campaign stops for local politicians. In the past, temples also served an economic function, with people from outlying areas bringing their produce on set days once or twice a month for sale in these interim markets.

Taiwan's folk temples have colorful decorations, with paintings, and bas-relief works depicting prolific scenes. Oddly enough, these scenes have little or nothing to do with religion, but come from commonly-known Chinese novels such as *All Men Are Brothers* and the *Romance of the Three Kingdoms*. Buddhist temples are more likely to use paintings with religious themes, mainly based on stories related to the life of the Buddha. The painters portray everything, including the landscape, in Chinese style, not Indian.

Among the most outstanding temple decorations seen in Taiwan are the colorful ceramic figures called *chien nien* found on temple roofs. Chien nien, which literally means 'cut and glue', were first used in China during the Qing Dynasty to decorate temple roofs. While they are quite striking visually, those with a preference for simpler things may find this folk art a bit gaudy. However, an examination of the development of this art can add to one's appreciation.

Chien nien are usually based on history, literature, myths, religion or auspicious symbols, including pagodas, dragons and phoenixes. The art originated in Guangdong Province and on the mainland chien nien are found mainly in the south. They were later introduced to Fujian, and then to Taiwan during the latter years of the Qing Dynasty.

During the boom in temple construction in the 1920s, many prominent chien nien masters crossed the Taiwan Strait to work on the new structures. These craftsmen represented two styles, the Guangdong school, mainly from Shantou City, and the Fujian school, primarily Quanzhou. These styles in Taiwan can be further broken down into the Southern Ho and the Northern Hung, a reference to two famous craftsmen, Ho Chin-lung from Guangdong and Hung Kun-fu from Fujian. Ho is known for his partiality for military figures and Hung for the creation of civilian figures. Most of the surviving chien nien craftsmen in Taiwan today are either the apprentices of these two men, or have learned from other students of these two styles.

The early chien nien were made from flawed or broken ceramic and porcelain bowls. Lime, asbestos, syrup and honey were mixed, making a soft plastic mass that was modeled into rough human, animal and plant shapes. The 'skeletons' were originally made of iron wire, although today it is more common to use cement and stainless steel wire to create the basic shape. While still damp, the figure would be covered with ceramic fragments, taking on a more identifiable form. The rest of the figure was then made from bowl fragments, which had to be carefully shaped before being added to the wet figure. A special clipper had to be used, with pieces taken from different parts of the bowl depending on the shape and effect desired.

Bowls from China and Japan were usually used. Japanese bowls were thinner and easier to cut and shape, but the colors faded quickly under the hot sun. Chinese bowls, on the other hand, were more weather resistant, but were so thick they were difficult to cut.

Chien nien are normally placed along the main swallow-tailed ridge of the peaks of temple roofs, and on the hanging ridges that extend down the front of the roof.

The center of the ridge is the most important section of the roof. In the coastal provinces of southeastern China the practice of putting a pearl flanked by two dragons on the ridge is quite common. The pearl is said to be miraculous and a relic of Buddha, and when it is arranged between two dragons is said to represent Buddha and Buddhism. The dragons are the guardians of Buddhism. The pagoda is an importation from India where it is a symbol of Mt Meru, the axial mountain of the universe connecting heaven and earth. The pagoda is seen as a staircase to heaven. The Chinese believe that mountains can control unlucky influences on earth and since a pagoda is a mountain symbol it is used for this purpose. The small pagoda seen on the ridge of a roof is used for repelling evil influences.

Three gods are often depicted on the roof, representing wealth, posterity and longevity. The God of Longevity is shown with a staff in his right hand and a peach, the symbol of long life, in his left. The God of Posterity carries a child in his arm, and the God of Wealth holds a *ju-i*, an s-shaped ornamental object, formerly a symbol of good luck. The Chinese characters for *ju-i* mean 'as you wish'.

Chien nien temple roof decoration

No Cha, one of the most popular figures from Chinese mythology, is a child god who can perform miraculous deeds with his wheel of fire, magic bracelet and spear. He is often found on the ridges of side halls either alone or riding a dragon. The mythical phoenix is said to appear only in times of prosperity and peace and so is an auspicious symbol. It is often portrayed gazing at a ball of fire and can be used to substitute for the two dragons chasing the blazing pearl on the ridge center.

Buddhist temples usually do not have chien nien, but those that do generally choose designs based on Buddhist scriptures.

The art of chien nien has undergone dramatic changes since first being introduced to Taiwan hundreds of years ago. After the Japanese left the island in 1945, the use of Japanese bowls declined. Now, colored glass is more commonly used in place of bowl fragments due to its low cost, ready availability and ease in working with it. Experts lament this change, saying that the glass chien nien are too transparent and flat and that the colors are too gaudy. Furthermore, ceramic pieces are now mass-produced, and this has also reduced the aesthetic attraction.

There are only a handful of chien nien craftsmen left in Taiwan and none known to be still practicing the trade on the mainland. Fortunately, there appears to be more appreciation today of the artistic value of the figures and so temples undergoing renovation are being more careful to remove the chien nien from the roof and to store them in a safe place until it is time to remount them.

Other symbols are also placed on temple roofs. The *hu lu*, or double-chambered gourd, is an object of magic and mystery. It was originally a flask for water and wine, or a container for herbs. The interior was believed to be a miniature mountain paradise into which a soul could enter and wander about in a state of bliss. According to local lore, an evil spirit can be captured and trapped inside the hu lu, and so its presence on the roof serves to frighten evil spirits away from the temple.

Fish tails and dragon tails are said to be capable of producing waves and rain and so are put on temple roofs to offer protection from fires.

Unfortunately, many of Taiwan's old temples have been damaged by the ravages of time and nature, or have fallen into ruin due to neglect. While many temples have been renovated over the years, often the work was done improperly, with concrete and metal replacing the stone and wood originally used. As a result many temples have lost much of their traditional appearance.

Chinese Food

When refugees from all over China migrated to Taiwan three decades ago, with them came the unique culinary styles of every mainland province. Internationally, the widest range of superb Chinese food accessible to Western tourists is undoubtedly in Taipei. Within blocks of each other are clusters of excellent restaurants offering the fiery cuisine of Sichuan Province, mouth-watering Peking duck, delicately prepared Shanghai-style seafood, exotic Cantonese delicacies, Mongolian barbecue and firepot, and native Taiwanese and Hakka food.

If possible, dine in the company of Chinese friends during your stay in Taiwan. And insist that they order what they like—or else you may end up with sweet-and-sour pork and fried rice selected by polite acquaintances trying to anticipate the taste of foreigners. Taste a dish before asking what it is: pig's stomach and duck blood taste much better than they sound. Chinese meals are perfect for this kind of exploratory dining because dishes are ordered communally and guests help themselves from the collection placed in the center of the table as the meal progresses.

It is good manners only to take from each dish what can be eaten immediately; do not accumulate a great pile of food on your side plate. In fact, side plates are absent in some restaurants and you are expected to use your rice bowl (filled with rice) as only the temporary resting place for food morsels on their way from dish to mouth. A general rule of thumb for table manners is to watch your Chinese friends and act accordingly. Even in some of the classiest restaurants, sipping soup straight from the soup bowl and spitting bones on to the table-cloth are not uncommon. On the other hand, after-dinner toothpick manoeuvres must be discreetly shielded from view by the free hand.

If you cannot dine with Chinese acquaintances, do not be afraid to venture out on your own. After deciding what type of regional cuisine you want, order what seems to be a fair sampling of the menu—for instance, one meat dish, one fish dish, one vegetable dish, a soup, and so on. Chinese menus are usually arranged under these headings and all well-known restaurants in Taipei have English translations. In deciding on quantity, a basic guideline for a small group is to order small portions of as many dishes as there are diners, plus one soup. For larger groups, several dishes should be ordered in medium or large portions. You can also ask about specialities of the house. In Taiwanese restaurants, the quality of the service and the trappings do not always reflect the quality of the food so taste first before passing judgment. You should make advance reservations for the more popular restaurants.

In Taiwan the most popular regional cuisine is from **Sichuan Province** in southwest China. Spicy and richly flavoured, this cuisine makes liberal use of hot peppers and may prove rather fiery to the uninitiated. Popular specialities include *kung pao* chicken (diced boneless chicken sautéed with chillies), duck smoked with camphor and tea, egg-plant with garlic and *mapo tofu* (diced beancurd sautéed with ground pork, garlic, scallions, ginger and lots of chilli peppers). Rice is offered but you might try *yin szu chuan* (silver silk rolls), a type of breadroll either steamed or deep-fried.

Cuisine from **Beijing** is mild but hearty. Wheat rather than rice is the staple and dumplings, breads and noodles feature prominently. The most famous dish—and justifiably so—is Peking duck. The meat and crisp skin of the duck is wrapped in thin crêpes of slightly griddled, unleavened dough after being dabbed with sweet bean sauce and garnished with scallion. Soup made from the duck bones is also delicious.

Hunan cuisine, like that of Sichuan, is known for its use of chilli peppers. A popular dish is honey ham.

The highlight of **Jiangzhe** cuisine (from Jiangsu and Zhejiang, two provinces located on the east coast of China), also known as Shanghai-style cooking, is seafood. Popular dishes are *xia pa* (fish jaws), vinegar fish and rock fish soup. Try also lion's head, pork meatball served on cabbage.

Cantonese cooking from southeast China is the best known provincial cuisine in most Overseas Chinese communities around the world. Sweet and colorful, Cantonese food is perhaps most famous for the brunchtime snack and tea morsels known in Cantonese as *dim sum* and in Mandarin as *dianxin*. Waitresses wheel carts holding endless varieties of Cantonese delicacies through the restaurant and diners simply select what they want from the parade of dumplings, sweet pastries, roasted meats and steamed treats.

Taiwanese cuisine is a branch of eastern Chinese cooking with a strong Japanese influence. It is light and liberally spiced with ginger and, like Shanghainese cuisine, often features seafood. Fried dishes are often cooked in pork fat. Try poached shrimp or squid, grilled eel, fried shrimp rolls, grilled clams, and turtle soup.

Hakka cooking is very earthy, representing their ties with agricultural society. Popular dishes include tripe, pig's knuckles, pig's tongue, pig's kidney, *kou rou* (fatty pork cooked with dried salted vegetable), pickled vegetables as well as other more standard Chinese dishes.

The hot pot, or firepot, is a popular winter dish, with vegetables, meat and seafood cooked together by you in a pot right at your table. At **Mongolian** barbecue restaurants for one price you can fill your bowl as often as you like with thinly sliced chicken, beef, lamb, a wide choice of vegetables and numerous condiments. The cook then stir fries it on a large stone grill.

Vegetarian cooking has long been a part of Chinese cuisine and contrary to popular opinion, it is anything but bland. *Sucai*, or vegetarian cuisine, is served at Buddhist temples and restaurants around the island. Try one of the island's vegetarian buffet restaurants which offer an interesting variety of dishes at very modest prices.

As a heritage from its 50-year occupation by Japan, Taiwan also has a wide range of Japanese restaurants, ranging from hole-in-the-wall places frequented by locals to palatial affairs in the major hotels.

TEAHOUSES

For years, teahouses in Taipei were small, dingy places where old men escaped for a pot of tea, a game of chess and small talk with friends. All this began to change around 1980, when a few shops opened to a young generation with a new-found respect for the past.

The growing popularity of teahouses marks a rekindling of interest in things Chinese among young people, a desire to balance the growing modernization of society with traditional aspects of Chinese culture. Teahouses have become places where people seeking to escape the pressures and fast pace of urban society can find peace and quiet, if only for a few hours, before heading back into the crowded city streets.

Teahouses in Taiwan come in a variety of shapes and sizes, ranging from Japanese-style houses with grass mats to modernistic art galleries to rustic farmhouses. The Tungpo Teahouse near National Taiwan University is often crowded with students who meet here to sip tea and talk as small birds fly around freely overhead.

A rustic house

Tungpo is designed with traditional Chinese red brick walls, cobblestone floors and Japanese *tatami* mats for guests to sit on. Folk artifacts displayed here were gathered by the owners who searched outlying villages and farms for old bowls, statues, stones, wood-carvings and temple accessories. Customers must get their own hot water for making tea, using a wooden ladle to dip water from a brick farmhouse stove in the rear of the shop. Genuine tea aficionados, who say tea is best enjoyed in pleasant surroundings and a tranquil atmosphere, will be disappointed, however, by the hustle and bustle of this lively teahouse.

The serene Wistaria Teahouse is a favorite of Chinese and foreign students, professors, artists and politicians. Chou Yu,

Tea utensils

its owner and former president of the Teahouse Owners' Association, has tried to create more than just a place to drink tea.

Chou, who says he considers the teahouse 'a small society,' laments that modern-day Taiwanese have become too materialistic and have lost the traditional Chinese sense of nature; he is using his teahouse to rekindle these forfeited feelings.

A proponent of Taoism, Chou has designed his place to reflect sensitivity toward nature. The garden has been laid out in accordance with the Taoist belief that nature is unfathomable and ambiguous. It has well-placed pockets of hidden spaces—a small spring, little ponds, secluded stone tables—which

continues on page 68

surprise the visitor at each turn. The fallen plaster and cracks on the wall left by a recent earthquake remain in place so people can see how man built the house and how nature has altered it. But nothing is ever explained or pointed out to the visitor. 'According to my philosophy,' he says, 'I always want to hide something and make people see it. This makes them more creative in the process.'

Most teahouses do not make much money. Their mainly young owners are not businessmen out to make a fast buck, but rather humans more interested in providing a congenial place for friends to meet and enjoy art, drama, poetry and traditional folk arts.

Although a visitor to Taiwan could not be blamed for assuming that coffee was the national drink, since coffee shops stand on almost every corner, the art of drinking tea originated in China, only later being transferred to Japan, where the highly ritualized tea ceremony still flourishes today. Historians say that tea was cultivated in China as early as AD 350. Lu Yu's classic, *The Art of Drinking Tea*, was written in the 8th century, when tea was made from pressed cakes of tea leaves.

The Chinese way of preparing and drinking tea is not as formal as in the Japanese *Chanoyu* tradition. China never developed an elaborate tea ceremony, which Chinese feel is contrary to the Taoist feeling of spontaneity and informality that they associate with drinking tea. They consider the art of tea as a release of creativity and imagination and a way to enjoy intimate friendship. Chinese tea drinking does not confine people to a tea room nor does it force them to follow rigid ceremony.

'Here the philosophy is different,' says Chou. 'We want the feeling to be natural and not designed. The Chinese style is more creative, spontaneous and interesting.'

John Blofeld, a true tea devotee, wrote in *The Chinese Art of Tea* that 'a whole range of pleasures involving ears, eyes, nose, palate and mood can be enjoyed by two or three people who have come together to make and drink fine tea.'

'For example there is music in the hiss and bubble of a kettle, a springtime freshness in the fragrance of the steam rising from the teacups, and a gentle exhilaration—too subtle to be apparent to a distracted mind—results from certain mysterious properties inherent in the tea itself....'

Tea

A visit to one of Taiwan's numerous teahouses will give you an opportunity to enjoy drinking tea the way Chinese connoisseurs do. In this style of drinking, known as *kungfu cha*, you will use a small teapot and tiny tea cups. This tea is not to be gulped down, but should be savoured. Kungfu does not just apply to martial arts, but to any activity that requires time and effort to master, from Taoist physical training to the art of brewing good tea.

As you will probably have to manage by yourself, a little advice is in order. Choose your type of tea from the many offered on the menu. First pour scalding water over the teapot to warm it. This is important because the pot used for kungfu tea is so little that the heat of the small amount of water used for each infusion disperses very quickly. The way to do this is to pour hot water into the empty pot until it runs out and into the tea boat in which the pot stands, and both are full. The pot is thus heated from within and without. Wait five seconds and then dispose of all the water.

Next fill the empty pot with tea leaves, half full if you are using a semi-fermented tea (oolong), or one third full if you are drinking green tea. The pot and tea boat are filled once again as before. Pouring should be done in a rotary motion to ensure the stream of water falls evenly on all the tea leaves. The lid is then immediately replaced. This first infusion is not drunk, but immediately poured away. This is known as 'washing the leaves', which stay in the pot for the second infusion, following immediately. The pot is refilled and the tea steeps as the host scalds the cups by pouring hot water into and over them in the tea plate. Scalding must take only 30 seconds to prevent the water in the teapot from lying on the huge pile of leaves too long, making the tea too strong.

The cups are now placed touching one another to facilitate pouring. The host dries the bottom of the teapot by running it around the rim of the tea boat in a counterclockwise direction, a welcoming symbol. Tea is then poured into the cups, a little bit at a time in each cup, rotating until each cup is full. This ensures that the properties of the tea remain equal in each cup.

As soon as the cups are returned to the table, another infusion is made. Altogether, there may be four infusions, not including the first discarded one. The first pot should steep for 30 seconds, the remaining three infusions for just ten seconds.

Most teahouses serve more than just tea. Some enhance the experience with popular snacks such as salted melon seeds, peanuts, toasted squid, dried beancurd, rice cakes and preserved fruits.

Traditional Taiwan Architecture

It has been said that traditional Chinese dwellings provided more than just protection from the elements. Those built in accordance with the dictates of traditional custom are thought to be an expression of Chinese society, a statement about the socio-cultural factors that linked the individual, family and society, tying them to their heritage.

For example, since old Chinese dwellings housed extended families ranging from a few dozen people to several hundred, they were larger than modern dwellings. To maintain the required distinctions in status between young and old, the honored and the lowly, architecture had to comply with the order of social precedence. Therefore, the roofs on the right and left wings, where sons and grandsons lived, were lower than the roofs of the central rooms which housed family elders.

Furthermore, in the agricultural society of the past, the extended family was an economic unit responsible for both production and consumption. The dwelling thus also included the means of production. A large landholder's house would contain a grain-drying area and a rent collection office in front of the main doorway, while a merchant's house would include storerooms and workshops.

Large family complexes also played a social and cultural role. The homes of the Lins of Panchiao and the Lins of Wufeng, for example, contained schools, opera stages, sewing rooms, etc. Traditional Taiwanese dwellings, therefore, sheltered not only families but customs, norms and religious practices as well, embodying a whole way of life.

Despite the island's breakneck pace of modernization, and poor attempts at renovation prior to the 1980s, many old dwellings have escaped the wrecking ball and the vicissitudes of nature and time, thanks to the hard work of architects, historians and others determined to preserve this part of China's heritage.

While northern Chinese styles have served as the prototypes for the development of architecture throughout China, a distinctive southern style has evolved over the centuries, with farm structures built by early Chinese immigrants in the 17th and 18th centuries in the styles of Quanzhou and Zhangzhou, Fujian, where most of the early migrants came from.

These pioneers did not construct permanent Chinese dwellings. There were few women here due to the rugged frontier life, difficulty in crossing the Taiwan Strait as well as to the Qing-dynasty policy of the late 1700s, which restricted the migration of women. Ancestral tablets, which signified family succession and continuity and determined where home was, were to stay on the mainland for the time being.

The immigrants considered themselves sojourners until they one day returned to their ancestral homes in China, or until they were well-established enough in Taiwan to lay the foundations of a nuclear family. Until then, shelter was their main concern, and the bamboo, reed matting and thatched grasses used by the aborigines were adopted by the Chinese as well.

The male–female imbalance began to shift toward the end of the 18th century as men returned to their native villages to find wives, or as they married sinicised aborigine women on the island. With the formation of families, the diminishing of ties to the ancestral village in China and the amassing of wealth, more substantial structures were needed, and people began to build more durable dwellings, usually following traditional precepts.

Shape, size and orientation were determined by mainland practices that emphasized symmetry and balance. The basic structure of the traditional house was rather uniform. It contained a walled enclosure surrounding several smaller buildings, which in turn encompassed one or more courtyards. The courtyard was called *jin*, or entrance, because it denoted a central building which must be entered to reach the back halls. In the center of the main building there was a large room, the central or ancestral hall, which held the ancestral altar, ancestral tablets and portraits of the ancestors. This room also served as a room for greeting guests, and for ceremonies such as weddings and funerals. The receiving of guests and ceremonies were transferred to other rooms later, if new rooms were added to the complex.

Traditional southern Chinese architecture

This core building was the nucleus to which ramified structures were attached, with the unit expanding as the family grew. The pattern evolved into an I- or an inverted U-shape (*sanhoyuan*), with the addition of wings built at right angles to the axis of the central portion. These side buildings, called *hulong*, or protector dragons, were used as bedrooms for younger generations, or as space for storage or cooking. If additional wings were built outside the hulong, they were called outer protectors. The left and right wings were normally equal in size and height in accordance with Chinese principals of balance and aesthetics.

The wings had accordant roof lines that were lower than the main and most important dwelling, which housed the ancestral altar. A formalized hierarchy of room use dictated that the oldest and most important members of the household occupied the bedrooms closest to the ancestral hall. The roofs of buildings decrease in height with the descending importance of their occupant, so that the building with the lowest roof would be that used by servants or for storage and other service functions. This system also created a hierarchy of privacy. The higher one's position in the family, the more courtyards one could enter, and the further one could proceed into the complex.

Between the wings would be one or more courtyards, which provided room for performing household chores outside the dark interiors, and which also served as a drying floor for agricultural goods.

As the family unit evolved through the marriage of sons, and as wealth and human relations allowed, the home expanded past the U-shape, with expansion happening either laterally or to the front. Farm houses tended to expand laterally, while domiciles of the aspiring or arrived gentry reached greater depths. Wings would usually be added on parallel to the basic wings in pairs.

A large number of rural dwellings are very narrow, stretching a long depth from the main entrance, rather than expanding laterally. These were usually not designed to meet the needs of a growing family, but to permit a hierarchy of ceremony and privacy not found in the more egalitarian farmhouse.

Although the houses found in Taiwan during the pioneer years were bamboo- and wood-thatched, these were gradually replaced by houses using sun-dried bricks, stone and eventually kiln-dried bricks. Tamped earth construction techniques were common in the drier areas of the mainland, but this was rare in Taiwan where pounded earth was vulnerable to frequent earthquakes and constant rain.

Sun-dried bricks were used well into the 20th century. These were sometimes cut from mud accumulations on the surface of paddy fields, stacked in rows and then covered with straw to dry for several weeks. More often, however, clay was dug from a pit at the front of the dwelling or taken from hill slopes on the edge of a river. The clay was mixed with rice straw or rice chaff to strengthen it, was moulded and cut,

Fengshui

When the well-known architect Han Pao-te returned home to Taipei from studying at Princeton and Harvard in the 1960s, his first assignment was to design a house for a relative who was a high-ranking government official. But just as the official was about to move in to his new house, colleagues criticized it as unfit; the *fengshui*, they said, was bad. To his deep embarassment, the newly grad uated architect was forced to invite a fengshui man, who didn't have the benefit of an Ivy League education, to look at his design and correct his 'mistakes'.

A palmistry chart, used to tell a person's fortune by the lines and marks on the palm

'That was when I realized the power of fengshui,' Han recalls. 'I began to study it right away.'

Fengshui, which literally means 'wind and water,' is the ancient Chinese art of geomancy. It is based on the belief that inanimate objects can affect one's life. People in Taiwan and other Chinese communities still use fengshui today to determine the positioning of graves, houses and other buildings, including office towers, and furniture and office layouts.

When modern highrises go up in Taipei, the builder routinely calls in a geomancer, whether he believes in fengshui or not, aware that a prospective occupant will call in his own geomancer to see whether the building has the right fengshui to help rather than hinder his fortune. Some construction companies even have fengshui experts on the payroll as consultants.

Despite the fact that modernization has overtaken Taiwan, the geomancy business has boomed in recent years, and Taipei alone is estimated to have 10,000 practitioners. Local psychologists point to the pressures and rapid change of modern society that induce people to turn to traditional practices like fortune-telling and geomancy for comfort and a sense of their roots.

Geomancers follow ancient guidelines, some based on common sense, in making their design recommendations. Raised ground, for instance, is consid-

continues on page 74

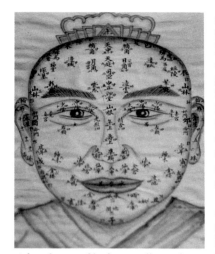

A face chart, used by fortune tellers to foresee the future of a person from facial features

ered a good place to erect a building; that stands to reason, particularly in flood-prone cities. When designing a house, geomancers generally recommend that its important area should be centrally located; that helps promote a close family unit. Mirrors with eight diagrams painted on them are commonly seen hanging over doors because people believe they deflect bad luck from a dwelling.

The color of a building can also come into play. Although most cultures consider fire-engine red loud and garish, it is common in Chinese communities, especially during important holidays, because it is the color of joy and festivity. Yellow was favored by ancient Chinese royalty, so it also enjoys popularity. Green is another auspicious shade, because of its connection with the earth, plants and fertility.

Real estate advertisements in newspapers frequently employ 'good fengshui' as a selling point and it is common for builders, developers and clients alike to move their doors from one location to another in an attempt to improve the fengshui. One restaurant moved its door from one side of the shop to the opposite side in hopes of turning business around. This evidently did not work and the restaurant soon changed hands. When the new owner took over he promptly returned the door to its original site.

Special rulers are sold for measuring the size of a family altar and the distance between the gods placed on it. If everything is not just right, a family or proprietor could be in for a spell of bad luck. One geomancer says that the removal of even a single misplaced nail can end problems.

Fengshui is taken seriously by all segments of Taiwan's society, from small village farmers right up to corporate decision-makers. When the Evergreen Group put up its new headquarters in Taipei in 1987, it erected a large white ship's mast in a small garden adjoining the building. Unfortunately, the mast was directly opposite the door of another building just across the street. The other company complained that the mast was 'like a dagger pointed at their offices,' thus ruining their fengshui. They demanded that it be moved, but Evergreen balked, saying it had no other place to put the mast. The dispute was only resolved when the complainant moved into a new office building.

Despite these stories, there is evidence that geomancy may be touched by charlatanism. Han says that geomancy today is arbitrary, has numerous interpretations, and that it is not uncommon for several geomancers to come up with totally different conclusions. In fact, fengshui was originally used only to determine the position of burial sites and did not include buildings or furniture until recent times, he says.

Han does not believe in fengshui, which he describes as a proto-science. But he says that a knowledge of it can produce a better understanding of Chinese culture. 'If you don't understand fengshui, you will still understand Chinese architecture, but you will miss a lot,' he says. 'Now when I look at the traditional Chinese environment, I understand it better.'

Present-day attitudes toward fengshui in modern Taipei can be summed up in the words of Chi Kang (223–62), one of the Seven Sages of the Bamboo Grove. 'I'm hesitant to make a hard and fast judgment. I wouldn't want to say that divination can tell your future, but I wouldn't want to say there are no unlucky houses either.' In short, it's probably safer to believe in fengshui than not to.

A Geomancer's compass, a tool to define suitable locations for houses and buildings

and then left to dry in the sun. The roof beams were directly propped up by the sun-dried mud walls. To prevent premature rotting of the timbers resulting from contact with the water-absorbent earthen walls, several courses of kiln-dried brick or stone were piled on top of the wall.

Every year, usually in May or June, the plum rains, which come when the plum crop ripens, bring a month or more of rain to southern China and Taiwan. Damage from rain was prevented by the use of broad eaves, a covering of plaited grasses, plastering of outer walls with lime cement or by adding a resilient veneer.

The use of more stylish tile and thin brick veneers indicated that the owner was newly prosperous. Thin square or rectangular tiles on old homes were fastened with a nail or wooden stake through the center, said to have been introduced by the Dutch during their occupation of the island. Fishscale tiles arranged like shingles are still seen on numerous structures in southern Taiwan. The old master masons also used *hung mao tu*, a mixture of brown sugar, glutinous rice and lime to cement the tiles onto the wall.

Kiln-dried bricks date back to the late 17th century but were not common until the 19th century. Many of the bricks used in old dwellings were imported to Taiwan from the mainland as ballast in trading ships carrying lighter necessities such as cloth back to the island. The ships bound for Taiwan from Fujian often needed ballast against the rough sea, and so stone, timber, tiles and other building materials were brought to the island in large quantities. Black bricks came from northern Fujian, while red bricks came from southern Fujian.

Although Taiwan was rich in forest land, the woods were inhabited by head-hunting aborigines. In those days, therefore, it was easier to use lumber shipped over from the mainland. There were generally two types, one from Fuzhou and the other from Minnan. Fuzhou, in northern Fujian, was famous for its pine and fir and the houses there were largely left unpainted to show the fine grain of the wood. Minnan, however, produced a poorer grade and so paint was used extensively to make up for its deficiency. The special shade of blue seen in many homes of Taiwan's gentry was one of the most popular colors used in southern Fujian.

The skills of local builders in those days were inferior to those of Quanzhou and Zhangzhou craftsmen. Many of the large rural farmsteads around today, such as the Wufeng Lins, the Panchiao Lins and the Taipei Lins, were built under the watchful eye of mainland masters and artisans who were brought in with the materials from the mainland. With both material and craftsmen from Fujian, the building styles of southern China were faithfully reproduced here in Taiwan.

But the construction of Chinese houses requires more than the use of carpenters and masons. *Fengshui* (literally wind and water), or geomancy, a popular but compli-cated set of rules based on the ancient belief which contends that inanimate objects can influence one's life, also applies to location and things outside the house such as railroad tracks, power lines and graves. Fengshui was used to determine the selection of building sites, their orientation, the number and sometimes even the purpose of the rooms.

Physical dimensions were also carefully determined. The Wen Kung scale, an esoteric measuring scale, was used to ensure all heights and depths of rooms conformed to auspicious measurements. The scale, also known as the Lu Pan scale, is divided into eight sections of four units each and the various lengths on the scale were believed to be related to the future fortune of the owner of the house. Auspicious and inauspicious measurements are marked on the ruler and unlucky measurements had to be avoided at any cost, lest the occupant meet with misfortune, and possibly even death. The central halls and bedrooms in Taiwan houses were therefore all of specific pre-determined proportions, and so fairly uniform.

These frontier mansions clearly reflect orthodox domestic architectural principles, as well as attempts to incorporate elements of temple styles. Thatched roofs were most common, except for the tiled roofs of some gentry families and temples, and even as late as 1952, 45 per cent of rural dwellings in Taiwan had thatched roofs. New-found wealth, improved social status or rank acquired by passing the civil examinations, were often indicated by the transformation of a thatched roof to a more substantial one.

In China a person's standing was indicated by the style of roof on his house, and this was strictly regulated by Beijing. Two basic roof styles are found in Taiwan: swallow's tail and horseback. The swallow's tail, marked by raised sweeping ends, was restricted to temples and the houses of government officials. Common people used the unrestricted horseback style, which as its name implies was rounded and raised much like the back of a horse. Those who came to Taiwan in the 16th and 17th centuries mainly settled in the south around Tainan, the seat of the government at that time. The sumptuary laws governing housing during the Ming and Qing dynasties were therefore more carefully observed in the south.

Taiwan's frontier *nouveau riche* in the north, far from the reach of the government, boldly flouted these regulations, erecting dwellings with swallow's tail roofs as well as other styles and decorations prohibited in China and southern Taiwan.

The roof frame was made up of a series of columns held in place by tiers of beams. The weight of such roofs led to the use of small windows to lessen the strain on the walls. Small windows had the added benefit of keeping out intruders and subtropical thunder showers, but they make the interior very dark.

Horseback roofs, now commonly seen all over the island, normally have supportive ridge poles running the length of the roof which are tied to the walls using a device called the 'iron scissors,' said to be another legacy of the Dutch. Decorative embellishments can be seen at the ends of most horseback roofs. Carved or ceramic dragons, phoenixes and other auspicious animals were placed along the ridge of some roofs. Auspicious fruits such as peaches and pomegranates, as well as flowers, weapons and other symbolic objects, can also be seen on the tops of dwellings.

The profusion of symbolic house decorations reveals the deep faith in religious beliefs, spirit worship, geomancy and folk superstitions. Houses in Tainan's Anping District, for example, had reflecting walls across the front courtyard and directly opposite the main entrance, or wooden screens between the front gate and the entrance to the first court to protect the dwelling from intruding evil spirits. A carved lion's head brandishing a sword in its mouth was placed over the main doorway, and a tai chi symbol painted on the ridgepole served the same purpose.

Over the ancestral hall the family would hang a *pa kua*, or eight trigams, an antidote for evil influences resulting from location or the construction of a new building close by. This is usually employed when there are mutually antagonistic situations, such as when a door faces another door across the lane, or when a lane leads directly to a doorway. A small mirror was often hung above the door where it is seen by many Chinese as an effective deflector of malevolent spirits. These mirrors are quite common today, even in modern high-rise buildings in Taipei.

In the Lin family complex in Panchiao some of the walls are decorated with various types of auspicious tile designs. Octagonal tiles signify good luck from the eight directions, hexagonal tiles symbolize the shell of a turtle, and thus longevity, round tiles represent perfection, and double round tiles double perfection. Tiles in the shape of ancient Chinese coins signify wealth.

The rapid transformation of Taiwan in recent decades has almost completely erased the culture and lifestyle of the past. Fortunately, many old houses remain today, their presence whispering secrets of days gone by. With even just a smattering of knowledge about their function and structure, one can begin to understand these whisperings and the environment that produced them.

The Arts

CHINESE OPERA

Up until the introduction of Western drama to China, all Chinese drama was operatic in nature and presentation. Although the use of conversational dialogue was not unknown, it was never seriously developed.

Chinese opera, which embraces all forms of traditional Chinese drama, can be traced back to the second millennium BC. However, regular professional performances did not begin until the 12th century AD, when cities with large populations began to emerge. At this time, Chinese opera was a composite art form comprising singing, dancing and acrobatics.

Chinese opera has several regional forms, each of which has developed separately. Peking (Beijing) opera, the most common form today, originated in 1790 when the nation's top regional theatrical companies gathered in Beijing to celebrate the birthday of Emperor Chien-lung (1711–1799). Many of the companies stayed in the capital after the festivities ended, continuing to give performances at the court and for the general public. Peking opera eventually prevailed over the other regional opera forms, mainly due to its unique aria style and arrangement.

The stage in Chinese opera is similar in all the genres. It is almost completely bare, with only symbolic and functional props. The costumes are colorful and elaborately embroidered, but no effort is made to achieve historical authenticity. The costume patterns and designs are based partly on Ming-dynasty fashions and partly on convention, regardless of the historical period in which the opera is set. Nor is any attempt made towards realistic lighting. Night scenes are presented with full lighting.

There are four major categories of role in Peking opera: male, female, painted face and the comic. Each is further divided according to age, status and occupation. The painted face usually includes bandits, schemers and traitors. The comic can be identified by the white patches of paint on the nose or around the eyes.

Peking opera has been the most famous genre in Chinese theater for two hundred years, but now faces increasing competition from television and videotapes. This has led some opera troupes to experiment with new forms. In 1987 *Kingdom of Desires*, an adaption of *Macbeth*, was performed by a local opera troupe. Several Western plays have also been adapted for Peking opera, such as Eugene Ionesco's *Chairs*. The recent opening to mainland China has made it possible for operas by mainland playwrights to be staged in Taiwan theaters, and this has helped to revitalize dying interest in the art form.

Peking opera is now mainly popular in Taiwan among intellectuals and opera connoisseurs, and can frequently be seen on stage and on television. There are four prominent professional opera troupes on the island, affiliated with the army, navy, air force and the Ministry of Education, as well as many private troupes.

Taiwan has two schools dedicated to the training of actors and musicians: the National Fuhsing Dramatic Arts Academy and the Kuokuang Drama and Fine Arts Experimental School, operated by the armed forces. Both accept students at the age of nine and offer nine years of training. Two schools offer advanced college-level training.

TAIWANESE OPERA

Kotsaihsi, or Taiwanese opera, was adapted from the type of song brought to the island by immigrants from Fujian Province in the late Ming and Qing dynasties. The songs were in the Fujian dialect, and most described the feelings of early immigrants who worked hard to clear land for settling and planting.

This art form quickly grew in popularity, and gradually incorporated the faster rhythms of local folk songs. Although the operas were originally performed without musical accompaniment, string instruments were later added. In the early days, operas used simple costumes and easily understood gestures and expressions dramatizing every-day life. These performances were put on in town squares or in front of temples, where people gathered to enjoy the show.

Kotsaihsi was later influenced by the more animated Peking opera, increasing its popularity. Farmers organized their own theater groups, performing outdoors and in public theaters. With the arrival of television and movies, however, kotsaihsi was rejected as unsophisticated and lost its position as the dominant form of entertainment. To win back its audience, opera performers perfected their skills and explored ways to suit the changing tastes of viewers. One idea they came up with was to put women in leading roles. Other innovations included the use of scripts, modern writing and directing methods, the use of modern dialogue in place of narration, and improved costumes and sets. Kotsaihsi has been revived, and is now a popular form of nightly TV entertainment. Outdoor performances have not died out and kotsaihsi can still be seen at temples and public places where neighborhood residents, from grandparents to grandchildren, crowd the sidewalks to enjoy one of the island's few institutions of the past.

PUPPET THEATRE

It is not known for sure when *putaihsi*, the traditional Taiwanese hand puppet theater, first started. However, one legend claims that it was originated some 300 years ago by a man called Liang Ping-lin. Liang was on his way to Beijing to take the annual civil service examination when he dreamed of an old man who read his palm

Colorful Taiwanese puppets

and predicted 'Success is within your palm'. Liang assumed this meant he would pass the examination, but he failed. He returned home and took up puppetry, later giving performances based on traditional themes. His reputation spread and soon people came from far away to see his shows. Liang then incorporated carving, embroidery, music and other arts into puppetry, and it is in this form that putaihsi was transported to Taiwan by early immigrants from Fujian Province.

Modern day puppets are smaller and less well-made, and today's hand puppet theater no longer strictly follows the classical rules, which regulated when puppets were to enter, exit, sit and walk. However, this folk art is still popular on the island, and several schools have set up hand puppet troupes, keeping the art alive for generations to follow.

MUSIC

Traditional Chinese music in Taiwan can be divided into two categories. The first developed from music played by folk groups, comprising from three to ten people. The performers are generally elderly and mainly play folk tunes or themes from Chinese operas. The modified Chinese orchestra is a response to changes in society, playing traditional Chinese music and adaptations of folk songs, as well as classical and symphonic compositions. There are three professional Chinese orchestras in Taiwan giving frequent performances.

DANCE

Dance in China can be traced back to the Shang and Chou periods of the first millennium BC, when it was divided into two categories, civilian and military. The later subjugation of China by border peoples led to the introduction of folk dance forms of various peoples of Central Asia, which were merged with indigenous dances of the Han Chinese. This continued into the Tang Dynasty, which was the golden age of Chinese dance. The imperial court gathered the top dancers of the country to perform the lavish 'Ten Movement Music' dance, which incorporated elements from China, Korea, Xinjiang, India, Persia and Central Asia. This form of dance made use of colorful costumes, poetry, songs and a dramatic plot, combined with background music to create an artistic performance rich in style and content. It was a predecessor of modern Chinese opera.

Dance in Taiwan has become a multifaceted art form. Students of dance usually begin with ballet and modern dance, only later progressing to traditional Chinese dance. They then look for new directions for Chinese-style body expression with an open mind to experimentation. Lin Hwai-min's Cloud Gate Dance Ensemble was built on a foundation of modern dance, and gradually absorbed elements from traditional Chinese opera. The New Classical Dance Troupe also takes modern dance as its starting point, combining it with traditional ethnic and Taiwan aborigine folk dance.

FILM

Taiwan once had a well-deserved reputation for churning out low-quality kungfu flicks and sticky romantic films. While films of the past were not allowed to deal honestly with the problems of modern society, a new generation of directors came on the scene in the 1980s and took advantage of the trend toward political liberalism to turn out realistic films which examined aspects of society considered taboo just a few years ago. Young directors began developing their own styles, and found a wealth of material in Taiwan's *hsiang tu* (native soil) literature, which focused on local themes, working-class characters and social issues.

Some suggested Taiwan films are:

Jade Love, a gripping film about spurned love, is based on a novel by Pai Hsien-yung, considered to be one of the best contemporary Chinese writers.

The Sandwich Man, three short pieces about Taiwan in the early 1950s, based on short stories by Huang Chun-ming, one of the island's most famous authors.

City of Sadness, winner of the Golden Lion Award for best film at the Venice Film Festival in 1989, deals with the turbulent transition period when the island was returned to Chinese rule in 1945. The infamous February 28 Incident, in which thousands were killed, serves as background. Directed by Hou Hsiao-hsien, one of the island's handful of talented young directors.

Several other movies by Hou are bitter-sweet searches into family relationships in the past based on Hou's own experiences growing up in a small town in Taiwan: *Summer at Grandpa's*, the semi-autobiographical *A Time to Live and a Time to Die* and *Dust in the Wind*. *The Boys of Fengkuei* is about three boys from a fishing village in the Pescadores who run off to the bright city lights of Kaohsiung.

Another excellent young director is Edward Yang. *That Day on the Beach* tells the story of a young woman who leaves her home and domineering father to marry her lover. The marriage collapses and she finds that the new, free world is more than she bargained for. Also by Yang are *The Terrorizer*, *Taipei Story* and *A Brighter Summer Day*.

Films that focus on rural life in Taiwan include: *A Flower in the Rainy Night*, which examines the plight of a young woman given away as a child and then sold by her foster parents to a brothel at the age of 14; *Dull Ice Flower*, a moving story about a poor boy from a small village who wants to be an artist, provides an interesting look at village life in the 1960s.

Since almost all Chinese films have English subtitles, it is possible for foreign visitors to gain rare and extraordinary insights into the local culture through its films. MTV centers (MTV stands for movie television) are places where you can choose a video cassette for viewing in a small private room that can sit one to several persons. Solar System, in Taipei, is considered the best MTV center in Taiwan. It has some 15,000 Chinese and foreign titles, including a good collection of classic films, documentaries, cartoons and shorts, and 66 private rooms.

Folk Arts

With the transition from an agricultural to an industrial society, many traditional folk arts have begun to decline, and even disappear. The government and the Council for Cultural Planning and Development have made a special effort to encourage the protection of folk arts and folk crafts. The Ministry of Education has helped by presenting awards to those contributing to the preservation and transmission of traditional folk arts. More importantly, the ministry has encouraged schools to include traditional folk arts in physical education and art classes to ensure their natural survival.

Two of the most common folk art performances are the dragon dance and the lion dance, an indispensable part of Chinese New Year and other important celebrations. The Chinese revere the dragon, which symbolizes power, dignity and good luck, and the dragon dance has been popular since the Song Dynasty. The dragon can be from nine to 24 sections long, with each section stretching from five to six and a half feet, supported by up to 100 strong members. The lion dance is more common, partly because it requires less members and can be performed in a smaller area. One person manipulates the head, and one the tail. A third person sometimes carries a silk flower ball or wears a mask of the laughing Buddha, teasing the lion into action.

Chinese games dating back thousands of years remain popular with young people in Taiwan. Diabolo is a barbell-shaped hollow toy that is manipulated on a string tied to two sticks. The player spins the diabolo on the string, working it from side to side, sometimes flinging it high into the air and then catching it again on the string. The hollow diabolo emits a humming sound as it spins back and forth. Shuttlecock kicking, another popular game unique to China, is played by children on the street. A small weighted object with a feather attached for balance is kept in the air by kicking it with the side of your foot, or is kicked back and forth from player to player. Surprisingly, jumping rope is also an old activity from China, and is practiced much the same as it is in the West. While Chinese tops resemble those in other countries, the Taiwanese variety range from small to giant ones, weighing as much as 50 kilograms and requiring several people to lift and throw them.

Paper-cutting, which dates back to the Tang Dynasty, is another popular folk art. Delicate paper-cuttings using traditional or decorative themes are displayed on windows during the Chinese New Year. Paper-cuttings can be purchased in department stores and art shops.

Chinese knotting was once used in China for record keeping, large knots representing major events and small knots less significant ones. Over the centuries, knotting became more complex, with different knots signifying different things, such as a girl's eligibility for marriage, or an official's position at court. Jade and precious stones were also sometimes interwoven with knots. Today Chinese knotting is used to make necklaces and bracelets, and also serves as wall hangings or decorative embellishments for fans, sachets, lanterns, window shades and traditional musical instruments. Many shops in Taiwan specialize in this art, for example the Museum of Chinese Knotting Art, Basement, 21st Century Building, 207 Tunhua North Road in Taipei.

Chinese embroidery is related to traditional clothing. When Taiwan was first settled by Chinese immigrants, women had to make their own clothing, often using embroidery for decoration. They became quite skilled at this art, using a wide variety of threads and patterns based on traditional Chinese motifs, such as dragons, phoenixes, fruit, flowers and butterflies, as well as religious themes. Although embroidery is no longer a necessary skill for people in Taiwan, it remains an important art in making traditional opera costumes, temple tablecloths and clothing and decorations used in parades and religious ceremonies.

Taiwan's many temples display the adeptness of the Chinese in the art of wood and stone carving. Sandalwood, known for its fine grain and fragrance, is most popular for carving miniature and delicate figures. Camphor wood is used as the raw material for the bulk of woodcarving. It is valued because of its resistance to pests, and its thick trunks and gnarled roots and branches. The entire tree is used, from its roots to its branches, and nothing is wasted. Wood is transported to carvers where it is first dried and sprayed with varnish to preserve it. It is then carved into a rough image, after which finer knives are used to do detail work. A large piece can take months to complete, while smaller pieces are finished in just a few days. When the carving is completed, the piece is sandpapered and then polished or painted. Some of the best work appears in religious carvings, of gods and goddesses for example, and in carved pieces in temples such as stone columns encircled with writhing dragons, or wall engravings.

Stone carving has been practiced here since the days of the first immigrants, when the finest stone from the mainland was transported to Taiwan in ships as ballast.

One of the few remaining folk artists that can still be regularly seen on the streets and in the night markets of Taiwan is the dough sculptor, who uses a mixture of flour and glutinous rice to turn out colorful animal and human figures. The dough sculptor boils these two ingredients together for a few minutes, and then adds sugar, banana oil and food coloring. He takes out a wad and molds it into a ball, carefully shaping the nose, eyes, lips and whiskers. After the face is complete, the sculptor uses green, yellow and purple rice dough to make the clothing and ornaments. He continues to add various pieces here and there, finally turning out a colorful human or animal figure, much to the delight of the children crowding around his pushcart.

Aboriginal wood carvings, Sun Moon Lake

Another itinerant folk artist is the candy sculptor. The candy man uses molten sugar to form a hollow ball around his thumb. Before it hardens, he stretches the mass until it resembles a narrow tube. Next, the mass is carefully placed in a mold powdered with corn starch to prevent it from sticking to the surface. Placing the candy-fashioned tube into his mouth he begins to blow slowly until the sugar fills the mold. When the candy is inflated he places a bamboo stick in it to serve as a holder.

Festivals

There is a rich folk heritage of traditional festivals and celebrations still kept alive on Taiwan today. Traditional celebrations, especially *paipais*, religious observances, follow the lunar calendar and thus vary from year to year. The visitor should check beforehand. In addition, some festivals and government holidays do not occur every year. Apart from the occasions listed below, Taiwan's aborigine tribes observe their own festival periods; information on these is best obtained in Taiwan at the time of your visit.

■ JANUARY–FEBRUARY:
Chinese Lunar New Year: This occurs in either January or February and is the most important holiday of the year, observed by the Chinese with their families. The public holiday lasts for three or more days starting with Lunar New Year's Eve. This is a bad time to travel around the island as much of the urban population returns home, traffic is horrendous and almost everything is closed down. Taipei becomes very congested for about a week before the holiday as companies rush to finish last minute business. Expect to pay a hefty surcharge to taxi drivers during the first two days of the holiday.

Preparations begin well in advance, when people buy food and new clothing, get their hair cut, thoroughly clean house and pay off the year's debts. In the weeks leading up to New Year's Eve, a holiday atmosphere is evident as people rush around snapping up snacks, candy and colorful decorations with auspicious meanings.

After a family reunion and banquet, the new year is ushered in with the thunderous roar of exploding firecrackers and screaming rockets. This cacophony continues until after dawn, and then sporadically on the following days. Customs for the new year include enjoying big family feasts, offering sacrifices to the gods and giving children red envelopes containing 'lucky money'.

Movie theaters and major restaurants are essentially the only businesses open during the holiday. From the sixth to the 12th day of the new year, parades and folk activities are held in front of the Presidential Office Building, Chiang Kai-shek Memorial Hall and Sun Yat-sen Memorial Hall in Taipei. People return to work between the fifth and eighth day, but the holiday atmosphere lasts through the Lantern Festival, the 15th day of the first lunar month.

The Lunar New Year starts on January 23, 1993 and February 10, 1994.

■ FEBRUARY–MARCH:
Lantern Festival: This marks the end of the traditional new year holiday. The Chinese used to believe they could see celestial spirits by the light of the first moon of

the new year and lit torches to help visibility. Colorful lanterns, carried by small children through the streets in the evening, are now used to symbolize this belief. Taipei's Lungshan Temple has an impressive display with a contest for the most fancifully fashioned lanterns. A parade of colorful floats decorated with traditional and modern themes drives around Taipei in the evening.

The Taipei Lantern Festival, featuring thousands of elaborate lanterns, lion and dragon dances, folk arts demonstrations, acrobatic performances and ceremonial temple processions, is held at the Chiang Kai-shek Memorial Hall. It changes its theme each year and combines tradition with technology, art, sound and light.

Yenshui 'rocket hives' fireworks show: A unique celebration coinciding with the Lantern Festival. According to legend, nearly 200 years ago the people of Yenshui petitioned Kuankung to help fight a plague which had ravaged the town. In response, the god designed rocket hives—miniature multiple rocket launchers which each fire thousands of mini-rockets. The three-day battle ended successfully on the Lantern Festival and ever since Yenshui has marked the anniversary with a lavish display of rocket hives.

Each year thousands of visitors crowd the town, staying up the entire night to watch the fireworks. Be careful. The shower of rockets spews in all directions, and even with helmet, goggles and thick clothing, injuries and burns occur.

The Lantern Festival is on February 6, 1993 and February 24, 1994.

■ MARCH–APRIL:

The Birthday of Kuanyin, the Goddess of Mercy: Celebrated on a large scale in Taipei's Lungshan Temple, her birthday occurs without the continual explosion of firecrackers that accompanies the birthdays of other deities. This is because Kuanyin is so pure that it is unnecessary to ward off evil spirits, as none would dare to approach her. Her birthday is marked by chanting ceremonies to soothe the souls of the dead and by the release of wild animals (birds, turtles, and so on). Fishermen also hold celebrations at Kuanyin temples near seaports.

Kuanyin's birthday falls on March 11, 1993 and March 31, 1994.

April 5: Tomb Sweeping Day: A time for families to visit the resting places of their ancestors to pay their respects, clean the graves, place fresh flowers and perhaps plant a few new bushes or trees. Offerings of sacrificial paper money are burned in the belief that the smoke will carry the essence of the money to their ancestors in the spirit world. A quantity of meats, vegetables and wine, often a complete dinner, is arranged on a tray and placed in front of the tomb, where the spirits can consume the essence of the food. The food, minus its essence, is later taken home and eaten.

Tomb Sweeping Day in Taiwan is celebrated annually on April 5, or April 4 in a leap year. It is both a traditional Chinese festival and a contemporary national holiday in Taiwan.

■ APRIL–MAY:

The Birthday of Matsu, Goddess of the Sea: This occasion is celebrated in the close to 400 temples in Taiwan dedicated to Matsu, with the biggest observance at the Matsu Temple in rustic Peikang attracting pilgrims from many other Matsu temples around the island. Each year thousands of people walk from the town of Tachia, 100 kilometers to the north, stopping at 16 Matsu temples along the way during their one-week pilgrimage. Throughout the night statues of Matsu are carried down the street and into the temple, amid billowing incense smoke and exploding fireworks. Meanwhile, on side streets there is a carnival-like atmosphere as children in costumes atop floats are driven around the city, tossing candy out to the crowds, and, oddly enough, scantily-clad dancers and singers perform from the back of trucks elaborately decorated with flashing lights and mirrors. During this period the temple is active 24 hours a day: in the courtyard are martial arts, lion dances and other performances, while operas are presented on an open stage opposite the temple. Amid a din of bells, drums and firecrackers, pilgrims attend a steady succession of rituals within. The temple's Matsu images make inspection tours of the town.

Matsu's birthday falls on April 14, 1993 and May 3, 1994.

Chinese New Year decorations on sale in Tihua Street, Taipei

TAIWAN FESTIVALS TABLE

FESTIVAL	DATE (Month)	LUNAR DATE (Day/Month)
Lunar New Year	Jan/Feb	1/1
Lantern Festival	Feb/Mar	15/1
Birthday of Kuanyin	Mar/Apr	19/2
Tomb Sweeping Day	Apr 5th	-
Festival of the God of Medicine	Apr/May	15/3
Birthday of Matsu	Apr/May	23/3
Birthday of Sakyamuni	May	8/4
Lukang Folk Arts Festival	May/Jun	2/5
Dragon Boat Festival	May/Jun	5/5
Birthday of the City God	Jul/Aug	13/6
Chinese Valentine's Day	Aug/Sep	7/7
Chung Yuan Festival	Aug/Sep	15/7
Mid-Autumn Festival	Sep/Oct	15/8
Birthday of Confucius	Sep 28th	-
National Day	Oct 10th	-
Birthday of Chingshan Wang	Nov/Dec	22/10

ABORIGINAL FESTIVALS	DATE-MONTH	LOCATION
Flying Fish Festival	Apr/May	Lanyu (Orchid Island)
Ami Harvest Festival	Aug/Sep	Hualien
Festival of the Little People	Nov/Dec	Nanchuan Township, Miaoli County

Chinese mythological character made of food

Festival of the God of Medicine: One of the more interesting of Taiwan's traditional festivals is celebrated each year to honor the 10th century healer, Wu Pen. The festival is held at Hsuehchia, on the banks of the Chiangchun River in Tainan county. The Tzu Chi Temple, which sponsors the annual festival, dates from the first day of Taiwan's conquest in 1661 by Koxinga.

The great procession honoring the God of Medicine stretches over three kilometers and includes floats covered with fresh flowers and legendary figures, statues of the God of Medicine atop elaborate sedan chairs borne by believers, and troupes of acrobats. This parade is perhaps the largest gathering of acrobats in Taiwan.

The procession begins at dawn, led by a group known as the 'centipedes'. Worshippers prostrate themselves all along the route and allow the centipedes to trample them in the belief this will drive out evil spirits. The procession stops at the Tzu Chi Temple for extended rites and then retraces the steps of Koxinga and his conquerors from the temple they founded to their landing place on the riverbank, where more ceremonies are held.

The Medicine God's birthday is also celebrated at Taipei's Pao An Temple. The procession is on April 2, 1993 and April 21, 1994.

The Birthday of Sakyamuni: Buddhist monks and nuns celebrate this day by reciting Buddhist scriptures, purifying themselves by observing strict rules of abstinence and bathing, and by releasing captured animals, such as turtles, fish and birds. A small statue of young Sakyamuni is bathed in a basin during a temple ceremony. Thousands of candles are lit in temples. The birthday of Sakyamuni falls on May 28th, 1993 and May 18th, 1994.

■ JUNE:

Dragon Boat Festival: The legend behind the colorful Dragon Boat Festival concerns a famous Chinese poet named Chu Yuan, who lived during the Warring States period (403–221 BC). A loyal court official, he was discredited by rivals and lost the trust of his king. Unable to regain the king's favor, the despondent poet drowned himself on the fifth day of the fifth lunar month in the year 277 BC.

The common people who lived in the area respected the exiled official so much that they jumped into their boats and rushed out to save him. Unable to do so, the people threw bamboo stuffed with cooked rice into the water so that the fish would feed on the rice rather than the body of their hero. The annual Dragon Boat Festival commemorates this unsuccessful rescue attempt, which evolved into the present custom of eating *tzungtzu*, glutinous rice filled with pork, bean paste or peanuts, wrapped in bamboo leaves.

Since antiquity the Chinese have believed that the fifth lunar month is a pestilential period. Sanitation is stressed, medicines are added to food, aromatic branches are hung above doors, and beautifully embroidered protective amulets or sachets containing spices or medicines are fastened to the clothing of children.

The festive boat races are held on rivers and lakes around the island, as well as on the sea in the Penghu Archipelago. Large crowds attend the races in Taipei, Lukang, Tainan and Kaohsiung, where teams from all over the world compete.

The boats are called after the mythical dragon creature believed to have dominion over water. The heads and tails of the dragons are affixed to the boats only for the races and must then be brought to life. Amid burning incense and exploding firecrackers, a Taoist priest dots the eyes of the dragons with paint, after which sacrificial paper money is placed in the dragons' mouth and thrown into the water to dispel any evil spirits lurking nearby.

This festival is a public holiday, and is also observed as Poet's Day. The Dragon Boat Festival falls on June 24, 1993 and June 13, 1994.

Lukang Folk Arts Festival: Hundreds of thousands of visitors from around the island cram the tiny town of Lukang for its annual Folk Arts Festival, which exhibits a variety of Chinese arts, including lantern making, top spinning, candy and dough sculpture, paper cutting and folding, oil paper umbrellas, kite flying, macrame, wood carving and puppet shows. There are also dragon boat races, tug-of-war contests, dragon and lion dances, stilt walkers, drum dances, Chinese music and opera performances, parades of temple gods, as well as floats featuring various themes from traditional Chinese life.

The four-day Lukang folk arts festival begins three days before the Dragon Boat Festival.

Birthday of the City God: The City God, whose origins date back over 4,200 years, protects the city from danger, guards it from enemies and can, when necessary, alter the weather to avoid natural calamities. The god and his disciples also tend to the task of judging good and evil and sending unworthy souls off to hell.

The Hsiahai Chenghuang Temple, at 61 Tihua St, Section 1, has been famous for its annual celebrations, held on the god's birthday for over 100 years. An image of the City God parades the streets followed by costumed people with painted faces (who represent the City God's assistants). Other activities include lion and dragon dancers, and worshippers carrying small lanterns or incense burners. The parade ends amid the thunderous roar of exploding fire crackers, which signals the start of a big feast.

The City God's birthday is on August 1, 1993 and July 21, 1994.

■ AUGUST–SEPTEMBER:

Ghost Month: On the first day of the seventh lunar month, the gates of Hell open wide and the spirits are allowed a month of feasting and revelry in the world of the living. To ensure that the ghosts enjoy a pleasant vacation, lavish feasts are set out, paper 'spirit money' is burned for their use, and Taiwanese operas are performed.

The climax of Ghost Month comes at the **Chung Yuan Festival,** on the 15th day of the lunar month, when great sacrificial feasts are laid out in temples and elaborate chanting ceremonies for the dead are conducted by Taoist and Buddhist priests.

To insure that the ghosts do not get lost on their way to these feasts, lanterns are attached to tall bamboo poles in temple courtyards to act as beacons for the wandering spirits. Lanterns are also floated on lakes and streams due to a Chinese legend which asserts that the spirits of people who have drowned are confined to the place where they died unless they can find substitute victims. A bad time to go swimming.

This special month is celebrated most actively in Keelung, and the festivities always attract thousands of visitors. The Chu Pu Tan Temple in Keelung's Chung Cheng Park is well-known for its elaborate spirit feasts. Another highlight is the annual parade through the streets of Keelung to Patoutzu or other nearby harbors, where bright lanterns, many of which are shaped like little houses, are set afloat.

Ghost Month starts August 18, 1993 and August 7, 1994.

Chinese Valentine's Day: This falls on the seventh day of the seventh lunar month. An ancient Chinese legend tells of the cowherd and the weaving maid, who incurred the wrath of the gods and were banished to widely distant stars. Each year, on the seventh day of the seventh lunar month, sympathetic magpies form a bridge between the stars, which allows the couple to meet again.

Chinese Valentine's Day is on August 25, 1993 and August 14, 1994.

■ SEPTEMBER–OCTOBER:

The Mid-Autumn Festival (Moon Festival): On the 15th day of the eighth lunar month, this festival observes the biggest and brightest full moon of the year, the harvest moon.

The Moon Festival can be traced back to legendary Hou Yih, a talented architect who built a palace of jade for the Goddess of the Western Heaven. In reward, she gave him a pill with the elixir of immortality, warning him not to take it until he had fulfilled certain conditions. Hou Yih's ever-curious wife, Chang O, found the pill and promptly swallowed it. As punishment, she was banished to the moon where, according to tradition, her beauty is at its most radiant on the day of the Moon Festival.

The festival is a public holiday marked by family reunions, moon-gazing, and the consumption of moon cakes, round pastries stuffed with red bean paste and egg yolk, or fruits and preserves. Moon cakes are distributed between friends and relatives, a widespread custom which helped to launch a revolution in ancient China. The Mongols, alien conquerors, established the Yuan Dynasty (AD 1279–1368) to rule over a weak and divided China. A warrior named Chu Yuan-chang decided to free his country of the Mongols. He wrote a message of rebellion and had copies placed inside moon cakes, and in this way led a popular uprising that overthrew the invaders.

Visitors in Taipei during the Moon Festival can join hundreds of other moongazers at the Chiang Kai-shek or Sun Yat-sen Memorials, and in the city's larger parks such as Yangmingshan, Youth Park and New Park.

The Moon Festival falls on September 30, 1993 and September 20, 1994.

September 28: The Birthday of Confucius: Also known as Teachers' Day, this holiday is celebrated with a dawn ceremony, parts of which date back 3,000 years, at Confucian Temples around the island. The celebration includes a ritual dance, costumes, music and other rites.

The most elaborate of the ceremonies takes place at Taipei's Confucian Temple, at 275 Talung St. Admission is by ticket only. Tourists should request tickets as far in advance as possible because it is difficult to get tickets for this popular celebration. Call the Tourism Bureau or the temple's management office at (02) 592-3934. If you cannot get a ticket, dress rehearsals are open to the public. This is also a public holiday.

October 10: National Day, or **Double Ten,** commemorates the Wuchang Uprising on October 10, 1911, which led to the overthrow of the Manchu dynasty and the establishment of the Republic of China on January 1, 1912. The celebration is marked with huge rallies and parades, folk dances, acrobatics, lion and dragon dances and displays of martial arts in the plaza in front of Taipei's Presidential Office Building. A huge fireworks show over the Tamsui River ends the day.

■ NOVEMBER–DECEMBER:
Birthday of Chingshan Wang: Chingshan Wang is believed to be able to cure illnesses. He was brought from mainland China's Fujian Province by Qing-dynasty fishermen, who built a temple for the god in Taipei's Wanhua district. At that time Wanhua was stricken by a deadly plague, and patients who worshipped at Chingshan Temple claimed miraculous cures. This ensured the temple's popularity.

The god's birthday falls on the 23rd day of the tenth lunar month, though Wanhua residents traditionally celebrate the event one day earlier when thousands of worshippers flock to the temple to mark the birthday, and statues of gods from other

Wanhua temples arrive to help Chingshan Wang inspect his domain. The celebration includes a big parade by Chingshan Wang and 30 other gods who are carried in sedan chairs, along with traditional Taiwanese folk music and folk arts performers, followed by devotees dressed as helpers of the various gods. Households in the area light lanterns, decorate their doorways with red drapes and set out tables laden with sacrificial offerings. As the parade passes, residents set off firecrackers to welcome the gods, and lavish feasts are held that night.

The Chingshan Wang Temple is at 218 Kuei Yang St, Section 2, Taipei. The birthday is celebrated on December 5, 1993 and November 24, 1994.

Burning of the Wangyeh Boats: A bizarre ceremony is held every three years in Taiwan, when worshippers place food, images of deities and other offerings on a huge, lavishly decorated boat resting atop a small mountain of paper 'spirit money' and, at the auspicious hour, set it on fire. The ceremony has its roots in ancient Chinese history, and many stories are told about the details of this grand spectacle.

The boat burning has traditionally been associated with appeasing the gods of pestilence, known as Wangyeh, and the ritual burning signifies the banishment of disease.

Two of the biggest ceremonies are held in Pingtung in southern Taiwan and in Chiating in central Taiwan. The ritual boat burning is known as *chien chiao*, and is usually held during the ninth lunar month, which corresponds to October or November. Divining blocks are used to determine the exact date. The event lasts seven days and the boat is burned between 3 and 4 am on the last day.

Tourists should be prepared to make an early start in order to witness the beginning of the 8 am ceremony. Images of Wangyeh are placed in sedan chairs and paraded through the streets, along with the boat, to a nearby river or the sea. As the solemn procession moves toward the water, worshippers sweep the path in respect for the gods or as penance for past wrongdoing. The boat is then set on fire.

The Tainan ceremony will be held on May 23, 1994, and the ceremonies in Pingtung and Chiating will be held in October or November, 1994.

■ COLORFUL ABORIGINAL FESTIVALS

The most impressive of the traditional aboriginal activities are the different tribal festivals, of which the harvest festivals are generally the most important. Rich in pageantry, the spirited celebrations provide visitors with a glimpse of the aborigines' colorful traditional clothes, their beautiful singing and dancing, and their vivid culture.

Ami Harvest Festival: Possibly the largest regular aboriginal gathering is the annual festival held in Hualien in late August or early September (the dates are set each year in mid-July by tribal officials). The festival lasts seven days. On the first day, the chief calls all of his men to prepare themselves for the festival. On the second day, hunters present their offerings to the chief, who on the third day metes out either praise or punishment to the hunters, depending on their success. On the fourth day, men of lower tribal ranking come together to sing and dance. The men of the higher ranks do not sing until the fifth day, and on the fifth day both men and women dance together in the square in front of a shrine. The festival comes to an end on the seventh day.

Flying Fish Festival: The annual Flying Fish Festival of Orchid Island's Yami tribe is based on an ancient myth about a talking fish named Blackfin, who laid down a strict set of rituals and taboos about catching the fish, which today remains a vital part of the Yami diet. The festival takes place during the second or third month of the lunar calendar. The rules say that on the first day of the flying fish season all males must put on their most beautiful clothing and jewelry, and their silver helmets and sail out to sea in their boats and entice the fish to appear. The rules also require that all fish drying racks be destroyed, and that fences be built around each house. No strangers are to visit on this day. And no tribes people are to throw stones into the sea.

Festival of the Little People: This is one of the most interesting festivals in Taiwan. The Saisiat people, a small tribe numbering less than 3,000, inhabit Hsinchu and Miaoli counties in the north. The festival is celebrated every other year on the 15th day of the tenth lunar month throughout this region, but the celebration in the area facing Heaven Lake in Nanchuan Township, Miaoli County, is said to be the most complete and beautiful. According to the most plausible story explaining this festival, some 400 years ago the Saisiat suffered from undernourishment due to their lack of farming skills. In the mountains they inhabited there was a pygmy tribe called the Ta Yih, which was strong and skilled in farming, and shared their knowledge with the Saisiat. Unfortunately, the Saisiat later had differences with the pygmy tribe and exterminated their helpers. Afterwards the Saisiat worried that the spirits of the Ta Yih would take revenge and so established a colorful ceremony to appease the grieving pygmy spirits.

The week-long festival has five parts: invitation, salutation, meeting, entertainment, and expulsion of the spirits of the small people. The festival begins with songs and worship to invite the wronged pygmy spirits to join the festivities, at which time everyone faces east to welcome the spirits. The host tribesmen then serve generous helpings of rice wine and dancing continues until dawn. At sunrise on the final day, the celebration reaches its climax with a rite exorcising the pygmy spirits. The tribal leader's family members place a small tree over their spirit shrine, and young tribesmen jump up to snatch pieces of the tree and throw them into the eastern sky, a symbol of the exorcism of the evil spirits. This goes on until the tree is bare, and then the same young people perform a ferocious ritual dance.

Fruit on sale at a night market in Taipei

Night Markets

One of the best traditional shopping experiences in Taiwan is to visit a bustling night market. Nearly every night, these make-shift shopping centers pulse until midnight with a carnival atmosphere of bright lights and crowds of people buying or browsing. The markets offer fun, bargains and a lot of local color, and generally sell a variety of traditional products, casual clothes, novelty items and food. There are no set prices, but since most vendors speak only Chinese, pen and paper are helpful for bargaining. Only Taiwan currency is accepted and unsatisfactory buys cannot be exchanged.

Hot Springs

Taiwan sits atop a large thermal region and hot springs are found in nearly all parts of the island. More than 100 sources have been discovered, and 40 have been developed into resorts. The springs can be divided into two categories based on their origins: meteoric water or volcanic water. Meteoric water is surface water that penetrates inside the earth, is heated, and then rises again in the form of a spring. Volcanic waters are those near volcanoes. Yangmingshan National Park is famous for its hot springs, which contain noticeable quantities of sulfur, characteristic of volcanic water. Sulfur springs are said to be therapeutic for arthritis. Carbonate is the major mineral found in the hot springs in eastern Taiwan. Carbonate springs are known as 'beauty springs' because they are said to improve the condition of one's skin. Iron and magnesia are other common minerals in spring water.

A hot-spring bath should not last more than 15 minutes at any one sitting, and the temperature should not exceed 45°C (113°F). Those with heart disease and hypertension are advised to check with a doctor before bathing in a hot spring.

Northern Taiwan

Northern Taiwan, flanked from west to east by the Taiwan Strait, the East China Sea and the Pacific Ocean, is an area of historic sites, elaborate temples, hot spring resorts, beautiful coastal rock formations and towering mountains, all a short distance from the capital city of Taipei.

Taipei

Once called the 'Ugly Duckling of Asia,' Taipei is one of the fastest growing cities in the region. High-rise office buildings, condominiums, and modern department stores today stand on land that was covered with rice paddies just 20 years ago.

Despite these rapid changes, Taipei remains Chinese at heart, maintaining a traditional lifestyle and culture reminiscent of days long past. Look around and you will see devout Buddhists praying in crowded temples where the air is thick with the smell of incense; small shops selling herbal medicines that have been used for thousands of years; people in parks singing Chinese opera and playing traditional instruments; hawkers of traditional wares and snacks pushing their carts through the bustling city streets; shopowners laying out tables piled high with sacrificial foods or burning ritual money in front of their stores on religious days.

Taipei does not make a good first impression. However, while many are disappointed at first glance, those who take time to scratch the surface of the city, to understand a little of its history, to wander down its back alleys, and to sample its small restaurants and teahouses, will discover that there's much more to the city than meets the eye.

Taipei has many attractions, one of the most important being the National Palace Museum, which houses the world's largest collection of Chinese art. In addition, the city boasts a number of valuable historical sites such as the Qing-dynasty North Gate, and dozens of temples, such as the 255-year-old Lungshan Temple, and the sprawling Yangmingshan National Park, just 30 minutes from downtown Taipei. Often overlooked are the quaint teahouses, coffee shops, and some of the best Chinese restaurants in the world.

HISTORY

Taipei developed rather late by the geological yardstick. The city occupies a triangular basin, actually a tectonic depression that was a huge lake some four billion years ago. Only after long periods of geological evolution did the depression become alluvial. In

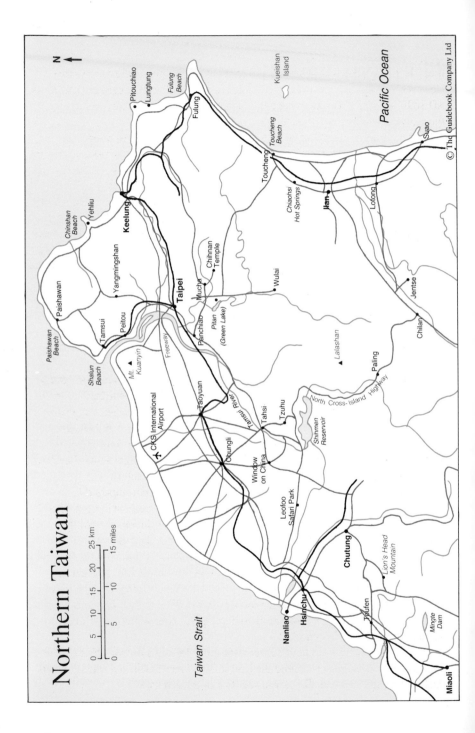

time, the lake gradually disappeared as a result of an uplifting of the earth's crust. However, scholars say that the center of the basin was still waterlogged as recently as AD 1697, when the Pingpu aborigines inhabited it. And just a century ago, much of the central part of the city was still muddy paddy fields.

It is not known exactly when people began settling in the Taipei basin. It is known that large numbers of Chinese left the mainland and sailed across the Taiwan Strait during the Ming Dynasty (1368–1644). Records indicate that boats from mainland China first sailed into the Tamsui River to fish and trade in 1521.

In 1661, Cheng Cheng-kung (Koxinga) arrived in Taiwan to drive the Dutch off the island and to establish a base for the overthrow of the alien Qing government. More importantly for Taipei, Koxinga laid the foundation for the development of the city. He assigned General Huang An to command the army and naval forces at Tamsui, along the Tamsui River. Huang's soldiers were later ordered to reclaim land along the banks of the river as far as Chihlansampo.

Chinese settlers sailed up the Tamsui River, first settling in Hsinchuang where they established a farming community. In 1709 reclamation was extended from Hsinchuang, today a suburb of the city, to Mengchia (present-day Wanhua). Here, the early immigrants from Quanzhou, Fujian Province, established the first Chinese community in the heart of Taipei, complete with temples and businesses.

In those days the Tamsui was wide and deep enough for ships to navigate easily up and down the river. The early settlers rowed across to the opposite bank to trade with the island's aborigines who brought their produce in dugouts. Since so many canoes crowded the river at that spot, the place soon became known as Mangka, which means 'canoe' in one of the aboriginal languages. The name, pronounced Mengchia in Mandarin, was eventually adopted by both the aborigines and the Chinese traders to refer to the entire area, which is today called Wanhua.

Expansion continued gradually. In 1737, the city grew to encompass the Wenshan and Sungshan districts, and Mengchia had already become a prosperous center of trade with a large community. A year later, the inhabitants erected the Lungshan Temple in honor of the Goddess of Mercy. Today it remains one of Taiwan's most popular temples. By 1853, Mengchia had reached the peak of its prosperity. Ships crowded its port and thousands of shops and trading firms lined its streets. Around this time the area also developed a certain notoriety for licentious nightlife that still exists. In that same year, the natives of Quanzhou engaged in internal fighting and one faction broke away to develop Tataocheng (today's Yenping district), to the north of Mengchia.

The Taipei city wall was built between 1882 and 1884 at a cost of 420,000 silver dollars. It ran 15 kilometers around the city, stood 15 meters tall, and was 12 meters thick. An artillery turret to discourage attacks topped each gate.

Taiwan became a province in 1886 and its first governor, Liu Ming-chuan, transferred the seat of the capital from Tainan in the south to Taipei in the north. A noted reformer, the new governor immediately began setting up railroad, postal, and telegraphic services. A year after his arrival, Liu turned on the first electric light, making Taipei the first city in all of China to be electrified. In 1889, China's first train made its maiden trip from Taipei to Keelung.

Chinese rule over the island was not to last for long, however. In 1895, Taiwan was ceded to Japan following China's defeat in the Sino-Japanese War. A group of literati in Taipei known as the Peony Poets' Club declared the establishment of the Republic of Taiwan, and although Japan's superior military easily defeated the movement, sporadic resistance continued for years.

By the turn of the century it became impossible for ships to enter the port and Mengchia entered a period of decline. The first obstruction was a sandbar which developed about 100 years ago. As the Tamsui River became increasingly shallow, ships could no longer freely sail in and out of the harbor. A second hindrance was the building of a railway bridge at Tachiaotou; this bridge prevented ships from sailing into the area. Although the railway bridge was later converted into a drawbridge, much of the business had already moved.

The Japanese made Taipei the seat of their government on the island and proceeded to change the face of the city. In 1900, workers began tearing down the city wall to make way for an expansion program and the construction of Taipei New Park. It took 11 years to demolish. Only four of the original five gates remain standing, and to enable traffic to move past them unimpeded the gates have been made the centerpieces of busy traffic circles. Streets in Mengchia and Tataocheng (Yenping) were modernized and these districts merged with Taipei to form a bigger city.

The city was rebuilt by the Japanese to look like a European-style colonial capital, with wide avenues, tidy parks and grandiose public buildings. Most structures were built in the post-renaissance style popular in Japan at that time, and many are still used today as government offices. The Taiwan Tobacco and Wine Monopoly Bureau, National Taiwan University Hospital, the Control Yuan, the Taipei Guest House, and the Taiwan Provincial Museum, all built between 1901 and 1906, testify to the Japanese desire to develop the city.

In 1945, the island was returned to Chinese rule, following Japan's surrender to Allied forces. When the mainland fell to Mao Zedong's communists in 1949, the nationalist government and more than two million Chinese fled to Taiwan. Taipei was made the temporary capital of the Republic of China in December 1949, marking the beginning of a new phase in the city's history.

Shen Pao-chen, the Manchu court's Imperial Commissioner for Formosa, 1874, taken by M Berthaud

Taipei remained a backwater town for the next 20 years, however, with its residents relying on pedicabs for transportation as late as the mid-1960s. Change gradually came in that same decade as the island's economy began to take off, helping Taipei to make the transition from a small, functional town to a cosmopolitan city, attracting more and more people from rural areas to the glitter of modernity and the promise of a brighter future.

In 1967, Taipei became a special municipality, giving it the same status as a province, and making its mayor equal in rank to a provincial governor. The city's area was also expanded almost fourfold.

The Japanese designed Taipei to comfortably accommodate about 600,000 people, but by 1963 its population had already climbed past the million mark, had doubled again by 1975, and in 1992 stood at more than 2.6 million, with close to one million motorcycles, cars, and trucks, competing on the city's jam-packed streets with more than 30,000 taxis. The rapid growth spurred demand for housing and office space. Surrounded by mountains, Taipei had only one way to expand and that was up. Tens of thousands of modern high rise buildings and hotels have gone up around the city, radically changing its face, but not its heart.

THE CITY

Taipei is divided into several sections, each with its own unique atmosphere. It is not an exceptionally large city so many sights are easily reached on foot. Chungshan Rd runs north and south and is the east–west divide of the city. Therefore, streets running from east to west across the city have the word east or west added to their names, indicating which side of Chungshan Rd they run. North and south are divided by Chunghsiao Rd, with streets running to the north and to the south being so designated. For example, Fuhsing North Rd and Fuhsing South Rd are divided at Chunghsiao Rd. Nanking East Rd and Nanking West Rd are divided by Chungshan Rd. Major streets are also subdivided into sections 1, 2, 3, 4, and so on.

The numbers of lanes and alleys, sometimes difficult to see from a taxi, roughly follow the order of building numbers. In other words, lane 265 would be somewhere around building number 265. The same system works with alleys, which run off lanes. Building, lane, and alley numbers are written on the small blue metal signs which hang near the entrances to shops and buildings.

A knowledge of Chinese geography will help you get around the city. Most streets are named after places, rivers and mountains on the mainland and their location roughly corresponds to the map of China. Streets named after northern Chinese cities will be found somewhere in the north of Taipei; places in the south of China occupy the city's southern reaches. For example, Beiping (Beijing) Rd is in the far north of the city, while Kwangchou (Guangzhou) St is in the south.

Chiang Kai-shek Memorial (above); *The National Theater* (below)

Taipei's long-awaited rapid transit system is behind schedule, but once completed will go a long way in alleviating current transportation headaches. The first service to begin operation is the 24-kilometer elevated Mucha line, using a system already installed in France. Automatic driverless trains on rubber wheels will begin carrying as many as 10,000 passengers an hour in late 1992. A heavy-rail line to Tamsui, north of the city, will open for business in late 1994 and will hook up with the Hsintien line, extending the Tamsui line to the south of the city in mid-1995. A third line running from Nankang to Taipei's city center will begin operating in late 1995, and will connect to Panchiao in 1998.

WALKING TOURS

Three city tours are provided below. Each tour explores side streets and alleys with quaint houses, interesting restaurants and shops, and temples.

■ OLD TAIPEI (4–5 HOURS)

Although the center of commercial activity has shifted eastward in recent years and away from this part of town, government offices remain here and a number of historical sites can still be found in the old downtown area. Most of the buildings constructed during the early years of the Japanese occupation (1895–1945) are European-style, a form popular in Japan at the turn of the century.

Begin your stroll at the **Taipei City Hall**, 39 Changan West Rd. This structure was built in 1920 by the Japanese as an elementary school. There are several traditional shops in the area. The **Taiwan Handicraft Paper Manufacturing Co**, 47–2 Changan West Rd, was opened by the Japanese in 1935 and still makes handmade paper. Other paper shops on this street sell a wide variety of Chinese paper-cuttings. The **Lin Tien Cooperage**, on the corner of Changan West Rd and Chungshan North Rd, is one of the few remaining bucket-makers in Taiwan. Mr. Lin, the proprietor, proudly points to the old clock on the wall when asked how long his shop has been in business; 1928 is painted on the dust-covered face, the year his father opened the shop. This store is a reminder of old Taipei. Its worn brick walls are pockmarked from decades of being hit with tools and buckets, the dark stairs at the back of the shop are worn smooth from countless footsteps, and the rough, uneven floor is covered with wood shavings. The small shop is piled high with wooden buckets and pails, leaving Lin little room to work. He has resisted selling the valuable property, and his son says that he will take over the family business when his father retires, keeping alive this family tradition for a third generation.

Walk south down Chungshan North Rd toward Chunghsiao West Rd and you will soon come to the Japanese-style **Wu Mei Hotel**. In 1913, Dr Sun Yat-sen, father of the Republic of China, was on his way to Japan and stopped over in Taiwan. He stayed at this hotel, now reconstructed in a lovely garden with a small pavilion and pond.

Cross Chunghsiao West Rd and then cross to the opposite side of Chungshan South Rd. The red brick building at this intersection is home to the **Control Yuan**, the nation's highest supervisory body. The building was built in 1915 to serve as an administrative headquarters for the ruling Japanese. The large dome, surrounded by smaller domes, appears to be Byzantine or Eastern European in style. Fortunately, when a wing was added to the building in 1987, designers utilized the original materials and style, using the same red brick with gray trim and circular windows.

The **Parliament Building**, one block south of the Control Yuan, was a school during the occupation. The **Chinan Presbyterian Church**, next door to the Parliament, was built in 1916 for professors teaching at National Taiwan University Hospital and Medical School, just a few blocks away.

Continue down Chungshan South Rd past the Ministry of Education, then reach the **Chinese Handicraft Mart**, a government-sponsored store that sells a wide variety of Chinese handicrafts.

The old **National Taiwan University Hospital** on the opposite side of the road was built by Kondo Julo, a Japanese architect who specialized in hospital architecture. Notice the building's Ionic columns on the second level and the pediment on the top level. The huge lobby with its impressive high curved glass ceiling and rows of archways is also worth a look.

Walk down to the next intersection to a traffic circle built around the **East Gate**. The old city wall originally ran along the street connecting this gate with the other city gates; the enclosed area was the center of Qing government.

Look south and on the left you will see the imposing **Chiang Kai-shek Memorial Hall**, completed in 1980. The white marble memorial hall, the centerpiece of the complex, stands 76 meters tall and overlooks small ponds and manicured gardens. The hall is almost 23 stories tall and at the time of its completion was the tallest structure in Taipei. There is a museum on the ground floor of the memorial hall with photographs and personal belongings of the late generalissimo, including his uniforms and medals. A 25-ton bronze statue of President Chiang stands on the main floor, where a military honor guard keeps a permanent vigil. An impressive precision change of guard occurs every hour on the hour.

In front of the hall and just behind the 30-meter-tall Ming-style arch at the main entrance are two large palace-style Chinese buildings, the **National Theater** and **National Concert Hall**. These buildings were added to the complex in 1987. Leading international and local artists perform here regularly.

The memorial park is busy from the crack of dawn until late at night. Chinese gather here every morning before work to exercise, dance, sing Peking opera, or play

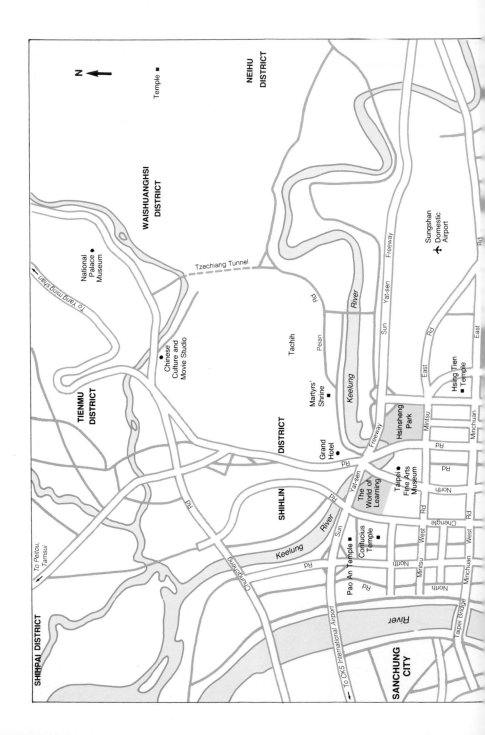

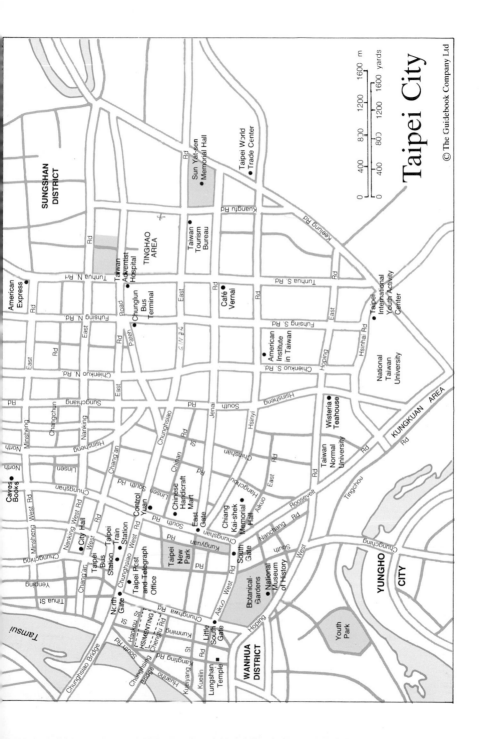

Taipei City

© The Guidebook Company Ltd

SUNGSHAN DISTRICT

WANHUA DISTRICT

YUNGHO CITY

KUNGKUAN AREA

TINGHAO AREA

Tamsui

Sun Yat-sen Memorial Hall

Taipei World Trade Center

Taiwan Tourism Bureau

American Express

Taiwan Adventist Hospital

Chunglun Bus Terminal

Café Vernal

Taipei International Youth Activity Center

American Institute in Taiwan

National Taiwan University

Caves Books

Wisteria Teahouse

Taiwan Normal University

Chinese Handicraft Mart

City Hall

Control Yuan

Chiang Kai-shek Memorial Hall

Taipei Train Station

Taipei Bus Station

Taipei Post and Telegraph Office

Taipei New Park

East Gate

South Gate

North Gate

Little South Gate

Botanical Gardens

National Museum of History

Lungshan Temple

Youth Park

Scale: 0 400 800 1200 1600 m / 0 400 800 1200 1600 yards

traditional instruments. Throughout the day newlyweds arrive for wedding photos and senior citizens come to stroll, or gather in the shade for a game of chess. The Memorial Hall is open from 9 am–4:30 pm, and the park complex is open daily from 5 am to midnight.

Opposite the Memorial Hall is the modern **National Central Library**, opened in 1986. It houses 12,000 rare Chinese books, including more than 600 Song and Yuan-dynasty texts, ancient stone rubbings, Buddhist scrolls from Dunhuang, wooden and bamboo tablets inscribed during the Han Dynasty (206 BC–AD 220) and a large collection of contemporary Chinese and English books.

Walk back up Chungshan North Rd toward the East Gate and pass the Ministry of Foreign Affairs on the left.

If you stand at the intersection and look north across the street you will see the **Taipei Guest House**, a French renaissance building. It was completed in 1912; a high wall makes it only partially visible from the street. The building, considered a fine example of Japanese workmanship, was originally the residence of the Japanese governor-general, but the Ministry of Foreign Affairs claimed it after Japan's surrender and turned it into a posh lodging for visiting VIPs.

Turn west and you will see the **Presidential Building**, a tall renaissance-style building at the head of the street. This structure took seven years to complete and was opened in 1919 as the Japanese governor-general's office. At that time, its 66-meter-high central tower made it the tallest building in Taipei. During the Japanese occupation, the building was a symbol of colonial authority. Allied bombers damaged the structure during World War II, but it was later renovated. Every day at sunrise the national flag is raised here in a solemn ceremony, and lowered at sunset. On both occasions the national anthem is played and all traffic in the area comes to a halt.

On the north side of the street, surrounded by a fence, is **Taipei New Park**, a good place to watch the Chinese at play. Activities begin at sunrise as peddlers lay out their goods—herbs, ointments, tea, socks, shoes, pens, nail clippers—at the entrance. Hundreds of people, young and old, come here every morning to exercise before heading off to work or school.

Enter through the gate that faces Hengyang Rd and bear right around the outdoor theater. On the theatre's side is a memorial arch (*paifang*), in honor of Hung Teng-yun, a native of Fujian who moved to Taiwan with his father when he was 13. Hung, a successful businessman and philanthropist, contributed money and laborers for construction projects in Taipei. Governor Liu Ming-chuan asked the Qing government for permission to build the paifang in 1887, and a year later it was erected on Shihfang Street (now Hsiangyang Rd). It was moved to its present location in 1905. A tablet under the top eaves explains that this paifang honors Hung's concern for public welfare. Scrolls on both sides of each pillar tell of Hung's virtuous deeds. An imperial decree, once on the center base under the top eaves, has disappeared.

On the east side of the park is a large pavilion surrounded by four smaller pavilions. The bust of a famous figure in Taiwan's history occupies each pavilion: Lien Ya-tang, historian of Taiwan; Chiu Feng-chia, who fought against the Japanese; Liu Ming-chuan, Taiwan's first governor; and Koxinga, the Ming-dynasty general who forced the Dutch off the island.

North of the pavilions, over the path that runs near the street, is another memorial arch. **Huang's Virtuous Paifang** was built in 1882 by Wen Tien-hsi in honor of his mother Huang Chi. She was born in Fujian in 1820, but later emigrated to Mengchia (Wanhua) with her husband, the son of a wealthy merchant family. Legend says her husband worked himself to death preparing for the rigid civil service examination. Huang Chi, just 28 at the time, vowed she would raise the children by herself and remain filial to her in-laws.

Imperial permission was granted to build a paifang and memorial temple, and in 1882 craftsmen from Quanzhou were hired and stone was brought from China for construction of the paifang. However, the temple was not finished until after the island was ceded to Japan. The Japanese demanded the land for official use and the temple was torn down and rebuilt in Yuanshan Park. In 1901, the paifang was moved here. The tablet and inscription under the bottom eaves tell us that this paifang was built to honor the virtuous Huang Chi. Scrolls on the front and rear sides of the pillars tell stories of her deeds, which were used to educate the public in the mores of traditional society.

The domed building just inside the main gate is the **Taiwan Provincial Museum**, a neo-Greek structure with fluted Doric columns built in 1915 by the Japanese. In the lobby of the museum are huge columns on marble bases which form the foundations for the building's huge stained-glass dome. The first floor holds art exhibitions and the second floor has an anthropological exhibit. The entrance fee is NT$5.

Leave the museum and turn left through a small gate that leads to the other side of the park. Here you can usually find artists at work painting portraits and martial artists practicing their routines. By the fence stand two old locomotives, the first ones used in China. One was built in England in 1872, the other in Germany in 1887. Both were retired in the 1920s. Next to the trains are several Qing-dynasty cannons.

At the rear of the park is a monument to General Claire Chennault. During World War II Chennault organized the Flying Tigers, a group of volunteer American pilots who flew for the Chinese air force against the Japanese. There is a statue of General Chennault here, said to be the only secular statue of a foreigner on the island.

Leave the park through the main gate on Hsiangyang Rd, turn left and proceed to the intersection of Chungking South Rd. Then turn right and walk up to Chunghsiao

Ju Ming

Chinese have for centuries dismissed sculpture as more craft than art form, in no way equal to painting and calligraphy—the embodiment of Chinese culture—and certainly not worthy of the attention of true connoisseurs of Chinese art.

It is remarkable, then, that this centuries-old prejudice should be dispelled by an unknown sculptor from a poor village in northern Taiwan.

Ju Ming, considered the best Chinese sculptor of the 20th century, was born in a farmhouse in Tunghsiao, Miaoli County in 1938, the last of 11 children. His success as an artist was in no way to be expected.

Ju Ming was not a bright student. His grades were not good enough to get him into middle school, and so at the age of 13 he went to work as a clerk in a general store, using his spare time to weave hats for his father's bamboo shop. Fortunately, when Ju Ming was 15, his father had the foresight to apprentice him to Li Chin-chuan, one of Taiwan's most famous traditional wood carvers. As an apprentice he had to do a lot of mundane chores unrelated to carving. He was not paid, but was given simple food and a stipend for haircuts.

At that time Master Li was working on a new temple, sculpting birds, flowers, phoenixes and dragons in the traditional style. In Taiwan it is not unusual for carvers to spend one or two decades working on the carvings for a temple. Ju Ming turned out to have a talent for carving, and after completing his apprenticeship of three years (plus four months as compensation for holidays) he set up his own workshop and was soon prospering as a master craftsman.

He eventually became bored with this work. It was basically commercial, and since the styles were passed down from generation to generation there was little room for creativity. Furthermore, carvers were somewhat lower than carpenters on the social scale, considered little more than laborers. At the age of 30, Ju Ming realized he wanted to do something more fulfilling, but that if he were to make the transition from craftsman to artist he would have to find a new master. In 1968, he and his wife and children moved to Taipei where he became apprenticed to Yang Yuyu, a well-known Taiwanese architect and sculptor who had studied in Tokyo and Rome.

Despite his 15 years of experience, Ju Ming once again had to work as a traditional apprentice—making tea, sweeping floors and running errands, all without payment. His relationship with Yang was well worth the humbling experience. Yang provided Ju Ming with encouragement and direction. He arranged Ju Ming's first solo exhibition at the National Museum of History in Taipei, where his exhibit of water buffalo, chickens and a variety of historical figures carved in camphor wood won him wide acclaim around the island.

Yang's most important advice came in the mid-1970s when he suggested the wiry Ju Ming take up *taichi*, an ancient form of Chinese shadow boxing with a meditative quality, to strengthen his body and develop mental discipline. Through the practice of taichi Ju Ming came to understand the union of the body, mind and nature, and immediately went to work figuring out how to capture the delicate, but powerful, movements of taichi in wood. This was not difficult. The slow movements and loose fitting garments worn by taichi exponents lent themselves naturally to the sculpture of Ju Ming.

'In the movements and gestures of taichi he found a theme so natural to his Chinese spirit that it seems astonishing that no Chinese sculptor has ever explored it before', wrote Michael Sullivan, a Chinese art historian.

Looking at these graceful, delicate works, one has the impression that Ju Ming gave intense thought to each cut. This is not true. He achieved his goal by eliminating smooth polished surfaces; he abandoned his chisel for a chainsaw, ripping the wood open with a manual crank-spreader, hacking and gouging the wood, sometimes tearing it apart with his bare hands. He followed the natural grain of the wood so the movements and gestures of the figures became more expressive and intense. The finished product had a rawness that showed the strength of the material and the sense of energy of the movement.

A Taichi sculpture by Ju Ming *continues on page 112*

Ju Ming once said of his style: 'I use a dumb method, and that is speed—sculpting at high speed. When one sculpts at high speed, cutting strokes follow closely upon each other and attention is focused on the fleeting moment. At every split second the blade changes the form, and the mind does not have the chance to reconsider. It is the power of instinct that brings the work to completion. One forgets oneself in the act and one's conscious knowledge is not allowed to interfere with one's instinctive powers.'

A trip to New York in 1980 was to have a profound effect on Ju Ming, resulting in his first departure from Chinese themes. The first Living World series (1980–82) was inspired by his stay in New York, which was a threatening place for Ju Ming. The faceless figures in this somewhat theatrical series, standing alone or in groups, appear anonymous, detached and dejected. The wood is raw and exposed, as if it had been attacked indiscriminately.

The second Living World series, begun in the mid-1980s, features life-size bronzes based on ceramic technique. While this series bears a similarity to the first in its sense of silence, it shows a greater depth and maturity and a stronger emotional and artistic awareness.

'There are many who feel that Ju Ming is repetitious, that he has taken the easy way out and is churning out that which is a proven success,' says Ian Findlay Brown, editor of *Asian Art News*. 'This is clearly not true. His vision is constantly evolving as he works to master his forms and material completely as an artist.'

Brown points out that Ju Ming's third Living World series is as dynamic as any of his earlier works. Made from twisted stainless steel (using a machine of his own invention which rolls and cuts sheet steel) and thick nylon rope, this series focuses on people alone. While bearing a resemblance to the first Living World series in wood, the color is from colored rope, not paint, and the figures are very impersonal and more alienated than his earlier pieces.

Brown says that in the decade to come Ju Ming will take to a new creative path that may include more ceramics and painting.

Ju Ming's main accomplishment, writes Michael Sullivan, is his contribution to making sculpture 'a creative art form expressive of Chinese feeling.'

'The achievement of Ju Ming, quite apart from the stunning power and beauty of his work is that, more than any other living Chinese sculptor, he has found in his own cultural heritage a natural—one might even say inevitable—source for the creation of a formal language that is both contemporary and Chinese'.

East Rd. Finally, turn left again to the **North Gate**. This important gate, built in 1882, was the 'lock' on the door to the territory within, according to an inscription above the portcullis. Thick walls run close to the edge of the eaves, blocking the sides and leaving only narrow openings. This is known in Chinese as *chienlou*, or arrow tower, a design seldom seen in other structures in Taiwan from that period.

Chinese custom dictates that forts, like other structures, should be oriented in accordance with the principles of geomancy. As a result, North Gate does not strictly face due north, but several degrees to the east. Characters inscribed over the portcullis give the name of the gate and the date of its construction. The other city gates were improperly renovated in 1966 and lost their original appearance; North Gate is thus the only gate that retains its original Qing-dynasty form. Unfortunately, an overpass built alongside the gate in the 1970s ruins the view.

Cross the street to Chunghwa Rd, which runs parallel to the train tracks, to reach the famous **Chunghwa Market**, also known as Haggler's Alley or the China Bazaar. According to one old saying, everything eventually makes its way to Chunghwa Market. A variety of small shops sell antiques, coins, stamps, clothes, electronics, computers, tapes, records and food. Adjacent are numerous fortune-tellers, tailors, and other businessmen in this three-storey, eight-block-long row of buildings. Chunghwa Market, now dingy, was one of the most popular shopping centers in the city in bygone days.

The buildings are all connected by bridges on the upper floors. The **Genuine Peking Restaurant**, located in the seventh row on the second floor, is known for its Peking duck. This simple restaurant is still popular with Beijing residents of the city, who come here for authentic northern Chinese dishes.

On the second floor of block eight is a store that sells costumes and other items for Peking opera. This is said to be the only place left on the island that makes shoes for the opera.

Refugees from mainland China who flooded Taiwan after the communist takeover in 1949 were the first to settle the area. Temporary houses were hastily thrown up along the railroad tracks to accommodate these people and before long, more than 1,600 shacks littered the site between North Gate and South Gate.

As the number of residents grew, peddlers began to congregate here and the situation worsened. Chiang Kai-shek ordered the area redeveloped to provide proper housing for its inhabitants. The present block of buildings was completed in 1961, and has now become an eyesore. The government has been trying to tear down the structure for several years, but residents oppose the plan.

At the intersection of Chunghwa Rd and Chengtu Rd, just behind the Chunghwa Market, is the busy **Hsimenting District**. Take time to walk around the narrow streets crowded with fast-food shops, restaurants, movie theaters and countless clothing stores. Hsimen (West Gate) was the site of the former gate, torn down during the Japanese occupation. Return to Chunghwa Rd and continue south to **South Gate**, then bear left and walk to the **Little South Gate**, the last of the five city gates that were once joined by the city wall.

■ TIHUA STREET (CLOSED ON SUNDAYS) (1 HOUR)
Although the 'good old days' are long gone, Tihua St, in one of Taipei's oldest districts, remains nestled in a time warp. Here old world businesses survive in buildings that date back to the early years of this century. They sell traditional Chinese goods, such as colorful bolts of cloth, bamboo crafts, Chinese cooking utensils, dried foods, and herbal medicines and other traditional remedies. Many shops continue to turn out handmade goods, from quilted blankets to coffins. Li Tien-lu, Taiwan's most famous puppeteer, once said 'On Tihua St you can buy everything you need from birth to death.' The street is also known for its contribution to the arts; many famous Taiwanese writers, poets, composers and artists come from this proud old area.

Tataocheng, as the area was once known, began to develop in 1851 when Lin Lan-tien, a native of Fujian, established three shops here to carry on trade with mainland China. When the Tamsui waterway at Mengchia silted up, businessmen looked upstream for a place to load and unload ships. They found a spot near Tihua St and Tataocheng soon became the new city center. In 1887, Governor Liu Ming-chuan made Tataocheng the residential area for foreign businessmen, attracting even more ships to the port.

The area's prosperity was hit hard during the Japanese occupation when sedimentation of the river ended its reign as a major shipping center. Businesses were forced to move to present-day downtown Taipei. Following the retreat of the nationalists to Taiwan in 1949, Tihua St won a new lease on life. The government forbade all contacts with the Chinese communists, but realizing the importance of herbs, many of which were not grown in Taiwan, decided to allow imports from the mainland to arrive through middlemen in Hong Kong. Tihua St became the center of this trade, and managed to remain an important wholesale center for sundry goods, herbs and medicines.

The opening of travel to China in 1988 allowed mainland goods to become more easily available, so the area's fortunes took another turn for the worse. Recent interest in nostalgia, which has spurred numerous books and films about old Taiwan, has created renewed interest in Tihua St. The city attempted to tear down the houses to widen the street in the late 1980s—with the support of many residents—but fortunately, architects and historians managed to convince the government to renovate the area instead.

The street and its surrounding alleys are extremely narrow, reputedly because

Chinese medicine and dried goods on sale in Tihua Street

they were designed for rickshaws and not cars. On holidays—especially the Chinese New Year—this area is packed with shoppers and stays open almost around the clock. If you are in Taiwan during the week before Chinese New Year, be sure to visit Tihua St.

The street is noted for its Gulangyu-style architecture, a hybrid of traditional southern Chinese architecture and rococo. When Fujianese merchants travelled to Southeast Asia in the late 1800s, they were impressed by the colonial buildings they saw. Upon their return to China, they combined foreign styles with the popular architecture of southern China, developing the hybrid Gulangyu style which they later brought to Taiwan. The red brick buildings have a store in front and a living area at the back. Though very narrow, they are surprisingly deep. Some buildings even have courtyards and a small garden in the center.

Instead of standard doors, many of the houses have wooden slats that slide into place and are locked with thick planks. The old overhead brick arches covering the sidewalks protect shoppers from the rain.

A walk through the area provides an opportunity to step back in time, and since this tour covers Tihua St linearly, it is impossible to lose your way. Begin at the intersection of Nanking West Rd and Tihua St, just a few blocks east of the banks of the Tamsui River where ships from mainland China once unloaded their goods. This walk only goes as far as the Taipei Bridge; all of the shop numbers refer to Section 1. Look for even numbers on the right side, odd on the left.

Stores on the first three blocks specialize in cloth although there are a few that sell Buddhist religious items.

Three blocks north of Nanking West Rd is a large white-tiled building on the right. This is the new **Yung Le Market**, a modern market where today's urban housewives shop for a wide variety of fruit, vegetables and meat on the first floor. Live chickens are butchered on the spot. On the second floor are more than 100 stands selling different kinds of textiles, including material for suits, dresses, cotton-padded blankets, curtains, etc.

From the first floor, walk out the rear entrance to an old market that still operates directly opposite the modern market. It has stores that process and sell fresh Chinese herbs.

Return to Tihua St. The next building on the right (61 Tihua St, Section 1) is the diminutive, 130-year-old Hsiahai Chenghuang Temple, or **Temple of the City God** (see page 56). The City God is in charge of Taipei, working in heaven in the same capacity as the local magistrate would in the world of mortals. This is why the temple layout resembles that of a city magistrate's office. The birthday celebration of the City God, on the 13th day of the fifth lunar month (usually in June), is one of Taipei's biggest annual festivals. It has been held here for over 100 years (see page 91).

In the 1800s, a man named Chen escorted a gilded image of the god from his native home in Tungan County, Quanzhou Prefecture. The image was first worshipped in his bakery as a family deity. The shop prospered and residents of the area believed it was due to the god's blessings so the community contributed funds for a temple for the city god. When a clan fight broke out in 1853 between different groups of immigrants, the natives of Tungan were defeated and driven to the Tataocheng area. The image was once again placed in a bakery run by a member of the Chen family. The bakery proved too small so in 1859 this structure was completed.

In front of the temple several hundred red lanterns hang from the ceiling, donated by people praying for peace. Inside on the main altar are 200 religious statues, more than in almost any other temple on the island. The statues have been donated to the temple by Buddhist worshippers to thank the gods for answering their prayers.

The two fierce deities to the right and left of the altar are General Hsieh and General Fan, the City God's bodyguards (see page 58). The temple's west side is the place of worship for the 38 Tungan warriors who lost their lives in the 1853 fight in Mengchia to protect the Chenghuang image and their fellow clansmen.

Turn right upon exiting the temple and continue north on Tihua St. From the stores on both sides of the next several blocks come the pungent smells of spices, Chinese medicines, dried foods and herbs imported from China and other countries. Here Chinese druggists fill prescriptions, taking various herbs and medicines, such as medlar, juniper berry, antlers, dried lizards, and scorpion tails, from small drawers behind the counter where they are neatly stored. They then grind the substances before wrapping them in newspaper cones for customers.

Huge slabs of lumber lie outside the coffin maker at No. 174. The Chinese make coffins out of rounded tree trunks, which are often carved and painted in rich colors. According to a sign over the door of the I in Feng Yi Shop at No. 214, the family began selling bamboo and wooden utensils in 1906. The store sells baskets, buckets and bamboo steamers. An array of hand-painted paper and plastic lanterns in many shapes and sizes can be found at No. 310, one of the few companies in the city that manufactures them. Although the lanterns are made elsewhere, the painting is done here. The shop has been in business for more than 80 years, and is now run by the third generation of lantern painters.

The shop at Nos. 303–305 sells Chinese cooking utensils. It is crammed with woks, bowls, plates, steamers, clay pots and other kitchen items. A few doors away at No. 333 is a man who makes cotton-padded blankets by hand. Blankets can be made to order; the price depends on the weight of the cotton. An old-fashioned ice factory at No. 345 evokes the days when big blocks of ice were delivered door-to-door for use in ice boxes.

Turn right at the Taipei Bridge on Minchuan West Rd. Here are several artisans at work carving wooden and stone Buddhist statues. This is the end of the tour, though you might want to explore the nooks and crannies among the small streets that cut through Tinhua St.

■ WANHUA (3 HOURS)

Many visitors enjoy strolling through Wanhua, Taipei's oldest district. Here a proliferation of noisy markets, shops selling temple accoutrements, herbal medicine stalls and houses built in the old architectural style hint at the roots that underlie Taipei's increasingly modern exterior. Wanhua, between Chunghwa Rd and the Tamsui River, is the home of the Lungshan Temple, the oldest and most famous Buddhist temple in Taipei, and numerous other venerable temples.

In the night market along this street, open-air foodstalls, hawkers, fortune-tellers and snake vendors compete for attention in a carnival atmosphere. The Chinese believe that consuming snake soup of a blood-and-bile mixture improves eyesight and general health. Little or no English is spoken here; if people object to your photographing them it is advisable to stop.

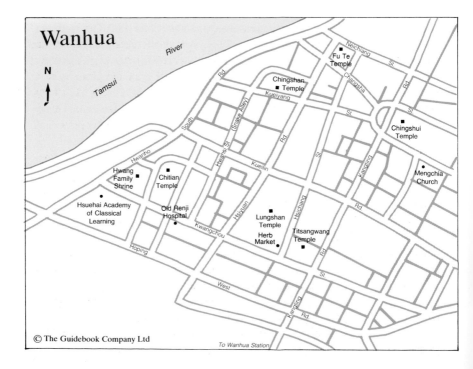

This tour begins at the intersection of Kwangchow St and Hwanho South Rd, not far from the banks of the Tamsui River.

One block south of Kwangchow St at 93 Hwanho St, Section 2, is the **Hsuehai** (Sea of Learning) **Academy of Classical Learning**. Constructed in 1843, it is the only establishment of its kind still intact in the city. The main hall was a lecture room, the rear hall was dedicated to Chu Hsi (1130–1200), the famous neo-Confucianist, and the side wings served as a dormitory for teachers and students.

During the colonial period the Japanese confiscated the building and turned it into an army barracks. Later it was turned into a Japanese language school. A man named Kao, impressed with the temple's good fengshui and history as a school for classical studies, bought the property and converted it into the Kao Ancestral Temple, its other name. When Hwanho South Rd was widened in 1973, the entrance and front house had to be torn down. As a result, the entire building was demolished and rebuilt on its present site. Unfortunately, it has lost much of its original look. The building today has three main houses, two corridors and two wings, and is still the ancestral temple of the Kao family. Scrolls hanging above the main hall to encourage students to work hard, written by Chen Wei-ying, who became dean in 1864, are the only reminder that this was once an academy.

Return to Kwangchow St and walk down the first alley on the left to the **Hwang family shrine**, which dates to the 1830s. This temple, recently renovated and covered with a fresh coat of paint, looks much newer than it actually is. The huge beams and other wooden parts under all that paint were shipped from mainland China more than 150 years ago. On the main altar are dozens of ancestral tablets placed there by families who share the surname Hwang. There are numerous colorful murals on the walls depicting famous stories from Chinese history. The temple also houses a nursery school.

Leave the temple and turn right for one block to Hwanho South Rd, then turn right at the first lane. One block in and on the right is the **Chitian Temple**, built in 1786 and said to be the only temple in the Wanhua area dedicated to Matsu, Goddess of the Sea and patron saint of Chinese sailors.

According to a popular story, in the late 1700s, when Mengchia engaged in extensive commerce with mainland China, a vessel known as the Red Ship transported timber. Once, while at sea, the Red Ship suddenly ran into a storm. The ship's frightened crew prayed to Matsu to protect them. Miraculously, the men escaped harm and safely reached shore. To thank the goddess for her holy intervention, people built a temple of worship in a timber yard. Originally made of wood, the temple has been rebuilt several times and is now made mainly of concrete. Matsu sits on the main altar wearing a crown of pearls. To the right and left are her fierce bodyguards. The green one is General Thousand Miles, the red one is General Favorable Winds.

Turn left when you exit the temple and continue down the lane until you rejoin Kwangchow St. Families still occupy the traditional red brick Chinese houses here. At Kwangchow St turn left again. In the evening hundreds of peddlers come here with their carts piled high with food and goods. On the street's left side is a restaurant that specializes in venison. Animal lovers beware; you may see live deer in cages being butchered on the spot. Snake dishes are also prepared here in the evening at little roadside stands.

One block ahead on the right is the old **Renji Hospital**, site of the former Mengchia Foundling Hospital. In 1870, donations were solicited from wealthy businessmen in the Mengchia area for the construction of a hospital for abandoned children and the children of people too poor to take care of them. During the occupation, the Japanese forced the people to turn it into Renji Hospital. They destroyed the former building. Of the original foundling hospital, only the granite tablet at the front door remains.

Next on the left is the infamous Hwahsi St, better known as **Snake Alley**. The city government turned the street into the Hwahsi Tourist Night Market in 1987, dividing it into sections A and B. A roof was erected over the street, touristy Chinese gates were added at the ends, and many of the store fronts were modernized, diluting Snake Alley's formerly pungent flavor. Many of its restaurants continue to serve snake, turtle and other exotic dishes, but the method of preparation is cruel. Snakes are the main attraction. Ominous cages with writhing snakes are piled on the sidewalk behind the snake handlers. The snakes are slit down the middle while still alive, and the blood and bile squeezed into a glass where it is mixed with herbs and kaoliang, a fiery brew made from sorghum. The Chinese believe this tonic is good for the eyes, lower spine and sexual performance. The snake meat is then cooked and served. Squeezed in between the restaurants are body builders and martial arts practitioners selling special health tonics.

Toward the end of Section A on the right, is the street's most famous restaurant, **Tainan Tantsumian**. With its baroque glass chandeliers, French provincial carpets, white columns and gold-trimmed ceilings, this expensive seafood palace seems out of place amid the run-down surroundings. Food is served on expensive Wedgewood china and water poured into crystal glasses. The padded stools around each table are the only concession to local tastes.

A bit beyond Section A is Taipei's most notorious red light district. On the left, a maze of winding side streets are the haunt of an estimated 1,000 prostitutes who loiter in front of red-lit doorways attempting to lure men into the tiny rooms of their seedy brothels.

Walk back down Hwahsi St to Kwangchow St and turn left. Cross the first major intersection to find **Lungshan Temple**, at No. 211 Kuangchow St. Completed be-

Sing song girls in Wanhua's red-light district, in the late 1800s

tween 1738–40, it is the city's oldest and most popular temple and one of the finest examples of temple design on the island. Lungshan Temple is an ornate structure dedicated to Kuanyin, the Goddess of Mercy, and houses many lesser deities as well. On festival days, when the air is thick with incense smoke, devotees flock here to make offerings and ask for divine guidance. On the roof of the main hall is a pagoda that represents the staircase to heaven. The temple is also renowned for its stone sculptures, especially the 12 columns with winding dragons, wood carvings and bronze work.

Beyond the second gate many people can be seen throwing divining blocks to determine their fortune, while others make fruit offerings to the gods. Further inside, at the main and rear altars, people burn incense at large brass urns. The Goddess of Mercy sits on the main altar surrounded by other gods. The Chinese are tolerant and this explains why Taoist and other folk deities are worshipped here alongside Buddhist deities. An altar at the rear of the temple houses Taoist deities like Matsu, the Goddess of the Sea, and Kuankung. The temple is open from 7 am–10 pm.

Turn left after leaving the temple and take another left at the first lane to the open-air herb market, where pungent medicinal roots and plants are on sale. Walk straight across the market to 245 Hsichang St and enter the front yard of the **Titsang-wang Temple**. Legend says Titsangwan was born in Korea and sailed to Chiuhua Mountain in China in 653, that he sat on Chiutzu Peak for 75 years and finally reached enlightenment. He is said to have been instructed by the Buddha to save all sentient beings, so he frequently appears in Hades to save the sorrowful souls there.

He is also called Youmingchaochu, or Master of Hades. The temple was built in 1828. In the evening, a night market for clothing sets up on this section of the street.

Walk down Hsichang St to Neichiang St and turn left. A few blocks away is a small park with a temple on one side. This is **Fu Te Temple**, established in the 1930s for the worship of the Earth God. The temple was originally on Hsichang St but shifted to its new location a few years ago. It was originally part of a gate which was locked at night to protect residents from attack by bandits, pirates and rebels. Hundreds of statues of the Earth God have been left here temporarily by local people who are away from home and cannot attend to him properly.

Follow Hsiyuan St to Kueiyang St. One block to the right at No. 218 is **Chingshan Temple**, founded in 1856 and known for its fine stone carvings in a strong Japanese ornate style. The main deity here is Chingshanwang, the protector of three counties in Fujian Province. He is thought to be a judge in Hades who presides over the fate of souls, and is similar to the City God, though responsible for the whole nation. Chingshanwang is believed to be the apotheosis of General Chang Kun of the Three Kingdoms Period (220–65), a man of great intelligence, honesty and bravery. The first of many temples built in his honor was constructed during the Song Dynasty (960–1279).

According to legend, a statue of this god was being transported by fishermen from Fujian to a temple in Taiwan in 1854. After reaching shore, the people carrying the statue to its new home suddenly found they were unable to move it any further beyond a spot on what is today Hsiyuan St. After burning incense and using divining blocks to determine the cause of this phenomenon, they learned the god wanted to have his temple built on this street. Shortly after, an epidemic broke out in the area and everyone who prayed at the new temple was saved. This story made the temple famous and more and more believers came to worship. Local gentry raised funds and in 1856 the temple was moved to its present site to accommodate the crowds of worshippers.

Walk back down Kueiyang St under the round red brick archways, past the numerous fruit and food stalls. At Section 2, No. 94, find the gleaming, modern **Mengchia Church**, site of an older church built in 1879 by Geoge Leslie Mackay, a Canadian missionary. Until the late Qing Dynasty, people in Mengchia were anti-Christian and Mackay met strong opposition when he first arrived to preach. But he persisted and eventually succeeded in building his church, which was torn down in the mid-1980s to make way for this new structure.

Walk back to the intersection of Kangting Rd and Kueiyang St, turn right and walk one block to **Chingshui (Clear Water) Temple**, one of three major temples in Taipei (the other two are Lungshan Temple and the Paoan Temple). Built in 1790, it is a blend of Buddhist and Taoist elements. The main god is Chen Pu-tsu, the protector of Anhsi County immigrants. Chen was born in Fujian in 1037 and became a monk at a young age. In 1083 a serious drought was ended by Chen's prayers for rain. Local people, considering this a miracle, built a house for him on Penglai Mountain. A fresh spring flowing from a rock in front of the house became known as Chingshui, or clear water. Chen became known as the founder of Chingshui.

Natives of Anhsi immigrated to Taiwan in 1787 and built a temple dedicated to Chen. Completed in 1790, the temple was damaged by a typhoon in 1817 and later burned down during clan fights between immigrants from different counties in Fujian. The temple was rebuilt in 1875 after eight years of work. The stone carvings on both pediments beside the corridor are of the Chia-Ching period (1796–1820) and are the temple's oldest remains.

Seven Chingshui founder statues were brought to Taiwan from the mainland and the one from Penglai Mountain is considered the most efficacious. People from the temple say that when some major event—good or bad—is about to occur, the god's nose falls off as a sign. When the event passes, the nose automatically reattaches itself. Any attempt to put the statue's nose back on before the right time is fruitless. In the main temple hall is a large tablet dedicated by Emperor Kuang Hsu of the Qing Dynasty.

From the temple gate find a taxi, or turn left on Kangting Rd and return to Kwangchow St, just a few blocks east of Lung-shan Temple, for another look at the temple. Or else, take a longer stroll through one of the two night markets in the area. On Kuangchow St every evening hundreds of peddlers set up stands selling food, clothes, tools, toys and much more.

Many city buses go to the Wanhua area.

The neons of Taipei reflected after rain

TEMPLES OF TAIPEI
■ PAOAN TEMPLE
61 HAMI ST

The Paoan Temple, built by immigrants from Tungan, Fujian Province, in 1805, is considered one of the island's outstanding temples. This Taoist temple contains ornate, intricate carvings and visitors should examine the columns decorated with writhing dragons and the ceilings adorned with wood carvings of lions, flowers and figures from Chinese mythology. The yellow tile roofs and eaves are lined with hundreds of miniature figures. The huge, colorful mannequins used in the temple's parades and ceremonies are kept in the inner courtyard, and the embroidery on their costumes is delicate. The main deity of Paoan Temple is Paoshengtai, a legendary doctor and herbalist. Other deities worshipped here include the God of Agriculture, the God of Good Fortune, Ju Lai Fo, and the Goddess of Birth and Fertility, Chu Sheng Niang Niang. Young wives pray to the latter for the birth of sons.

During the occupation the temple was requisitioned by the Japanese as a language school and factory for bamboo mats. In 1917, after years of petitioning the Japanese, permission was given to restore the temple. Two years later Paoan Temple regained its former grandeur.

Across the street from Paoan Temple is tranquil **Longevity Garden**. The park is laid out in traditional Chinese style with trees, shrubs, flowers, and man-made streams and ponds crisscrossed by bridges and platforms. Turtles and huge frogs often come out of the water to sun themselves on the rocks and ledges. In a corner of the park is a stage where Taiwanese opera (*kotsaihsi*) is sometimes performed, and where members of the Talungtung Old Folks Club play the theatrical *peikuan* music.

■ CONFUCIUS TEMPLE
275 TALUNG ST

A short distance from Longevity Garden is the peaceful and dignified Confucius Temple. It was built in 1854, destroyed when the Japanese invaded Taiwan in 1895, and then rebuilt on this same site in 1925. This complex is a good example of traditional Chinese architecture, and its gardens are well landscaped. Unlike Buddhist and Taoist temples, you will find no statues, lanterns or colorful decorations in a Confucius temple. The temple is usually devoid of visitors except for one day a year, September 28th, the birthday of Confucius. On that day a colorful rite honoring China's most famous master takes place (see page 93).

City buses to the Confucius and Paoan temples include 0 North, 2, 24, 41, 201, 246, 288, and 303.

■ HSING TIEN TEMPLE
  261 MINCHUAN EAST RD

The Hsing Tien Temple is dedicated to Kuankung (Kuanyu), the God of War and patron of businessmen (this explains why so many Mercedes Benz are double-parked outside the temple). Kuankung, easily recognizable by his red face, is a prominent figure in the Chinese classic *The Romance of the Three Kingdoms*. Fortune-tellers crowd the streets and underground walkways surrounding the temple, which is on the corner of Minchuan East Rd and Sungchiang Rd.

■ LUNGSHAN TEMPLE
(See page 130)

■ YUAN TUNG TEMPLE

Vegetarian meals are offered at the Yuan Tung Temple, a Buddhist nunnery in Chungho, just 20 minutes by taxi from downtown Taipei. Meals are served at noon and in the early afternoon. There is no set menu or prices; eat what you get and pay whatever you feel is a fair price. The Chinese building below the parking lot is a memorial to the soldiers who died fighting against the Chinese communists for Ta Chen Island in 1955. Take city buses 201, 241, 242, or 244.

■ CHIHNAN TEMPLE

High on the slopes of Monkey Mountain is Chihnan Temple, dedicated to Lu Tung-pin, one of the Eight Immortals of Chinese mythology who is worshipped by both Buddhists and Taoists (see page 57). Known as the Temple of a Thousand Steps, its nickname derives from the 1,275 stone steps that were once the only way up. The temple provides fine views of the Taipei Basin.

The temple's origin is obscure, though one popular account tells of a gambler who sought refuge on Monkey Mountain to escape his debts. He became a hermit and spent his time making wood carvings of Lu Tung-pin. The carvings were so beautiful he began worshipping them. Woodcutters and hunters soon reported seeing a Taoist who bore a close resemblance to the god Lu. More and more people heard this story and headed up the mountain to burn incense to the god, and before long a path was worn between Mucha and the hermit's hut. In 1891 people from the village of Chingmei raised funds for a proper temple and the first hall was soon built. Lu Tung-pin has a reputation for answering the prayers of the faithful. The temple has received generous donations, which it has used to expand this complex. In 1968 the five-storey imperial-style Lin Hsiao Pao Tien was added, dedicated to the Jade Emperor, and in recent years several other structures have been built.

Temple paintings and wall friezes, Paoan Temple, Taipei

Divining blocks are used to communicate with most gods, but the Chihnan Temple offers another medium for reaching Lu Tung-pin. It has a special 'dream room' beside the main altar for those who want to experience prophetic dreams. To do so, a guest must eat only vegetarian food for three days prior to dreamtime to make sure he is physically and spiritually clean. Then, on the appointed evening, he must kowtow at the altar, burn incense, and tell Lu his problem. The dreamer then goes to the room to sleep and wait for a message from Lu. After each dream the guest throws crescent-shaped divining blocks that indicate whether the dream is the correct one. If not, the dreamer goes back to sleep to dream again. Dream interpreters are on hand at the temple.

Chinese believe that unmarried couples must never go to Chihnan Temple together. Lu Tung-pin, an amorous god, becomes extremely jealous when he sees couples together at the temple and is said to use his supernatural powers to drive the lovers apart.

Countless tales recount Lu's many successful sexual encounters with beautiful maidens and goddesses, and there are several about his longing for the beautiful Kuanyin, the Goddess of Mercy. One story tells how a lovesick Lu was spurned by Kuanyin. The goddess created a river between herself and Monkey Mountain and lay down on the river's far side, beyond the frustrated Lu. The river is the Tamsui and the mountain is Kuanyin Mountain, which bears a resemblance to the reclining goddess. Huang Chun-ming, a famous novelist, once wrote that if you look at Kuanyin Mountain from the bend in the road just before entering the city of Tamsui, you can see what looks like Lu's hand creeping up one of Kuanyin's breasts.

Just behind the temple is a small zoo called Chihnan Tourism Paradise. It has a variety of birds, deer, monkeys, pigs and rabbits. Admission NT$20.

Chihnan Temple is in the suburb of Mucha, 19 kilometers southeast of Taipei. A taxi ride from downtown costs around NT$200 and takes half an hour. Reach the temple by city buses 236 and 237, or Chihnan buses 1 and 2, which leave from Tacheng St, north of the main post office and North Gate.

The following unique temples are interesting and deserve mention.

■ TEMPLE OF THE GOLDEN BUDDHA

In 1954, Abbot Tzu Hang, a well-known Buddhist monk, died at the age of 60. Following his instructions, his upright body was placed in an urn which was buried for four years. When the urn was unearthed and opened, it was discovered that his body was preserved, despite the fact that no embalming methods were used. The body was then covered with gold leaf and now sits in the Temple of the Golden Buddha in Hsichi, a Taipei suburb. Take the Keelung bus from East Station in Taipei and get off at the first bus stop in Hsichih.

■ TEMPLE OF THE EIGHTEEN PRINCES

This is one of two temples in Taiwan dedicated to a dog. The Temple of the Eighteen Princes, situated on a cliff overlooking the north coast, is the burial place of a dog and 17 fishermen who perished together in a shipwreck more than 100 years ago. The temple is popular with taxi drivers, prostitutes, gangsters, and gamblers—people who feel spurned by more orthodox deities. They drive to the temple in droves after the bars and nightclubs close to reverently place cigarette butts—not incense—in front of the statue that marks the grave. 'He likes anything bad,' confided one devotee. Worshippers buy a red cloth at the temple and use it to rub the granite statue's head. These red cloths, miniature statues and medallions with the dog's picture are frequently found in taxi cabs, cars and trucks. Several of Taiwan's businessmen are said to have made their fortunes after visiting the shrine. Gamblers have hit a lucky streak, prostitutes have found honest husbands, and unemployed workers have found jobs.

According to legend, a local fisherman saved the dog from a wooden junk that splintered in a storm. Seventeen bodies later washed up onshore, and as the villagers dug a grave by the coast, the dog jumped into the ditch to die with his masters. A lantern was hung over the grave to commemorate the dog's loyalty, and for years fishermen used the lantern as a guide in rough weather. The temple, only built in 1961, was enlarged in 1975 and began staying open 24 hours. To get to the temple take the Chinshan bus at Tamsui.

■ LIAO TIEN-TING TEMPLE

Liao Tien-ting Temple near Tamsui is dedicated to a thief known as the Robin Hood of Taiwan. Liao was born in central Taiwan in 1883, was orphaned at a young age, and began earning a living aged seven, tending cattle. He came to Taipei when he was 12 to learn kungfu from a master. Like Robin Hood, Liao soon used his skills to steal from the rich—the Japanese in this case—to give to the poor. He was eventually betrayed by a friend, arrested, and executed in 1909. His temple, located in Pali across the Tamsui River, was not built until after the Japanese withdrew from the island. Today it is a popular place of worship for local thieves. Ironically, some of them have reportedly been picked up here by the police. Buses running from Beimen (North Gate) to Pali pass the temple.

Lungshan Temple

In 1885, as French marines prepared to attack Taipei, volunteers from the Mengchia district rushed to the defense of the city. The offical emblem carried into battle by this battalion was an image of the Lungshan Temple.

That a rendering of the temple was chosen is not surprising. Built in 1738 when Mengchia was at the peak of its prosperity, the temple quickly became the heart of the area's religious, social, commercial and even judicial affairs.

Before long the temple's reputation spread throughout Taiwan, becoming a magnet for worshippers from all over the island. Today, it ranks as one of the oldest and largest of the more than 5,000 temples and shrines on the island and is considered one of the best examples of traditional Chinese temple architecture.

The roots of Lungshan (literally 'Dragon Mountain') can be traced back to Fujian Province. In the early days when traders plied between the mainland and Taiwan, a merchant from Quanzhou in Fujian traveled here. While passing through Mengchia he stopped to relieve himself.

In order to avoid committing a sacrilege, the merchant removed the sacred incense pouch that hung around his neck and placed it on a stalk of bamboo while he urinated. The pouch came from the Lungshan Temple in Quanzhou and the merchant wore it everywhere he went. This time, however, he absent-mindedly left it hanging on the branch.

As the story goes, people in the area noticed a bright light shining among the bamboo and became frightened. Soon their curiosity got the best of them, though, and they crept closer for a better look. When they reached the stalk of bamboo, they discovered the pouch, which was inscribed with the following words: 'This pouch of incense ash originated from the Goddess of Mercy of the Lungshan Temple.'

Taking the shining pouch to be nothing less than a miracle sent down from heaven, the people spread the word of its existence, attracting scores of pilgrims. The inspired locals then decided to erect a shrine on the spot, an exact replica of the temple in Quanzhou dedicated to the Goddess of Mercy. They imported every piece of timber and stone from Fujian. Not a single nail or a drop of glue was used. Instead, the pieces were expertly fitted together and within three years the structure was completed.

During the next two centuries the temple was damaged four times. The first incident occured in 1815 when an earthquake leveled the Mengchia area, including the temple. According to contemporary reports, the statue of the

Goddess of Mercy survived unscathed and remained on its pedestal amid the surrounding devastation. News of this miracle attracted more pilgrims.

The temple was damaged again in 1867 when a strong typhoon slammed into the island. Craftsmen managed to restore the temple, aspiring to emulate the original design using the same materials wherever possible. But by 1919 it was falling victim to time and nature; its paintings were fading and wooden beams rotting.

Craftsmen repaired the temple once again, making it sturdier to help it withstand the elements, but soon the temple would face the destructive might of man and machine.

On June 8, 1945, with the end of World War II approaching, Allied bombers struck the Mengchia area where Japanese troops were billeted, hitting the main hall of the temple. The temple was destroyed, and anything that managed to survive the initial blast was reduced to ash by the ensuing fire. The flames from the incendiary bomb were so hot they melted the iron railings surrounding the camphor wood statue of the Goddess of Mercy. Once again, however, the statue itself reportedly remained unscathed on the main altar amid the ruins.

Although the Mengchia (now Wanhua) area is no longer as economically, socially or culturally important as in years past, the Lungshan Temple persists as a stronghold of Taiwanese traditionalism, a hub of religious and secular activities. Worshippers crowd through its gates every night and neighborhood residents sit in the coutyard every evening relaxing and chatting with friends. And no serious politician misses an opportunity to make a campaign stop at the temple.

*Worshipping at the
Lungshan Temple, Taipei*

MUSEUMS, SHRINES, HISTORICAL SITES

■ SUN YAT-SEN MEMORIAL HALL

This memorial to Dr Sun Yat-sen, father of the Republic of China, is in a large park. The hall contains a 19-foot bronze statue of Dr Sun, historical photos, exhibition and lecture halls, and an auditorium. A half-hour multi-media show (in English) acquaints visitors with the story of the man who led the 1911 revolution against the Qing Dynasty. Sun Yat-sen is today held in high esteem in both China and Taiwan.

The park has large expanses of grass, a huge fountain in front and a small man-made lake hidden off to the side (with a bridge leading to a tiny pavilion in the center). Early risers gather on the spacious grounds daily at sunrise, and the park is a popular gathering place on weekends, when children come to fly colorful Chinese kites in the shapes of dragons, snakes and butterflys.

The Sun Yat-sen Memorial Hall is located at the end of Jenai Rd, Section 4. The building is open daily from 9 am–5 pm. The grounds never close. The memorial is close to the Taipei World Trade Center (TWTC) complex. City buses to the memorial include 27, 31, 33, 55, 70, 207, 212, 232, 235, 240, 259, 263, 266, 269, 270, 281, 282, 284, 288, and 504.

■ TAIPEI WORLD TRADE CENTER

A short walk from Sun Yat-sen Memorial Hall is the Taipei World Trade Center. Its frequent trade shows in the huge Exhibition Hall feature sporting goods, automobiles, high fashion, etc; all open to the public. Current shows are advertised in the two English-language newspapers, and schedules are available from the Tourism Bureau. The World Trade Center is located at 5 Hsinyi Rd, Section 5, and is open daily from 8 am–5:30 pm and from 8:30 am–noon on Saturday. Children under 15 are not allowed to enter the exhibition hall.

■ CHINESE ARMED FORCES MUSEUM

The Chinese Armed Forces Museum, 243 Kueiyang St, Section 1, is just off of Chung-hwa Rd. This museum houses thousands of pieces of Chinese military paraphernalia, including reproductions and paintings of famous battles, weapons, uniforms, books, and even the pen used to sign the surrender document with the Japanese at the end of World War II.

■ TAIWAN PROVINCIAL MUSEUM

(See page 109).

■ BOTANICAL GARDENS

The charming Botanical Gardens, located on Nanhai Rd south of the downtown area, have a beautiful lotus pond and 700 species of plants, including tropical varieties and orchids. This pleasant, relaxing place is worth a visit since it is also the site of an old Qing-dynasty building, the National Museum of History and the National Science Hall.

■ HSUNFU YAMEN
An important historical site in the Botanical Gardens is the Taiwan Puchengshihszu Office Building, also known as the Hsunfu Yamen. The *puchengshihszu* was an official who headed the civil affairs department in the provincial government of the Qing Dynasty. In 1893 a building was erected for this department near the present Taipei Police Station. After Taiwan was ceded to the Japanese two years later, the structure was used as the temporary office of the Japanese governor-general until the official office was completed in 1919 (the present Presidential Building). The Hsunfu Yamen was turned into the Japanese army headquarters in 1931, but shortly after was torn down. Part of the building was saved and reassembled in the Botanical Gardens. The site is known for its colorful door gods and Chinese garden.

■ NATIONAL MUSEUM OF HISTORY
The National Museum of History, 49 Nanhai Rd, stands in front of the Botanical Gardens. This small, unpretentious museum houses an impressive collection of more than 10,000 Chinese artifacts and is well worth visiting. The collection includes embroidery, imperial robes, oracle bones, religious implements, bronzes, earthenware and special exhibits of contemporary Chinese painters. Clear but brief descriptions in English are provided.

On the first floor is an oil portrait of the Empress Dowager Tsu Hsi of the Qing Dynasty, painted by the American artist K.A. Carl in 1903. Mrs Carl was introduced by the US representative in China, and spent one year at the Summer Palace in Beijing finishing the portrait of the empress, who was 70 years old at the time. The painting is mounted in an elaborately carved redwood frame decorated with dragons, roughly two and a half meters by six meters. This portrait is on extended loan from the Smithsonian Institute in Washington DC.

Also notable are Song-dynasty tomb guardians, figurines of beautiful, chubby women, and tricolor Tang-dynasty horses and camels. A cafeteria on the second floor at the back of the building overlooks a lotus pond.

Photography is permitted. The museum is open daily from 9 am–5 pm. Admission is NT$10.

■ POSTAL MUSEUM
The Postal Museum, a short walk from the Botanical Gardens, is a must for stamp

collectors. It displays the history of ancient China's postal service, Chinese and foreign stamp collections, and has a library. The museum is open from 9 am–5 pm. 45 Chungching South Rd, Section 2.

■ BUTTERFLY MUSEUM
The Butterfly Museum, at Chengkung High School, 71 Chinan Rd, Section 1, is open, by appointment only, from 9am–5pm. Tel 396-1298

■ TAIPEI FINE ARTS MUSEUM
The Taipei Fine Arts Museum, just below the Grand Hotel at 181 Chungshan North Rd, Section 3, has 24 galleries displaying the work of modern artists.

■ THE ARTISTS' CLUB
Next door to the Fine Arts Museum is the Artists' Club, located in an ornate, European-style building. On the first floor is a coffee shop and video room. On the second floor is a room for specialized art materials, a small library and an exhibition area. The house, a potpourri of architectural styles, has fancy brickwork on the lower story and a mock-Tudor upper story, topped with a stained-glass dormer window. It was built for a tea merchant between 1915 and 1920, and was perhaps designed by a Japanese architect. The house served as the residence of officials, was bought by the city government in 1979, and later renovated.

■ THE WORLD OF YESTERDAY
Opposite the Taipei Fine Arts Museum, on the site of the old Taipei Zoo, is The World of Yesterday. Designed for children, the complex offers a glimpse of Chinese history and culture through displays of mythology, ancient toys and games, traditional handicrafts and folk culture. On Sundays and holidays, Chinese opera and other performances are presented on an outdoor stage in the cultural section, and live demonstrations of crafts and folk arts are held in the handicrafts section. A replica of an ancient Chinese city gate is the entrance to the mythology area. The structures in The World of Yesterday are constructed in the traditional architectural style of Fujian Province.

The World of Yesterday is one of three sections that eventually will make up the Taipei Children's Recreation Center. The other two are The World of Today (an amusement park) and The World of Tomorrow (focusing on science). The park is open from 9 am–5 pm daily, except Monday. Admission is NT$20 for adults and NT$10 for children.

■ YUANSHAN SHELL MOUNDS
At 66 Chungshan North Rd, Section 3 is the Yuanshan Shell Mounds, one of Taiwan's

earliest archaeological sites. It consists of two different strata. The upper layer is a culture of crude, colorless pottery found in the shell mounds and called the Yuan-shan Shell Mound Culture. Carbon 14 dating places the Yuanshan Culture at 2,500–4,800 years ago. The shell mound is mainly made of cockles and a few marine molluscs, discarded by ancient inhabitants after eating. In addition, food residues, pottery and stoneware have also been found in the shell mounds. The lower layer is characterized by cord-marked pottery, a type found in neolithic cultures, and is called the Tafengkeng Culture. The giant ti stone found here, one of the world's largest whetstones, was used by neolithic men to grind rocks, bones and horns into tools. The site has been designated an Historical Site of the First Rank.

■ NATIONAL REVOLUTIONARY MARTYR'S SHRINE

On Peian Rd is the National Revolutionary Martyr's Shrine, dedicated to Chinese who gave their lives in the 1911 revolution. This huge red and gold complex in the classical style of Chinese palace architecture reproduces famous structures of Beijing. Behind the two large brass-studded doors is the main shrine where the names of the heros are inscribed. The shrine was once closed in the afternoons, reportedly because the late President Chiang Kai-shek enjoyed quiet afternoon strolls here. An impressive changing of the honor guard takes place every hour. The shrine is open from 9 am–5 pm.

■ THE NATIONAL PALACE MUSEUM

The National Palace Museum (see page 136) houses the world's largest collection of priceless Chinese art treasures, spanning almost 5,000 years of Chinese history. Most of the more than 620,000 pieces in this museum came from the Chinese imperial collection, begun more than 1,000 years ago.

The pieces not on display are stored in temperature-controlled tunnels behind the main building, surveyed by a US$3 million security system. All-weather infrared and microwave scanners constantly monitor and record activity inside and outside the vault. The storeroom also has an automatic fire-extinguishing system. Visiting art experts are required to take special precautions. Not only are they prohibited from handling silk items, they must also refrain from speaking, despite wearing surgical masks, to ensure that human breath does not contaminate any of the precious material.

The imposing building has glazed tile roofs and moon gates. The museum has space to exhibit 15,000 pieces, and changes its regular exhibits once every three months. At that rate it would take more than ten years to view all the items. If you plan to take in everything on display at the National Palace Museum, expect to make several trips. There are daily guided tours in several languages; English-language

THE NATIONAL PALACE MUSEUM

It reads like the script of *Raiders of the Lost Ark*. The world's greatest collection of Chinese art treasures, some pieces thousands of years old, is precariously carted over mountains, across deep rivers, and up and down the country's rugged roads, to evade capture by the Japanese and later by the Chinese communists.

Amazingly, this priceless collection of masterpieces makes its way safely to Taiwan in 1949, just before Mao's forces complete their takeover of the mainland. This long and arduous journey has to be one of the great adventure stories of the world.

The collection dates back to the Song Dynasty (960–1279), when Emperor Tai-tsung instructed officials to comb the country for outstanding paintings and calligraphy. The mass of art they brought back gradually grew to include porcelain, carvings, enamelware, lacquerware, books, jade and more; but down through the ages only emperors, their courts, and high officials were permitted to gaze upon these wonders.

The 1911 revolution led to the overthrow of the Qing Dynasty, though the victors allowed Henry Pu Yi, 'the last emperor', to remain in the Forbidden City. In 1924, however, the nationalist government suddenly gave the deposed emperor just 24 hours to leave. As soon as the emperor, his wife, consorts, concubines, servants and 480 eunuchs had left, the doors of the palace were sealed and guarded by police. Art experts—the first commoners except for imperial employees to enter the premises—then began the arduous work of cataloguing the entire palace collection, a monumental task that took two years. In October 1925, the government exhibited these treasures of Chinese culture to the public, the first time in Chinese history that commoners were allowed to lay their eyes on the imperial collection.

On September 18, 1931, fighting broke out between Chinese and Japanese troops, instigated by Japanese officers who claimed the Chinese had attacked them along a railway line outside Mukden (Shenyang). Japan moved quickly to mobilize its forces to take control of all of Manchuria. Chinese officials realized that it was only a matter of time before war reached Beijing so they began making plans to remove the most valuable pieces in the imperial collection from the path of advancing Japanese soldiers.

On the evening of February 5, 1933, wheelbarrows started shuttling back and forth between the Forbidden City and the train station. Some 19,557 crates were moved, in five different batches, the beginning of a 16-year odyssey and one of the most exciting episodes in the history of art.

Officials requisitioned two entire trains for the trip to Pukou, across the river from Nanjing. There, officials waited a month before they received instructions to load the crates on a ship bound for Shanghai, where they were stored in a warehouse in the Western concessions.

Four years later, the collection was transferred again, this time to a new temperature-controlled facility in Nanjing. But before workers had time even to think about putting the collection on display, another incident occurred on July 7th, 1937. Japanese troops took control of the Marco Polo railway bridge near Beijing. The fighting that followed the Marco Polo Bridge Incident marked the first real battle of World War II, and the threat of war once again endangered the collection.

Just before Shanghai and Nanjing fell, the collection was moved again. Eighty boxes shipped to the library at Hunan University in Changsha barely escaped destruction on two occasions. Just after the crates arrived, that city's train station was the target of a bombing. Anxious workers hurriedly shipped the treasure to Guiyang, capital of Guizhou Province, just one day before bombs leveled the Hunan University library.

Guiyang officials charged with the complex job of keeping track of the collection's movements decided to store some of the crates in underground Buddhist caves near Anshun, but workers soon realized the dampness could damage the art. Orders then came to transfer the crates to Hanzhong. Since there was no railway line, trucks had to be used. Three hundred trips were made to transport 7,000 crates across snow-swept roads in the dead of winter. At times, the snow fell so hard that drivers were unable to see the road. Forty-eight days later, the objects arrived in Hanzhong, just as the treasures' protectors learned that the collections' intended home in Hanzhong had also been bombed.

The next destination was Chengdu, Sichuan Province, some 525 kilometers and five bridgeless rivers away. It took ten months to finish the arduous journey; several trucks overturned along the way, but miraculously, not a single item was damaged in transit. However, in Chengdu the bombs threatened again. The crates were now moved 150 kilometers southwest to Emei in July 1939, where they remained until the end of the war in 1945.

Meanwhile, as Japanese soldiers marched into Nanjing, throwing the city into chaos, another batch of crates was shipped by boat to Hankou. Later, 10,000 additional crates were sent to Chongqing, but had to be rerouted to Leshan in September 1939 after more bombing. One of the vessel's tow ropes

continues on page 138

The National Palace Museum

broke loose and the ship carrying the crates appeared certain to run aground on the rocks. Fortunately, it struck a soft spit of sand instead.

The collection survived that incident and was eventually transported back east to Nanjing in 1947. According to accounts of the voyage, one crew member spent the entire three-month trip on his hands and knees fighting off termites intent upon damaging the crates. On December 9th, 1947, the collection was deposited in the Nanjing Museum, where the first exhibition in a long time was held the following year.

Within a year, however, the collection was again uprooted when it became apparent that communist Chinese forces would soon evict the nationalist government. On a cold, rainy winter day in early 1949, as communist forces marched from the north, petrified families of nationalist Chinese military men rushed on to a ship at the port of Nanjing. The crowd occupied space intended for some 2,000 crates from the dynastic collection on its way to Taiwan. Navy

Commander-in-chief Admiral Kuei Yung-ching attempted to order the men, women and children off the ship. But when the refugees began crying loudly as he boarded the ship, Kuei found himself at a loss for words. After thinking the situation over for a brief moment, Kuei ordered that the officers' and sailors' quarters be opened for these people, and that the collection be placed in the cargo hold, on the deck, in the dining hall and in other nooks and crannies of the ship. Despite their efforts, 700 crates had to be abandoned to make room for the anxious refugees on this last ship to safety.

The bulk of the collection—5,000 crates—made it to Keelung in February 1949. It was stowed away in a warehouse owned by the Taiwan Sugar Corp in Taichung until 1965 when the National Palace Museum in Taipei finally reached completion.

All in all, the collection covered some 10,000 kilometers, through 23 cities and towns, over 32 years from the day it first left the Forbidden City in 1933. Incredibly, not a single piece had been damaged during the ordeal.

(Clockwise) *Wen-yuan Pavilion edition from the Ssu-k'u ch'uan-shu (Complete Library of Four Classifications); silver raft by Chu Pi-shan, Yuan Dynasty; jadeite cabbage with grasshoppers*

tours begin at 10 am and 3 pm. Photography is not allowed in the museum, but cameras can be checked in at the entrance. The museum has a Chinese tea room, a restaurant and a gift shop selling good, inexpensive reproductions and souvenirs.

The museum is open daily from 9 am–5 pm. Admission is NT$30. It is located in the thickly wooded hills of Waishuanghsi, 15 minutes by taxi (NT$200) from most parts of town. City buses going to the museum are 213, 255, and 304.

■ CHIHSHAN GARDEN

Outside the museum is the beautifully landscaped Chihshan Garden, built in the tradition of the great gardens of China. It has a pond, tree-lined paths, and pavilions, and covers 16,000 square meters. No metal nails were used in any of the structures in the garden, nor has anything been painted. All joints are cut to fit together by pegs and holes. Admission is NT$10.

■ CHINESE CULTURE AND MOVIE STUDIO

The Chinese Culture and Movie Studio, just a few minutes from the National Palace Museum, is a movie set with replicas of old Chinese buildings where Chinese movies and television programs are filmed. If lucky you may see a movie being filmed, though the site is mediocre. The set is open daily from 8:30 am–5 pm, but closes between noon and 1 pm. Admission is NT$80. The adjoining wax museum displays historical Chinese figures. Admission NT$30.

■ CHANG TA-CHIEN RESIDENCE

This former residence of the late, great Chinese painter, Chang Ta-chien, is open Monday through Saturday by appointment only. 2, Lane 342, Chinshan Rd, Section 2. Tel 841-1234.

■ FU HSING CHINESE OPERA MUSEUM

The Fu Hsing Chinese Opera Museum, located at the National Fu Hsing Dramatic Arts Academy, displays all kinds of Chinese opera equipment, including colorful costumes, headgear, weapons and musical instruments. Visitors are shown a film on opera and then receive a guided tour of the displays. After touring the museum, visitors watch a performance at the operatic school, one of only two in Taiwan. The museum is open on Tuesday, Thursday and Saturday, and only accepts group tours by appointment. The school's address is 177 Neihu Rd, Section 2. Tel 790-0234.

■ LIN AN-TAI MANSION

The Lin An-tai Mansion, a 30-room estate with intricate stone and wood carvings, is a classic example of Qing-dynasty architecture. The Lins were a rich merchant family from Fujian Province. The family's wealth is symbolized by the sweeping swallow's-tail eaves of the roof. This embellishment of status was in fact a violation of Qing sumptuary laws which dictated that only officials of a certain rank could employ such eaves. Wealthy families in northern Taiwan commonly ignored the rules. The house was first built around a square, with additions later built on two sides. All corridors lead to the courtyard, which served as the center of family life. The mansion has an ancestral shrine, four main bedrooms, work rooms and sitting rooms. The two kitchens in the rear corners of the house were possibly used by different branches of the extended family.

Built in the 1820s, Lin An-tai Mansion was originally located on Szuwei Rd. After the government decided to widen Tunhua South Rd, it was agreed to move the house. In 1978, experts spent five painstaking months dismantling and cataloguing the house piece by piece. Planners and government officials then spent five years arguing about where the house should be rebuilt. Once the present site in Pinchiang Park was chosen, workers spent 20 months reassembling the 20,982 planks and beams, 38,096 bricks, 240,050 tiles, 95 windows, and 32 large wood carvings. The Lin An-tai Mansion is open daily, except Mondays, from 9 am–4 pm. Admission is free. The mansion can be reached by city buses 21, 33, 35, 72, 222, 283, and 286.

■ LIN FAMILY GARDEN

The 1.2-hectare Lin Family Garden was built on the eve of the Sino-Japanese War, sometime between 1888 and 1893, and literati considered it to be 'the most picturesque garden in northern Taiwan.' The Lins migrated to Taiwan from Fujian in 1778 and amassed a fortune in the wholesale rice business. The garden took three generations of Lins almost 40 years to complete.

When the Japanese occupied the island, the family fled to the mainland and the garden was confiscated for use as a villa. The garden was seriously damaged by refugees who squatted there after World War II, some using the ponds to raise ducks, others converting pavilions into toilets. The Lins donated the garden to the government in 1976, and the restoration, begun in 1982, took four years at a cost of US$4.5 million. The garden follows classical Chinese principles and is perhaps the finest example of landscaping on the island.

The first building is the Chi Ku Shu Wu, or **Ancient Library**, which reflects Southeast Asian influences transplanted to the island by travelling merchants. This library once contained several thousand manuscripts, diaries and paintings, some dating back to the Song and Yuan dynasties. They have since disappeared.

Next is the **Fangchien Pavilion** and another pavilion, in the adjoining pond, where the Lin family entertained guests and enjoyed traditional performances. Walk down the winding path to the Lai Qing Ke, or **Hall of Approaching Greenery**, a two-storey pavilion used to meet important guests. The upper floor has an excellent view of the surrounding green countryside, hence its name. The Kai Hsuan Yi Hsiao, or **Pavilion that Brings Smiles**, is in front of the guest house; it once featured comic operas.

The largest pond in the garden is the **Great Banyan Shaded Pond**, filled with carp and surrounded by banyan trees. Beside the pond is a man-made mountain that resembles the land around the Lin family's ancestral home in China. The **Hall of Stable Tranquility**, used for guests and banquets, is the biggest house in the garden.

The Lin Family Garden is at 9 Hsimen St in the suburb of Panchiao, southwest of Taipei. The garden is open Tuesday through Sunday from 9 am–5 pm, but is closed Mondays and on the day immediately following a holiday. Admission is NT$60. Panchiao is ten minutes from Taipei by train. The walk to the garden from the Panchiao train station also takes ten minutes; numerous signs point the way. Buses 307 and 310 go directly to Peimen St, where the Lin Family Garden is located.

■ TAIPEI ZOO

Taipei's new zoo moved to the suburb of Mucha in the late 1980s. It is open daily from 8:30am–4:30pm. Admission in NT$40. To get there take city buses 236, 258, 282, or 291.

■ TAIPEI CITY TEAHOUSE AND MUSEUM

This museum displays antique tea processing machinery and has a pleasant teahouse. Open daily 1 pm–8 pm. 8–3, Lane 40, Chihnan Rd, Section 3, in the suburb of Mucha.

■ ART GALLERIES

Hanart Taipei: 104 Chungshan North Rd, Section 5.
Tel (02) 882-9772
Caves Art Center: B1, 138 Chunghsiao East Rd, Section 1.
Tel (02) 396-1864
Chung Shan Gallery: 505 Jenai Rd, Section 4.
Tel (02) 702-2411
Crown Art Center: 50, Lane 120, Tunhua North Rd.
Tel (02) 716-8888
Hsiung Shih Gallery: 10th Fl, 385 Tunhua South Rd.
Tel (02) 772-1158

SHOPPING

Taipei's old shopping areas are around Chungshan North Rd and its side streets, the Hsimenting, or Westgate, area, and the Chunghwa Market, also called Haggler's Alley, on Chunghwa Rd.

Chunghsiao East Rd, Section 4, on the city's newly developed 'East Side,' has now taken over as the main center for fashion shoppers. This area is known among some expatriates as the New Ginza. Prices in large establishments, especially department stores, are usually fixed and are rather high.

Bargain when shopping in smaller stores, especially for antiques and curios. The standard rule of thumb is to offer half the original price and then work towards a compromise. Be very careful when buying antiques because many fakes appear to be authentic.

CLOTHES: Many visitors have clothes custom made in Taiwan. Tailors are especially numerous on Linsen North Rd around the President and Ambassador hotels. Most hotel arcades also have tailor shops as well. Women may want to order a made-to-measure *chipao* (*cheongsam*), the form-fitting Chinese-style dress that rarely fits when bought ready-made. Numerous sewing shops can be found on Poai Rd, Hengyang Rd, and in Hsimen district, where chipaos of silk and satin are made.

CRAFTS/ANTIQUES: Calligraphy tools, known as the Four Treasures of the Studio, include the writing brush, inkstone, inkstick and paper. A wide variety of writing tools, many exquisite in themselves, can be found in shops along Chungching South Rd. **Kander Arts and Antiques**, 230 Chunghsiao East Rd, Section 4, has a large selection of these items.

Chinese name chops have been used as a form of signature for thousands of years. People in Taiwan still use their personal name chops to finalize contracts, sign documents, cash checks, and for other purposes. Name chops made from buffalo horn, ivory, jade, hardwood, or plastic can be carved with your name in Chinese or English. Chop carving is a minor art form and many people collect chops the way others collect stamps. Name chops can be made around the city, but carvers proliferate on Hengyang Rd near New Park. One old shop is **Tien Shih Chai Co**, 45 Hengyang Rd. Tel 311-1606.

Handmade paper is available at the **Taiwan Handicraft Paper Manufacturing Co**, 47-2 Changan West Rd, first opened by the Japanese in 1935. This light, almost translucent paper is tough and durable. Cotton or *kozo* paper can be used for making clothes, and *hsuan* paper is used for scrolls and art paper. The company's handmade paper can also be used to make handsome cards and books. Several other paper shops are located on this street. They also sell a wide variety of Chinese paper cuttings. Chinese kites can be purchased at **Rising Sun Kite Handicraft Co**, Room 702, 42 Sungchiang Rd.

Under the Kwanghwa Bridge at the intersection of Shinsheng South Rd and Pateh Rd is the **Kwanghwa Market**. Old Chinese and foreign language books and magazines, inexpensive computers, electronics, handicrafts and Chinese antiques can be found in this market. Be careful when purchasing antiques however, as some of the items are simply good reproductions.

The **Chinese Handicraft Mart**, 1 Hsuchow Rd (at the corner of Chungshan South Rd) and the **Taiwan Crafts Centre**, 7th Fl, 110 Yenping South Rd in the Rebar Department Store, (both government affiliated) offer an array of products including ceramic ware, furniture, jewelry, art reproductions, and marble products from the quarries of Hualien on the east coast.

At the **China Pottery Arts Co**, 14 Chungyang South Rd, Section 2, in Peitou, you can watch craftsmen produce pottery and porcelain right in the factory. An adjoining showroom displays hundreds of items for sale. Yingko, a center for the pottery industry in Taiwan, is 40 minutes south of Taipei (see page 154).

The **National Palace Museum gift shop** sells replicas and souvenirs based on the museum's famous art collection. The National Museum of History, 49 Nanhai Rd, also sells good reproductions of famous works of art. Cloisonne can be found in a number of stores on and around Chungshan North Rd, Section 4, and Linsen North Rd. Hand-knotted Chinese carpets are available at the government-run **Chung Li Rug Factory**, 2–4, Lane 27, Chungshan North Rd, Section 2. Jade is sold at the **Holiday Jade Market** under the Chienkuo Expressway at the intersection of Chunghsiao East Rd and Jenai Rd. This open air market is open Saturdays and Sundays only. Taiwan's jade is dark green nephrite, a type of genuine jade, but Chinese prefer the light green variety from Burma, and consider it the only true jade.

In Taipei many shops specialize in Chinese knotting, or macrame. Perhaps the largest is the **Museum of Chinese Knotting Art**, located in the basement of the 21st Century building, 207 Tunhua North Road.

BOOKS: While Taiwan has given up its title as the book pirating capital of the world, specially priced Taiwan editions of many popular books are available at **Caves Books**, 103 Chungshan North Rd, Section 2. This bookstore also carries a wide variety of books on Taiwan and other Asian countries, as well as a good collection of popular paperback titles. Tel 537-1666.

TEA: Taiwan has grown tea for centuries. Since the Chinese communists took control of the mainland, Taiwan has diversified and increased its crop and now produces counterparts of some of the finest mainland types. Quality Taiwan teas are available in bulk, tea bags, or gift containers, and at prices ranging from remarkably low to ridiculously high. Taiwan has several types of tea, each processed in a different manner; prices are determined by the different grades, tastes and varieties. The most

expensive teas can cost as much as NT$10,000 a pound, though good teas can be bought for about NT$40 per ounce.

Some popular teas are: *Lung Ching*, or Dragon Well, a green (non-oxidized) tea with a slightly bitter taste. *Ching Cha*, or green tea, is 20 per cent oxidized and tastes fragrant and cool. *Tung Ting*, with 40 per cent fermentation, tastes bitter, but has a sweet aftertaste, a characteristic appreciated by tea connoisseurs. *Tieh Kuanyin*, or Iron Goddess, is 50 per cent oxidized and is sweet and heavy, appealing mainly to older people in Fujian and Taiwan. Oolong tea, known in the West as the Beauty of the East, is 70 per cent fermented and is sweet, mellow and not bitter. Black tea, so-called in the West because of its dark brown, wholly oxidant leaves, is known in Chinese as *hong cha*, or red tea, due to its dark red color, and is good either hot or cold.

Most tea stores in large cities have at least one clerk who speaks some English. After you select some types which appeal to your sense of smell, you can sample them in the store, and then purchase the ones you like best. In addition to tea, many shops sell attractive gift packs of traditional tea sets and accessories which make ideal gifts or souvenirs. Some larger shops will even show you the steps of the traditional tea ceremony while you sample the teas. An old and reliable chain of tea dealers is **Ten Ren Co**, found all over the island.

FURNITURE: Traditional Chinese furniture is generally made with wood imported from Southeast Asia, such as rosewood, ebony, sandalwood and teak. The wood is soaked for three years, dried naturally, and then baked in kilns for two months. Furniture is pieced together with wooden nails, stakes, and glue—absolutely no nails are used—and then varnished seven or eight times. Furniture shops are clustered on Changsha St and Chilin Rd in Taipei, and on Chungshan North Rd, Section 5 in Shihlin.

■ NIGHT MARKETS

Taipei has several good night markets, and every visitor should try to visit at least one of them.

The **Shihlin Night Market**, Taipei's biggest, lies just north of the Grand Hotel. Since the majority of shoppers are students, prices are among the lowest to be found anywhere.

Kungkuan Night Market borders the campus of National Taiwan University, running along Sections 3 and 4 of Roosevelt Rd. Most of the businesses here cater to students. Numerous restaurants fill the area, from international fast food chains, to moderately priced foreign restaurants to small, inexpensive Chinese eateries. Bookstores and movie theaters that show current international films in English are nearby, as well as many small boutiques and gift shops.

Another student night market is the small **Shihta Night Market** next to Taiwan

Normal University on Shihta Rd, just off Hoping East Rd.

The **Hwashi Street Night Market**, also known as Snake Alley, is in the western part of Wanhua, just a few minutes walk from Lungshan Temple. Best known on the street are the infamous snake shops. Ox testicles are also available and are said to be quite good for one's health. See page 120 for a more detailed description.

Wanhua is the oldest district in Taipei, and its night market is one of the best traditional night markets. The **Wanhua Night Market** is between Kangting Rd and Kuangchou Rd.

Chingkuang Night Market is near the intersection of Nungan St and Shuang-cheng St, just off Chungshan North Rd; it mainly sells food.

The **Jaoho Night Market** is Taipei's newest. The 500-meter-long market is divided into three sections. The eastern section begins in front of the Tzuyu Temple, opposite Sungshan Train Station, and has about 100 stands selling clothing, fruit and toys. The western section has about 40 food vendors, and in the central section there are Chinese folk artists producing dough and sugar candy sculpture, macrame, calligraphy, and Chinese paper-cutting. Open 5 pm–midnight on weekdays, and noon to midnight on holidays.

ENTERTAINMENT

The National Theater and National Concert Hall, located in the Chiang Kai-shek Memorial Hall complex, are the venues for big-name international and Chinese performers. Well-known international orchestras, musicians and dance companies perform here regularly. Chinese music, opera, dance, and other traditional Chinese performing arts can also be enjoyed here. Similar programs are held at Sun Yat-sen Memorial Hall. Check the community page of the *China Post* and the *China News* for the latest information on entertainment in Taipei.

■ CHINESE OPERA

Opera performances are held at the Sun Yat-sen Memorial Hall, Jen Ai Rd, Section 4, every Saturday afternoon at 2 pm and 4 pm. Admission is free. Opera can also be seen at the Armed Forces Cultural Activities Center, 69 Chunghwa Rd, opposite the Chunghwa Market. Performances usually begin at 7:30 pm daily; tickets sell for between NT$100 and NT$300. Operas are also occasionally put on at the National Theater, in the Chiang Kai-shek Memorial Hall complex. Chinese opera is highly stylized and employs classical Chinese that is unintelligible even to most locals. While few foreigners find themselves able to sit through an entire performance, everyone should sample a little of this colorful and ancient art form. The most popular operas with foreigners are those based on the classical novel Journey to the West, featuring the humorous antics of the impish Monkey King and amazing Chinese acrobatics.

■ TEAHOUSES

Teahouses, once the reserve of old men, have made a comeback in Taiwan in recent years. Among the best are:

Wisteria, No. 1, Alley 16, Hsinsheng South Rd, Section 3

Located near National Taiwan University, Wisteria pioneered the teahouse revival in Taipei. It is housed in an old Japanese-style structure with hundreds of potted plants in its yards. Some floors are covered with tatami mats, so remove your shoes upon entering. Private rooms for small groups are available.

Tungpo, 784 Tingchow Rd

This teahouse has red brick walls, cobblestone floors and mats on the floor. The folk artifacts displayed here were discovered by the owners who searched outlying villages for old bowls, statues, stone and wood carvings and temple accessories. Birds fly freely around as you sip tea. Customers use a wooden ladle to get their own hot water from a brick stove at the rear. Tungpo is a favorite with students.

Café Vernal, 2nd Fl, 110 Jenai Rd, Section 4

Café Vernal provides rooms with tables and chairs or rooms with tatami mats on the floor. The warm decor is a hybrid of Japanese and Chinese styles. Private rooms for small groups are available.

■ PUBS

Dozens of pubs have opened around the city in the past decade, offering food, music, darts, and a convivial atmosphere. An imported beer in a simple pub costs perhaps NT$70, and as much as NT$120 in a larger place with a band. Most expatriates frequent the pubs around Shuangcheng St, between Chungshan North Rd and Linsen North Rd, behind the Ambassador Hotel, an area once popular with American GIs and affectionately dubbed the 'Combat Zone'. The most popular establishment is **The Farmhouse**, with live music most nights beginning at 9:30 pm and jazz on Sunday afternoons at 3:30 pm. If the music is too loud, head to the downstairs bar, which has pool tables and a quieter atmosphere.

The Ploughman group of pubs, with traditional English atmosphere, are conveniently located around the city. They have live music and have been popular for many years: **The Ploughman**, 9, Lane 25, Shuangcheng St; **The Farmhouse**, 5, Lane 32, Shuangcheng St; the **Ploughman's Inn**, 8, Lane 460, Tun Hua North Rd; and the **Ploughman's Cottage**, 305 Nanking East Rd, Section 3.

Foreigners studying Chinese and teaching English in Taipei frequent a string of pubs around Roosevelt Rd and Hoping East Rd, close to National Taiwan University and National Taiwan Normal University. **The Roxy**, 22 Hoping East Rd, Section 1, is a small pub with a large record selection. Another Roxy at 4, Hsinsheng South Rd, Section 3, just south of Hoping East Rd, has dancing. The **Feel More Jazz Pub**, at the intersection of Roosevelt Rd and Jeelung Rd, has a highly agreeable atmosphere and good live jazz Wednesdays through Saturdays.

The best discos are located in the hotels, such as the **Kiss Disco** in the Mandarin Hotel, 166 Tunhua North Rd. A less pricey disco is **Whiskey a Go-Go**, 65 Shinhai Rd, Section 3, behind National Taiwan University.

Also popular are Chinese beer houses that have spread around the city since the early 1980s. Beer houses—many have tables on the sidewalk—specialize in (watery) draft beer and seafood. Their main concentration is on Anho Rd in Taipei, and on Chungcheng Rd in Tienmou.

■ MTV

A popular form of entertainment in Taiwan is MTV, or Movie Television. MTV centers have private rooms where you can rent a movie on video cassette or laser disc for viewing with a few friends. The charge is about NT$120 per person and includes a free coffee, tea or soft drink. There are hundreds of these places; just look for the bright neon signs beaming the MTV symbol. Solar System, Hsinyi Rd, Section 4, has an amazing collection of videos and laser discs from both Asian and Western countries.

■ KTV

KTV, or Karaoke Television, is a cousin of MTV. These sing-along clubs are patterned after the karaoke bars in Japan. KTVs offer private rooms with TVs, music videotapes and a microphone so you can sing along with the bouncing ball. Like MTVs, KTVs are everywhere. Look for the KTV neon lights.

YANGMINGSHAN

Yangmingshan is just 30 minutes from downtown Taipei and has long been a favorite mountain getaway of Taipei residents. Hotels offer hot spring baths and blind masseurs. The scenic ride up Yangteh Rd travels along a tree-lined highway with wonderful views of the city far below. The residential area of Yangmingshan (Green Grass Mountain), is dotted with the beautiful homes and suburban villas of Taipei's wealthy residents.

Halfway up Yangmingshan is the house of China's great humorist and writer, the late Lin Yu-tang. It has been converted into the **Lin Yu-tang Memorial Library** and time appears to have stood still here. Lin's library and bedroom have been left largely untouched. His pipe, Chinese brush and inkstone lie in their regular place, while his clothes still hang neatly in the closet. Handwritten and typed manuscripts are displayed in glass cases. The late essayist and novelist is buried in the garden behind the house. The Lin Yu-tang Memorial Library is open daily from 9 am–5 pm, except Mondays, holidays, and the 16th of each month. Take bus 301 or 260 and get off at Yungfu Station. The house is at 141 Yangteh Rd, Section 2.

The second point of interest is **Chinese Culture University**, whose traditional architecture and white roofs are easily spotted from the city below. After the main road turns left you will next pass the China Hotel, and hat-shaped **Shamao Mountain**. Next reach the original Yangmingshan Park, built by the Japanese, a particularly beautiful place during spring when the azalea and cherry trees are in bloom. But the real beauty of the mountain lies ahead in the National Park.

Yangmingshan National Park is famous for its fresh mountain air, waterfalls, volcanic craters and sulfur springs. The park is an excellent place for hiking and has numerous peaks, two of which are more than 1,000 meters tall. There are also waterfalls and hot springs, some of which can only be reached on foot. The park covers more than 11,000 hectares, and its volcanic past can be seen (and smelled) in its valleys, plateaux and peaks.

Development and hunting have depleted the area's stock of animals, but there remain Formosan macaques, Formosan civets, muntjacs, wild boars, hares, some 88 species of birds, monkeys and snakes, as well as numerous other mammals and reptiles. In winter the park can be cold; it is the only place near Taipei where snow falls, albeit rarely.

Walkways and trails to the park's main scenic spots offer ideal hiking for a couple of hours or a full day. Most of the peaks are easily climbed, but a few military areas and nature zones are off limits.

■ MT TATUN

In a saddle between Chihsingshan (Seven Star Mountain) and Mt Tatun lies **Chutzuhu (Bamboo Lake)**. The bamboo remains, but farmers drained the lake long ago. The only water left in the valley now trickles through rice paddies or gushes along swift streams. From here two main peaks—Mt Tatun and Chihsingshan—can be climbed easily.

Mt Tatun has a road to the peak as well as two footpaths, one running parallel to the road, the other ascending from the far side. The Mt Tatun–Mt Mientien area is the park's best location for watching birds and butterflies (there are over 150 butterfly species here).

■ CHIHSINGSHAN (SEVEN STAR MOUNTAIN)

A paved trail that leads hikers through thick stands of bamboo to the seven peaks of

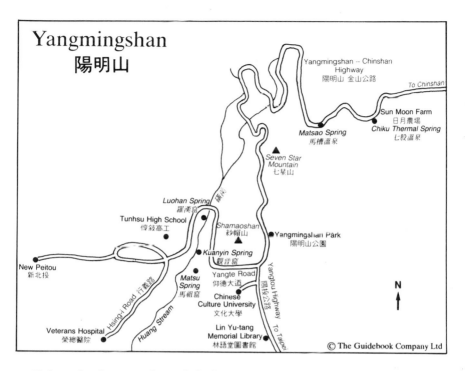

Yangmingshan
陽明山

Yangmingshan – Chinshan Highway
陽明山 金山公路

To Chinshan

Sun Moon Farm
日月農場

Chiku Thermal Spring
七股溫泉

Matsao Spring
馬槽溫泉

Seven Star Mountain
七星山

Luohan Spring
羅漢窟

Tunhsu High School
惇敘高工

Shamaoshan
紗帽山

Yangmingshan Park
陽明山公園

Kuanyin Spring
觀音窟

New Peitou
新北投

Matsu Spring
馬祖窟

Yangte Road
仰德大道

Yangtou Highway To Taipei
仰德公路

Chinese Culture University
文化大學

Hsing-i Road 行義路

Huang Stream

Veterans Hospital
榮總醫院

Lin Yu-tang Memorial Library
林語堂圖書館

N

© The Guidebook Company Ltd

Chihsingshan begins at the road's highest point, between Taipei and Chinshan. A huge sulfur pit has scarred the entire mountainside; it has steaming fumaroles lined with sulfur and pools of water hot enough to boil an egg. At 1,200 meters, this is the park's highest point. The path is steep and moderately difficult. From the top, visitors have breathtaking views of the Taipei Basin to the south, Tamsui to the west, and coastal villages and the sea to the north.

■ HIKE TO CHINESE CULTURE UNIVERSITY

An enjoyable 1.8-kilometer hike to Yangmingshan begins in Tienmu, just north of Taipei, and finishes at Chinese Culture University on the mountain. Take a bus to the traffic circle in Tienmu where you will find two streets going uphill. Take the street on the right to a flight of stone steps that lead up to the forest. Soon reach a fork in the road; the road to the left returns to Tienmu, the fork to the right continues to Shantzehou and Chinese Culture University. Buses to Tienmu are the 220, 224, 267, 268, 601, and 603, all of which go to the traffic circle.

■ YANGMINGSHAN HOT SPRINGS

A creation of several volcanoes that became extinct thousands of years ago, the mountain massif has many volcanically active areas and hot springs. These springs are concentrated in three groups: one in the valley of Huang Stream at the foot of Shamaoshan (Mt Shamao), one in Yangmingshan Park, and another along the highway that connects Yangmingshan with Chinshan.

The three major springs below Shamaoshan are named after deities: Matsu Spring, Kuanyin Spring, and Luohan Spring. Paths connect the three. Matsu Spring is in the lower reaches of Huang Stream, while Luohan Spring is located much further up. Each has two public baths, one for men and one for women. Several private baths exist near Matsu Spring as well. Kuanyin Spring, located at mid-stream, has two public and one private bathing house. Beside murmuring Huang Stream is a teahouse where you can enjoy hot tea after a relaxing soak.

The Yangmingshan spring area has two public baths beside Yangming Lake in the park's front section.

Matsao Spring, located along the Yangmingshan–Chinshan Highway, has 24 single baths and one large public bath. Sun Moon Farm, near Chiku Thermal Spring, has 27 single baths and two public ones. These rustic, but clean baths are in the midst of an alluring grove of trees with walkways.

The charge for public baths runs from NT$20–25 per person.

If possible, avoid Yangmingshan on Sundays when all of Taipei appears to be heading up the mountain.

GETTING THERE—YANGMINGSHAN AND THE SPRINGS.
Take the 301 city bus which goes up Yangmingshan's main road. This bus originates on Chunghsiao West Rd and runs along Chungshan North Rd, where you can board at several stops. If you are in Peitou, take city bus 230 and stay on to the last stop. The path behind the bus station leads to the main gate of the park in ten minutes. The ride from downtown Taipei takes about 45 minutes. A taxi up the mountain costs about NT$200.

To get to the Huang Stream hot springs take bus 219 from Peitou. Get off at Tunhsu Senior High School and follow the path into the valley. City bus 301 goes to the hot spring in the front section of Yangmingshan Park. The best way to get to Matsao and Chiku Thermal Springs and to Sun Moon Farm is to drive along the highway that leads to Chinshan.

TOURIST FARMS

It is possible to pick fruit at one of Taipei's five suburban tourist farms. A small fee is charged to enter the farms. There is no charge for tasting, but a price is charged for fruit taken out of the farm.

The **Peitou Orange Farm**, 18 kilometers from Taipei, welcomes visitors to wan-

Yangmingshan

der through the groves with knife and plastic bag to pick oranges and strawberries. The oranges grown here mature in winter. Take bus 218 to Peitou, then take a minibus in front of the Peitou District Office to Chingtien Temple, 15 minutes away, then walk five minutes down the road to the orange grove. Open from January to April.

The **Mucha Tea Garden** is famous for its Iron Goddess (*Tieh Kuanyin*) tea. The garden does not permit visitors to pick tea. However, paths through the fields are open and tourists are free to watch the farmers plant and harvest the crop. Sample the different kinds of local tea and buy it here cheaper than in the city. Take bus 251 or 236 to the last stop, National Chengchi University, and change to the smaller No. 10 bus which goes right to the farm. Open from 10 am–4:30 pm daily.

Taipei's Southern Environs

■ PITAN

South of Taipei is Pitan, or Green Lake. The Chinese consider Pitan's facilities for swimming and boating and its amusement park to be outstanding attractions, though most Western visitors cannot figure out why. Pitan is not worth visiting unless you are heading to Wulai, the most accessible aborigine area near Taipei.

The Hsintien Bus Co has buses to Pitan which leave every 10 minutes from Kungyuan Rd in front of New Park, and which also stop at Wulai.

■ WULAI

An hour south of the capital city is the resort of Wulai, home to 3,000 aborigines of the Atayal tribe. Wulai has a suspension bridge, a gorge, one of the island's highest waterfalls, a lake, an amusement park, a scenic railway leading to an aboriginal village featuring song and dance shows for tourists, and a cable car.

To get to the waterfalls look for the bridge near the small Wulai bus terminal. After crossing the bridge, head down the small street lined with souvenir shops to the electric mini-train. The train will take you to the base of the waterfalls. A cable car here will carry you to the top of the waterfalls. A round-trip ticket costs NT$130. At the top is Dreamland, a small amusement park.

The aborigines at Wulai put on commercial dance shows. To see a genuine village take the bus from the main Wulai Station to Hsinhsien Village. Bring your passport and apply for a mountain pass from the police station next to the bus station. Buses leave Wulai at 6:30 am, 12:30 pm and 5 pm.

Another place to see less commercialized aborigines is Doll Valley, a 4-kilometer walk from Wulai. You will need a Class B mountain permit to go there, but this can be easily obtained in Taipei or from the police station near the Wulai bus terminal.

Avoid Wulai during weekends and holidays because of the crowds. To get there, take the same bus that goes to Pitan (see above).

■ YINGKO

Yingko, a 30-minute train ride southwest of Taipei, is Taiwan's pottery center. This small town makes a wide variety of traditional and modern pottery, but specializes in the production of hand-painted replicas of Ming and Qing vases that once decorated the imperial palaces of Beijing. The town's narrow streets are lined with shops selling porcelain, simple earthenware tea sets and delicate statues. Wenhua Rd, in front of the train station, is known as Pottery Street. It is possible to tour some of the factories to watch potters working at clay and artists painting vases. The China Art Ceramic Co, No. 19, Lane 223, Chungcheng 1st Rd, welcomes visitors without prior arrangement, and has English-speaking guides. An information desk at the town hall can arrange tours of other factories as well. Tel (02) 670-3300 or 679-3891.

Just off the main street is a temple dedicated to Sun Tzu, the famous military strategist of the Warring States Period (475–221 BC) and author of the Chinese military classic, *The Art of War*. One source says the temple is actually dedicated to Sun Pin, a descendent of Sun Tzu, also known for his military genius. The temple, tucked against the hillside, is easily spotted from a distance because of a large statue of Sun Tzu on the roof. The temple's eaves and stone columns are decorated with intricate sculptures and carvings from Chinese mythology. There is a garden on the south side of the temple.

Frequent trains run to Yingko from the Taipei Train Station.

■ SANHSIA

The Qing-dynasty town of Sanhsia, just a short trip from Yingko, is famous for its architecture. The village looks much as it did at the turn of the century, with rows of brick houses lining the narrow, winding streets.

The town's main attraction is **Tsushih (Divine Ancestor) Temple**, dedicated to Chen Chao-ying, a Song-dynasty loyalist who fought the takeover of China by the Mongols in 1277. Chen's example is said to have inspired his descendants to carry on his mission, which they did by establishing the Ming Dynasty in 1368.

In recognition of his contribution, the Ming emperor deified Chen and a temple honoring him was built in Fujian. Immigrants to Taiwan brought an image of the Divine Ancestor when they settled in Sanhsia. This temple, built in 1770, also contains Buddhist relics brought over from Fujian. Tsushih Temple has excellent wood and stone carvings, among the best examples of temple art in Taiwan.

The village was the headquarters of the anti-Japanese resistance in northern Taiwan after the Japanese occupation began in 1895. In retaliation the Japanese burned the temple down. During World War II, the temple was destroyed again by allied bombers. It has been under reconstruction since 1947; this long period of work, due for completion in 1995, is partially due to the demand for thoroughgoing artistic integrity. New decorations still planned for the temple include intricately carved stone and bronze columns, eight bronze statues, carved stone lions and exquisite bronze bas-reliefs depicting historic and legendary scenes, as well as elaborate camphor wood carvings. Some of the island's best carvers work at the back of the temple and visitors are welcome to watch them as they practice their craft.

Sanhsia can be reached by bus from Taipei. Although the distance is short, the trip can take 1–2 hours depending on the traffic. Plan at least an hour to tour the temple, with a little time to walk around Sanhsia. Buses leave from behind the Presidential Office Building in Taipei.

■ TAHSI

A short drive through the green mountains and fertile valleys southwest of Yingko and Sanhsia are several areas of interest. The town of Tahsi is noted for its turn-of-the-century architecture, delicious dried beancurd, Chinese wooden furniture and giant spinning tops. The town was once the site of a busy seaport, and its shipments of wood, camphor and tea brought great prosperity to the area. The people used their wealth to build magnificent houses in the architectural style of their native Fujian Province. Distinctive Western-style baroque facades, decorated with plants, animals and birds, were added around 1920. This style of architecture is concentrated on Hoping Rd, a three-minute walk from the bus station.

Dried beancurd is the town's best known product, and the entire process, from the soaking of beans to squeezing, boiling, solidifying, forming, preserving and drying, can be seen in many shops. Tahsi's excellent water is said to be part of the secret of its tasty dried beancurd.

The furniture shops are located mainly on Hoping, Chungyang, and Kangchuang roads, and much of the work is done right there in the shops. Tahsi's giant tops are not for children. In fact, the biggest tops weigh as much as 80 kilograms, requiring the cooperation of several strong men. On Sunday afternoons it is possible to see people practicing in front of their houses.

Just past Tahsi is Tzuhu, or Lake Mercy, the final resting place of Chiang Kai-shek.

■ TZUHU

On the way to the Shihmen Reservoir you will pass peaceful Tzuhu; a mausoleum ˋ here holds the sleek black granite sarcophagus of President Chiang Kai-shek who died in 1975. Formerly a meditation retreat of Chiang, who liked the area because it was reminiscent of his family home in China, Tzuhu is considered only a temporary resting place by the Chinese who followed him to Taiwan. Some are still determined that his remains and those of his son, Chiang Ching-kuo, who is buried nearby, will one day be returned to Nanjing, the former Kuomintang capital.

A pleasant path leads through bamboo groves and acacia trees to the lake, then on to the villa. You must present your passport at the security desk near the snack bar before entering the mausoleum.

GETTING THERE

Take a train or bus to either Taoyuan or Chungli, where you can transfer to a bus to Tzuhu. From Tahsi take a bus or a taxi to nearby Tzuhu.

■ SHIHMEN RESERVOIR

The Shihmen Reservoir, a two-hour drive southwest of Taipei, is the largest lake in northern Taiwan. It has a pleasant view and an impressive dam. The area also has a recreation area with an amusement park, nature trails, restaurants and boat tours of the lake.

Take a train or bus to Chungli, 36 kilometers southwest of Taipei, and transfer to a local bus for the ride to the reservoir. Buses and taxis are also available in Tahsi.

■ LEOFOO SAFARI PARK

Near Shihmen Reservoir is Leofoo Safari Park, an outdoor wildlife park popular with families. You can drive through the park in your own car or on a tour bus and observe 47 species of animal, including cheetahs and lions, in a natural habitat. The park has a petting zoo filled with baby animals for young children. It is open from 9 am–4:30 pm daily. Admission is NT$185. Leofoo is about 90 minutes south of Taipei.

Transportation to the park is operated by the Leofoo Hotel on Changchun Rd in Taipei at the intersection of Sungchiang Rd. Buses leave at 9 am and the price of a ticket includes round-trip transportation, admission to the park and a tour. If you travel there on your own, go to Chungli and take the bus from the terminal opposite the train station.

■ WINDOW ON CHINA

Window on China is a miniature village with about 100 well-known structures from China's and Taiwan's past and present, captured on a scale of 1/25. In one stop you can tour China's Great Wall, Forbidden City and Temple of Heaven. Replicas of Taiwanese structures cover the island's entire history from its early colonization by mainland emigrants to the present day. Early buildings include an old Dutch fort and the former British consulate in Tamsui.

Thousands of living trees and shrubs were carefully shaped and grown to the correct sizes to complement the various buildings, and special mosses were grown on some reproductions to give the appearance of age. The exhibits are populated by more than 50,000 tiny figures, all done perfectly to scale and outfitted in costumes completely faithful to their eras.

Window on China is essentially a masterpiece of kitsch. If you want to make the trip, try to tie it in with visits to nearby Tahsi, Tzuhu, Shihmen Reservoir or Leofoo Safari Park.

GETTING THERE

Take a train to Chungli, then transfer to a bus at the Hsinchu Bus Co terminal near the train station.

■ NORTH CROSS ISLAND HIGHWAY

The North Cross Island Highway (Highway 7) is a wonderful mountain road that begins in Taoyuan and climbs over the hills above Shihmen Reservoir. The highway branches at Chilan; the north branch turns to the east coast at Ilan and the south goes higher into the mountains, where it eventually intersects with the Central East–West Cross Island Highway at Lishan (see page 188). A hostel at Paling Mountain is a good place to begin a day hike. Just north of Paling is the Lalashan Forest Reserve, 19 kilometers down a gravel road. The reserve requires a mountain permit, which can be acquired on the road.

North Coast Highway

The North Coast Highway traverses one of Taiwan's most beautiful areas. The road, known as Route 2, begins in the historic city of Tamsui, northwest of Taipei, and winds its way around the northernmost tip of the island, finishing in the port city of Keelung on the northeast coast. Some tour operators offer guided coach tours along the route, but to enjoy the sights at your own pace, you will need your own car or motorcycle.

To reach the North Coast Highway drive north on Chungshan North Rd to Shihlin. After crossing the Fulin Bridge, turn left and proceed straight to Wenlin Rd, which will take you to Peitou.

Peitou is a small, picturesque town 13 kilometres northwest of Taipei, known for its hot springs resorts. During the Japanese occupation the town was a popular Japanese spa. Later it served as a rest and recreation center for Americans fighting in Vietnam. This explains why the town once had a notorious reputation as a red light district. This is no longer the case. Industry and building, including a subway linking the town with Taipei, are changing Peitou's once charming atmosphere.

The **Taiwan Folk Arts Museum**, 32 Youya Rd, exhibits Taiwanese and aboriginal crafts, including statues of folk gods with English explanations, a traditional bridal carriage, Taiwanese puppets and musical instruments. The museum has a room displaying aboriginal artifacts. Next to the museum is a handicrafts shop, a Chinese teahouse, and a Mongolian barbecue. The hot spring facilities are no longer open. The museum is open daily; admission is NT$50 for children and NT$80 for adults. Tel (02) 891-2318.

Also in Peitou is **Hell's Valley**, a hot spring resort with water hot enough to boil an egg. Located off Chungshan Rd, just northeast of Peitou Park.

City buses 216, 217, 218, 219, 223, 302, and 308 all go to Peitou from Taipei. Take city bus 230 from the Yangmingshan bus terminal near the main gate of the park.

After passing the huge Datung plant, continue along Bailing Rd past the Kuantu Bridge (do not cross the bridge). From this point on just follow the signs to Tamsui.

As you drive up the east bank of the Tamsui River towards the town, notice **Kuanyin Mountain** looming in the distance across the river; it slopes up from the west bank and rapidly rises more than 600 meters, with views of the mouth of the Tamsui River, site of numerous naval battles when colonial powers were seeking to conquer the island. The mountain is named after the Goddess of Mercy because the shape of the mountain bears some resemblance to this popular goddess.

Eight paths lead to the top; it takes 1–2 hours to reach the peak. Most people drive to Lingyun Temple, halfway up the mountain, and begin the climb there. The temple serves vegetarian meals every Sunday from noon–2 pm. Food stands at the top sell soft drinks, noodles and other snacks.

To get to Kuanyin Mountain, take a ferry across the river or a bus that crosses the Kuantu Bridge. The Sanchung Bus Co operates a direct service from Taipei, with buses leaving from the terminal on Tacheng St, just north of the main post office and North Gate. Take the bus to the last stop and follow the road for 10 minutes to a stone path on the right. From here it takes 40 minutes to Lingyun Temple.

Kuantu Natural Park, situated at the confluence of the Tamsui and Keelung rivers, is an ideal place to watch the many migratory birds that winter in Taiwan. The park is divided into several sections, including an ecological preserve, recreation area and bird sanctuary.

TAMSUI (TANSHUI)

An easy stroll through the narrow, bustling streets of Tamsui gives visitors a feel for the town's history. Many of the old shops along the main road have reasonably priced antiques, and the town's old Matsu Temple is decorated with magnificent sculptures and carvings. From the temple courtyard one can look down over the narrow streets to the harbor below. Two colleges and a hospital built in the late 1800s by Western missionaries are located here.

■ FORT SAN DOMINGO

The Spanish, the Dutch and the British occupied Fort San Domingo for over three centuries; its history is evoked in different periods and styles of European architecture, and its fortunes help one understand Taiwan's links to Western powers.

In the 16th century, Western maritime powers began opening trade routes to the Far East. The Dutch and the Spanish were quick to establish a foothold on Taiwan, with the Dutch in Tainan in the south, and the Spanish dominant in the north. Both countries chose harbors as their base, and built forts and other defenses. Little remains of the walls of Fort Zeelandia and Fort Provintia in the south, and nothing of Fort San Salvador at Keelung. The only site that has been entirely preserved is Fort San Domingo.

The fort, located on a strategic ridge overlooking the Tamsui River, was built by the Spanish in 1629 as they expanded their territory from Keelung, which they occupied three years earlier. The materials used were mud bricks, reeds, bamboo and timber. After the garrison suffered serious casualties in an attack by local aborigines in 1636, the Spanish rebuilt the fort and made the walls much higher, this time using stone blocks with lime mortar.

Despite these improvements, Tamsui fell to the Dutch in 1642 when the Spanish were driven out of Taiwan. The Dutch rebuilt the fort, which then became known

160

The official seal of the British Consulate in Taiwan, Qing Dynasty

among local Chinese as Hung Mao Cheng, or the Fort of the Red Haired Barbarians. A new stone foundation was laid in 1644, and large quantities of lime and bricks were shipped from the mainland. In 1662, the Dutch were evicted from Taiwan by Koxinga, the Ming-dynasty patriot, but before abandoning the fort they sabotaged parts of it. The fort then suffered a lengthy period of neglect.

The signing of the Sino-British Treaty of Nanjing in 1842 marked a turning point for Fort San Domingo. This treaty, together with treaties signed with other major powers of the day, led to the opening up of Chinese ports to foreign trade and the establishment of consulates. Tamsui, a major port at the time, was opened to foreign trade in 1860.

The British set up a consulate there, established by the naturalist Robert Swinhoe, for whom a species of Formosan pheasant is named. Swinhoe had been unable to find accommodations onshore and so set up his office on the ship *Adventure*. In 1867, the Chinese leased the fort to Britain in perpetuity. A boundary stone with a British royal monogram and the date 1868 stands on the east side of the consulate, marking the year the lease began. In 1891 an elegant brick edifice was built just to the east of the fort, complete with colonnaded verandahs around the building. This was the new consulate and living quarters for the consul and his staff. The fort no longer functioned as a fort and was simply incorporated into the consulate.

The British remained at the fort until 1972, when they broke relations with Taiwan and turned it over to Australia. Within a few months Australia broke off diplomatic relations, also to recognize Beijing, and the site was entrusted to the United States until the Taiwan government formally resumed possession in 1980. The restored site is open to the public, and the government has designated it an Historical Site of the First Rank.

South Gate, built of stone slabs at the fort's entrance, was part of a wall constructed in 1724 when the site was occupied by Chinese soldiers. Four gates originally stood at each of the cardinal points, but only this one has survived. A number of old cannons still stand under the terrace, as if ready for action. The Dutch removed the original cannons when they withdrew, so these were probably brought from nearby Chinese gun emplacements. One inscription states that the cannon was manufactured in the 18th year of the Chia-ching Emperor (1813).

The fort's exterior has been renovated several times, changing its outer appearance, but the interior and the foundations date back to the Spanish and Dutch presence. The exterior today has many features found in traditional castles such as Tiverton and Bodiam in southern England. Two of the four rooms on the ground floor were used as prison cells after the fort was renovated by the British. The doors still have peepholes and small openings for passing food. During the latter years of the 19th century, British subjects guilty of crimes were imprisoned in the fort.

The consulate building has two storeys, receptions rooms, a dining room, a study downstairs and bedrooms upstairs. In the center of the entrance hall is a stone spiral staircase with a delicately carved wooden banister. The red bricks, shipped from Amoy (Xiamen), were handmade and used with mortar made from a compound of sugar, glutinous rice, and lime—a mixture said to dry even harder than cement. The walls are half a yard thick; British units of measurement indicate a British architect designed the building. Small ventilation apertures in the basement in the shape of a Chinese coin make it likely that Chinese craftsmen were employed.

The ceilings on the verandahs on the first floor employ a rare architectural feature using corrugated-iron arches. These arches are supported by I-shaped iron brackets which are flat on top in order to form the floor of the second floor verandah. This technique, designed as a fire prevention measure, was first used in Taiwan in this building.

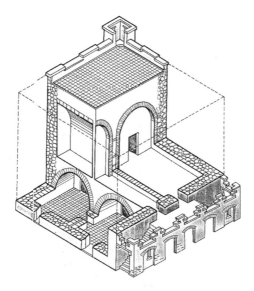

Architect's sketch of Hung Mao Cheng

Notice the semi-circular arches of the ground floor colonnade. They stand in contrast to, though complement, the complete circular archways above the colonnade. The colonnades, characteristic of Victorian architecture, provide shelter from the sun and rain. The exterior masonry and the keystone, made from a block of gray stone taken from Mt Kuanyin across the river, are also noteworthy. The 12 bas-relief designs above the pairs of double columns in the colonnade are carved in three dimensional brickwork and take the form of roses, the emblem of England. The monogram above the keystone includes the building's year of construction, 1891, and the initials for Victoria Regina, showing that it was built during the reign of Queen Victoria (1837–1901).

Admission is NT$20. The grounds are open from 9 am–5 pm. The fort is closed Mondays and on the day following national holidays.

A pleasant 20-minute walk to the fort from the train station passes through a fishing village where Hollywood crews filmed waterfront scenes for *Sand Pebbles*, the epic movie that starred Steve McQueen.

If you have time, walk up the hill on the coast to the pleasant campus of **Tamkang University** overlooking the beach. The buildings on campus blend Chinese and modern architectural styles. At **Shalun Beach**, where the Tamsui River reaches the ocean, you can swim, surf, and windsurf.

The nearby **Taiwan Golf and Country Club** was built in 1919, midway through the Japanese occupation. Nicknamed the 'Shady Lady of Tamsui', many consider the tree-lined course Taiwan's best.

One of the real attractions here is the sunset view from the banks of the Tamsui River as fishing boats return to port. Tamsui is now a fishing village (its name means fresh water) with many fine seafood restaurants. Chihnan Bus Co runs buses to Tamsui; they leave from the area near North Gate. Take either Chihnan 2 or 5. From Tamsui return to Route 2 heading northeast to reach the ocean in about 15 minutes. The road follows the coast all the way to Keelung.

A nice white sand beach north of Tamsui with good facilities is **Paisha-**

Old British Consulate, Tamsui (left);
newlyweds pose for a wedding photo under the arches of this grand building (above)

wan, a popular place for surfing, windsurfing and hang-gliding. There is a small fee to enter the area. Shower and changing facilities are provided.

The next major landmark on the route is **Shihmen (Stone Gate)**, at the northern-most tip of the island. The area is named after a huge gap in a rock, formed over the ages by the action of pounding waves. It marks the boundary between the Taiwan Strait to the west and the East China Sea and Pacific Ocean to the east.

From Shihmen continue along Route 2 for about 20 minutes to **Chinshan**, a fishing village with a park and an excellent beach. In addition to swimming there are facilities here for boating, water skiing, surfing and camping. Chinshan also has a swimming pool and hot spring baths. The admission fee for the beach is NT$40 and for the swimming pool NT$100. The Chinshan Youth Activity Center near the beach has dormitory rooms, doubles and bungalows. Reservations are a must during the summer.

Chinshan is easily reached by local bus from either Tamsui or Keelung. From Taipei a bus leaves from the Chunglun Bus Station on Pateh Rd and goes over Yangmingshan.

The next point of interest on the highway is **Yehliu**, a famous sightseeing attraction. The northeast monsoon wind and sea have worked together to create a gallery of rock formations. The formations have names based on their shapes, including Queen's Head, which resembles a profile of Egyptian Queen Nefertiti, Cinderella's Slipper, and Dinosaur. A stone bridge leads past a tidal pool to a narrow promontory with magnificent views of the coastline. A footpath runs steeply up to a lighthouse at the end of the promontory.

Yehliu (Wild Willows in Chinese) takes its name from the adjoining fishing village, where you can visit **Ocean World**, an aquatic park with trained dolphins, other sea mammals and diving acts. It is about an hour from Taipei.

About two miles east of Yehliu is **Green Bay**, a popular recreation area. It has a good beach and rents equipment for windsurfing, para-sailing, hang-gliding, sailing, scuba diving and fishing. In addition, there is an amusement park for children and several dozen bungalows along the beach.

KEELUNG

The last stop on this tour is the busy port city of Keelung, overlooking the East China Sea. The city has a population of 350,000 and is the second largest port in Taiwan.

Keelung has a colorful history similar to that of Tamsui. A few traces of this turbulent history remain. The city encircles a large natural harbor that was a base for 16th-century Japanese pirates. It was later invaded by the Spanish, Dutch, French and Japanese.

The Spanish first landed in the area in 1626 when searching for a natural harbor from which to expand their trade in the Far East. It was once known as Santissima Trinidad, a name given by a Spanish expeditionary force from the Philippines that occupied the seaport and stretches of the nearby coast. The Spanish built many forts, but they have since been destroyed. At that time, only a small number of Chinese and aborigines lived in Keelung, a hiding place for Japanese pirates. The Spanish were defeated 18 months later by the Dutch who ruled the city until 1662, when it was finally returned to China.

Keelung remained in Chinese hands until August 1884. In that year China and France fought a war over the disputed Yunnan–Indochina border. Three French warships bombarded the seaport, and French marines occupied it until peace was restored eight months later. The city was lost yet again in May 1895 to a Japanese expeditionary force, led by General Kitashirakawa, an imperial prince, who died six months later in Tainan (of malaria).

From the heights of **Chungcheng Park** you can get a panoramic view of the harbor clogged with freighters, and the gray box-like buildings of the city. Finding the park is easy. A conspicuous 22-meter-tall white statue of the Goddess of Mercy perches on the mountain top. For an even better view, especially at night, climb up the steps inside the hollow statue.

Many old cannons and buildings from the Qing Dynasty and Japanese occupation can still be found in the park. At the foot of the mountain is a cemetery for French soldiers killed during the 1884 attack on Keelung. The French government maintains the cemetery.

On a mountain opposite the Grave of the National Heroes at Tashawan is the **Erhshawan Gun Emplacement**. At the beginning of the Opium War in 1840 the British planned to attack Taiwan. The local magistrate ordered the construction of the parapet to improve the island's defenses. He installed a battery of eight cannons as well.

The British army's first attack occurred in August, 1841, but the local army, under the command of a Manchu general, put up strong resistance, sinking several enemy warships and taking a number of British prisoners. In 1843, after several unsuccessful attempts to seize Taiwan, the British withdrew. From Keelung, the Japanese expanded their control to the whole island and ruled Taiwan until 1945.

Seagate Fortress, built between invasions during the 1840s, lies on a hill overlooking the harbor's eastern side. A hilltop on the western side offers fine views from the remnants of a Dutch fortress.

Nearby is the **Cave of the Immortals**, a narrow cleft in a hill containing Buddhist shrines and sculptures. Keelung's 200-year-old **Pingan Temple** contains images of the Earth God and his wife, their faces blackened by two centuries of incense smoke.

Hoping Island, located at the harbor's eastern edge, has stones carved by nature, and is popular for picnicking, fishing and rowing. **Fantze Cave**, perhaps created by the Dutch, is situated on a hill with fine sea views.

The city has several good restaurants, though you might want to try its night market instead. It specializes in fresh local seafood. Keelung's most popular dining spot is **Miaokou**, or Temple's Mouth, a large cluster of food stands selling fruit, seafood, chicken rolls, and other Taiwanese snacks and desserts. The temple referred to is the Shengwang Temple, which enshrines the Divine Ancestor of the people of Zhangzhou in Fujian Province.

Keelung is one of the world's wettest cities, with rain falling on an average of 214 days a year, mainly between October and March. Frequent trains and buses ply the route between Keelung and Taipei. Buses leave from Taipei's East Station.

It takes only 30 or 40 minutes to drive back to Taipei from Keelung on the North–South Highway. Alternatively, you can continue southward to the Northeast Coast National Scenic Area.

The Romance of the Rails

Upon entering the railway station at Twatutia, my attention was at once attracted to the locomotive which was to carry us to our destination. Never in my experience had I seen one in like condition. The brass work had turned to a dirty black, the iron work to a speckled brown, and, like a wounded warrior, it was bandaged from head to foot. Still with all its blemishes it held steam, and a grimy Chinese was shoveling in coal at a fearful rate, that there might be no deficiency.

Fearful of the consequences, but unshaken in my resolve to ride to Kelung, I entered an affair which resembled a stock car fitted with seats. Having provided myself with a first class ticket, which created considerable astonishment, I took a seat in the small compartment, and was soon joined by a greasy railway guard and a conductor whose only claim to respectability was a very unsanitary silk-jacket which had long since lost its beauty. Upon my arrival being proclaimed throughout the car, other unsavory individuals gave me their company, and to my chagrin I observed that they were permitted to avail themselves of this privilege though possessed of only second class tickets. The car was now fast filling up with all sorts of animal freight. A crate of chickens, two baskets of vegetables, and all sorts and varieties of boxes, bundles, and other goods. There seemed to be no rule as to what should be carried in the coaches, and in the present instance it was difficult to tell which had been given the preference—live stock, freight, or human beings.

We now got under way and whizzed along the richly cultivated plain stretching Kelung-wards from Twatutia. For the first few miles all went smoothly, and then we commenced to negotiate the mountain passes; at least so it would seem to one inattentive to the passing landscape. But to my surprise I found we were still on the level plain and that the curves and grades could not be attributed to any irregularity in the earth's surface. Still they were there, and away we went swinging around at a high rate of speed with the passengers clutching on to the seats and windows, and in a few moments swinging back into line again. On looking out of the rear coach *the track appeared something like a pair of gigantic cork-screws flattened out.*

Now the conductor awakened to his duties and commenced the collection of fares, first going through and collecting tickets and fares from such as were willing to deliver or pay the equivalent in full, and then starting after the deliquents. They compromised a large proportion and appeared greatly opposed to adding their mite to the collection. Still our conductor was obdurate and stuck to each one until he got something out of him. The passengers commonly produced a small string of cash which they handed to the conductor who made a rough estimate of their value, ordinarily to find a great shortage. He then demanded the balance due and the wrangling commenced. At it they went at the top of their voices until the passenger by dealing out a few cash at a time had paid somewhere near the amount, or by greater vocal power had worn out the conductor. It is quite safe to say that not a single individual of this class paid the full amount nominally know as the fare.

Having disposed of this, the conductor next tackled the destitutes; at least such they were according to their own distressing tales. Three or four of these refused absolutely to produce anything, and the wrangling recommenced. The conductor now searched the clothes of the offenders, and to me it appeared that affairs were coming to a crisis. But I was wrong. From a gesticulating, raving madman who it appeared nothing but blood would satisfy, the conductor instantly assumed a most perfect composure, as though his work had been one round of pleasure, and then seizing a chicken from one of the deliquents, a sort of combination pillow and small trunk from a second, and a roll of filthy clothing from a third, he returned to my small compartment, tranquil and apparently satisfied. Whether or not the stuff was redeemed on the arrival of the train at Kelung I cannot say.

James W Davidson, Consul of the United States for Formosa,
The Island of Formosa, 1903

Northeast Coast National Scenic Area

Enchanting landscapes, magnificent seashores, and charming rural towns highlight the Northeast Coast National Scenic Area, just southeast of Keelung. A visit to this area can be completed in one day if you drive your own car.

Pitouchiao is noted for its resemblance to a nose and for its grassy terraced fields. A zigzag road leads to steep cliffs dropping headlong into the Pacific Ocean. A lighthouse sits ahead at the end of the cliff path.

One kilometer south of Pitouchiao is the scenic area of **Lungtung Cove**, where white sandstone rises from the sea displaying magnificent patterns of erosion. Lungtung, the highest peak on the Northeast Coast Highway, has sheer cliffs and is one of Taiwan's best rock climbing areas.

Lungtung can be reached by bus from Keelung. Get off at the town of Lungtung and walk back toward the tunnel that the bus passed through. In front of the tunnel is a path that descends to the right. Take this path down to the water and when you reach the coast turn left and walk until you come to the rock climbing area.

Three kilometers down the highway is the fishing village of **Homei**, formerly known as Wentzuken. Nearby is **Chinshawan**, a summer resort. **Aoti**, a major stopover on the highway, 2.6 kilometers further south, has inexpensive seafood restaurants and a camping area right on the beach.

A system of wooden pavilions and walkways lends a Chinese character to the new **Yenliao Seaside Park**, which boasts the island's finest seashore leisure facilities. The beach has showers, changing rooms, and tables and chairs for eating and relaxing. Equipment for water sports can also be rented.

Japanese expeditionary forces landed here in May 1895 to begin their conquest of the island. A monument has been erected to those who sacrificed their lives fighting the Japanese.

White sand and azure water make **Fulung** one of Taiwan's best beaches. It stretches several kilometers and is divided into internal and external sections. The internal section is for windsurfing and the external for swimming; waves are good enough for surfing. Rustic bungalows, cottages and camping areas are available at reasonable prices. Rates are often discounted on weekdays and during the off-season. Beach equipment can be rented.

Fulung is close enough to Taipei for a day trip and is easily reached. It is about an hour by train from the capital. Alternatively, take a bus to Keelung and transfer to a local bus going to Fulung.

Taiwan's largest camping area is in the most beautiful part of the Northeast Coast National Scenic Area, **Lungmen Riverside Park**. It is a good place for water sports, camping and bicycling. Campsites include a grassy meadow, wooden lean-tos and a car-side camping area. Four central cooking sites are the only places in the park where cooking and fires are permitted. The service center has a dining hall, grocery store and equipment rental. The park's water area offers paddle boats, canoes and rowboats. A bicycle path running between the park and camping areas will eventually connect with Yenliao and Fulung. Lungmen has a 24-hour guard service to protect campers.

The 200-year-old **Tsaoling Historic Trail** is an easy eight-kilometer stroll through the hills overlooking the coast. Qing-dynasty monuments and tiny Earth God shrines dot the footpath. The true attractions, however, are rippling creeks, tranquil farm-land, verdant valleys, dense woods, bamboo groves and stunning ocean views from the ridge. Stone benches and wooden pavilions provide places to rest and picnic. The northern end of the trail can be reached from a narrow paved road that branches off the coastal highway about one kilometer north of Fulung. Two kilometers down the road is a temple, directly opposite the road to the mountain trail.

Santiaochiao, 8.4 kilometers south of Fulung, juts out into the Pacific Ocean and is Taiwan's easternmost point. A lighthouse aids fishing boats in the area. Traces of an old Spanish town can still be seen on the mountain slopes.

Continue along the coastal highway to the waterfalls and hot springs of Chiaohsi in Ilan County, then proceed down the stunning east coast to Hualien and Taitung. Or else follow the inland route (Highway 9) through the steep mountains back to Taipei.

Ilan, Hsinchu and Miaoli Counties

ILAN COUNTY
■ CHIAOHSI
Chiaohsi, known as Little Peitou, is famous for its hot springs, though there are better hot spring resorts elsewhere on the island. If you stop here, visit **Wufengchi Waterfalls**, a 50-minute hike or a quick taxi ride above the town. Local trains from Taipei serving the east coast stop in Chiaohsi. Buses running between Taipei and Suao also stop here.

■ TAIPINGSHAN
Taipingshan is the closest rugged mountain to Taipei. Despite its proximity, it remains quiet, clean and undisturbed. Consider a hike to lovely **Tsuifeng Lake**.

Take the main road back down the mountain for eight kilometers to **Jentse's** hot

springs. From Jentse you can get a bus to Ilan (city). Avoid Taipingshan in the winter months when it rains frequently. A Class B mountain pass is required to hike up Taipingshan, and this can be obtained in Tuchang on the way. Remember to bring your passport.

Travelling to Taipingshan is inconvenient, which largely explains why it has managed to remain relatively unspoilt. There is no public transport to the mountain; the one daily bus from Ilan goes only as far as Jentse. From there you must walk or hitchhike the rest of the way. The bus from Ilan to Jentse leaves at 7:50 am.

■ SUAO

The sleepy town of Suao has a fine natural harbor, now Taiwan's newest and fifth largest international seaport. The town was originally settled by immigrants from Quanzhou, Fujian Province. During the Qing Dynasty, a man named Su led a small band of immigrants to the area. The name of the town derives from combining Su's name and the word *ao*, (harbor).

Suao is the northern terminus of the **Suao–Hualien Highway**, a spectacular cliff-side road (see page 232). Suao is also the northern terminus of the North Link Railway that connects Taipei with Hualien in the southeast.

Try one of the town's cold mineral spring baths, located on Lengchuan Rd opposite the train station. The water is said to be good for skin diseases and general health. Its primary mineral content is carbon, leached out of stone into geothermally heated groundwater two kilometers below the surface. Other minerals in trace amounts include sodium, potassium, magnesium and calcium. Sanitized and filtered cold spring water is also available for drinking, although the taste is strong and slightly sour. The most interesting bathing place is the wooden bath house built by the town government. You can bathe in an open public pool for NT$40—one for men and one for women. Most people bathe naked. A private wooden room with a small pool costs NT$80 for 40 minutes.

Two cold spring pools nearby can be used for free. The water is the same as at other sites, but there are no facilities for changing. The pools, stone-lined rectangular holes in the ground with tin walls, are used primarily by old men. Concrete steps beside the old baths lead up to two pavilions that offer nice views of the harbor and town.

More interesting than the town of Suao itself is the old-fashioned fishing harbor at **Nanfangao**, situated behind the international freight harbor, about two kilometers from the center of town. Two large temples stand in front of the harbor, both dedicated to Matsu, the Goddess of the Sea. The **Chingai Temple** has 95 religious images rought from the Matsu Temple in Meizhou, Fujian Province, forerunner of all Matsu temples. The smaller **Nantien Temple** houses a large number of religious items. The plaza in front of the temple turns into a busy night market in the evening. You will also find several seafood restaurants here.

GETTING THERE
Chunghsing buses leave Taipei's North Station several times each hour for Suao. A direct train service runs to Suao from Taipei.

HSINCHU COUNTY
■ HSINCHU (CITY)
There is not much to see or do in Hsinchu, capital of Hsinchu County. It is the home of Taiwan's Science-Based Industrial Park, as well as Chiaotung University and Tsinghua University, Taiwan's two best technical institutions. Consider a visit to the small Hsinchu Zoo (slightly run-down), or the Confucius Temple, both just a 10-minute walk southeast of the train station.

An interesting place is the large Chenghuang Temple, the City God Temple, known for its adjoining restaurant area. This is a popular place where locals go to eat delicious Hsinchu specialties, such as *gongwan* (meat balls) and *mifen* (a type of vermicelli). However, it is dark and dingy here and the food is very local, appealing only to adventurous gourmets. Chenghuang Temple is downtown near the intersection of Chungshan Rd and Tungmen St, a 10-minute walk northeast of the train station.

■ LION'S HEAD MOUNTAIN (SHIHTOUSHAN)
Buddhist temples, shrines, and monasteries, evoking the flavor of ancient China, dot the cool, verdant hills of Lion's Head Mountain, which straddles Hsinchu and Miaoli counties. Resembling a reclining lion, this mountain has a cluster of some dozen temples, the oldest of which is about 70 years old. Many are set into shallow caves on the slopes of the mountain. The ride leading to the temples goes through a scenic tea growing area inhabited by Hakkas.

The hike begins at a stone arch at the entrance. Shops here sell drinks and food and maps of the mountain. The path leads up to the **Moon Viewing Pavilion** at the summit, then leads down through flower-scented forests and bamboo groves. The walk takes around three hours.

A night at one of the mountain temples is a rare chance to experience life in a Chinese temple as it has been lived for thousands of years. **Linghsia Cave**, **Chinkang Temple**, **Hai Hui Temple**, **Chuan Hua Hall**, **Fu Tien Kung** and **Yuan Kuang Temple** usually provide food and spartan but clean lodging, which includes a tatami room with quilts, and vegetarian dinner and breakfast, for a suggested donation of about NT$200. If you stay for lunch you should pay an extra NT$50. If you stay for just one meal the suggested donation is NT$50. You are expected to finish everything in your rice bowl, or you may well be scolded by one of the nuns for wasting food. Separate chopsticks are placed beside each dish for transferring food to your rice bowl, so do not stick your own chopsticks into the dishes from which everyone eats. Also, men and women, even if married, are not allowed to sleep in the same rooms. This does not apply to young children. No alcohol is allowed and quiet is expected around the temples and at night.

Yuan Kuang Temple is the best place to stay. It was formally known as Shih Yen Tung Temple, or Lion's Cliff Cave Temple, because it is built in a cave. The spot was discovered in 1894 by a man looking for a place to meditate. He was the first monk to stay on Lion's Head Mountain.

The monks and nuns spend their time harvesting and curing tea, caring for the temple, cooking and working in the hillside fields behind the temple where they live. This area is off limits to visitors, unless you are invited.

The temple has built a large complex on the mountain slope for guests. Try to arrive before dark as dinner is served at about 5:30 pm; the custom is to bathe before eating. Monks and nuns knock on doors just before 4 am, summoning visitors to the

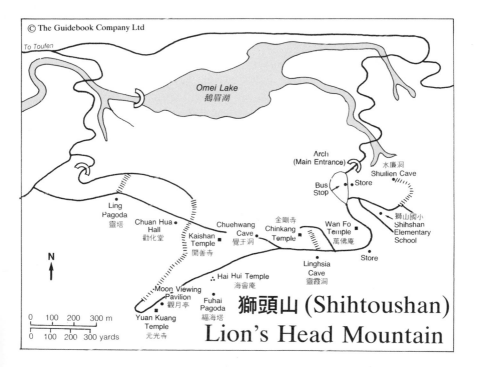

pre-dawn Buddhist service. No one cares if you sleep in, but breakfast is served promptly after the service at around 5:30 am.

To depart, take the steps down the other side of the mountain, a short 20 minute walk that passes newly renovated, gaudy temples. These include Chuan Hua Hall, with a large courtyard and a good view of the Ling Pagoda and mountain scenery below, and Fu Tien Kung, known for its colorful murals. Both of these sites provide food and lodging.

The last religious structure is a damaged six-storey pagoda at the town of Omei, where you can catch a bus to Toufen. From there frequent buses travel to Taipei.

GETTING THERE

There is no direct transportation to the mountain from Taipei.

First take a bus or train to Hsinchu, an hour south of Taipei. Then go to the Hsinchu Bus Co terminal opposite the train station and catch a bus to Chutung. From Chutung get a bus to the foot of Lion's Head Mountain. It is also possible to take a bus to Toufen, and then switch for a bus to the mountain. This will leave you at a different side of the mountain, closer to the Yuan Kuang Temple. Get off the bus and find shops and a set of steps on the left side of the road with an archway overhead. Make sure the bus driver knows you are heading for Lion's Head Mountain because the next stop is much further down the road. Avoid the mountain during crowded weekends.

MIAOLI COUNTY

■ **SANYI**

Sanyi is a center for wood carving and wooden furniture. The town was established around the turn of the century when a Japanese discovered that the strong-smelling wood in the area was actually camphor wood. He opened a wood carving business, which soon prospered and was followed by others. The carvers, now using imported wood from Indonesia and the Philippines, create a wide range of subjects, from lifelike animals to Buddhist figures.

Only local trains stop here, and they are infrequent. Take a train or bus from Taipei to Miaoli City, then transfer to a local bus to Sanyi.

A view of the coast along the Suao–Hualien Highway

Central Taiwan

Central Taiwan, bordered on the west by the Taiwan Strait and on the east by the Pacific Ocean, is an area of spectacular and varied natural beauty, with fertile plains and highlands that include Northeast Asia's highest peak. Two of the island's five international seaports are located in Central Taiwan, Taichung on the west coast, and Hualien on the east. The coasts are linked by the Central East–West Cross Island Highway, one of Asia's most beautiful mountain roads. Its most travelled stretch, the Taroko Gorge section along the eastern end, is a natural wonder. Another point of interest is a narrow gauge alpine railway that leads to the highest railway station in East Asia.

Taichung

HISTORY

Five centuries ago, Taichung was no more than an aboriginal village inhabited by the Pingpu tribe. In 1721, a boatload of settlers took off from mainland China for Taiwan. They established a village called Tatun (Big Mound), named after a nearby hillock. The first city government was established in 1889. By 1895, when the Japanese began their 50-year occupation of the island, Taichung had already become a proper city. The Japanese renamed it Taichung (Central Taiwan). Some older residents still prefer to use the old name.

CITY SIGHTS

Taichung, a bustling metropolis and the economic and communications center of central Taiwan, lies just two hours south of Taipei. It has a population of more than 762,000, and is the third largest city on the island after Taipei and Kaohsiung. The city's importance increased in 1976 with the opening of an international seaport, 25 kilometers west of the city.

Taichung is a convenient stepping-off point for visits to the East–West Cross Island Highway, as well as a hub for visits to Sun Moon Lake, Hsitou Forest Recreation Area and other locations in west-central Taiwan.

■ TAICHUNG PARK

Taichung Park, also known as Chungshan, or Sun Yat-sen Park, is an example of classical Chinese landscaping. The park, built in 1908, covers 20.2 hectares in the center of downtown. A small hill in the park is the hill (*tatun*) that gave the city its

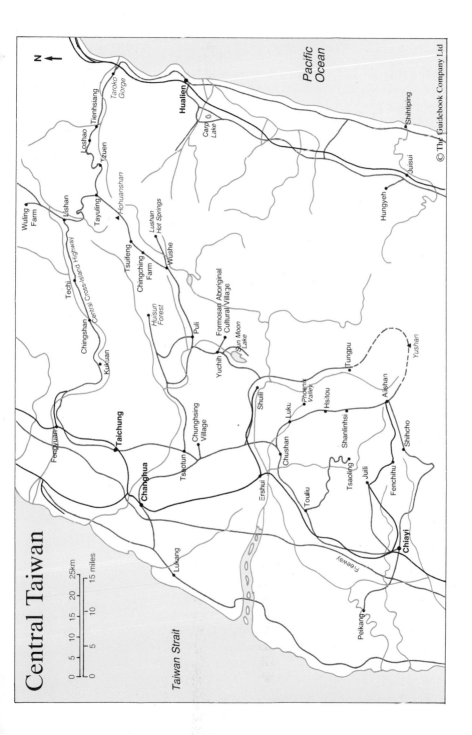

Central Taiwan

Taiwan Strait

Pacific Ocean

© The Guidebook Company Ltd

0 5 10 15 20 25km
0 5 10 15 miles

N

Taroko Gorge
Tienhsiang
Loshao
Zuen
Hualien
Carp Lake
Shihtiping
Juisui
Hungyeh
Wuling Farm
Lishan
Tayuling
Hohuanshan
Techi
Central Cross-Island Highway
Tsuifeng
Chingching Farm
Lushan Hot Springs
Wushe
Chingshan
Huisun Forest
Kukuan
Puli
Formosan Aboriginal Cultural Village
Sun Moon Lake
Yuchih
Tungpu
Yushan
Fengyuan
Taichung
Chunghsing Village
Shuili
Phoenix Valley
Luku
Hsitou
Alishan
Tsaotun
Changhua
Chushan
Shanlinhsi
Shihcho
Ershui
Touliu
Tsaoling
Juili
Fenchihu
Lukang
Peikang
Freeway
Chiayi

original name. On top of the hill is **Moon Viewing Pavilion**, the only remnant of the old city wall's North Tower. It was built in 1889 and later destroyed during the Japanese occupation.

This is a serene place to escape the busy city traffic. It is also a good place in the early morning hours to watch people practice *taichichuan*, (Chinese shadow boxing), martial arts, aerobics, and even ballroom and disco dancing. During the day local musicians play and sing traditional Chinese and Taiwanese songs. There is a lake in the park with Chinese-style bridges and pavilions, surrounded by a walkway. The park is on Kungyuan Rd, opposite the Park Hotel.

■ CONFUCIUS TEMPLE

Taichung's Confucius Temple is relatively new, but still adheres to traditional rules of architecture. A special ceremony here on September 28th celebrates Confucius' birthday. It includes ancient rituals, music, and costumes, and great pains are taken to strictly observe traditional practices.

The Confucius Temple is located on Shuangshih Rd, in the northern part of the city. Red buses 10, 11, 40 and 46 all go there.

■ MARTYRS' SHRINE

On Lihsing Road, near the Confucius Temple, is the Martyr's Shrine, a good example of traditional Chinese architecture. The shrine is dedicated to the memory of 72 patriots who were beheaded by the Qing government in 1911 for their role in the attempted overthrow of the dynasty. A ceremony is held here every year on Youth Day (March 29).

■ PAOCHUEH TEMPLE

The Paochueh Temple, 140 Chienhsing Rd, also in the northern part of Taichung, has a memorial bell tower and a 31-meter-tall Milofo. Better known as the **Laughing Buddha** because of his gleeful smile, Milofo sits on a huge pedestal in a corner of the temple compound. Smaller statues of Milofo grace different parts of the temple. Three other Buddhas sit in the main shrine, protected by fierce guardian deities.

Take green buses 6, 14, 16, and 17.

■ TAICHUNG SCIENCE MUSEUM

The Taichung Science Museum is a hands-on learning museum with up-to-date scientific equipment and exhibitions. Its Space Theater is very popular. The museum is located at 1 Kuanchien Rd. Take green buses 22, 46, 47, or 48.

■ TAIWAN MUSEUM OF ART

The museum has 24 galleries specializing in works of modern artists. Open Tuesday to Saturday, 9 am–5 pm; Sunday from 9 am–8 pm. Admission is NT$10. The museum is next door to the Taichung Cultural Center.

■ TUNGHAI UNIVERSITY

Tunghai University has numerous buildings constructed in the architectural style of the Tang Dynasty on its 140-hectare wooded campus. An exception is the modern-looking Luce Chapel, designed by the Chinese-American architect I. M. Pei; it symbolizes a pair of hands folded in prayer.

Take green bus 22 or red bus 38 to the campus.

SHOPPING & ENTERTAINMENT

The main shopping area is along Chungcheng Rd, near the train station. More interesting is the night market on Chunghua Rd. The street is quiet during the day, but around 6 pm hordes of vendors set up on the street, selling a wide variety of clothing, toys, household goods, local snacks and much more. There is an open-air market near Tsuyu Rd. An interesting night market opens in the evening near the intersection of San Min and Kuang Fu Roads.

■ SNACKS

Taichung is famous for its local snacks, including cold papaya milk, sweet bean ice, meatballs, sun cakes, and Yihsin dried beancurd; these are available in shops around the city.

According to local lore, papaya milk, which tastes as good as a cold milk shake, originated in the city when Chen Hong-tsun thought up the recipe to make better use of the produce from his papaya trees. Chen's son still sells the drink that made Taichung famous at a stall at 125 Chunghua Rd, Section 1, in the night market area.

Sweet bean ice is also a local invention, a concoction of shaved ice smothered in different kinds of beans and fruit, a popular summer dessert. The original is still sold in a market behind the Jenyu Bus Station.

Meat balls are usually consumed with soup, and have a unique flavor. The best in the city are sold in a little restaurant on the corner of Taichung and Fuhsing Roads.

Sweet, flaky pastries called sun cakes are available at Taiyang Tang, 23 Tzuyu Rd, Section 2. Yihsin bean curd, flavored with special spices, was developed over 50 years ago by Hsueh Chun-ho and he still turns it out at a shop on Lachin St.

■ PUBS

Pubs in Taichung are concentrated on Taichung Kang (Harbor) Rd near the National Hotel. Try **J.D.**'s, the **Heidelberg**, and **Cheers**!

Bali Hai: 225 Taichung Kang Rd, Section 1

The Wagon Wheel: 229 Taichung Kang Rd, Section 1

Alt Heidelberg: 13 Kuanchien Rd.

Blue Bat: Basement, 247 Taichung Kang Rd, Section 1

■ DISCOS

The following discos are popular, and are conveniently located at the same address, 115 Luchuan West Street. Some have a cover charge.

DD, 9th floor

Telstar Disco, 10th floor

Golden Butterfly Dance Hall, 7th floor

GETTING THERE

Taichung is connected to different parts of the island by bus and train. There are three bus stations in the city, all quite near the train station. Buses for Taipei leave from the bus station in front of the railway station; southbound buses for Chiayi, Nantou, Tainan and Kaohsiung leave from the station behind the train station; buses for Sun Moon Lake, Wushe, Lishan and Hualien depart from the bus station two blocks north of the train station.

AROUND TAICHUNG

■ LIN FAMILY GARDEN AND MANSION

Nine kilometers south of Taichung on Route 3 in the town of Wufeng is the Lin family complex. The Lins of Wufeng were among the richest and most powerful families in Taiwan, and their position demanded sumptuous dwellings; they spared nothing to make their home the finest that could be built. The old buildings here were constructed about a century ago at the foot of a mountain. This time of gracious living demanded exquisite workmanship and only the best materials. The finest species of trees were felled on the mainland, shipped to the island and used whole for columns and beams, or cut into boards. Bricks were molded and fired in kilns built especially for the building, as were the red tiles for the roofs. Beautifully painted porcelain tiles from Fujian were embedded in concrete posts or made into decorative wall panels. Artisans from mainland China were hired to produce intricately carved furniture, window panels and other decorations, and skilled painters were engaged to paint roof beams, walls and doors, producing paintings of gods to protect their houses and inhabitants.

Taichung

Chienhsing Rd

Paochueh
■ Temple

Chungcheng
Park

N

Science
Museum

Martyr's
■ Shrine

Confucius
■ Temple

Stadium

Kungyi Rd

Hsiangshang Rd

Taiping Rd

Kungyuan

Chingwu Rd

Taichung
Park

Lieniwu Rd

Cultural
Centre

Nanching Rd

Wuchuan West Rd

Railway
Station

Nantun Rd

Chienkuo

Chunghsiao

Chiencheng

Jenho Rd

Chunghsing
University

© The Guidebook Company Ltd

| 0 | 200 | 400 | 600 | 800 | 1000 m |
| 0 | 200 | 400 | 600 | 800 | 1000 yards |

The complex is now in a state of serious decay. Nevertheless, the buildings remain some of the best examples of late Qing-dynasty architecture on the island. The complex is divided into three units: the **Ching Hsun Tower** and **Ching Jung Studio** (also called the Upper House), **Kung Pao Official Residence** (the Lower House), and **Lai Yuan**, a traditional Chinese pleasure garden, behind the mansions. The Official Residence was once the home and office of a Qing official and is Taiwan's best preserved building of this type. Only Lai Yuan is open to the public.

In the beginning two brothers, Lin Tang-pang and Lin Tien-kuo, each had their separate establishment. Ting-pang, the elder brother, was head of the Lower House and lived in the Old Hall situated to the right of the Kung Pao Official Residence. Tien-kuo headed the Upper House, and lived in what is today Fourth Grand Aunt's two-storey mansion. The later mansions were added as the family grew.

In the mid-19th century, when Wufeng was frequently attacked by aborigines and people from neighboring villages, the two-story building at the center of the complex was used as a watchtower, arsenal and place of safety for women and children. The Kung Pao Official Residence was later used by Lin Chao-tung, the grandson of Tang-pang, and a Qing government official. One *faux pas* was the placement of two carved stone lambs at the main entrance of Kung Pao. While stone lions were a symbol of the residence of an official, stone lambs were traditionally used to mark the graves of great men.

The Ching Hsun Tower was rebuilt in the 1920s after being damaged in an earthquake. Lin Wen-chin, Tien-kuo's youngest son, brought honor on the family by climbing the traditional ladder of success in China, garnering the coveted *chu jen* degree. In honor of his mother he built Lai Yuan.

During these early days, the first courtyard bustled with activity, with servants taking care of chores, and traders, messengers, soldiers, and an occasional peasant passing in and out of the courtyard amid the shouts of the Lin children who took their lessons in rooms beside the court.

The buildings are now occupied by the impoverished descendants of the early Lins, along with an assortment of squatters, most of whom claim kinship with the original residents by the mere fact of sharing the same surname. (Lin is one of the most common of Chinese names.)

The graves of the original Lins sit on the hillside behind the Mingtai High School, which now occupies Lai Yuan. The garden fell victim to a bulldozer when the school was built, and little remains of its original splendor except for a water pavilion overlooking a broad pool and the Five Cassias House, a two story building a few steps away.

GETTING THERE

Buses leave Taichung frequently for Wufeng on their way to Puli and Sun Moon

Lake. Get off at the Wufeng stop. The Upper House is on Laiyuan Rd, just one block
east of Route 3. The Lower House is a few steps south of the Upper House, at 24
Minsheng Rd. Lai Yuan Garden can be reached by following Laiyuan Rd for about
400 meters as it winds toward the hills.

■ CHUNG HSING VILLAGE

Chung Hsing Village, seat of Taiwan's provincial government, and the Provincial
Assembly Hall in the nearby town of Wufeng, are situated 22 kilometers south of
Taichung.

■ TSAOTUN

Tsaotun Village, about 20 kilometers from Taichung, holds the **Taiwan Provincial
Handicraft Exhibit Hall**, displaying local handicrafts and modern products, such as
bamboo ware, rattan furniture, Chinese lanterns, lacquer ware, ceramics, stonecraft,
wood carvings, jewelry, cloisonné and other items.

Central East–West Cross Island Highway

The Central East–West Cross Island Highway, an engineering marvel, snakes its way
from Taichung in the west through the rugged Central Mountain Range to Taroko
Gorge on the east coast. The highway stretches 192.8 kilometers across the island,
traversing various climates, snow-capped mountains, alpine forests, rocky ravines,
hot springs, rushing rivers and mountain lakes.

The road was built to open the area to fruit farms, animal husbandry, logging and
tourism, but was also part of a scheme by Chiang Kai-shek to develop the island's
infrastructure, with the dream of retaking the Chinese mainland.

Some 10,000 veterans of China's civil war worked 46 months to complete the
highway at a cost of US$11 million.

Using hammers, chisels and pick-axes to carve the highway and tunnels out of
the tough rock by hand, an estimated 460 workers—survivors of years of combat in
China—lost their lives to landslides and falling rocks during the nearly four years of
construction. It was completed in 1960.

When the road was finished, several million dollars in US aid went into planting
fruit groves and distributing small farms to destitute aborigines and soldiers from the
road crews. Today, high in the mountains, these veterans, the latest Chinese arrivals
to the island, live and farm on the steep mountain slopes side by side with aborigines,
Taiwan's earliest inhabitants. Some shacks can only be reached by riding up in metal
baskets that dangle precariously from motorized cables.

One indication of the danger of driving along this beautiful, but dangerous, highway, is the small pieces of gold paper that are seen along most of the 196 kilometers of the route. This 'spirit money' is thrown out of the windows of vehicles by superstitious drivers, a payment to the gods for protection.

Buses operate in both directions along the highway, and the trip costs NT$300. Buses leave from Taichung for Hualien at 7:15, 7:50 and 9:30 am. Buses from Hualien to Taichung leave at 7:30, 8 and 11 am. If you have a choice, start from Taichung, as the scenery becomes more and more beautiful as one moves from west to east.

Although the eight-hour bus ride can be accomplished in one day, consider stopping somewhere along the way to enjoy the beauty of the region.

Hotels exist at the major stops on the highway, at Kukuan, Lishan, and Tienhsiang. There are China Youth Corps hostels strung along most of the route. Phone the hostels in advance for reservations and to see if their kitchens are open. On the weekends the hostels are sometimes full, and during the weekdays often deserted. Food is not served at every hostel on weekdays, although instant noodles are usually available. The youth hostels are open to all people, regardless of age.

To walk the entire highway route, which few people attempt, takes five to seven days. However, it is worthwhile to walk one or more sections. Hostels or hotels stand every 15–30 kilometers. The route from Tehchi Dam to Lishan has some of the most beautiful scenery. If you walk, be sure to take a rain coat. In the winter, take a coat or heavy sweater; a light jacket or sweater is recommended for the summer, especially at higher elevations. A good flashlight is also a must, as many of the tunnels are dark, with water-filled pot holes, and it will alert speeding drivers to your presence. Water and food are not always available so take along a flask, some dried fruit, and other basic supplies.

From the west the highway begins in Tungshih, a fruit and timber marketing center 25.8 kilometers northeast of Taichung. Rice fields and orchards cover most of the first 20 kilometers from Tungshih. Large parts of the western lowlands are planted with apple, starfruit, pear, peach and plum trees. Hundreds of thousands of plum buds are brought down from the highlands, where the fruit grows plumper and sweeter, and are grafted on to the trees in January, then individually wrapped in protective bags that are removed only when the buds flower in March.

This section of the road follows the Tachia River, which is crossed in many places by rustic suspension bridges. This is the most inhabited part of the highway, but there are few stores. Trucks piled high with every imaginable household item, from brooms to knives to plastic buckets, ply this half of the highway, selling their goods to the frontier residents. The sign on one restaurant just before Kukuan advertises rabbit and fragrant meat, a euphemism for dog meat, which is a popular, but illegal,

Central East-West Cross Island Highway

台灣中部東西橫貫公路

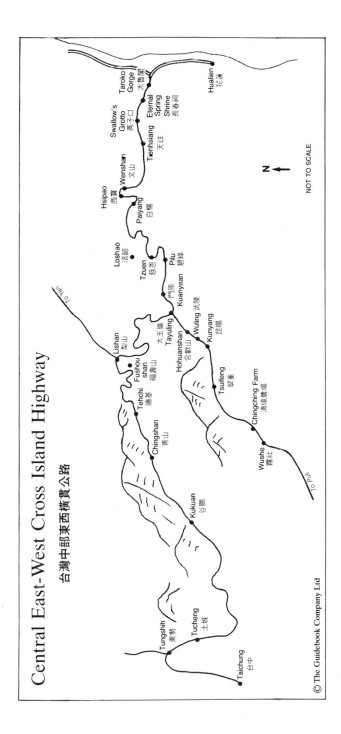

Taichung 台中
Tungshih 東勢
Tucheng 土城
Kukuan 谷關
Chingshan 青山
Tehchi 德基
Fushou Shan 福壽山
Lishan 梨山
Tayuling 大禹嶺
Hohuanshan 合歡山
Kunyang 昆陽
Wuling 武陵
Kuanyuan 關原
Tsuifeng 翠峰
Chingching Farm 清境農場
Wushe 霧社
Pilu 碧綠
Tzuen 慈恩
Loshao 洛韶
Paiyang 白楊
Hsipao 西寶
Wenshan 文山
Tienhsiang 天祥
Swallow's Grotto 燕子口
Eternal Spring Shrine 長春祠
Taroko Gorge 太魯閣
Hualien 花蓮

To Ilan 往宜蘭
To Puli 往埔里

N

NOT TO SCALE

© The Guidebook Company Ltd

winter dish in Taiwan. Several restaurants along the road to Kukuan serve fresh rainbow trout.

■ KUKUAN

Kukuan (750 meters), a popular hot spring resort, means 'valley pass' and is 34 kilometers from Tungshih. The scenery improves here, but the small town, lined with cheap gift shops and small restaurants, is disappointing. The restaurants serve mushrooms and vegetables native to the mountain area, as well as fresh mountain trout, deer, serow and wild boar.

A river rushes through the town and hot spring water is piped into the hotel rooms. There are no natural outdoor hot spring pools here.

The main attraction is **Dragon Valley Waterfalls**, a short 1.7-kilometer hike through Dragon Valley. The walk begins across the teak footbridge (near the Dragon Valley Hotel) which crosses the Tachia River. Pass a small zoo and a botanical garden with sculpted bushes and bougainvillea and follow the concrete path; it is covered by a concrete roof supported by concrete logs, guarded by concrete rails and polls, punctuated by concrete pavilions—the only way to reach the spectacular falls. They plunge some 80 meters over a rock face in two strong streams, throwing up clouds of mist that form rainbows when the sun is right. The walk takes about one hour there and back.

Another nearby site is **Mt Pahsien** (Mountain of the Eight Immortals) **Forest Recreation Area**. Once one of Taiwan's largest forestry stations, it is now logged out and has been redeveloped into a recreation area with lush vegetation, two mountain streams and a camping area. If you have a full day to spare you can climb Mt Pahsien (2,400 meters). Most visitors make the 4.5-kilometer trip to Mt Pahsien Forest Recreation Area on foot.

After leaving Kukuan, the highway begins its steep ascent into the sublime Central Mountain Range. Along the way to Tehchi, 28.1 kilometers from Kukuan, is a fork in the road. A sign indicates that Tehchi can be reached by taking either way. The lower road is 16 kilometers, the higher 19 kilometers. The higher road passes the Chingshan Youth Hostel, 5.6 kilometers from this point, which commands a good view of mountains and the clear water of the Tachia River. One of Chiang Kai-shek's numerous holiday residences is located in the vicinity. The lower road goes past the imposing 180-meter-tall Tehchi Hydroelectric Power Dam, built in 1972 by the Taiwan Power Co on the Tehchi Reservoir, a 14-kilometer-long artificial lake. Both roads eventually merge.

The town of Tehchi has little more than a bus station and squalid restaurant. About three kilometers east of the bus station is the pleasant Tehchi Youth Hostel, situated on a hill overlooking the Tehchi Reservoir.

Chiang Ching-kuo and engineers mapping out the route of the new highway

Chiang Ching-kuo, Chiang Kai-shek, and Madame Chiang inspect work along the Central East–West Cross Island Highway, 1957

Just outside Tehchi is Chiayang, one of the few 'towns' along the highway. As the road winds 20 kilometers upwards towards Lishan, so too do the orchards.

■ LISHAN

Lishan (Pear Mountain, 1,945 meters) lies at the upper reaches of the Tachia River and is the halfway point on the East–West Highway. This was once a major aboriginal settlement of the Tayal tribe.

Lishan, the most developed town along the road, has several hotels, lodges, restaurants and shops dotting the mountain slopes. It is a sleepy farming area where vegetables and cold weather fruit are grown, such as peaches, pears and apples. However, fruit sold locally is sometimes much more expensive than that sold in supermarkets in urban areas. Fruit can be bought more cheaply at nearby Fushou Mountain (see below).

The region provides magnificent views of the **Hsuehshan massif**, often covered with snow in winter, and the blue waters of the **Tehchi Reservoir**, well below the town.

On a hill overlooking the main street is the **Lishan Cultural Museum**, featuring photographs of the highway crews, a large model of the entire highway, as well as a collection of aboriginal artifacts, farm tools, clothing and photographs. Behind the museum, down a long flight of broken stone stairs, is a temple dedicated to the memory of the veterans and engineers who lost their lives building the highway. The museum is a 20-minute walk from the Lishan Guest House.

Six kilometers above Lishan is **Fushou Mountain**, the site of farm houses and flourishing fruit orchards run by retired soldiers. To get here, walk about one kilometer east down Lishan's main road until you reach a Christian church on the left. On the right is a road that leads to the mountain. After cresting the brow of the hill above the town, the road levels out and, after passing expansive grasslands, fruit orchards, deep valleys and distant peaks, a fork to the right leads to **Tienchih (Heavenly Pond)**. Chiang Kai-shek chose this beautiful area for one of his summer residences. His modest two-storey wooden house is open to the public.

The main road continues to Huakang, a small town where there is another fork. One branch peters out on the flanks of Hohuanshan, the other snakes precipitously down through a valley of aboriginal villages. This road eventually joins up with the main road from Hohuanshan, and 80 kilometers further on reaches the aborigine town of Wushe.

From Lishan, the north branch of the East–West Highway runs northeast to Ilan (see page 169).

Fruit seller, Lishan

The hills of Lishan, dotted with farms

■ TAYULING

A little over 30 kilometers from Lishan is Tayuling, at 2,565 meters the highest point on the East–West Highway. The tall mountains to the south are Mt Chilai and Ho-huanshan, whose peaks are often hidden by fog. The landscape here has changed to extensive grasslands and forests of fir and hemlock. The area is named after Tayu, founder of the Xia Dynasty (c. 2205–1766 BC), who faced enormous engineering difficulties when harnessing the Yellow River, as did the engineers on this highway.

The road drops quickly after Tayuling, falling 2,000 meters in just 70 kilometers. There are no supplies until just before Wenshan, 50 kilometers away. **Kuanyuan,** just five kilometers east of Tayuling, has dense forests frequently shrouded in fog and clouds, bringing to mind Chinese landscape paintings. There is a youth hostel at Tzuen, 23 kilometers away, and further on at Loshao (spelled Roshao on the road sign), 41.7 kilometers from Tayuling. About 10 kilometers outside Tienhsiang is a pavilion along the roadside from where you have a bird's eye view of the village. Looking down from high up in the mountains, notice the Hsiangteh Temple, Tien Feng Pagoda, and the suspension bridge, well-known landmarks of Tienhsiang.

From Tayuling, the south branch of the East–West Highway runs southwest to Wushe (see page 191).

■ WEN SHAN HOT SPRINGS

Three kilometers outside Tienhsiang on the main road lie Wen Shan Hot Springs. There are no inside bathing facilities here, so bathe in the open air. Head down the steps towards the river, cross a suspension bridge, and then follow a small road to the hot springs.

■ TIENHSIANG

Tienhsiang (450 meters) is nestled in a verdant valley. This village has a handful of houses, small restaurants, the Tienhsiang Lodge, a China Youth Corps hostel, and a Catholic and a Protestant hostel. The area promises several interesting walks.

If you walk down Tienhsiang's main road you will see the Tienhsiang Lodge on your right and the suspension bridge on your left. Across the suspension bridge is a path leading to a pagoda and temple on the hillside. The pagoda offers views of the surrounding countryside. Early morning is the best time to walk around here, as the first rays of sunshine illuminate the shrouded mountains.

From Tienhsiang the road continues for 19 kilometers past breathtaking scenery to the mouth of Taroko Gorge (see page 232).

AROUND TIENHSIANG

Water Falls: About one kilometer up the main road from Tienhsiang is a tunnel on the left with a red gate just wide enough for a person to fit through. A six-kilometer walk from here leads to a waterfall where you can cool off. Tunnels along the way may be wet and dark in places, so bring a flashlight.

Hike: Take the road toward Taroko Gorge until you reach the Taroko Gorge National Park headquarters. A trail starts behind this building. Bear to the left at an intersection several hundred meters from the start. This forest hike will take you to the Wenshan Hot Springs, and then three kilometers back to Tienhsiang. The entire walk takes four hours.

Tienhsiang and Taroko Gorge can be reached by bus from Hualien.

NORTH BRANCH OF THE EAST–WEST HIGHWAY
The north branch of the Central East–West Highway runs 111.6 kilometers from Lishan to Ilan on the island's northeast coast. Along the way are Wuling Farm and Hsuehshan.

■ WULING FARM
Wuling Farm, a government orchard established for veterans, is the starting point for some of the best hikes in Taiwan. People climbing Hsuehshan, at 3,884 meters Taiwan's second highest mountain, usually spend the night here before making the final ascent. Other hiking destinations in the area are Yensheng Waterfall and Taoshan (Peach Mountain).

Wuling can be reached by bus from Lishan. The buses leave at 8 am, 10:10 am, noon, 1 pm, 3 pm and 4:50 pm.

■ HSUEHSHAN
You need a mountain pass to climb Hsuehshan. The hike takes about 12 hours; there are two huts on the route where you can rest for the night. The first is Chika Shan Zhuang, where water is available, two hours from the starting point. The second is San I iu Jiu Shan Zhuang, without water. Be sure to bring along basic equipment, warm clothing, a sleeping bag and food.

SOUTH BRANCH OF THE EAST–WEST HIGHWAY
The south branch of the East–West Highway extends southwest for 42.2 kilometers from Tayuling (see page 190) to Wushe.

■ WUSHE
Wushe is a cool mountain resort on a high ridge. Green Lake, a reservoir in the valley below, can be reached by walking down the road that runs through the village.

Wushe is also an aboriginal village, the site of a bloody uprising against the Japanese in 1930. The Japanese swiftly retaliated, leaving more than 1,000 aborigines dead. A plaque in the village commemorates the battle.

Buses to Wushe, Chingching Farm, and Tsuifeng, the start of the hike to Hohuanshan, leave from Taichung several times a day. Other buses go from Puli at the
Nantou Bus Co terminal.

AROUND WUSHE

Lushan Hot Springs: Lushan is not on the south branch of the East–West Highway,
but is just nine kilometers east of Wushe. This hot spring mountain resort is situated
on both sides of a deep gorge. The town's two sections are connected by a suspension
bridge. Hot spring inns perch on both sides of the gorge.

Upstream along the gorge is a restaurant sitting on the cliffs. You can buy eggs
here to boil in the steaming hot springs. Early descriptions of Lushan make it sound
quite idyllic, though now it is ill-maintained and rather dirty.

Buses leave Wushe for Lushan approximately once an hour. Direct buses also
leave from Taichung.

Chunyang Hot Springs, in a village of the Atayal tribe, is just three kilometers
from Wushe. The area has managed to escape crowds of tourists and is peaceful and
undisturbed.

Buses for Chunyang leave from Wushe and Lushan.

■ FROM WUSHE TO HOHUANSHAN

At the toll booth at Wushe, the road ascends rapidly to Green Lake. After passing
Yushih (1,748 meters), you will catch a glimpse of **Chingching Farm**.

Chingching is a group of farms running along the road between Hohuanshan and
Wushe. The area is known for its cows, a rare site in Taiwan, and orchards where you
can pick your own fruit for a reasonable price. After Chingching Farm, the road
changes from tarmac to gravel and becomes steeper and narrower.

Pass through Sungkong, the Alpine Botanical Center of the Agriculture Dept of
National Taiwan University and Meifeng Farm, an experimental farm of the college of
agriculture of National Taiwan University.

Tsuifeng (2,306 meters) is the start of the six-hour hike to Hohuanshan. This is
the last point that cars can reach during the snow season without tire chains. From
here you will pass Hsinjenkong (2,506 meters), Yuanfong (2,756 meters), with its
dense pine forests, Kunyang (3,091meters), covered with short arrow bamboo, and
finally Wuling (3,275 meters), just two kilometers south of Hohuanshan.

WULING

Wuling, not to be confused with Wuling Farm on the highway's northern branch, is
the highest point on this branch of the highway at 3,275 meters.

Scenic Tehchi, Central East–West Cross Island Highway

BO YANG

Bo Yang, a bespectacled, mild-mannered writer in his 70s, appears anything but belligerent. Yet, his provocative writing style has rankled Chinese governments on both sides of the Taiwan strait, and has infuriated Chinese around the world.

The anger is caused by Bo Yang's refusal to accept what is irrefutable to most Chinese—that Chinese culture, a source of pride for centuries, is superior to all others.

In fact, Bo Yang delights in telling Chinese about the shortcomings in their culture. Chinese are too loud, cruel, selfish and too willing to tolerate abuse of power by authority, he argues. He describes Chinese culture as stuck in the soy sauce vat, and says that only when Chinese realize this will they reform themselves. He hopes to bring about this realization through his writing.

'It's like holding up a mirror to the Chinese,' he writes. 'It's only when the Chinese can face themselves, and realize they're sick, that they can get on well.'

In an interview with the *Far Eastern Economic Review* Bo Yang explained that Chinese history showed that China had missed out on three critical ingredients: democracy, human rights and a belief in equality.

'The history of China is like a car that runs in circles, over and over the same ground. The history of the West started as a car too, but somewhere along the way it came up with the ingredients for making a plane. Then it took off to heights China could not reach.'

And he lays the blame at the feet of none other than China's master sage, Confucius, and his followers.

'In the two and one half millenia since his death, China's literati did little more than add footnotes to the theories propounded by Confucius and his disciples....The minds of the literati were stuck on the bottom of an intellectual stagnant pond, the soy sauce vat of Chinese culture.'

For many years Bo Yang contemplated writing a book called *The Ugly Chinaman*. He gave a speech in the United States in 1984, which was later made into an essay published in *Pai Shing Semi-Monthly*, a Hong Kong magazine. The essay, entitled 'The Ugly Chinaman', was soon being passed from hand to hand among intellectuals and students on the mainland, and in almost no time at all created a furor. The Ugly Chinaman essay in turn evolved into a book, a collection of Bo Yang's musings on history, politics and culture, which sold more than 120,000 copies in Taiwan alone, and was read by an unknown number of people on the mainland. An English translation was published in mid-1992.

In *The Ugly Chinaman*, Bo Yang argues that China's cultural tradition has discouraged independent thinking, encouraged excessive fear of authority and inhibited the development of democracy.

'How is it possible for such a great people to have degenerated to such a state of ugliness?' Bo Yang asks. 'Not only have we been bullied by foreigners; even worse, for centuries we've been bullied by our own kind—from tyrannical emperors to despotic officials and ruthless mobs....'

The Ugly Chinaman was temporarily banned in mainland China in early 1987. However, bootleg copies soon surfaced on college campuses and among intellectuals around the country. When the author went to China in November 1988, after Taipei lifted the ban on travel to the mainland, his first visit home in four decades, admiring students travelled by bus and train from far away to meet with him.

Bo Yang, whose real name is Kuo Yi-tung, was born in Kaifeng, Henan Province, in 1920. A staunch nationalist and an ardent anti-communist, he joined the Kuomintang (KMT) when he was 18. Following graduation from National Northeastern University, he taught at a number of universities in China. When the communists defeated the nationalist government in 1949, he was among 2 million mainlanders who retreated with the KMT government to Taiwan.

In the 1950's Bo Yang showed a knack for writing *zawen*, or satirical essays, a style made popular by Lu Hsun (1881–1936), with whom he is frequently compared. His early writings were attacks on communism. In the 1960's, however, he began writing a daily newspaper column called *Idle Gossip*, in which he turned his pen on the negative aspects of Chinese culture, and corruption and abuse of power within the government, the police and the KMT.

The essays won him admirers, but also enemies. Influential people, who felt they had been the target of his scathing attacks, pressured newspapers not to publish his articles. Others saw his criticisms of Chinese culture as an attempt to undermine public morale. Bo Yang was unfazed, confident that his strong anti-communist credentials would protect him.

The authorities were looking for an excuse to silence Bo Yang, and it came, oddly enough, in the form of a Popeye comic strip. In 1967, Bo Yang was responsible for getting this comic strip from King Features Syndicate in New York, and for supplying a Chinese translation for the *China Daily News*. Unfortunately, one particular translation made him vulnerable.

In the offending comic, Popeye and Junior are alone on a deserted isle.

continues on page 196

Popeye announces that he will run for president and that he will hold a democratic election with one restriction: no vote for Junior. Unfortunately for Bo Yang, the Generalissimo saw the comic strip as an oblique attack on himself.

Authorities charged Bo Yang with 'defaming the leadership' and 'complicity with the communists'. He was hauled in for several bouts of interrogation, before being arrested in March 1968 and sent to trial. The trial focused on charges that he was a communist agent, with little mention of Popeye.

Bo Yang's fate was sealed after he signed a confession admitting to taking part in a communist conspiracy. The prosecutor asked for the death sentence, but Bo Yang was fortunate to be sentenced to ten years in prison, later reduced to eight. After the sentencing, he announced that the confession was obtained through torture, during which his leg was broken beneath the knee by his interrogators, and that he was promised he would be released if he 'confessed'. Despite getting the support of leading overseas Chinese scholars, his pleas for release fell on deaf ears.

After spending four years in a Taipei prison, Bo Yang was transferred to a maximum security prison on Green Island, off the southeast coast of Taiwan. Originally known as Fire Scorched Island, Green Island was where all the major political prisoners were kept until 1990.

Bo Yang later wrote that while confined to the island he came to the realization that there was no difference between the KMT and the communists. This realization in turn led him to search for a cultural explanation. The answer he found was the lack of democracy.

'I have discovered that God has predestined some people like me for jail, whether the jail be in Taiwan or the China mainland', Bo Yang wrote in *The Ugly Chinaman*. 'But why does speaking the truth lead to such unfortunate circumstances? My answer is that this is not a problem of any particular individual, but rather of Chinese culture as a whole.'

Although he was due to be released in March 1976, Bo Yang was instead placed in solitary confinement, and not released for one more year. When he was set free on April 1, 1977, he had spent a total of nine years and 26 days behind bars. During this period he wrote poetry and three books on Chinese history, including one of his most famous, *An Outline History of the Chinese People*.

He now devotes his time to writing history. In 1994, Bo Yang hopes to complete his translation into modern Chinese of the Song-dynasty treatise *Zizhi Tongjian (A Comprehensive Mirror of Government)*, Sima Guang's political history of dynasties from the Warring States Period (770–221 BC) to the Song Dynasty—a project that he began in 1983.

Paranoia

Chinese culture is infected with a virus of neurotic anxiety which has been passed down from generation to generation and which even today resists cure. People say that if someone is a miserable failure you can simply blame his ancestors, but there is a major flaw in this statement. Can you blame the son for contracting a hereditary illness? And are his parents even at fault? We shouldn't blame our parents, nor should we blame our ancestors; if we must lay the blame somewhere, it should be with the culture that our ancestors have handed down to us. This huge country, with one quarter of the world's population, has sunk into a quicksand filled with poverty, ignorance, struggle and bloodshed, from which it is extremely difficult to escape. When I observe the way people in other countries carry on interpersonal relations I become very jealous. The traditional culture which has brought about the present situation in China has conferred upon the Chinese people a wide variety of unseemly characteristics.

One of the qualities for which the Chinese people are notorious is a propensity for quarreling among themselves. A Japanese person on his or her own is no better off than a pig, but three of them together make a dragon. In Taipei, if three Japanese people are in similar businesses, they will take turns making sales. With Chinese businessmen, if X is selling something for 50 dollars, Y will sell it for 40; if X is selling for 30 dollars, Y will sell for 20. Every Chinese person is a dragon in his or her own right. Put a Chinese person in a research institute or an examination hall where no interpersonal relationships are involved, and they can produce impressive results. But put three of these dragons together and they're about as good as a pig, or an insect. This is because of their addiction to quarreling. But if you tell them that, they'll write a book about 'The Importance of Cooperation' for your benefit.

Chinese people are hard put to admit their errors and produce a myriad of reasons to cover their mistakes. There's an old adage: 'Contemplate *errors behind closed doors'. Whose errors? The guy next door's, of course! Chinese don't admit their mistakes because somewhere along the line they lost their ability to do so. Though we don't admit our mistakes, they still exist, and denying them won't make them disappear. Many Westerners have said to me, 'It's hard getting to know Chinese people: you never know what's really on their minds.' I reply, 'You think you have problems? When Chinese people speak with other Chinese, it's nearly impossible to know what's going on.' Dealing with the Chinese is just like chasing after a woman: it's all too easy to say or do the wrong thing at the wrong time. If everyone in China continues to act like a pursued woman, can we ever correct our mistakes? Rarely does a day go by when it isn't necessary to try to puzzle out what's going on in someone's mind. With friends, this is relatively unimportant. But in the case of people with whom you must establish close contact, such as officials or people with power and money, you must be particularly vigilant about fathoming their thoughts. What an incredible waste of energy! Consider the popular saying: In China it's easy to get things done, but difficult to do things right. When it comes to getting things done in China, 2 plus 2 equals 4. But in dealing with others, 2 plus 2 may equal 5, or 1, or 853. For when you so much as speak the truth, others may accuse you of attacking, or even overthrowing the government.*

Since it seems as if the Chinese people have never had a healthy sense of self-respect, it is immensely difficult for them to treat others as equals: if you aren't my master, then you're my slave. People who think this way can only be narrowminded in their attitude towards the world and reluctant to admit their mistakes. Worse, though, is the way an unending series of mistakes has created a condition of paranoia in so many Chinese people. This mental climate is a fertile breeding ground for despots and tyrannical officials, and there is little hope that this particular species will soon die out in China. In traditional Chinese culture, the virtues of 'acting wisely and playing it safe' are echoed time and again.

To illustrate this, here's a story called 'The Art of Buying Watermelons': A shop owner said to one of his clerks, 'Go out the door and head west. When you get to the first bridge, you'll see someone there selling watermelons. Buy me a four-pound melon.' The clerk went out the door and headed west, and returned to the shop empty-handed. The owner swore at him and told him he was a dumb fool. The clerk replied, 'Actually, they're selling melons to the east.' 'Why didn't you go there then?' 'You didn't tell me to.' Though the owner swore at him once again, he actually regarded the clerk as an ideal employee because of his naïveté, obedience and lack of imagination. But had the clerk, noticing that no melons were available in the west, headed east and discovered a heap of sweet and inexpensive melons for sale, the owner would probably have said the following to him upon his return: 'You're brilliant! That was an excellent decision you made. If only everyone who worked here was as smart as you. You're absolutely indispensable to me,' though in truth he would never trust a clerk with such a wild imagination. A slave with a mind of his own is a dangerous person to have around; such a person should consider himself lucky if he doesn't get killed.

How can people raised in a culture like this cultivate the habit of independent thinking? Because Chinese people lack this capacity, we have bad taste and poor judgement, fail to discriminate between good and bad, muddy the distinction between right and wrong, and act without a set of standards. The only way to improve the situation of the ugly Chinaman is for each of us to cultivate our own personal taste and judgement.

Bo Yang, *The Ugly Chinaman*, translated by Don J Cohn

■ HOHUANSHAN (MT HOHUAN)

Hohuanshan, 3,416 meters tall, is the most accessible high peak area in Taiwan. Literally Mountain of Harmonious Happiness, it is one of the few places on Taiwan to see snow. Skiing is possible in January and February. However, the region is usually very crowded with people anxious to see snow during the winter, so autumn, quieter and more beautiful, is actually the best time for a visit.

Pine Snow Hostel is the only place open all year round offering food and lodging, so book in advance. From the hostel it is a one-hour hike to the highest summit in the area.

An unpaved road runs nine kilometers northeast from Hohuanshan to Tayuling on the East–West Cross Island Highway. Kenankuan, often hidden under layers of thick clouds, is a well-known landmark on this section of the road. From Tayuling (see page 190) you can catch a bus to Tienhsiang, Taroko Gorge, and finally Hualien, less than two hours away. Or you can take the longer route westward back to Taichung, a day's ride away.

If you approach Hohuanshan from Tayuling during the snow season, Tayuling will be the last place you can reach by car. After reaching here you will have to continue on foot, or hire a taxi fitted with chains. The road is very steep and dangerous when covered with ice or snow. Taxis can also be hired in Wushe and Lishan for the trip to Hohuanshan.

Changhua County

CHANGHUA CITY

Thirty minutes southwest of Taichung City lies Changhua City. The only worthwhile attractions here are Pakuashan, with its 30-meter-tall concrete Buddha sitting on a lotus dais, and the Confucius Temple.

■ PAKUASHAN

The inside of the giant Buddha is hollow and has an internal staircase that leads to different floors, each featuring a different aspect of Buddha's life, from birth to enlightenment, and finally entry into nirvana. Behind the Buddha is a large Buddhist temple.

■ CONFUCIUS TEMPLE

The Changhua Confucius Temple was built in 1726 by a county magistrate and has since undergone eight renovations. The scale of the temple complex is even grander than that of Tainan's Confucius Temple. Since the buildings were designed for use as the Changhua County School, various constructions were forbidden by custom. As a result, the style of a four-sided courtyard, reserved for the higher-level prefectural school, was not used here, and the east and west sections of the complex are independent of the main structure. Furthermore, many important features of the complex were demolished during the Japanese occupation and the temple today is only two-thirds of the original size.

The Gate of the Sage, located directly before the Hall of the Sage, has five doors, with the central door marked by a pair of stone drums that emphasize the position of this central gate. The emphasis on the center is also seen in the roof design with its tripartite symmetry.

The Hall of the Sage is the focal point of the complex. Here a plain vermilion tablet represents the spirit of Confucius. The temple has adopted a double eaves, hip-and-gable formula, with porticos on four sides. The pair of dragon columns supporting the entrance are sculpted from high quality white Quanzhou stone; the quality of the work and delicacy of detail is quite unusual. The sides of the hall's brick platform use a style of brickwork known as jutting-and-concave bond, in which the bricks are first laid according to a desired pattern, with the remaining spaces filled with white lime. Another pattern seen in the platform is the elongated swastika design, symbolizing an infinite supply of good fortune. This design is not found in any other Confucius temple on the island.

The east and west galleries house ceremonial tablets honoring the memory of great Confucians of the past.

Lukang (Deer Port)

According to historical records, Chinese first arrived in the Lukang area around 610 during the Sui Dynasty. Pingpu aborigines had occupied the area since early times. The town of Lukang was not established until the 17th century. Most early Han immigrants settled on land near the mountains because water was more easily available. As a result, Lukang was the only town on the coast in the early years of the Qing Dynasty.

There are several explanations for the town's name. One claims the name derives from Lu-tsai-kang, the original aborigine name that was possibly kept by the Han Chinese. According to another theory, the town took its name when disembarking immigrants saw the many deer that lived in the area. Others say the port's shape resembled a deer. Finally, some say that Lukang was a rice growing area with many rice storehouses (lu).

Lukang was one of Taiwan's three earliest ports, along with Tainan in the south and Mengchia in the north. When restrictions on emigration were relaxed during the reign of Emperor Kang-hsi (1662–1722), waves of Chinese immigrants from Fujian

Lukang

© The Guidebook Company Ltd

poured across the Taiwan Strait. The majority passed through Lukang, and when formal business dealings between the mainland and Lukang began in 1684, this was the port of entry and exit for most goods.

By the mid-1700s, Lukang was a major center of commerce and shipping, with junk-borne trade with Fujian Province bringing Taiwan's produce to the mainland and returning with manufactured goods, immigrants, artisans and, as ballast, the shaped stone that was used as a construction material and is still in evidence in some of Lukang's buildings and pavements. An estimated 100 ships of all kinds sailed into Lukang from the mainland each day during the peak years between 1780 and 1840, when, with a good wind, the trip could be made in a day. The town's population grew to 200,000, and it became the island's largest port and second largest town after Tainan.

In those days, shipping companies concentrated just north of the harbor. They operated fleets to Quanzhou and Xiamen, and as far north as Tianjin. The area was extremely busy, with coolies moving goods from place to place, wharf workers loading and unloading ships, clerks checking goods, sailors enjoying shore leave, and loud discussions about the price of goods and delivery. On commercial Wufu St (today's Chungshan Rd), shoppers and sailors jostled for space with one another, bargaining with the merchants. At the food market at the street's far north end, hungry fishermen sold their catch, and sailors looked for a variety of foods not normally in their shipboard diet.

The port fell into decline and was later abruptly closed by the Japanese at the beginning of their 50-year occupation of Taiwan in 1895. Silt and sand had built up and the port was no longer useful for shipping. The population of this sleepy town is now only 80,000; most depend on fishing and aqua-culture to earn their living.

Lukang, which in the early years had close ties to the Fujian cities of Quanzhou and Zhangzhou, has preserved much of its history in its narrow streets, architecture and shops. When trade with the mainland ended in 1895, companies that engaged in trading began manufacturing handicrafts such as furniture and wooden articles, and Lukang soon became a center of handicraft production. Artisans continue to work at crafts introduced to the island by their ancestors, making furniture, incense and religious items such as carved statues.

■ THE LUKANG FOLK ARTS MUSEUM

The best place to start your visit here is the Lukang Folk Arts Museum. The museum contains a replica of the city as it looked in the 1700s and other displays about the town's early years.

The museum is housed in two buildings with 30 rooms. The buildings were once the home of the Koo clan, one of the island's early wealthy families, whose descendants are today among the most important business leaders in Taiwan. The Koo family donated the buildings and most of the articles in 1973 to preserve Taiwan's cultural heritage. Most of the items date from the mid-Qing Dynasty to about 1920.

Ku Feng Lou, the smaller building to the right, is an 18th-century wood and brick structure of the southern Fujian style. It was the original home of the Koos, and the kitchen and living room show how people lived 200 years ago.

Yang Lou, literally 'foreign building', is a European structure designed by Nagano Uhezi, a Japanese architect who also designed the Presidential Office Building in Taipei. On display are some 6,000 items. On the first floor, separate rooms display documents and historical photographs, clothing, and theatrical and musical instruments. On the second floor is the Koo family bedroom, furnished with classical furniture and decorated with intricate wood carvings. In addition there is a meeting room, guest reception hall, ladies' bedroom, pantry, and a room that exhibits Qing-dynasty documents, poetry, calligraphy, government decrees and even a contract for selling one's wife.

The museum's address is 152 Chungshan Rd, but the entrance is down an alley to the left of a police station on Chungshan Rd; the museum is on the left. The entrance fee is NT$100 for adults and NT$60 for students. The museum is open from 9 am–5 pm on weekdays, and to 6 pm on holidays.

■ 'SEE NO SKY' STREET

Lukang's main street is Chungshan Rd, once known as *bu jian tian*, or 'see no sky' street. The road was formerly much narrower, curved like a crescent moon and paved with red bricks. Then called Wufu St, it was divided into five sections, each specializing in different commodities. One dealt in marine goods, another in cloth and dyeing, and another in medicines. Wooden gates erected at intervals provided protection against bandits, and those entering in the evening had to know the password.

The roofs of the buildings extended from each side and another roof was built over the middle of the street, forming an arcade—hence the name. The roofs were pulled down in 1934, but a walk around this main street and its winding alleys—with colored wall tiles, latticework windows, decorated eaves, fancy brickwork and inscriptions carved in stone—is still rewarding.

■ LUNGSHAN TEMPLE

Leave the museum, return to Chungshan Rd, turn left and walk several blocks to San Min Rd. Here stands Lungshan Temple, the oldest standing Buddhist temple in Taiwan. Lukang has some 70 large temples, but this is the most famous. It is a classic of temple architecture and has been designated one of the island's Historical Sites of the First Rank.

The temple was built in 1653 at another location, then rebuilt at its present site in 1786. It was erected by early settlers in gratitude to Kuanyin, the Goddess of Mercy, for their safe voyage across the dangerous Taiwan Strait. As Lukang was a commercial port of considerable importance, local gentry, prosperous merchants and shipowners were more than willing to contribute to the temple's construction. The temple, modeled on the famous Kai Yuan Temple in Quanzhou, Fujian, ancestral home of many of the townspeople, was most likely built by experts from that city. Craftsmen from Fujian and Guangdong arrived to do the more specialized work. Great care was taken to ensure that only the best materials were used, and the key materials—brick, stone, fir—were imported from the mainland.

In 1977 workers restoring the temple unearthed four stone inscriptions carved in rare black marble. The inscriptions included the names of sponsors of the temple from Quanzhou and Xiamen, as well as the details and expenses incurred in the purchase of bricks, tiles, timber and paint, and the cost for casting the temple's bronze bell. The inscriptions provide valuable information regarding the transport of materials and the type of construction during the large-scale refurbishment of 1829.

Four types of stone sculpture were used in the Lungshan Temple, employing techniques that date back to the Song Dynasty. A technique called 'water grinding with sunken pattern' can be seen in the whorled stone drums beside the central portal of the Hall of Five Gates. Here the stone is first ground smooth, then the pattern is incised so that light hits at a certain angle to bring out clearly in shadow a three-dimensional effect. The woodcarving belongs to the Quanzhou school, characterized by a loose and airy layout with careful regard to distinction between primary and secondary motifs.

Despite several renovations, the temple's original design and appearance have essentially been preserved; it is a model for students of classical Chinese architecture.

Lungshan Temple consists of a forecourt, a temple gateway, right and left retaining walls, the Hall of Five Gates, a theater, and the Hall of Worship, Great Hall and Posterior Hall.

The gateway was most likely built in 1786 and is considered an outstanding piece of Qing-dynasty architecture. Its double roof rests on 12 columns arranged in four groups of three. Four cylindrical columns hold up the upper roof and eight square columns support the lower roof. The stone pedestal at the foot of the columns is carved with a double lotus design, rarely seen in early Taiwanese architecture.

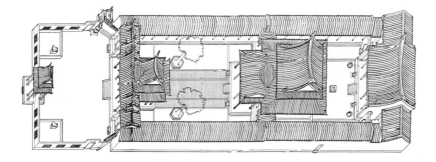

Lungshan Temple, Lukang

Just inside the gateway at the front of the forecourt stand two stone lions. The inscription at the base notes that they were donated in 1789. According to one story, two residents of Quanzhou ran into a storm while making the crossing to Taiwan. They eventually reached land safely after making a vow to Kuanyin. They later donated this pair of stone lions to the temple in thanks.

Beyond the forecourt is the expansive and majestic Anterior Hall, also known as the Hall of Five Gates because of its five doorways. The courtyard in front of the hall is paved with granite brought from Quanzhou in the 18th century. The sloping flight of steps in the center is called the Imperial Way, because it is the route used by a sedan chair carrying gods in processions. The deities Wei-to and Chia-lan, two popular door guardians, are painted on the central door, while other door gods are painted on the remaining four doors. A banyan tree sits in the central courtyard. Note the high relief wall sculpture of a *qilin*, an auspicious mythological animal. Its finely molded body and intricately carved head are classics of Qing artistic technique. Also noteworthy is the dragon column carved in fine Quanzhou stone. The dragon raises its head upwards, while its mate writhes downwards with its head near the base of the column; iconographically, this is called 'grand pandemonium in heaven and earth.' The octagonal window lattices form the Eight Trigrams motif, a symbol from the *I Ching*, or Book of Changes. Notice the four sea dragons circling around a yin-yang medallion, with a pair of auspicious carp and green bats in the corners.

The theater stands just inside the Hall of Five Gates and faces the Great Hall across the central courtyard. The theater symbolizes the role of drama in entertaining the gods. Operas and religious dramas are presented here on festival days. The theater's ceiling is an octagonal *plafond*, conforming to a pattern called the 'spider's web.' The design is supported by an interlocking network of elaborately carved brackets arrayed in and around 16 main buttresses which meet at the crosspiece. In the center is a painting of a dragon. The multi-tiered splendor of the rooftop hints at the connection with the free forms of Chinese calligraphy. The upward and outward curve of the eaves in the area in front of the theater widens the field of vision for spectators. It is still possible to hear impromptu performances of *nan-kuan* music, an aristocratic genre of classical Chinese music, presented in the theater by local musicians; the scene brings to mind visions of an imperial past.

After the central courtyard steps lead up to the Hall of Worship, situated just in front of the Great Hall. A huge incense burner stands here, and a pair of meticulously carved stone dragon columns rise in the center, belonging to the mid-Qing style.

The roof of the Great Hall, the highest in the complex, is supported by 40 columns. The central altar is dedicated to the worship of Kuanyin, and the right and left side altars are dedicated to two popular Taoist gods, Ching-chu-kung, an earth god, and Chu Sheng Niang Niang, who presides over the birth of sons. The temple's prize possession is the Great Bell, which hangs inside the Great Hall. The two-meter-tall bell measures 1.2 meters in diameter and weighs more than 500 kilos. The bell was cast in Ningbo, near Shanghai, and is the largest temple bell in Taiwan. After leaving the Great Hall enter the rear courtyard, where you will see the Dragon's Eye Wells.

The Posterior Hall, previously called the Hall of the North Pole, is dedicated to Hsuan-tien Ta-ti, a Taoist deity. Flanking him are the Dragon Spirit, Wind Spirit and the Turtle and Serpent Commanders.

■ YI LOU

A short distance from Lungshan Temple, just north of Chungshan Rd, is No. 5 Meishi St, a red brick building with a tower containing a round latticed window. This is Yi Lou, or Memory Tower, formerly the home of a devoted young husband and wife. One day before leaving home on a long business trip the husband planted a carambola tree in front of the window, telling his wife that whenever she saw the tree she could think of him. The husband never came back and his faithful wife spent the rest of her life sitting at the window staring at the tree and yearning for his return. The wife is long gone, but the window and the luxuriant carambola tree remain.

Spider's web plafond, *Lungshan Temple, Lukang*

■ NINE TURNS LANE

Nine Turns Lane, a red tile lane marked by old brick walls, courtyards and traditional architecture, has been preserved in its original form. At one point, a platform about three meters high straddles the lane. This is said to have been the meeting place for poets and literati.

■ BREAST-RUBBING LANE

One of Lukang's narrowest lanes is 'breast-rubbing lane', so called because two people attempting to pass have to turn sideways and 'rub breasts' as they go by.

■ YAOLIN ST

Walk up Chungshan Rd to Minchuan Rd, turn left and walk until you come to a small red-tiled street on the right called Yaolin St. It is known for its old buildings and is protected by the government. The area was renovated in the late 1980s, and some of the houses were restored, while those which could not be repaired were completely rebuilt in the same style. Shops on this street sell folk crafts and antiques.

■ MATSU TEMPLE (TIEN HOU KUNG)

At the north end of Chungshan Rd is the Matsu Temple, named after the Goddess of the Sea, a popular Taoist deity in Taiwan. The temple was built on the coast in 1647 to enshrine the first Matsu statue brought from the founding temple in Meizhou. The temple was later moved inland and expanded on its current site.

On the main altar sits the image of Matsu, its once pink face now blackened by centuries of incense smoke. It is believed to have been brought to Taiwan in 1684 from the original Matsu Shrine in Meizhou by Admiral Shih Lang who secured Taiwan for the Qing Dynasty by defeating the last of Koxinga's troops.

At the rear is a Jade Emperor hall, with a tablet representing this supreme Taoist deity. The temple also has two guardians; Thousand-Mile Eyes, who can see a thousand miles, and Thousand-Mile Ears, who hears with the wind. Master artisans from China produced them, as well as the temple's ornate ceilings, dragon pillars, stone drums and lions and wall paintings. On the lower level of the temple's rear hall is the Matsu Culture Museum, which exhibits traditional Chinese goods.

The square in front of the temple is crowded with vendors and stalls, selling folk art and junk. Items sometimes found on sale here include colorful sachets worn by children to ward off evil, and dough sculptures. Snacks here include meat balls, vermicelli, ox-tongue cakes (named for their shape, not their ingredient), maid in the moon cookies, and, most famous, fresh oyster soup and oyster omelettes.

■ THE PHOENIX MOUNTAIN TEMPLE

This small temple, built by immigrants from Quanzhou, is notable for the colorful painted guards on its main doors.

■ SHOPPING

Lukang is famous for its handicrafts and folk arts, some of which have been handed down for generations. Products available include: carved wooden furniture, oiled paper and bamboo fans, Buddhist religious paraphernalia, wood carvings, incense, kites and more.

GETTING THERE

Buses leave Taipei's Chunglun bus terminal several times a day for Lukang. Buses also go from both Taichung and Changhua.

Chiayi County

CHIAYI CITY

Chiayi, with little to offer the tourist, is a jumping off point for trips to Alishan, Peikang, Kuantzuling, and Wufeng Temple. If you have time to spare, walk to Chiayi Park at the end of Chungshan Rd where you can see the Confucius Temple, Martyrs' Shrine and 12 cannons dating back to the Chia Ching period (1796–1820). The walk takes 30 minutes from the train station. In the evening, explore the night market on Wenhua Rd near the Chungshan traffic circle.

Chiayi can be reached by train, bus or airplane. Two bus stations flank the train station at its front. The one on the right as you face the station is the Taiwan Bus Co station, where you can catch buses to other cities. The bus station on the left serves Alishan, Peikang, and Kuantzuling.

■ WU FENG TEMPLE AND MEMORIAL PARK

The Wu Feng Temple, 12 kilometers east of Chiayi, is dedicated to the memory of Wu Feng, a Qing-dynasty official said to have given his life to convince local aborigines to abandon their custom of headhunting. He died in 1769 at the age of 71. A town and a temple have been named after him, and several movies made about his life.

Every Taiwanese schoolboy knows the story of Wu Feng. He was said to have been a kind mainland official who learned the local dialect and was loved by the aborigines. After failing to convince them to abandon a headhunting party, Wu offered to supply them with a victim who would ride down the road on a horse the next day with his head covered in a red hood. The aborigines hid beside the road waiting for their prey, and when the man with the red hood rode by they leapt out and in an instant cut off his head. After removing the hood and realizing that they had decapitated their beloved Wu Feng, they gnashed their teeth in sorrow and swore never again to practice headhunting.

Unfortunately, historians say that while there was a minor official named Wu Feng in Taiwan at that time, there is no historical evidence to support the story. They say this story may have been made up by the Japanese for propaganda reasons. It was further expanded by the nationalists when they began their rule of the island because the government saw itself, like Wu Feng, as bringing civilization to an uncivilized Taiwan.

Aborigines on the island complained for years about the story, which they say portrayed them in a bad light, and which made their children the brunt of teasing in local schools every year when the story of Wu Feng came up in lessons. They protested repeatedly, calling for the removal of the story from textbooks. Activists took a more radical route in 1988, pulling down a bronze statue of Wu Feng in front of the Chiayi Train Station and setting fire to the Wu Feng Temple. In 1989, with the support of scholars, the government agreed to wipe Wu Feng from the pages of history and to change the name of Wu Feng Township in Chiayi County to Alishan Township, despite complaints from the descendants of Wu Feng.

The Wu Feng Temple was built in 1820 and has been refurbished several times since then. It has been declared an historical site of the third rank. A tablet installed at the temple in 1952 contains the following inscription written by Chiang Kai-shek: 'Righteous Even at the Cost of His Life.'

Just behind the temple is Wu Feng Memorial Park. The Chinese garden and Fujian-style structures were designed by Han Pao-teh, a well-known local architect. There are two exhibition halls. The Chongjen Hall displays antique folk crafts, such as wood carvings, porcelain, paper lanterns and umbrellas, paper cuttings, dough sculptures and embroidery. The Hsiangyi Hall depicts the story of Wu Feng, and exhibits Taiwanese historical relics, daily goods used by the Taiwanese in the old days, household furnishings and historical photographs. The park contains a man-made lake, bridge and pavilion.

The site of Wu Feng's alleged decapitation is one kilometer south of the temple, and is now a Chinese garden. A pathway from the entrance is flanked by two palace-style walls and leads to a spacious octagonal garden with a bronze statue of Wu Feng sitting atop a horse.

GETTING THERE
Buses to the temple leave from the Chiayi County Bus Co terminal (next to the Chiayi train station) about once an hour.

Nantou County

Nantou is Taiwan's only landlocked county, and is perhaps the most scenic, containing Sun Moon Lake and the Hsitou Bamboo Forest Recreation Area.

Sun Moon Lake

A popular scenic attraction in central Taiwan is Sun Moon Lake, a favorite with Taiwan honeymooners. It is 80 kilometers southeast of Taichung, and the road there traverses some of the loveliest scenery on the island.

Sun Moon Lake was originally two separate bodies of water. They were joined together when a hydroelectric dam was constructed in 1939. The area was once a major aborigine settlement. Today, more than 1,000 aborigines live, farm and fish in a village near the lake's south side.

A good place to start a tour of the lake is the Sun Moon Lake Hotel. The road first goes to the **Wen Wu (Scholar Warrior) Temple**. This temple is dedicated to Confucius, master of the pen, and Kuankung and Yueh Fei, ancient masters of the sword who have become deities. The temple is located on a hillside, affording a panoramic

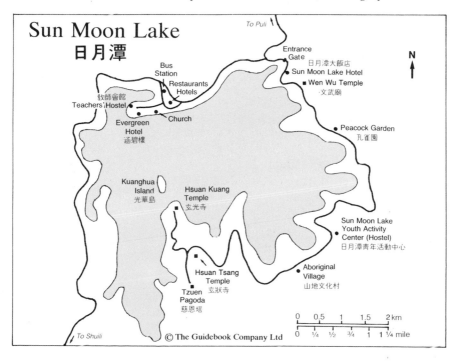

view of the lake from the terrace at the rear of the temple. Two stone lions flanking the entrance are said to be the largest in Taiwan, possibly even the world. The shrine to Confucius is located in the upper rear hall. The martial shrine, located just below, shows the subservient role of the sword to the pen in Chinese society.

Inside the martial shrine is red-faced Kuankung, and white-faced Yueh Fei. Two five-meter-tall painted door gods, carved out of solid camphorwood, stand guard at the entrance.

The complex has a complicated layout with several pavilions and halls connected by a maze of passages and stairways. The temple recently built a hostel and a restaurant that serves vegetarian dishes. South of here is **Peacock Garden**, home to hundreds of peacocks and other birds, and a butterfly collection.

Further on is **Tehua Village**, an aboriginal settlement. Some 1,000 members of the tribe live here (2,000 more live in another settlement on the lake), but the village no longer bears any resemblance to its original appearance. Restaurants and shops sell local products, such as royal jelly, honey, tea, cheap aboriginal items and a few authentic objects. Several kilometers from here is the Formosan Aboriginal Cultural Center (not to be confused with the Formosa Aborigine Cultural Village), a private tourist site near the lake, now in disrepair.

Sun Moon Lake (above and right)

Hsuan Tsang Temple, on a hill near the lake's southern end, holds a shard of the skull of Hsuan Tsang (Hsuan Chuang), the Tang Dynasty monk who brought Buddhist scriptures from India to China. His story has been immortalized in the classic *Journey to the*

West. A gilt image of a reclining Buddha and a statue of Hsuan Tsang are in the main hall of the temple. On the second floor is a shrine dedicated to Kuanyin, the Goddess of Mercy. The piece of Hsuan Tsang's skull is kept on the third floor. The relic was reportedly stolen from China by a Japanese during World War II, but was returned to Chiang Kai-shek by a Japanese monk in 1955.

Atop a hill behind the Hsuan Tsang Temple is the most prominent landmark at the lake, the nine-tiered **Tzuen Pagoda**. This pagoda, built in 1971, is an impressive example of pagoda architecture. It stands 46 meters tall, the tallest in Taiwan. Those who climb the 154 steps to its top will be rewarded with a beautiful view of the lake and surrounding mountains. The pagoda was built by Chiang Kai-shek in memory of his mother.

Row boats can be rented to visit **Kuanghua Island**, a tiny wooded isle in the middle of the lake (NT$60 per hour). Boat tours of the lake are also available for groups of two or more.

It takes a day to walk around the lake. Public buses stop at all the major points of interest around the lake as far as the Hsuan Tsang Temple, from 8 am–5 pm. Service is infrequent. Taxis can be hired for a tour of the area, as can motor scooters (about NT$500 for eight hours).

GETTING THERE

Sun Moon Lake is two hours from Taichung by bus. The fare is NT$74, and the buses leave from the bus station to the left of the train station four times daily. Two direct buses leave Taipei each day from the North Bus Station, near the Taipei Train Station. The trip takes four hours and costs NT$234.

BETEL NUT

Betel nut has been chewed by people throughout much of Asia since ancient times, and its use in China dates back to the Tang Dynasty (AD 618–907), when it was sent annually in tribute to the imperial court as a delicacy.

Today in Taiwan politicians present it to prospective voters, gangsters exchange it when concluding deals, and families hand it out like candy at weddings.

The popular concoction, called *binlang* in Taiwanese, is a masticatory made with the seed of the betel palm, a sliver of the fruit of the betel piper (a relative of the pepper), and a dab of lime paste (calcium oxide, not the fruit), with various herbs and other flavorings thrown in. The mixture is frequently wrapped in a leaf, which gives it an even stronger taste.

Known locally as Taiwanese chewing gum, betel nut has rapidly gained in popularity around the island, much to the dismay of health and agriculture officials.

While doctors say it is unhealthy and should be banned outright, tax officials bemoan millions of dollars lost in evaded taxes, and agriculture officials liken growing it for profit to growing opium, saying it is equally harmful to society.

Government officials worry that the practice will ruin the island's image. A common scene in Taiwan: a taxi driver pulls up to the curb, rolls down the window, and expectorates a mouthful of a blood-like substance onto the ground at the feet of a horrified foreigner. Unsightly red betel nut stains are commonly seen on sidewalks, streets, in elevators and in ashtrays.

While there are no hard figures for sales, the total retail value was estimated at more than US$3 billion in 1990, more than triple the US$1 billion recorded in 1987, with farmers earning an estimated US$285 million for the year.

The island has 55 million betel nut trees that produce each year about 1,000 betel nuts for each of the island's 20 million inhabitants. Despite this volume, Taiwan sometimes faces shortages. In recent years, officials have intercepted tons of *binlang* being smuggled into the island to make up for seasonal shortages.

According to a survey carried out by a Taipei advertising company, there are more than 70,000 betel nut stands on the island and telephone delivery is available in some areas. The habit is especially popular with people who work long, irregular hours, such as farmers, fishermen, and taxi and truck drivers, because the nut contains a narcotic stimulant and is believed to have some medicinal value.

Another reason for its popularity lies in its role in the local culture, especially in the south. While it is common today in the north of Taiwan to offer a guest a cup of tea or a cigarette, a visitor in southern Taiwan is more likely to have a betel nut thrust into his hand.

No respectable politician hits the campaign trail in the south without an ample supply of betel nuts to hand out to voters. In elections many male candidates take up the habit to be identified as a man of the people.

Hsu Hsiao-tan, a model turned nude dancer who made an unsuccessful bid for the Legislative Yuan, Taiwan's parliament, sold betel nut from the back of a truck in the southern city of Kaohsiung to finance her campaign.

Roadside betel nut stands in Taipei have increased rapidly in the past few years, with many stands now operating 24 hours a day. In Wanhua, one of the oldest and busiest sections of Taipei, one stand is said to sell US$1,000 a day worth of betel nut, for a daily profit of about US$400.

Betel nut is an easy crop to grow. Little manpower is required and damage from pests is minor. With the retail cost rising rapidly, the betel nut palm has become a veritable money tree. Production has risen sharply over the past decade, from 3,000 hectares in 1979 to 35,000 hectares in 1990, to the detriment of rice, pineapple and adzuki bean crops.

Betel nut often makes teeth fall out and stains remaining teeth a dark red; a dentist's nightmare. But far worse is evidence that betel nut contains a carcinogenic substance called arecoline and that its growing use is leading to a sharp increase in mouth, throat and stomach cancer. Doctors say that 91 per cent of oral cancer patients are betel nut chewers, and they also point out that the habit can also cause submucous fibrosis, a premalignant form of cancer that limits the ability to open the mouth, there is no known cure.

Despite the bad news betel nut aficionados chew on, refusing to believe the habit can cause cancer. Disturbing also is the fact that while the red 'betel nut smile' was once seen as the mark of an unskilled worker, more and more students, reporters, white collar workers and professionals are joining the ranks of the 'red lips tribe,' leading to what one magazine has described as 'betel nut culture.'

To meet overseas demand among Chinese and Southeast Asians, and to offset a supply shortage during the off season, Taiwan's ingenious entrepreneurs have hit on a new product: freeze-dried betel nut, available year-round.

■ AROUND SUN MOON LAKE

PULI

Puli, Taiwan's geographical center, is just north of Sun Moon Lake. Here is the Chengghuang Temple. Buses travel from Puli to Wushe.

HUISUN FOREST

Huisun Forest, located in a mountain valley north of Puli, remains untouched by encroaching commercialism and is a good place to hike, picnic and camp.

Two buses leave every day from Puli, at 8:40 am and 2:15 pm, for the 1 1/2 hour drive. Return buses leave Huisun at 10:30 am and 3:55 pm. On weekends buses are also available at Tsaotun, leaving at 8 am and 2:45 pm, and leaving Huisun for Tsaotun at 10 am and 4:40 pm. Admission is NT$40 for adults and NT$30 for students.

FORMOSAN ABORIGINAL CULTURAL VILLAGE

The Formosan Aboriginal Cultural Village is made up of nine reconstructed aborigine villages, featuring the culture of the island's 10 tribes (two of the tribes are combined in one village.) The best way to see the villages is on foot, walking the length of the footpath which begins beside the European Palace Garden leading up the west side of the valley, and then heading down the east side. The villages are scattered along the path and are modeled on structures once used by the island's aborigines. Each one has an explanation in Chinese and English detailing where this type of house existed and what it was used for. On weekends and holidays, aborigines sing and dance for the visitors. Tribesmen can be found in the various villages working at traditional crafts, such as carving, weaving and basketry. You can walk or take a minibus around the complex.

The administrators of the park seem confused about what they want the park to present. The first thing you encounter in the village is the immaculate European Gardens, and recently the village added two Disney-like attractions: 'Space Race,' a simulated spaceship, and 'Showscan Theater', a 25-minute program much like Space Race. What these two attractions have to do with aboriginal culture is hard to see. Both shows are included in the price of a ticket—NT$330 for adults.

From Taipei, buses for Puli leave every hour from the North Station, behind the Taipei Train Station. From Puli, the Nantou Passenger Bus Co has buses to the park about six times a day. The village, though close to Sun Moon Lake, has no direct buses to or from there. If you are at Sun Moon Lake, take a bus from Sun Moon Lake Village to Yuchih, where you can transfer to a bus for the aborigine village.

Hsitou (Chitou) Forest Recreation Area

The Hsitou Recreation Area, a secluded resort surrounded by ancient trees and cool,

Aboriginal village, Sun Moon Lake

fragrant bamboo forests, is one of the most serene, unspoiled sites on the island. Hsitou receives a lot of rain and is often shrouded in fog, adding a mysterious touch to its peaceful beauty. The forest area, originally set up by Tokyo Imperial University during the occupation, is now operated as an experimental forest zone by National Taiwan University. The area covers 2,488 hectares and has dozens of varieties of bamboo. Hsitou accounts for 40 per cent of all the raw and finished bamboo products in Taiwan.

The Chinese have a special affinity for bamboo, which explains the popularity of Hsitou. It is one of China's most important natural products, providing building material, raw material for paper, and even food. In literature and art bamboo is used to represent youth, modesty and old age. 'One can manage without eating', said the famous poet Su Tung-po, 'but one cannot manage without bamboo'.

Hsitou, sometimes spelled Chitou, offers quiet walks in its forests and groves of fir trees. Cars and motorcycles are banned from the park. The best time to enjoy a walk is in the early morning before the mountain mists roll in, when you can hear babbling brooks, singing birds and chirping insects.

The Chinese refer to refreshing walks in the forest as a 'green shower,' because it is felt that bathing oneself in nature is good for mind and body.

A 46-meter-tall cedar, 2.6 kilometers from the main gate, is estimated to be more than 2,800 years old and is one of the park's main attractions. According to local legend, a goddess who came to live in the world of mortals met a prince of the Bunun aborigine tribe. They fell in love and settled in Hsitou, but the goddess was called back to heaven and left the heartbroken prince, who stood gazing at the sky until one day he turned into the giant tree. The mirror left behind by the goddess later turned into Sun Moon Lake.

There are five trails within Hsitou, all marked by wooden signs: a path leading to the giant cedar tree passes a nursery, deer farm and gingko forest; between Tahsueh University Pond and the Youth Activities Center is a short trail where a large variety of plants grow; the Pine Woods short cut; the Brookside trail; and the Birdwatching trail.

Popular spots inside the area include University Pond, with its arched bamboo bridge, the Bamboo Cottage, and Deer Garden. The latter is closed to the public to protect the deer.

Plan to spend two days and one night at the park to experience its various aspects at different times of the day. Try to avoid weekends and holidays.

The entrance fee is NT$50, but hold on to your ticket if you leave the park to eat or go back to your hotel, since it is good for multiple entries during the day of purchase. Numerous restaurants outside the main gate sell tasty bamboo shoots, black mushrooms and other vegetables grown in the area.

From Hsitou, it is 20 kilometers to Shanlinhsi (see below), or a rigorous one-day walk to Alishan. The route between Hsitou and Alishan is a 40-kilometer-long nature trail.

GETTING THERE

Reach Hsitou by bus from either Chiayi or Taichung. Taichung has the most buses, leaving from the southbound bus station behind the train station. The road to Hsitou is lined with lush bamboo forests and tea plantations. If you are driving, consider stopping at Luku for a pot of famous Tungting oolong tea.

■ AROUND HSITOU

SHANLINHSI (SUN LINK SEA)

Shanlinhsi is a mountain resort with many paths for hiking, and is worth visiting if you are in nearby Hsitou. It has a waterfall and beautiful scenery and it is possible to hike up to Alishan from here, a 32-kilometer walk. You might prefer the easier down-hill walk from Alishan to Shanlinhsi. You can also walk to or from Hsitou along the highway, 20 kilometers away.

Buses to Hsitou also go to Shanlinhsi. It can also be reached by taking the right fork in the road to Fengshan.

PHOENIX VALLEY BIRD PARK

The Phoenix Valley Bird Park is the largest of its kind in Taiwan. It covers an area of 30 hectares and is home to 5,000 birds of 300 different species housed in 49 aviaries and four open spaces. It is located in the Phoenix Valley Scenic Area, 62 kilometers south of Taichung and 20 kilometers north of Hsitou. There are a few direct buses from Taichung and Chushan, a town at the base of the mountain below Hsitou.

ALISHAN (MT ALI)

Alishan is Taiwan's most famous mountain resort. It is the name of both a range of mountain peaks flanking the rugged north–south Central Mountain Range and a village linked by a narrow gauge alpine railway to the city of Chiayi.

The zigzag train ride from Chiayi to Alishan, the best part of the trip, takes almost four hours and involves dramatic scenery changes, from Chiayi's rice paddies, palm and betel nut trees, to the peak's cypresses and cedars. A broad highway now runs between Alishan and Chiayi, and other cities.

The railway was completed by the Japanese around 1912, opening up a rich supply of forestry resources. The railway station at Alishan is situated at 2,190 meters, said to be the highest railroad station in East Asia.

The train ride crosses 114 bridges and passes through 50 tunnels. At the front of

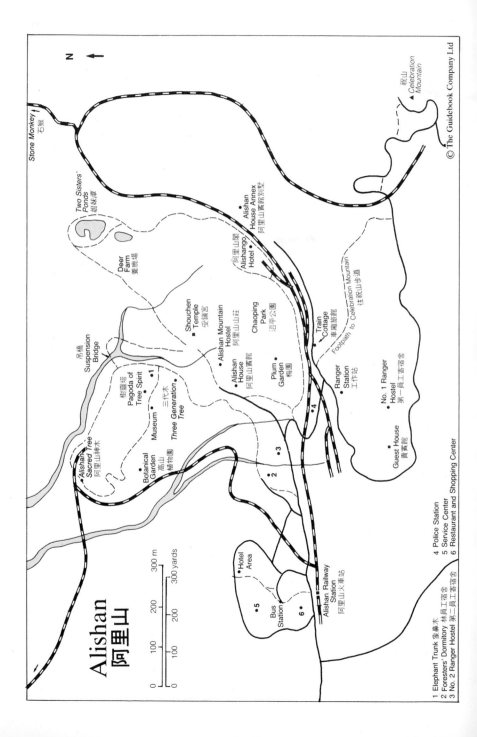

Alishan 阿里山

© The Guidebook Company Ltd

Stone Monkey 石猴

Celebration Mountain 祝山 ▲ Celebration Mountain

Two Sisters' Ponds 姊妹潭

Deer Farm 餵鹿場

Suspension Bridge 吊橋

Pagoda of Tree Spirit 樹靈塔

Three Generation Tree 三代木

Alishan Sacred Tree 阿里山神木

Museum 高山植物園

Botanical Garden

Shouchen Temple 受鎮宮

Alishan Mountain Hostel 阿里山山莊

Alishan House 阿里山賓館

Plum Garden 梅園

Chaoping Park 沼平公園

Train Cottage 車廂旅館

Alishango Hotel 阿里山閣

Alishan House Annex 阿里山賓館別墅

Footpath to Celebration Mountain 往祝山步道

Ranger Station 工作站

No. 1 Ranger Hostel 第一員工宿舍

Guest House 賓賓館

Hotel Area

Bus Station

Alishan Railway Station 阿里山火車站

N

300 m
300 yards
0   100   200
0   100   200   300

1 Elephant Trunk 象鼻木
2 Foresters' Dormitory 林員工宿舍
3 No. 2 Ranger Hostel 第二員工宿舍
4 Police Station
5 Service Center
6 Restaurant and Shopping Center

Alishan

each tunnel is a sign with three numbers. The top is the number of the tunnel, the middle its length in meters and the bottom the height above sea level at that point.

The railway passes through tropical, subtropical and temperate zones in just 72 kilometers. After leaving the city the train first passes through farm fields, and later past bamboo forests, papaya trees, banana trees, mountainside tea plantations, and the ubiquitous betel nut tree. You will also see several rustic villages. At several points the train must zigzag back and forth along two sets of tracks, because the area is too narrow for it to make a turn.

Alishan is often shrouded in mountain fog, giving it a misty, romantic feeling. Unfortunately, like so many other areas of Taiwan, it is becoming increasingly commercialized and crowded and has lost much of its original appeal.

A leisurely two-hour walk winds around Alishan. The walk passes by Plum Garden, Chaoping Park, Sister's Pond, a deer farm, the Shouchen Temple, a suspension bridge, and one of the highlights of the walk, the 3,000-year-old Alishan Sacred Tree, which was struck dead by lightning in 1947. Also along the route are Tse Yung Temple, the Botanical Garden, and a small museum. You will also see red cypress, cedar and pine trees, some thousands of years old. A map of the walk is available free of charge at the tourist center near the bus station.

The museum, built in 1912, displays Taiwan's flora and fauna, including stuffed specimens of the clouded leopard and Formosan bear, animals that once roamed the island in large numbers, but which are now rarely seen. There are also specimens of insects, butterflies, snakes, plants, wood and soil common to the area.

A few coal-burning locomotives, used until recently to carry lumber, are now on display and the original railway cars have been converted into a hotel, the Alishan Train Cottage.

A two-hour walk goes to the checkpoint at Yushan (Jade Mountain), but you must have a mountain permit to go further. The sea of clouds over Yushan is a magnificent sight, attracting hundreds of visitors every morning. Most rise before dawn to see the panoramic sunrise from nearby Celebration Mountain (Chushan). Hotels can arrange a minibus. Buses leave the hotels around 5:30 am and charge NT$150. A simple breakfast is offered for an additional NT$50, but food can also be purchased at Celebration Mountain. The walk to the mountain is about three kilometers; there are two routes—the road or a set of stone steps. Bring a flashlight.

There is a train to Celebration Mountain from Alishan, making one stop at the old station to pick up passengers. A round-trip ticket costs NT$100. The departure time varies depending on the time of the sunrise, which, unfortunately, it is often too cloudy to see.

GETTING THERE

A train leaves Chiayi for Alishan twice a day, at 8:55 am and 1:30 pm; on Saturday there is an additional train at 12:30 pm. A one-way ticket costs NT$373 (reduced for children) and can be purchased between 8 am and 3 pm. Tickets can be purchased three days in advance (call 276-8694 in Chiayi to make a reservation).

The two-hour bus ride from Chiayi costs NT$76. The bus leaves from the bus station beside the Chiayi train station at 6:30, 8 and 9 am, and 12, 1 and 4 pm. On Saturdays and Sundays there are also buses at 7 am and 2 pm. Check with the Tourist Hotline to check the schedules in other cities.

The charge for entering the Alishan Forest Recreation Area is NT$65.

The train ride to Alishan passes the small, rustic town of **Fenchihu**. There is nothing special here, except some pleasant hikes. One popular hike is to **Tatungshan** (Big Frozen Mountain at 1900 meters), two hours away. A short walk from the train station is a bamboo forest where you can see some rare square bamboo. Other popular hikes lead to a cave, **Tienchien Chikuan**, a three-hour round-trip, and **Mingyue Ku**, an overhanging rock. Some hotels organize hikes for groups of 30 or more.

Three buses a day go from Chiayi to Fenchihu, leaving at 9 am, 10 am, and 3 pm; the trip takes a little over an hour. Buses returning to Chiayi leave at 9:15 am, 12:30

pm and 5:15 pm. The bus from Chiayi to Alishan does not stop here, but all the trains to Alishan do.

Alishan has no banks, so be sure to bring enough NT dollars with you.

■ AROUND ALISHAN
STONE MONKEY
A scenic eight-kilometer train ride from Alishan, across 24 bridges and through 12 tunnels, brings you to Stone Monkey, a name derived from a nearby rock resembling a monkey.

The walk to Stone Monkey requires a mountain permit, and passes through several long, dark train tunnels, so bring a flashlight and watch out for trains. Trails from the train station lead to the resorts at Fengshan and Shanlinhsi—a day's walk. Signs along the way are written only in Chinese.

FENGSHAN
Fengshan is a 10-hour walk from Stone Monkey. A trail descends sharply near the train tracks. Walk down to the bottom and then turn right, until you reach a fork in the road and a road sign. The right branch goes to Shanlinhsi and Hsitou. The branch to the left of the road leads downhill towards Fengshan. Pass **Thousand People Cave** and **Tzuyu Waterfall**. At the bottom of the waterfall is a level dirt path. Continue on it and you will soon arrive at Fengshan. Ask in the town for directions to trails leading to Tzuyu Waterfall and **Shihpan Valley Waterfall**.

Fengshan can be reached by bus from Chiayi, but only if there are enough passengers. There is one bus a day for the four-hour trip. Call the Anhsing Bus Co, Tel (05) 222-3527, to make sure there is a bus. It departs from in front of the Yushan Hotel in Chiayi.

TAIHO MOUNTAIN HOSTEL
The Taiho Mountain Hostel is five kilometers from Fengshan. One interesting hike goes to Tafoshan, a three-hour trek. Do not confuse the Taiho Mountain Hostel with the town of Taiho, which is several kilometers further down the road.

JUILI
This quiet village is little more than a few houses, a school and several hotels, and while it cannot compare with Alishan, it is relatively untouched, and thus a good place for pleasant hikes and tranquility. You can walk from here to Taiho, Fengshan, Tsaoling and Fenchihu.

Juili can only be reached by bus. The Chiayi County Bus Co terminal, next to the

Chiayi Train Station, has buses leaving for Juili every day at 4:20 pm. Buses returning to Chiayi leave Juili at 5:50 am.

YUSHAN (JADE MOUNTAIN)

Yushan, or Jade Mountain, at 3,997 meters, is the highest peak in East Asia. Yushan's height posed a delicate problem for Japan when it annexed Taiwan in 1895—it displaced Mt Fuji as the highest mountain in the Japanese empire. The Japanese got around this by renaming Yushan 'Nitakayama,' or New High Mountain. The Chinese restored the original name, Yushan, after retrocession in 1945. Some foreigners refer to it as Mt Morrison.

The Yushan Range has 30 peaks. The slopes in the area rise sharply, from 800–3,997 meters, revealing different types of terrain, climate, flora and fauna. As the altitude rises, subtropical forests give way to temperate forests of broadleaf trees and conifers, which in turn give way to all-conifer forests and, finally, alpine vegetation.

Yushan provides a habitat for a wide range of wildlife, including animals rare to Taiwan. It is located in the Yushan National Park, which covers parts of Nantou, Chiayi, Kaohsiung and Hualien counties and has a total area of 105,490 hectares.

The walk up Yushan begins along a highway just in front of the village of Alishan. Two hours from this starting point is Tzuchung, a settlement between Alishan and Upper Tungpu, where police inspect mountain passes. A hostel provides food and lodging; many hikers spend the night here.

The next morning proceed to the saddle and continue for nine kilometers to **Paiyun Cottage** (3,600 meters), the last refuge before the final ascent. The views across the valley are spectacular, with wooded peaks, massive cliffs and an occasional waterfall. The path is arduous, but in good condition in most places, so not dangerous. The five hour uphill walk with a pack is quite tiring, making Paiyun (White Cloud) Cottage a welcome sight. Most climbers spend the second night here and get up around 3 am to climb the remaining steep 2.5 kilometers to the peak in time for sunrise. Near the top is a place dubbed Wind Mouth, where winds once blew a climber off the mountain. A covered fence now prevents such accidents.

The final 100 meters is a scary zigzag climb across a rock face, with anchored cables to aid climbers. The peak can only accommodate about 20 people. To the northeast is a line of mountains separated from Yushan by a sea of clouds, and to the west is Celebration Peak, the sunrise viewing point at Alishan, marked by lights. On the highest point of Yushan is a bust of Yu Yu-jen, late president of the Control Yuan, one of China's most renowned calligraphers, and an avid mountaineer. Most visitors walk back down the mountain to the **Tatachia Saddle**.

Vehicles can now drive right up to the Tatachia Saddle. You can also climb Yushan from Tungpu (see below), or descend to Tungpu. Along the way you will pass

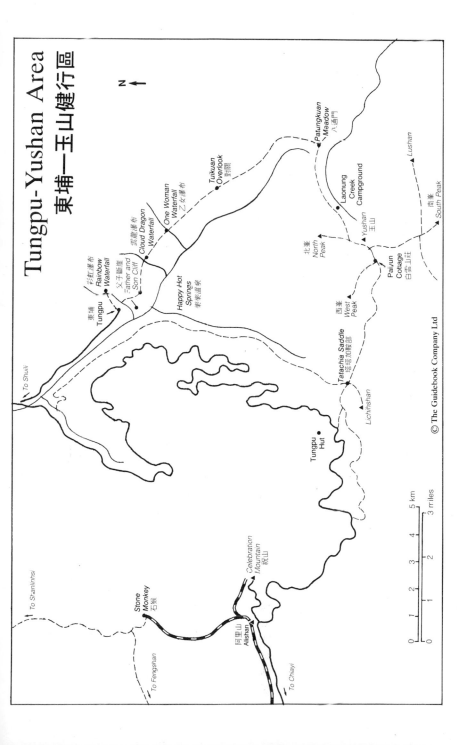

Tungpu-Yushan Area
東埔—玉山健行區

N

Patungkuan Meadow 八通門
Tuikuan Overlook 對關
One Woman Waterfall 乙女瀑布
Cloud Dragon Waterfall 雲龍瀑布
Father and Son Cliff 父子斷崖
Rainbow Waterfall 彩虹瀑布
Tungpu 東埔
Happy Hot Springs 東埔溫泉
Laonung Creek Campground
Yushan 玉山
North Peak 北峰
Pai'jun Cottage 白雲山莊
West Peak 西峰
Tatachia Saddle 塔塔加鞍部
Lichihshan
Lushan
South Peak 南峰

To Shuili
To Shanlinhsi
To Fengshan
To Chiayi

Stone Monkey 石猴
Alishan 阿里山
Celebration Mountain 祝山

Tungpu Hut

© The Guidebook Company Ltd

5 km
3 miles
0 1 2 3 4 5
0 1 2 3

Billowing clouds over Yushan

through **Patungkuan**, an alpine meadow with traces of a trail built at the end of the Qing Dynasty. The path through Tungpu does not go to Alishan.

A Class A mountain pass is needed to climb Yushan, obtainable from the ROC Mountain Climbing Society. In theory you must hire a guide, (see page 324). In Tungpu (see below) it is possible to hire guides from the Bunun tribe, known as the Sherpas of Taiwan. If you descend via Tungpu, your pass will have to be so endorsed.

Bring backpacking equipment, a flashlight, food, water and warm clothing. Even in summer, night temperatures can fall very low. Daytime, on the other hand, can get very hot, even in winter when snow and ice cover the peak. Autumn is said to be the best season for the climb.

TUNGPU

Tungpu, a mountain resort (1120 meters) with waterfalls and hot springs, is the home of the Bunun tribe. It is popular with hikers, but many of the trails are quite strenuous and steep and signs along trails here are only in Chinese.

An interesting hike from here is to **Rainbow Waterfall**, about a one-hour round-trip. Walk up the main street to the Shanghua Hotel, then head down the trail on the left side of the road. From Tungpu, a different, more dangerous route goes to Yushan (see above).

Tungpu can be reached on foot from Yushan or by bus from the nearby town of Shuili. Take the Tungpu bus from the Yunlin Bus Co terminal. Several buses a day go in both directions from around 7 am–5 pm. Shuili can be reached easily from Taichung; take the bus from the Kancheng Station (a short distance from the Taichung Station.) From Hsitou, take a bus from the bus terminal outside the main gate to Chushan, then switch for a direct bus to Shuili. From northern or southern Taiwan, take a train to Ershui and then a bus or the quaint little shuttle train to Shuili.

A Class B mountain pass (different than the one required for Yushan) is required to visit Tungpu (see Facts: Mountain Passes page 324). The pass can be obtained in either Taipei or at the Shuili police station, which is a necessary stop on the way to Tungpu. Hold on to the pass. You will have to return it to the police on your way back through Shuili.

■ AROUND TUNGPU

Patungkuan, or Eight Directions Pass, was once a vital mountain pass for controlling this vast area. During the Qing Dynasty and the Japanese period, governments stationed garrisons here.

The footpath to Patungkuan starts along a dirt path in Tungpu that drops slightly before winding around the mountain. You will soon come to a path on the left that climbs steeply at first and then becomes more gradual as it winds its way across a steep mountainside. **Father and Son Cliff** appears where the slope suddenly turns into a vertical stone face into which the path is carved. The path is a meter wide for most of the way, but in some places it is much narrower, and dangerous for inexperienced climbers. In some places steel chains strung along the path provide hand holds. Except for this stretch the path is well maintained. It crosses streams and passes waterfalls, some of which fall down the mountainside in several sections.

Beyond Father and Son Cliff is a fork in the road. Drop sharply down into the valley to **Happy Hot Springs**. A 30-minute walk down this path brings you to the river and a cable car that crosses the river. On the opposite side is a restaurant, a hostel, and a short distance on another cable car back across the river where there is a hot spring and interesting rock formations.

About four kilometers above Tungpu, back on the original path, is **Yunlung (Cloud Dragon) Waterfall** where the water drops 50 meters over a stone cliff under a wooden bridge before falling another 70 meters. A short distance above here is **Chiszu (Seven Threads) Waterfall**, a cascade with seven separate streams, some of which are hidden by the dense forest. It is also known as Yinu (One Woman) Waterfall because it supposedly bears a resemblance to veils worn by a dancing woman.

Some two and a half kilometers from Patungkuan is an area for camping and picnicking. About 200 meters down a side path from here is a place called **Kuankao** (View the Heights), with a road running to Hsinyi. To avoid the 14-kilometer walk up from Tungpu, arrange transportation at Hsinyi; this four-hour trip misses the waterfalls. Patungkuan is a further three kilometers above Kuankao. The path does not stop here, but can be taken to **Mt Hsiukuluan**, one of the tallest peaks in eastern Taiwan. A branch path on the right continues for 6.5 kilometers to Yushan's main peak. To continue past Patungkuan requires a Class A mountain pass and an accredited guide.

Yunlin County

TSAOLING

Tsaoling, situated in the far eastern corner of Yunlin County, has for the most part escaped the attention of international travellers. The attraction here is nature, pure and simple.

The area has had its share of tragedy. One day in 1941, Yunlin County trembled violently as an earthquake split the earth in two, tearing away part of a mountain and sending it crashing down into a valley. A natural dam was formed that blocked the

Chingshui River and formed a large body of water that became Tsaoling Lake. The lake lasted only 10 years before a week of constant rain collapsed the dam, carrying away 74 soldiers who had been struggling to keep the dam together. Another landslide in 1979 gave short rebirth to Tsaoling Lake. Within nine days the dam collapsed once again following torrential rains.

Tsaoling offers excellent opportunities for hiking. The village is built on a steep mountainside above the Chingshui River and consists of two connected parallel streets. There are three main attractions here.

The **Penglai Waterfall** is two kilometers east of the village along a paved road flanked by bamboo groves, betel nut palms, passion fruit vines, a deer farm and tea fields. The road, which begins in front of the Green Mountain Hotel, ends at a cable car terminal that ferries passengers across the valley in 10-person cars to a location near the riverbed below the falls. From here you can climb down to the stream, and if you are a good climber you can reach the foot of the waterfall. A second cable car takes visitors to the top of the falls. From here a small path leads travelers farther up the stream bed, where there is a magnificent view of the valley. A path from the lower cable car terminus also leads to the top of the falls.

The second attraction can be reached via the village's lower street. A long pathway, made mainly of concrete steps, leads steeply down to the river. The steps come to an end at the top of a huge rock face that falls at a 50-degree angle for no less than 140 meters. Two ropes hang down the face of the rock to help people make their way down safely. For added security, one of the ropes has safety nets on both sides. At the bottom the pathway leads down the river past snack shops. Half an hour later is **Water Curtain Cave**, where the path passes through a declivity in the stone behind the falls and the falling water forms a curtain.

At Water Curtain Cave, look for the lower end of a path that heads back up the mountainside. Follow it to **Frog Rock**, then come to **Fat Man's Misery**, consisting of several vertical cracks in the stone. Anyone considered even relatively fat should not attempt to pass through; in some places the opening is no more than 30 centimeters wide.

The last stopping place on this path is **Jade Valley**, where a stream rushes through narrow crevices. The path returns to the village, emerging behind the Rainbow Village Hotel.

The third scenic attraction is **Heartbreak Valley**, also known as Lost Soul Valley, three kilometers down a paved road from the western part of the village's upper street. This is the site of the landslides that created the natural dams of 1941 and 1979. The road ascends to a lookout point and a path that leads past several waterfalls.

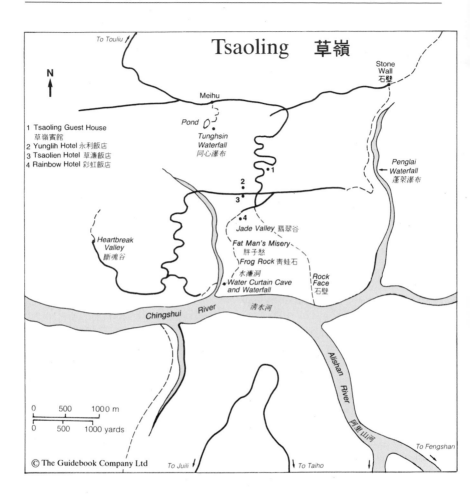

Tsaoling 草嶺

To Touliu

N

Stone Wall 石壁

Meihu

1 Tsaoling Guest House 草嶺賓館
2 Yunglih Hotel 永利飯店
3 Tsaolien Hotel 草濂飯店
4 Rainbow Hotel 彩虹飯店

Pond

Tunghsin Waterfall 同心瀑布

Penglai Waterfall 蓬萊瀑布

Heartbreak Valley 斷魂谷

Jade Valley 翡翠谷
Fat Man's Misery 胖子愁
Frog Rock 青蛙石
水濂洞
Water Curtain Cave and Waterfall

Rock Face 石壁

Chingshui River 清水河

Alishan River 阿里山河

0   500   1000 m
0   500   1000 yards

© The Guidebook Company Ltd

To Juili

To Taiho

To Fengshan

GETTING THERE

Buses leave Taipei's Chunglun Station for Touliu, Yunlin County, approximately once an hour. From the Touliu station walk three blocks to the Tsaoling Tour Bus Co at 47 Chungcheng Rd. Small buses leave here at 8:30 am and at 4 pm daily, with an extra bus on Saturdays and Sundays leaving at 12:30 pm.

PEIKANG

Peikang is a rustic old town about an hour's ride from Chiayi. The annual Matsu Festival (see Festivals, page 88) is the main reason for a visit.

Peikang's **Matsu Temple (Chao Tien Temple)** is the most extravagant of the island's 400 Matsu temples. Four stone lions and four gods sit atop dragons and guard the front of the temple. The double-layered roof of the front temple is especially colorful, even by Taiwanese standards, with hundreds of small ceramic figures amidst miniature mountains, palaces, pagodas and trees. The third and fourth buildings enshrine less important gods, and so have less ostentatious roof decorations. A small pagoda in the courtyard is for burning paper money.

The temple, formerly known as the Chao Tien Temple, traces its origins back to the arrival of a Buddhist monk in 1694. The monk brought with him an image of the goddess from a temple in her native town of Meizhou. Temporary housing was built for the statue, which is today the main image in this sprawling temple. Numerous renovations and reconstructions over the next three centuries brought the temple to its present size.

In addition to the many Matsu images housed in this temple there are separate altars for other gods, such as Kuanyin, the Earth God, and the parents of Matsu. In a small glass case several small crystal-like rocks are kept, found in the body of a monk who came from Fujian at the turn of the century. It is believed that these small crystals are only found among the ashes of cremated holy men, but some scientists believe such crystals are the result of eating beancurd, a mainstay of the Buddhist diet.

The temple is the site of Taiwan's largest celebration for Matsu's birthday. In the spring, thousands of worshippers walk in procession from Tachia to Peikang (see Festivals, page 88).

At the **Peikang ox market**, traditional trading and bartering methods are carried on that are rarely seen elsewhere. When the Chinese first came to Taiwan there were few horses, leaving all the heavy work to indigenous water buffalo. During the Qing Dynasty, aborigines captured wild buffalo, broke them, and then sold them to the Chinese. As more and more immigrants arrived, the demand for these animals rose and markets came into being. Transactions gradually got bigger, making the informal marketplaces too small. People began to meet at fixed places at regular times to buy and trade the beasts.

Mechanization of agriculture has diminished the use of oxen, leaving only three major markets; one at Peikang, one in Changhua County and another in Tainan County. On calendar days containing the numbers 3, 6 or 9 (e.g. 3rd, 9th, 13th, 16th), ox sellers from nearby towns come to the Peikang market for trading. Ox markets in other towns are held on different days to accommodate traders. The market in Peikang has existed for some 200 years, and is the largest on Taiwan. It is held on a large piece of ground on the left side of the Peikang Bridge. In the near future this market, too, will become a thing of the past.

GETTING THERE

Buses leave Taipei's Chunglun Bus Terminal every 20 to 30 minutes. The ride takes almost four hours.

Eastern Taiwan

Eastern Taiwan is cut off from the rest of the island by the tall peaks of the Central Mountain Range. Just 10 per cent of the island's population live on the mountainous east coast, a narrow strip of land between the coastal range and the sea, largely unsuitable for development and thus relatively free of pollution. Some of Taiwan's best attractions can be found here, including the Suao–Hualien Highway, Taroko Gorge and the East Coast Scenic Area.

The Suao–Hualien Highway

The Suao–Hualien Highway runs 88 kilometers along the east coast of the Central Mountain Range, high above the Pacific Ocean. As your vehicle swings around curves hugging the edge of this cliffside highway, those sitting on the ocean side will find themselves peering straight down several hundred meters to crashing ocean breakers. The highway has three sections: the northern section from Suao to Nanao, the middle section from Nanao to Hoping and the southern section from Hoping to the Chingshui Cliffs, the most dangerous and magnificent part of the road.

The road was built in 1875; in fact, it was a narrow trail carved into a vertical wall of stone above the Pacific Ocean. After three years of arduous work only a small path was completed. The road was improved by the Japanese in the 1920s and in the late 1980s became a proper two-lane highway.

The highway's tunnels and bridges account for almost 40 per cent of the route. The longest tunnel, 'Goddess of Mercy', runs for 7.7 kilometers. The road is frequently closed by rockfalls, landslides and the occasional earthquake or typhoon. The road descends several times to villages in the lowlands.

The trip can be made from either Hualien in the south, or from Suao in the north. Two buses make the trip each day from each direction, once early in the morning and once in the afternoon, taking three hours.

A rail line was completed in 1980, and most people travelling here take the train, which is faster than driving. Unfortunately, the train is farther inland and passes through numerous tunnels, bypassing much beautiful scenery.

Taroko Gorge

Taroko Gorge, a ravine lined with towering, 3,000-foot-tall cliffs, contains millions of tons of marble and is one of Taiwan's most scenic spots. The 19-kilometer stretch through the gorge is the most travelled portion of the Central East–West Cross island Highway (see page 183).

The road through the ravine follows the winding course of the Liwu River, the torrent of rushing waters that carved out the gorge. In places the cliffs have fallen, leaving huge slides of marble suspended like glaciers. There are 38 tunnels between Taroko and Tienhsiang, some with windows gouged out to provide light and ventilation.

At the eastern entrance to Taroko is a Chinese arch where many visitors stop to have their photos taken with aborigines, for a small fee.

West of the gorge's mouth, is the **Eternal Spring Shrine**, a memorial to the 460 workers who died during the construction of the highway. A waterfall cascades through the shrine from the mountainside, and stone steps lead up from the shrine to **Kuanyin Cave**, which contains a statue of the goddess and an engineering map of the highway. A tunnel footpath links the highway and the shrine. This is the last place to buy refreshments before Tienhsiang.

About seven kilometers from the Eternal Spring Shrine is **Swallows Grotto**, so named because of the countless swallows that fly about in the cliffside crevices and caves. The gorge here is so narrow that the sun only begins to shine through at noon.

Next pass the **Everlasting Bridge** and the **Tunnel of Nine Turns**, another engineering feat, which includes a string of short tunnels and windows cut out of solid marble. The **Tzumu Bridge**, a white marble structure, is eight kilometers east of Tienhsiang. Each end of the bridge is guarded by a pair of marble lions. On the far side of the bridge is a Chinese pavilion atop a rocky promontory. A small path leads up to it.

Just before Tienhsiang is Lushui, headquarters of Taroko National Park. A museum here exhibits aboriginal artifacts excavated from ancient villages in the park as well as utensils, clothing and other items used by the Ami and Atayal tribes that inhabit the area. An information center provides information and pamphlets in English for visitors.

The gorge ends in two kilometers at Tienhsiang (see page 190) where you can stroll over a suspension bridge to a temple and pagoda in the hills.

GETTING THERE

Taroko Gorge can be reached by bus or taxi from Hualien. Many people choose to make the trip from Taipei in one day, joining tours that arrange round-trip air travel to Hualien, transportation to the gorge, lunch at Tienhsiang, a visit to a marble factory and showroom in Hualien and a performance, albeit commercial, by aborigines at the Ami Cultural Village. Taxis charge about NT$1,500 for a round-trip visit to the

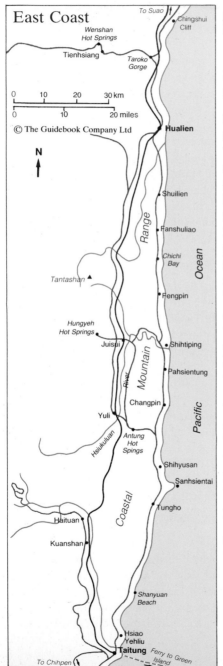

East Coast

To Suao
Chingshui Cliff
Wenshan Hot Springs
Tienhsiang
Taroko Gorge

0   10   20   30 km
0   10   20 miles

© The Guidebook Company Ltd

N

Hualien

Shuilien

Range

Fanshuliao

Chichi Bay

Ocean

Tantashan ▲

Fengpin

Hungyeh Hot Springs

Juisui

Shihtiping

Mountain

River

Pahsientung

Changpin

Yuli

Pacific

Hsiukuluan

Antung Hot Spings

Shihyusan

Sanhsientai

Coastal

Tungho

Haituan

Kuanshan

Shanyuan Beach

Hsiao Yehliu

Taitung

To Chihpen

Ferry to Green Island

gorge and Tienhsiang, stopping at popular sights along the way.

Hualien

Hualien, the capital of Hualien County, though rather small, is the largest city on Taiwan's east coast. It is also the site of one of the island's five international seaports. The county is the largest but least densely populated on the island and is largely dominated by the Central Mountain Range and other highlands. Its population of 360,000 includes about 80,000 aborigines, most of whom are members of the Ami tribe, the largest in Taiwan, with most of the remainder Atayal. Hualien is the starting point for tours of Taroko Gorge, the eastern end of the Central East–West Cross Island Highway, and the Suao–Hualien Highway.

Hualien has huge quantities of marble deposits and is an important producer and exporter of marble products: kitchen utensils, chess sets, hand carved figurines and furniture. These can be purchased in many shops in town and at the Retired Servicemens' Engineering Agency, 106 Huahsi Rd, near the airport. Marble is commonly used here to construct buildings, parks, sidewalks and monuments. Even the airport is built of marble.

Frequent aborigine performances take place at the Ami Cultural Village, though they are largely unauthentic

Rugged Taroko Gorge, carved by nature's hand

commercial displays. Tickets and transportation can be arranged through hotels and local travel agents. The best time to visit the area and see more genuine aboriginal culture is during the annual aboriginal Harvest Festival (see page 94).

As in other small towns and cities in Taiwan, taxis in Hualien do not use meters, so ask first what the charge will be for your destination. The charge for trips within the city is set, so you need not bargain.

GETTING THERE

Hualien can be reached from Taipei by train, or by bus via Suao, where there are two buses a day, one at 6:15 am and one at 12:00 noon. The bus trip takes three hours. Buses from Taichung travelling the scenic Central East–West Cross Island Highway take eight hours to reach Hualien. It is also possible to get a bus from Kaohsiung. China Airlines and Far Eastern Air Transport both fly from Taipei's Sungshan Domestic Airport to Hualien.

AROUND HUALIEN

■ CARP LAKE

Hualien's most popular recreational area is Carp Lake, a 45-minute bus ride southwest of the city. It lies in the foothills of the Central Mountain Range, and the main activities here are fishing, boating and hiking. Different types of boats are available for rent, but you must bring your own fishing gear; The carp weigh up to 25 kilos. A scenic path goes around the lake, and there are several interesting hiking paths behind the lake which lead up to nearby peaks. Nearby farms grow papaya, guava, tangerines, bananas and lemons. Buses for Carp Lake leave Hualien every hour on the hour.

East Coast National Scenic Area

The East Coast National Scenic Area is known for its beautiful scenery and miles of almost deserted black sand and pebble beaches. The area is a thin band of land running 170 kilometers north and south, reaching as far west as the mountain ridges and stretching to the sea. The outstanding scenery includes beaches, spectacular coastal views from mountain caves, interesting rock formations and coral reefs, picturesque fishing hamlets and aborigine villages. The Tourism Bureau manages the East Coast National Scenic Area and has plans to develop a wide range of facilities for camping, hiking, mountain climbing, bird watching, and water sports, including fishing, swimming, rafting and boating on inland rivers, and swimming, surfing, motorboating and sailing along the coast. Hotels and restaurants are also part of the development project. Nine areas along the coast will be developed as tourist sites.

Shuilien has been designated as an Ami aborigine village, though many Chinese live here and the village looks like any other in Taiwan. The area has a white pebble beach. Fanshuliao, a hilly area, is the site of a gorge cut by a winding stream. At Chichi Bay you will find a black sand beach for water sports. Shihtiping-Hsiukuluan boasts an aborigine village, coral reefs, rock formations, a fishing harbor, and the mouth of the Hsiukuluan River, popular with rafting enthusiasts (see below). At Pahsientung (Caves of the Eight Immortals) is a series of temples set in shallow caves, the ancient home of a Paleolithic people of the Changpin culture. These caves are important for archaeologists. If you climb up the steep steps leading to the temples you will be rewarded with a wonderful view of the coast. Shihyusan, or Stone Umbrella, named after a rock formation, is the site of a beach and quaint fishing village. Sanhsientai, or the Island of the Three Immortals, is a 28-hectare rocky island linked to Taiwan proper by a pedestrian bridge. The island has a lighthouse and rock formations. Chengkung is a picturesque fishing port on the coast famous for dried fish and other marine products. Tungho Bridge spans the Mawuku River near its mouth. Little Yehliu is known for rock formations and a park where old banyan trees grow out of coral. North of here is Shanyuan Beach, the only beach in Taitung suitable for swimming.

GETTING THERE

Buses serving this coastal route leave from Hualien and Taitung every 30 minutes. An inland route also connects the two cities, so be sure you get the ticket for the right bus.

■ HSIUKULUAN RIVER

This river offers exciting white-water raft trips that start near Juisui. The run manoeuvres through 23 turbulent rapids along this 24-kilometer route from Juisui to Big Harbor, where the river runs into the Pacific Ocean. It passes towering cliffs, spectacular rock formations and huge slabs of bright white marble.

The rafting season runs from April to October, though some people do the trip in the winter. The trip usually takes four hours. Rafting trips can be arranged by travel agents in Hualien; just look for the rafting photographs in the windows. Buses leave Hualien at around 7 am, arriving at Juisui about 9 am. You will be back in town by 5 pm. The cost of the rafting trip is NT$800; this includes transportation, equipment and lunch. You must also buy insurance.

Taitung

Taitung is a pleasant town on the island's southeast coast. Although sleepy today, it was the island's earliest settled area in prehistoric times. The aborigines who originally lived here have long since disappeared, yet the aborigines of Taitung County today outnumber all other aborigines in all of Taiwan's other counties. Taitung is not a popular tourist destination, but functions as a convenient jumping off point for visits to nearby interesting places, such as Orchid Island, Green Island, the East Coast National Scenic Area, the Southern Cross Island Highway and Chihpen Hot Springs. A few sites within the city are worth seeing if you have the time.

On Carp Hill, less than 10 minutes by foot from the bus station, is **Dragon Phoenix Temple (Longfeng Fogong)**, which can be seen from the city. The prosaic temple is not particularly interesting, although next to it is a pagoda with different deities on each floor. At the top are views of the city and the coastline, and on clear days it is possible to see Green Island. A beach at the end of Tatung Rd is a questionable place to swim. The shoreline here is turbulent and dangerous.

A few steps below the temple are several old locomotives. These trains lugged goods up and down Taiwan's railways for 60 years before being retired. Below them is

Taiwanese women in Taitung wearing the popular douli, *or conical hat*

the Martyr's Shrine, built in Ming-dynasty style.

The **Taitung Aborigine Folk Arts Museum** is located at No. 25 Nanking Rd.

GETTING THERE

Frequent buses and trains leave Taipei for Taitung (six hours by road, five by rail). Buses are also available from Kaohsiung on the southwest coast, and the trip takes four hours. Remember to get a seat on the coastal side of the bus. Far Eastern Airlines flies from Taipei four times a day.

AROUND TAITUNG

■ CHIHPEN HOT SPRINGS

For hundreds of years elderly aborigines have come to the banks of the Chihpen River in winter to dig shallow holes in the sand to let the hot water bubble up from the earth and soothe their aching muscles. Around the turn of the century the Japanese developed the area as a resort, giving it the name Chihpen, Source of Wisdom. Chinese still come to this valley of papaya, banana and betel nut trees to alleviate their pains in the hot springs. Like many other popular sites, avoid the weekends if possible.

The area can be divided into three sections. The first is centered around the Jyhbeen Hotel, the second is called Inner Spring, the site of several newer hotels and shops and the third section is the Forest Recreation Area, a short walk beyond section two. Several hotels have outdoor mineral pools which you can use

Fruit and candies on sale at the Taitung Night Market

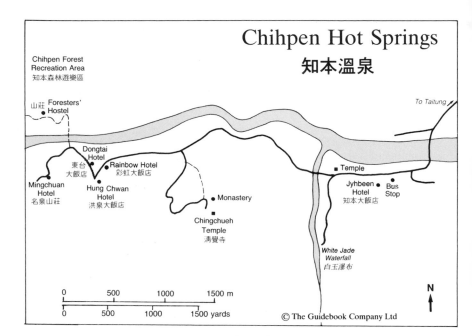

for free if you are staying at the hotel. Outside guests must pay NT$50. The pools are generally open from dawn to 11 pm. Bring a towel.

The Jyhbeen Hotel was once the most popular resort here, but is now run down and overpriced. The hotel has two outdoor pools, a hot one and a cool one big enough to swim in. Banyan trees hanging from the cliffs form a canopy over the pools. Several cheaper hotels are in this area, but they do not have outdoor baths. Small eateries and a few shops are near the Jyhbeen.

After you have enjoyed the soothing hot spring water, take a few hours to explore the area. A few minutes walk east of the Jyhbeen Hotel along the main road that follows the river, is a bridge. Look for a path on the left just before the bridge and turn left up this road. Continue to a fork in the road by a large tree. There are two waterfalls here. If you bear left and continue up the paved road you will soon come to the main **White Jade Waterfall**. Walk straight ahead along the narrow, broken path to soon reach a pleasant, smaller cascade.

Retrace your steps to the main road and continue along the river past a series of man-made tiered waterfalls. You will pass through fields where the fresh air is full of the fragrant smell of flowers. Ten minutes from the bridge is a settlement where a red archway stands over a road to the left. Walk under the archway and hike up to

Chingchueh Temple. A sign in front of the door asks you to remove your shoes and hat before entering. There are two famous Buddhist statues here. One is a three-meter, 1,000-kilogram bronze Buddha imported from Thailand, the other a white jade Buddha from Burma, which stands at 2.5 meters and weighs 4,000 kilograms.

A new hotel next to the temple is ending the quiet isolation the area once enjoyed. The temple has a dormitory and vegetarian dining room; it might be possible to arrange to spend a few days here.

If you return to the main road you will soon come to a residential area with several shops and hotels, an area more peaceful and natural than the area around the Jyhbeen Hotel. Up the road from here is the hillside **Forest Recreation Area**. There are no signs in English; just look for the wooden logs beside a set of steps heading down to a small suspension bridge. Buy a ticket to cross the bridge and enter the park. Admission is NT$35.

The Forest Recreation Area offers camping, picnicking and hiking through bamboo groves and dense forests. Near the area's top is **Thousand Root Banyan**, a giant tree with spreading roots that partially surround a pavilion. A hiking trail runs north along the river; you can swim near the suspension bridge.

GETTING THERE

Chihpen is 30 minutes south of Taitung; buses are frequent. The bus operated by the Tungtung Passenger Transport leaves from Hsinsheng Rd, opposite the bus terminal. A taxi to Chihpen costs about NT$350; be prepared to bargain. Buses leaving Chihpen for Taitung stop in front of the Tungtai Hotel and in front of a stall next to the Jyhbeen Hotel. Ask at the hotel for the schedule. In Taitung the bus stops in front of a small juice shop that serves excellent papaya milk shakes (papaya is a local specialty) and other delicious fresh fruit drinks. A bus from Kaohsiung also stops at Chihpen, though the bus stop is in the main town, three kilometers from the Jyhbeen Hotel. You can then pick up a bus coming from Taitung.

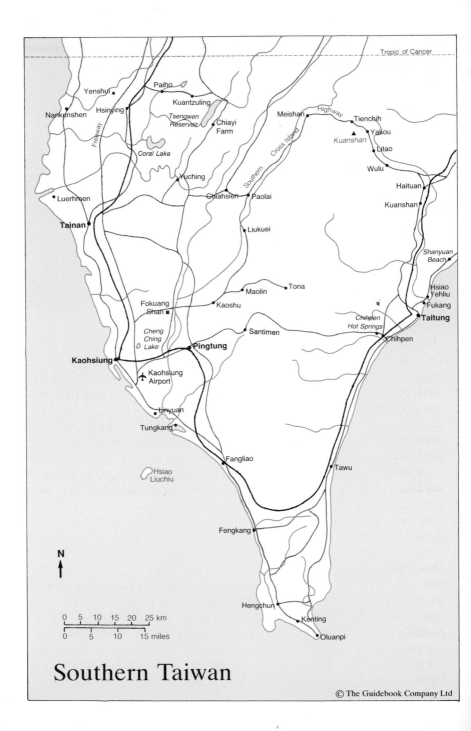

Southern Taiwan

Southern Taiwan

Southern Taiwan is a region of exceptional beauty, with lush green plains, white sand beaches and tropical forests. It is also a land of old temples and historic sites, as well as modern cities.

Tainan

Tainan, the oldest city in Taiwan, was the island's capital for 203 years, from 1684 to 1887. Today it is the fourth largest city on the island, with a population of 655,000. But unlike the other three major cities, Tainan is not a bustling metropolis with sky-scrapers, fancy shops and bumper-to-bumper traffic. This sleepy, orderly city is better known for its colorful history, kept alive by the many historical sites that dot its maze of tiny alleys, lanes and streets, and for the many old cultural and religious traditions that continue to thrive here.

HISTORY

The modern history of the area begins in the 1620s with the arrival of the Dutch. Anxious to establish a foothold from where they could develop trade with China, the Dutch occupied the Pescadores Islands (Penghu) after repeated requests for permis-sion to set up a trading post somewhere along the China coast were rejected by the imperial court in Beijing. The Chinese were not happy having foreigners in the Pes-cadores either, and suggested they set up in Taiwan instead. The Dutch accepted and sailed into a natural harbor on the island's southwest coast in 1624.

At that time, Tainan was already occupied by aboriginal tribes, Chinese settlers and a small number of Japanese traders. The Dutch built Fort Zeelandia in 1634 on a piece of land separated from the main island by a narrow peninsula. A smaller for-tress, Fort Provintia (frequently incorrectly spelled Providentia), was built on the shore of the main island across the harbor from Zeelandia in 1653. The Dutch probably would have remained on the island indefinitely had it not been for Cheng Cheng-kung, more popularly known in the West as Koxinga, a Ming-dynasty loyalist who wanted to use the island as a base for overthrowing the alien Qing Dynasty of the Manchus. Koxinga arrived on the island in 1661 at Luerhmen (Deer Ears Gate) with 30,000 soldiers in 8,000 war ships. He quickly seized Fort Provintia, but Fort Zeelandia proved more of a problem. The Dutch at this fort put up stiff resistance and managed to hold off its attackers for nine months before finally surrendering. Within one year of his arrival, Koxinga succeeded in forcing out the Dutch. Koxinga died at his residence in Zeelandia one year later, but his forces continued their fight against the Manchus for another 20 years until his grandson surrendered the island to Qing forces in 1683. The Cheng family name is closely linked with the history of the city.

CITY SIGHTS

Relics of the Dutch occupation include the site of Fort Provintia, now called Chihkan Tower, and Fort Zeelandia at Anping. Numerous Qing-dynasty structures stand in the city, as well as old temples. Tainan is known as the City of One Hundred Temples, but this is an understatement; there are some 300 temples here. While many of these historical relics have decayed or been pushed aside by modernization, traces of the city's past are still in abundance, fascinating reminders of Taiwan's links with China and the West. Of the Historical Sites of the First Rank in Taiwan, a third are located in Tainan: Chihkan Tower, Fort Provintia, Erh-kun-shen Fort, Shrine of the Five Concubines, Confucius Temple, Kuanti Temple and Great Matsu Temple.

Most of the important sites in Tainan are situated close to one another, though they are spread out over a large section of the city. For those who like to walk, the following pleasant walking tour can be easily completed in about five hours. The forts and the Koxinga Shrine each charge an admission fee (NT$20 for adults, NT$10 for students) and each has a one-page brochure in English that explains the history of the site. Be sure to ask for one when you buy your ticket.

■ FORT PROVINTIA (CHIHKAN TOWER)
212 MINTSU RD

The tour begins at Fort Provintia, a 15 minute walk from the train station, and just a few blocks up from the Far Eastern Department Store.

Fort Provintia was built by the Dutch in 1653, probably in response to a local uprising against the Dutch the year before. It was built facing Fort Zeelandia, just a few kilometers away. While Fort Zeelandia was the governor's central administrative building, Fort Provintia served as an office building for officials administering the island on behalf of the Dutch East India Company. The bricks used to build the wall were made with a curious mixture of sugar-water, glutinous rice paste and powdered clam shells—called *hung mao tu*, or Red Hair's clay, by local Chinese, Red Hairs being a reference to the Dutch. The wall was exceptionally strong. Its circumference ran some 450 feet. The north and south watchtowers, more than 36 feet tall, were known as the Red-hair Towers.

The fort fell quickly to Koxinga's forces soon after they landed in Tainan in 1661, and it was from here that Koxinga conducted his nine-month siege of Fort Zeelandia. After Koxinga drove the Dutch out of Taiwan, he briefly used Fort Provintia as the seat of his government and changed the name to Cheng Tien-fu.

After the harbor silted the space between Zeelandia and Provintia became dry land, the two forts lost their military importance and soon fell into decay.

Successive earthquakes laid to ruin the remaining rooms and chambers, leaving behind only the enclosure wall. In 1879, **Wen-chang Hall** and **Hai-shen Temple** were erected on Provintia's brick platform built by the Dutch. These buildings were renovated during the Japanese occupation, and used as a history museum. Another renovation was carried out after 1945, but unfortunately the work was not done properly and the original appearance was irrevocably lost.

Of the original Dutch fort, only a small portion of the wall—the platform's main entrance—remains. It was unearthed during the Japanese renovation of the structure. This wall, 300 years ago, received the brunt of the sea's high tides.

The two halls built in 1879 are still here and now house models of the original fort, paintings, models of turreted battleships and a few artifacts. An old well remains behind the buildings in the winding gallery attached to Wen-chang Hall. According to one legend, this was a secret passage to Zeelandia used by the Dutch to escape from Koxinga's forces. In front of the buildings are nine tortoise stelae, so called because they are set on the backs of stone tortoises. The stelae, with inscriptions in Chinese and Manchu by Qing Emperor Chien-lung, commemorate the defeat of the Lin Shuang-wen anti-Qing rebellion in 1788. Such commemorative stelae are valuable as they were seldom erected in Taiwan. In the courtyard is a replica of the Dutch surrender, with a statue of the Dutch bowing in submission to Koxinga. The Qing-dynasty stone lion and lioness at the front gate were damaged during World War II, but were later repaired.

Across the street from Fort Provintia is a tall red wall, the rear part of Kuanti Temple. Walk down Yungfu St beside the temple wall and turn right at the corner of the red wall to the temple entrance.

■ KUANTI TEMPLE (WU MIAO)
229 YUNGFU RD (CORNER OF MINTSU RD)

The Kuanti Temple is one of the best preserved and most beautiful temples in Tainan. It was built between 1660–1680, before the Qing government extended its rule over the island. The present structure conforms to the reconstruction of the final years of the Kang-hsi period (1662–1722). In 1727, the Kuanti Temple was designated as a site for official sacrifices, hence its current popular name, Kuanti Temple for Official Sacrifices. It is the best of the island's many Kuanti shrines.

The temple features long, narrow spaces, from the **Front Hall** to the **First Hall of Worship**, the **Second Hall of Worship**, the **Main Hall** and the **Posterior Hall**. The S-shaped feature visible near the roof's edge is a wall-lock—a device borrowed from Dutch architecture—used to ensure the stability of the iron rod that binds the roof-beams with the wall fabric. Notice also the octagonal column plinth in the Posterior

Chihkan Tower (above); *a Fish-eating-vine eave* (left); *Ching Dynasty Turtle stelae* (right)

Hall, with detailed relief decorations on each face, a feature rarely found in such contexts, and the finely carved stone drums flanking the central door of the Front Hall. An impressive feature of the temple is the tall red walls running around the complex.

Exit the temple and turn right down the narrow alley to the Matsu Temple next door.

■ THE GREAT MATSU TEMPLE
18, ALLEY 227, YUNGFU RD

The Great Matsu Temple, also called the Great Queen of Heaven Temple, sits beside the Kuanti Temple. It is one of many temples in Tainan devoted to Matsu, and its fine workmanship and detail make it one of the most notable temples on the island.

The temple was founded on the site of the residence of Prince Ning Ching, the pretender to the Ming throne. The prince was brought to Taiwan by Koxinga and in 1663, the royal residence was built for him and his household. In 1683, when the Qing forces defeated the last remnants of Koxinga's forces in a sea battle near Penghu, the prince, his five concubines and two servants (see page 250) committed suicide at the palace rather than suffer disgrace and captivity. The five concubines said good-bye to the prince and then hung themselves in formal dress. The 64-year-old prince publicly announced his decision, distributed his land, settled business affairs, invited his friends for a parting dinner and wrote some poetry before taking his own life by hanging two days later.

In 1683, General Shih Lang, an officer who had served the Cheng family (Cheng is the family name of Koxinga) before defecting to the Manchu side, commanded the Qing forces invading the Pescadores. In a sea battle he claims to have received divine assistance from Matsu, the Goddess of the Sea. Following his victory, Shih requested permission from Beijing to worship Matsu in an official ceremony. Permission was granted and he converted the prince's royal residence into a shrine to the goddess, which then became known as the Temple of the Princess of Heaven. In 1700, Matsu was elevated by imperial edict to Queen of Heaven and the shrine's title was changed accordingly—the first Matsu temple in Taiwan to have its name officially changed. In 1719, the temple was made a site for official sacrifices to be carried out regularly by the local magistrate.

In the inner palace, beyond the main hall, are three shrines dedicated respectively to Kuankung, Shangtikung and Kuanyin. Members of the prince's household and neighbors worshipped at these shrines. The Kuankung Shrine was the forerunner of the Kuanti Temple next door (both names refer to the same god). The gardens next to the residence were noted for their rare flowers and plants.

The seven beams and a flight of seven steps in the **Hall of Worship** are reminders that this was once the royal residence of Prince Ning Ching, features that make the temple unique in Taiwan. Other features of note are the tablets and plaques dating back to the Kang-hsi period (1662–1722), the 'resting mountain' roof on the front hall and the superb dragon pillars, sculpted in granite and inlaid with *qing cao* (green grass) stone, in the Hall of Worship. When the bells and drums hanging in the Hall of Worship are struck they can be heard for miles. The gallery running across the front of the **Front Hall** contains vivid sculptures of horses galloping, stopping, looking up and lying down. A dragon pair sculpted in relief on the temples were done by master craftsman Chiang, of Huian, Fujian, and are considered masterpieces of their kind in Taiwan. A stone stele erected by Shih Lang tells how Matsu helped him capture Taiwan. On this stele, time and nature have obscured most of the writing. A large statue of Matsu on the main altar is surrounded by dozens of smaller statues left by worshippers. The temple has undergone numerous renovations since 1740.

After leaving the temple retrace your steps to Yungfu Rd and walk south to Minchuan Rd. Turn left here and walk to the intersection of Chungyi Rd. Turn right down Chungyi Rd and within a few minutes you will see the First Commercial Bank and a lane on the left, where you will see the Tien Tan temple.

■ TIEN TAN (HEAVENLY ALTAR)
NO. 16, LANE 90, CHUNGYI RD

Tien Tan, a Taoist temple, was built during the reign of Tao-kuang (1821–1850) and is dedicated to the Jade Emperor, who is attended by a host of other Taoist deities. There is no image of the Jade Emperor in the temple; he is always represented by a spirit tablet. The temple was rebuilt after 1945, and now looks a bit modern and gaudy. There are some fine, detailed carvings here, though. The main altar holding the Jade Emperor's tablet is intricately carved in gold-painted wood. On one side wall is a fresco, a colorful painting of Hwa-to, a 3rd-century Taoist physician, operating on a wounded Kuankung, the famous military hero.

Exorcisms, trances, and other Taoist ceremonies are sometimes performed here at the rear of the temple.

Walk back out to Chungyi Rd, turn left and head down to Minsheng Rd. Make another left and walk to a traffic circle. Bear right past the Tainan City Government Office and walk down Nanmen Rd. A few minutes from here you will see a rust-red wall on the right. This is the wall of the Confucius Temple.

■ CONFUCIUS TEMPLE
2 NANMEN RD

This temple was built in 1665 by Cheng Ching (the son of Koxinga) after General Chen Yung-hua, one of his officers, made repeated pleas for such a temple to be erected in Taiwan. It was the first Confucius temple on the island, and its first phase consisted of only the free-standing offering hall, or Hall of the Great Sage, the main structure in all Confucius temples. It holds the ceremonial tablet to Confucius.

In the early 1700s, several other buildings were added to the complex. At the end of World War II, it was used as a military base by the Japanese. Their presence attracted allied pilots who bombed it on March 15, 1945. Several buildings were destroyed or damaged.

The complex underwent an extensive 10-year renovation that was completed in 1989, and it appears today much as it did in the Qing Dynasty.

The Confucius temple complex lies on a north–south axis with the major structures facing south, the prime compass direction in China.

THE GATE OF GREAT ACHIEVEMENT

The entrance-way is the Gate of Great Achievement, located at the southeast corner of the complex. The gate stands at a right angle to the inner courtyard entrance; it is considered disrespectful to have the entrance directly in front of the building where Confucius' spirit tablet resides. In accord with the rules of geomancy, this configuration forces people to approach the main hall by walking at right angles; evil spirits can only move in straight lines.

A sign over the gate proclaims 'Taiwan's First School,' a reference to the establishment of the National College that was opened here in 1671. A stone tablet at the front gate, known as the Tablet of Dismounting, has the following inscription in both Chinese and Manchurian: 'Officers, civil and military, soldiers and civilians, dismount here before entering.'

TEMPLE POOL

On the far south side of the complex is the half-moon Temple Pool, which provides balance to the layout. The temple was traditionally used for symbolic rituals. In former times, the Royal Academy in the capital was surrounded by water, so water came to symbolize success in official exams and academic pursuits. When scholars passed exams it was said that they had 'ruchih,' or 'entered the pool.' Successful examinees would pour some water from the pool on their hats as a the symbol of their scholarly achievement.

HALL OF THE GREAT SAGE

The temple's main structure is the Hall of the Great Sage. In front is a large dragon-like character carved from a single piece of granite imported from Fujian. This symbol is said to be the son of the dragon (the emperor), and symbolizes Confucius' rank as just below the emperor. Above the hall's sacred table honoring Confucius are several valuable wooden tablets presented to the temple by successive Qing emperors, written in the imperial calligraphy. A large plaque at the top is the calligraphy of Chiang Kai-shek. There is no statue of Confucius; he made it clear to his students that they were not to worship him after his death and that there should be no likenesses of him. Confucius is honored by the spirit tablet, inscribed with his name and titles. On the four slanting corners of the roof are rows of 'evil birds', symbolizing that the Master's teachings can even reform bad people.

EAST AND WEST CORRIDORS

The two buildings flanking the Hall of the Great Sage house the spirit tablets of Confucius' famous students and Confucian scholars.

On exiting the temple on Nanmen Rd, you will see a memorial arch opposite the temple's front gate with exquisitely carved figures. The arch is probably a commemoration of the renovation of the temple in 1683 (see Arches, below).

Turn right when you come out the main entrance of the temple and walk south down Nanmen Rd past Fuchien Rd until you reach an alley on the right. Down this alley is the imposing Great South Gate.

■ GREAT SOUTH GATE

The Great South Gate is the only city gate essentially preserved in its original condition. This is the only standing city gate in Taiwan with a double entrance and a protective outer gate. In front of it is a hall housing a large number of old stelae carved in the 18th and 19th centuries, most in commemoration of good deeds performed by local citizens.

Return to Nanmen Rd and walk for several blocks to Wu Fei St. Cross Nanmen Rd and walk down Wu Fei St to the park where the Shrine of the Five Concubines is located.

■ SHRINE OF THE FIVE CONCUBINES
1 WU FEI ST

This small, dilapidated shrine stands before the tomb of the five concubines of Ming-dynasty Prince Ning Ching. They all killed themselves rather than surrender to the Qing government.

Prince Ning Ching was a descendant of the royal Ming family, brought to Taiwan in 1662 by Koxinga. He lived in Tainan in a palace built for him and his household until the last remnants of Koxinga's forces were dealt a smashing defeat in the Battle of Penghu in 1683. The prince chose suicide rather than disgrace, and the five ladies took their own lives first as a sign of fidelity. They hung themselves dressed in formal robes in the palace hall and their bodies were buried in a tomb on Cassia Bud Hill. In

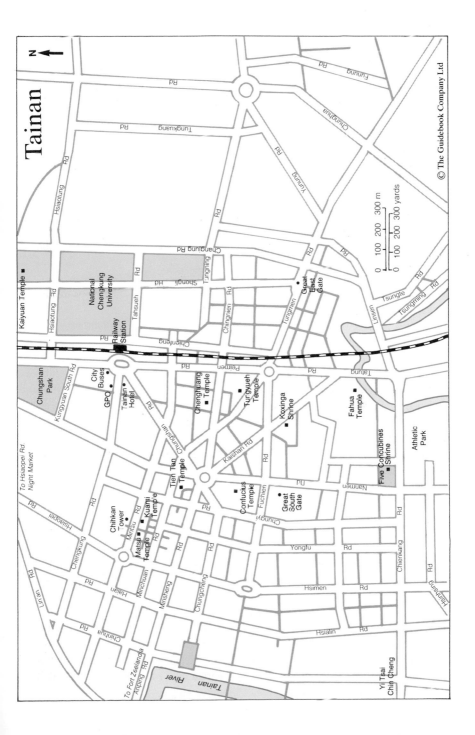

Tainan

N

© The Guidebook Company Ltd

Kaiyuan Temple

Hsiaotung Rd

Hsiaotung Rd

Tungkuang Rd

Rd

Hsiaotung Rd

National Chengkung University

Chungshan Park

Kungyuan South Rd

City Buses

GPO

Railway Station

Tainan Hotel

Chientang Rd

Peimen Rd

Chungshan Rd

Tansueh Rd

Chingnien Rd

Shangli Rd

Langning Rd

Changjung Rd

Rd

Rd

Turigmen Rd

Great East Gate

Yunung Rd

Chung-hua Rd

Funung Rd

Tsungle Rd

Linsen Rd

Tsungming Rd

Rd

Rd

0 100 200 300 m
0 100 200 300 yards

To Hsiaopei Rd.
Night Market

Hsiaopei Rd

Chengkung Rd

Mintzu Rd

Chihkan Tower

Matsu Temple

Kuanti Temple

Tien Tan Temple

Chenghuang Temple

Turgyueh Temple

Rd

Koxinga Shrine

Kaishan Rd

Fahua Temple

Athletic Park

Confucius Temple

Great South Gate

Fuchien Rd

Chungyi Rd

Namen Rd

Five Concubines Shrine

Chienkang Rd

Rd

Halan Rd

Minchuan Rd

Minchuan Rd

Minsheng Rd

Chungcheng Rd

Yongfu Rd

Hsimen Rd

Hsialin Rd

Chienkang Rd

Hsinghua Rd

Lin-an Rd

Chinhua Rd

To Fort Zeelandia
Anping Rd

Tainan River

Yi Tsai Chin Cheng

1786, two high officials visited Taiwan and were shown the tomb. To honor the memory of these women, orders were given to repair the tomb, set up a memorial tablet and establish a temple before the grave site. The inscribed tablets eulogizing the virtue and memory of the five concubines are inside the shrine. The four women painted on the doors are not the concubines, but legendary figures. Although the shrine is small and unimposing, the three-leaved door at the entrance is a sign of the status of the women as royal concubines.

On the right is a separate smaller shrine—the **Tomb of the Loyal Servants**— marking the burial place of two valets of the prince's household who joined their master in suicide. The shrine now sits in a deserted park.

Exit the park, turn right and walk until you come to a small street that bears left. Walk down it to Fahua St and the Fahua Temple; this temple is a little complicated to find, so ask for directions.

■ FAHUA TEMPLE
100 FAHUA ST

This structure, built in 1664, was originally a retreat for a scholar, a subordinate of Cheng Ching who arrived in Taiwan in 1663. It was converted into a temple in 1684.

At the temple's far right side is the **Butterfly Dream Garden**. On the left is the main temple that enshrines the Buddha. He is flanked by the large Great Heavenly Kings, two on each side, reaching almost to the ceiling. The building was destroyed by Allied bombers during World War II. Although reinforced concrete was used in the reconstruction, the original appearance was preserved. A seven-storey pagoda inside the garden contains the remains of the scholar who built the temple as his home. The temple is also known for its colorful murals. Banyan and bo trees stand in the courtyard.

When you leave the temple turn left and walk to Kaishan St, following the street around until you come to a red wall that surrounds the Koxinga Shrine.

■ KOXINGA SHRINE
152 KAISHAN RD

This tranquil garden shrine is devoted to the deified Ming-dynasty patriot, Koxinga. It was built in 1885 by Shen Pao-chen, an inspector general of the Qing court, under imperial edict. The decision by the Qing government to build the shrine signified that its Ming enemy had been forgiven and elevated to national hero and deity.

The original temple was the only one in Taiwan built in the Fuzhou style of architecture. Unfortunately, it was replaced with a northern palace-style building after 1945.

The main hall holds a large statue of a seated Koxinga. In the rear of the spacious grounds is an ancient plum tree, said to have been planted by Koxinga himself.

The complex also houses a museum. Although a bit dusty, it houses interesting artifacts and exhibits. On the first floor are prehistoric artifacts from the area, including ancient burial slabs. There are also paintings portraying life in prehistoric Taiwan. In the basement are cannons, grinding stones and stone carvings. On the second floor are reproductions of local forts, Qing-dynasty armor, clothing, bridal carriages, beds, coins and wood blocks. There are also paintings of the battle between Koxinga's soldiers and the Dutch, and of the foreigners' eventual surrender.

After leaving the shrine turn left and walk to the next main intersection which is Fuchien St. Turn right here, walk to the traffic circle and turn left down Minchuan Rd, Section 1, until you reach No. 110, the Tungyueh Temple.

■ TUNGYUEH TEMPLE
110 MINCHUAN RD, SECTION 1

The Tungyueh Temple was built toward the end of the Ming Dynasty and is dedicated to Tungyueh Tati, one of the kings of the netherworld. This dim, eerie temple befits a site devoted to the minions of darkness.

In the first hall on the right stand General Niu (Cow) and General Hsieh, two small cow-men, holding truncheons. On the left are General Ma (Horse) and General Fan, two small horse-men, holding weapons aloft. The generals appear ready to deliver punishment.

More dismal, however, is the second inner hall. Here murals depict scenes from Buddhist hells. Torture and punishment are carried out on humans as a table of heavenly judges looks on in approval. The scenes bring to mind Dante's Inferno.

The third hall is in stark contrast to the first and second. This area is very bright, painted in brilliant red and gold.

Taoist ceremonies take place at the temple every day, with chanting and blowing of buffalo horns to drive away misfortune and bring good fortune. It is sometimes possible to see exorcisms here, as well as people attempting to communicate with spirits.

■ CHENG HUANG (CITY GOD) TEMPLE
133 CHINGNIEN RD

All cities have a City God temple. Tainan's Prefectural City God Temple was constructed in 1668 during Cheng Ching's reign. A city is governed not only by its magistrate, but also by his heavenly counterpart, the City God and his assistants. While the magistrate is responsible for keeping the peace and upholding the law, the City God is responsible for people's souls, keeping a strict record of all those who have committed offenses or done good deeds. A huge abacus hanging inside the temple is used to tally a person's sins and good works.

The following important historical sites are located outside the city center and require a bus or taxi.

■ FORT ZEELANDIA (AN-PING FORT)
28 KUOSHEN RD, AN-PING DISTRICT

Now known as An-ping Fort, the Dutch began work on this structure in 1624, completing it in 10 years. It is the earliest fort in Taiwan, built on an offshore shoal at Yi-kun-shen, separated from the main island by a narrow expanse of water. First known as Fort Orange, the name was changed in 1634 to Fort Zeelandia.

The wall was made of red bricks brought here from Java by the Dutch. It stood more than 10 meters high, with a circumference of 846 meters. The fort was further protected by an outer wall three feet high. This grand structure was the home of the Dutch governor-general and the center of Dutch administration during their occupation of the island. Koxinga laid siege to the fort in 1661, but the Dutch managed to resist for nine months before surrendering and departing. Koxinga then declared himself king in 1662 and made Zeelandia his residence; he died here one year later at the age of 39.

In 1683, when the island was brought under Qing jurisdiction, the administrative center was transferred to nearby Tainan City. The fort was then made the Bureau of Military Supply.

As time passed and the harbor filled in, the fort lost all of its former strategic value. When the British invaded Taiwan in 1871, the arsenal inside the fort exploded and the walls were destroyed. Local people used the bricks and masonry as construction materials for their houses. In 1874 more materials were taken from here to build Erh-Kun-Shen Fort. After the Japanese occupation in 1895, the surviving remnants of the wall were torn down, the steps reconstructed, and a smaller enclosure wall added, making an elevated rectangular battlement.

All that remains of the original fort is a crumbling section of the old wall, a well, and the

An old cannon guards the ruins of Fort Zeelandia

semicircular base of a lookout tower. In 1920 the Japanese built European colonial-style buildings on the site. These today house models and paintings of the original fort, as well as displays detailing its history.

Take Bus No. 33 to the fort. A taxi from the center of the city costs about NT$80.

■ YI TSAI CHIN CHENG (ERH-KUN-SHEN FORT)
16 NANWEN RD

This fort was built in connection with the Moutanshe Tribal Incident of 1871. That year, a storm forced a group of fishermen from the Ryukyu Islands ashore at Heng-chun on the southern tip of Taiwan. After landing, the fishermen were slaughtered by aborigines from a place called Moutanshe. The Japanese government wanted to put the Ryukyus, then a Chinese protectorate, under their suzerainty, and so used the incident as an excuse to invade Taiwan in May 1874, winning suzerainty and other major concessions.

The incident made the Chinese government realize the weakness of the island's defenses, so it ordered Inspector General Shen Pao-chen, a native of Fujian and a reformer, to beef up Taiwan's fortifications. He believed China's future strength would depend on a build-up of naval armaments and sea defenses, and this fort was to be the first link of a wide defensive network for Taiwan. A French engineer was hired to design and direct the construction. Building materials were taken from nearby Fort Zeelandia, including fired bricks, and the work was completed a year later in 1875. The calligraphy engraved in the arches over the front and inner gates came from the brush of Shen himself. The four characters yi tsai chin cheng, literally 'golden fort lasting a million years,' were originally only meant as an auspicious inscription. They have now become the fort's official name.

The fort was enlarged several times, and by 1894 contained five muzzle-loading 18-ton cannons, four two-ton cannons, and four smaller 20-pound breech-loading cannons. The cannons were first fired by local patriots in their desperate attempt to resist the Japanese takeover of the island in the summer of 1895.

Some of the artillery pieces were sold during World War I to buy more modern arms, while others were melted down to make modern artillery during World War II. Those now on the site are copies of the lost ones.

The surrounding walls and moat have been restored to their original condition, and the cannons that once pointed menacingly out toward the seashore—now far away—look out over serene fishponds.

Yi Tsai Chin Cheng is only a short distance from An-ping, but public transportation to the fort is not convenient and so a taxi is the best way to get here. Ask the driver to wait while you walk round the fort—this takes about 20 minutes—as not many taxis come here.

■ KAI YUAN TEMPLE
  KAI YUAN RD

The Kai Yuan Temple, built in 1680, is an excellent example of Buddhist architecture. It was erected by Cheng Ching, reportedly as a retirement home for himself, although some say it was to be a home for his mother, Madame Kung, a concubine of Koxinga's. It was converted into a Buddhist temple 10 years later by the Qing government and a monk from Shanghai was installed as abbot.

Unfortunately, latter-day concrete additions detract from the temple's original beauty. A well in a room to the side of the last court was dug and used by Cheng Ching, after whom it is named. Behind the temple is a garden where monks grow their own food, and a three-tiered pagoda, repository for the bones of deceased monks.

The temple can be reached by buses 1, 6, and 17, which leave from near the train station.

■ CHUNG SHAN PARK

The pleasantly landscaped Chung Shan Park is just one block from the train station. The Respect Virtue and Venerate Literature Arch (see below), built in 1798, has been relocated to this park.

■ MEMORIAL ARCHES

Memorial arches were usually erected to commemorate good deeds. Four stone arches remain in Tainan today. The largest is the **Chieh Kuan Ting**, literally 'receive officials pavilion,' where all officials arriving in Taiwan were greeted by local dignitaries during the Qing Dynasty. It was erected outside the West Gate in 1784, but is now located at Chang Le St, Lane 143, in front of the God of the Wind Temple. The arch originally stood in front of the dock and officials disembarking from the mainland would meet local dignitaries under the arch, then walk into the temple where they would make offerings to the god for their safe journey. When returning to the mainland, the officials would leave by the city's West Gate, worshipping at the temple once again, this time praying for a safe journey home. The arch, 8 meters tall and 6.68 meters wide, is made of Quanzhou white stone, while the panels are carved of green stone.

A second arch is the **Respect Virtue and Venerate Literature Arch**, built in 1798 to commemorate the good works of Lin Chao-ying, a notable scholar. He contributed large sums of money for schools and once contributed all the funds needed for the renovation of the Confucius Temple. Originally situated in front of the Lung Wang Temple, the arch was later moved to Chung Shan Park in 1923 when the first site was turned into the Minsheng Circle, part of a Japanese urban renewal program.

Tainan's **Arch of Womanly Virtue** was erected in 1800 on a lane off Yuai St to commemorate the chastity and virtue of a Madame Shen. She married at 21, but was widowed six years later, pregnant and with one son. She not only raised her two sons, but gave them a good education, and attentively served her late husband's elderly parents. The story of her chastity and virtue spread far and in 1797 Emperor Chia-ching wrote a memorial extolling her.

The arch was put up on this spot three years later. It is small and simple, with only two columns. The top central tablet, indicating that the memorial was given by the emperor himself, has disappeared.

The **Pan Kung Arch** stands across the street from the main entrance to the Confucius Temple. The arch was probably built during temple repairs in 1683.

■ CITY GATES

The city wall was built much later than the original forts, since a city had to be fairly large to justify a wall. Construction of the first wall was started in 1723 following an anti-Manchu rebellion the previous year. This first wall was made of poles, thorny bamboo and other plants. A more sturdy wall of brick was erected in 1792 after Ming loyalist Lin Shuang-wen launched a rebellion and broke through the flimsy wall with artillery. The new wall was 5.5 meters high and six meters wide at the bottom. When no longer needed, it was allowed to decay and the Japanese tore down what was left around 1900.

All that remains of the original wall and eight gates are the Great South Gate (see page 250), Great East Gate and Lesser West Gate. The latter was dismantled and rebuilt on the campus of Cheng Kung University; the other two remain at their original locations.

SHOPPING & ENTERTAINMENT

The importance of religion in Tainan has ensured that folk arts continue to thrive. On the streets near major temples one can still see wood carvers, embroiderers and painters working in small shops turning out religious works for use in homes and temples, as well as makers of spirit money that is burned for the use of people in the afterworld.

■ HSIAOPEI NIGHT MARKET

The Hsiaopei Night Market is a large covered area with hundreds of stalls selling cheap clothing, everyday necessities and a wide variety of food. This busy market is a vibrant place to walk around in the evening when it is crowded with Chinese shoppers and diners. Food sold here includes seafood—squid, octopus, eels, clams, and oysters—and all kinds of meat, vegetables and desserts. In the winter stalls serve

The Avenging Angel

A group of young boys were running and hollering on East Market Street when they saw Hsiao Lo at the other end, walking toward them with glazed eyes. They came to a braking halt, and slowly jostled each other across the street to the front of the preserved fruits shop. They stared at Hsiao Lo, choking with mischievous laughter. An old woman came out of the shop. She glared at them angrily. "Vengeance will fall on the evildoer, debts will fall on the debtor. Now that Liu Lao-shih's back, the whole lot of you will have to pay!" She glanced up at the sky, then bent down to pick up the tray of orange peels that had been left drying in the sun. "The Boddhisattva has eyes," she muttered, as she carried the tray back inside.

The boys snuck up after Hsiao Lo and tiptoed behind him. As the k'u-lien tree came into view, the youngest one sidled up by Hsiao Lo and tugged at his pants. "Brother," he whispered, "don't go up there. That demon Liu Lao-shih is waiting for you."

Hsiao Lo looked over his shoulder. At the end of the street, the sun was still suspended over the horizon. The street was bathed in red. Over by the granary everything was quiet, except for the cawing of the black crows that wheeled about the branches of the k'u-lien tree. The tree, scorched by the sun for the past month, stood gaunt and lonely. A thin veil of golden dust now hung over it. Bent at the waist, it hunched toward the sinking sun, seeming to stare at it vacantly. Beneath the tree sat the napping man, his arms wrapped around his knees, hugging a sack to his chest.

The woman Chu came out of her teashop. She stood under the eaves complaining loudly about the heat. She craned her neck to look at the sun, then looked up at the mass of dark clouds gathered overhead.

"The weather's turning. If it doesn't rain soon, we might as well put a torch to the town and burn it all down." She emptied the basin of muddy water that she had brought out with her onto the ground in front of her shop. She had already noticed Hsiao Lo standing in the middle of the street, looking as if he had lost his soul.

The old fortune-teller walked across the road carrying a cup of tea. He kept his eyes on the ground as he slowly made his way, but glanced up to study the man sitting beneath the tree. "Liu Lao-shih commited murder and went crazy. The constables took him and locked him up tight. How could they let him escape a second time? It just doesn't stand to reason! And then, this man here doesn't look crazy at all. I think he's just a drifter passing through."

"If it is that crazy demon," said the woman Chu, "so much the better. As long as you've got a clean conscience, why should you care? Could it be, old sir," she laughed coldly, "could it be that you, too, were watching the parade in Wan-fu Lane that night?"

The fortune-teller's face stiffened. He looked over and spoke gravely. "I was watching them greet Kuan Yin from my doorstep. Not a drop of blood ever touched me. I'm white as innocence itself, and my conscience is clean." He uncurled a finger from around his cup and pointed at Hsiao Lo. "This little lout got himself drunk and went with Sun Ssu-fang and his gang. It's they who sinned, who brought us disaster, who summoned the plague demon to descend on us. It's they who dragged every frightened innocent in town into their evil mess!"

One of the men in the teashop stood holding his own porcelain teacup from home. He peered out from the doorway a long while, then burst out, "Vengeance will fall on the evildoer, debts will fall on the debtor. That cleaver of Liu Lao-shih's surely will not fall on an innocent body!"

The woman Chu walked to the back of her shop and filled a basin with water to splash on the ground under the eaves. Hsiao Lo's lone shadow was still stretched across the street. She went over to him and grabbed him by the arm. "Don't you know what's good for you?" she chided. "Standing out in the middle of the street attracting attention! If you could see how wretched you look standing out here! If that man were really Liu Lao-shih, he would've chopped you to pieces long before this!"

Without a word, Hsiao Lo followed her into the teashop. He sat down behind a table near the door and drew out the dagger from under his shirt. He placed it down softly on the table and sat staring at the half-dried dog blood smeared on its blade.

Suddenly, thunder rolled overhead. The woman Chu stood in the middle of her shop, holding herself very still, head tilted to listen. It came from far above the seven heavens, rolling and grumbling, like someone *being throttled. The whole town of Chi-ling paused, as if its heart had stopped beating. In front of the granary the street lay silent and empty. The crows, perched on the k'u-lien tree, flew up in confusion, flapping their wings and cawing with mounting urgency.*

"Its turned at last!" exclaimed the woman Chu, tossing aside the kettle and striding out under the eaves. All down the street, from the north end to the south, not even a single shadow of a man was in sight, except that of the one sitting beneath the k'u-lien tree. Beyond the town, the blood-red sinking sun ignited the western sky. It hung just over the horizon, glaring back through the centre of town to the k'u-lien, gaunt and lonely.

A bolt of lightning sliced the sky in two; the dagger on the table gleamed a cold blood-red. One by one, the men inside the teashop came out and huddled under the eaves. They sipped their tea and watched the white snakes slithering across the crimson sky. Fat drops of rain began to fall pattering down.

The man beneath the tree rose to his feet. He looked up at the flock of crows frantically beating their wings, seemingly bewildered by the wind and the rain. They scattered toward the west, a burst of black specks in the brilliant awesome sunset.

The man they feared to be Liu Lao-shih shook off the raindrops and wiped his hairy cheeks with the back of his hand. Throwing the sack over his shoulder, he walked out into the street, tucking his chin down on his chest.

Hsiao Lo felt for the dagger. He slipped out of the teashop and on to the street like a kite broken loose from its string.

The two of them stood in the middle of the street. The man slowly looked up at Hsiao Lo. The wind howled past the granary. The k'u-lien hunched toward the sun beyond the town, soughed as it scattered its yellow leaves over the ground beneath it. On one branch sat a lone crow. Its mournful cries mingled with the sound of the wind and the rain.

Slowly the man turned around, shrugged the sack on his shoulder, and heedless of the rain he began to walk away down the long street.

Li Yung P'ing, *The Rain from the Sun*,
translated by Candace Pong and Robert Eno

Chinese hot pot, a variety of meat, vegetables and seafood (you choose the ingredients) cooked in a broth at your table over a burner. One local specialty sold here is Tainan *tantzu mian* (noodles), named after the carrying pole that supported the ingredients and implements to prepare and serve the dish, formerly carted through the streets. These slightly spicy noodles, served with a meat sauce (and perhaps some shrimp) and garnished with onion and parsley, originated in the city generations ago.

Beside the night market is a modern shopping mall, with department store, shops, boutiques and fast food restaurants.

■ PUBS
Several pubs in the city are popular with the many Westerners teaching English here.

DIRTY ROGER'S
Roger, who is not dirty but actually very friendly, has been operating this warm pub for several years. He is here every night, sometimes performs comic routines in Chinese from behind the bar, and is more than happy to make friends and point visitors in the right direction around town. 104 Changjung Rd, Section 2. Tel 235-6527.

BAR FLY PUB, 22 Shengli Rd. Tel 236-9249

MACANNA BEER HOUSE, 117 Shengli Rd, near Cheng Kung University.

■ TEAHOUSES
Tao Hua Yuan serves Chinese-style tea at 18 Chienyeh St, near the intersection of Fuchien Rd and Kaishan Rd

GETTING THERE
Frequent buses and trains leave from Taipei, Kaohsiung, Taichung and Chiayi to Tainan.

AROUND TAINAN
■ LUERHMEN (DEER'S EAR GATE)
Luerhmen is the riverside site where Koxinga landed with his troops in 1661. The main tourist attractions are two large, new Matsu temples, separated by a few kilometers.

HEAVEN HOLY MOTHER TEMPLE
160 Chengpei Rd, Lane 245, Luerhmen, Tucheng, Annan District.
Situated next to Tucheng Village, this is said to be the largest Taoist temple complex on the island. It is easily recognizable by its shining gold roof tiles.

HEAVEN QUEEN MOTHER TEMPLE
236 Hsientsao St, Section 3, Lane 1, Luerhmen, Annan District.
This temple stands on the site of a much older temple structure. One of the Matsu statues in the main hall is said to have been brought to Taiwan by Koxinga; some claim it is 800–1,000 years old.

Buses for Luerhmen leave from the Hsingnan Bus Co terminal on Chungshan Rd in Tainan City. You can also take Tainan city bus No 29.

■ NANKUNSHEN
Nankunshen, built in 1662 and dedicated to five Tang-dynasty heroes, is one of the most active Buddhist temples in Taiwan. In the first hall are icons of the five heroes, in the second hall sit three statues of Kuanyin, the Goddess of Mercy, and in the third hall is the emperor of hell. On weekends thousands of Buddhists turn out to worship, setting off fireworks, holding parades and performing religious ceremonies. Shamans sometimes appear here as well. When possessed, they are said to take on supernatural strength, cutting themselves with knives and swords.

Frequent buses leave for Nankunshen from the Hsingnan Bus Co terminal in Tainan. The trip takes about 1 1/2 hours.

■ KUANTZULING
Kuantzuling is a small hot spring resort nestled in the mountains of Tainan County. It was once an impoverished farming area, but in 1898 Japanese troops stationed in the vicinity discovered mineral springs and developed the area into a resort. Most of the original, rustic, Japanese-style inns are gone now, replaced by modern establishments. Kuantzuling is known for the beauty of its scenery.

The water here is different from that of most mineral springs. Alkaline in nature, it has an unattractive, cloudy, gray look, though hot springs aficionados praise it for its therapeutic effects, saying it is good for skin diseases, arthritis, rheumatism, stomach problems, sore muscles and other ailments. The water, which comes from the ground at a temperature of about 75°C (167°F), is so hot it has to be mixed with cold water before being piped into the numerous hotels crowding the village.

The area is also known for its many temples. They are spread out over a wide area, so it takes several hours on foot to visit all of them. Taxis can be hired, but make sure you agree on the price and length of the hiring beforehand.

Red Hill Park is the starting point. Walk up the steps on the left as you leave town for 10–15 minutes to the park. It has pavilions, a children's playground and wonderful views of the nearby mountains, the coastal plain to the west and the Taiwan Strait beyond.

Karaoke bars are a growing element of Taiwanese nightlife

Head back down to the road and follow it up the hill, circling around to Kuantzuling Upper Village (the stone steps are a more direct route to the same destination). Follow the road outside the village for several kilometers until you see a turnoff to the left that goes to **Hsienkung Temple**.

Continue walking uphill on the main road to a tourist shop area with restaurants. Below on the left is **Fire and Water Spring**. Here jets of natural gas fuel eternal flames. They emerge with spurts of water from the bottom of a low rock face. Locals say the spring of fire and water is a divine manifestation and they offer incense and other sacrificial items here. You can catch a bus to the town of Paiho from here.

A 15-minute walk from here brings you to the dilapidated, but pleasant **Blue Cloud Temple**, built in 1701. Three kilometers down the road is the **Tahsien (Great Immortals) Temple**, built c.1702. It became a center of Buddhism in southern Taiwan after importing a white jade Buddha from India and an Amida (Future Buddha) from Japan. The temple is home to thousands of swallows that nest under its eaves, flying around the temple courtyard.

Near here is Hsientsaopu, a few kilometers below Kuantzuling and the main road. From here you can get a bus to Hsinying and Chiayi. From Paiho, however, there are more buses to Hsinying and Chiayi, as well as occasional direct buses to Tainan.

GETTING THERE

Travelers coming from the south can catch a direct bus to Kuantzuling in Hsinying, Tainan County. Those coming from the north can get a bus from the Chiayi Bus Co terminal on Chungshan Rd in Chiayi City.

■ TSENGWEN RESERVOIR

The Tsengwen Reservoir is in the western foothills of the north–south Central Mountain Range on the border of Chiayi and Tainan counties, about 60 kilometers northeast of Tainan City. After six years of construction ended in 1973, it surpassed Coral Lake as Taiwan's largest lake. The reservoir, created by damming the Tsengwen River, covers an area of 17 square kilometers.

Despite its isolation, thousands of visitors pour into the area every weekend to go boating in the lake, and to picnic, fish and enjoy quiet walks. The Tsengwen Youth Activity Center, a hostel operated by the China Youth Corps, is located on the river below the dam. Several hiking trails lead through the area, though only a few are marked.

The dam can be reached via a pleasant six-kilometer road that goes up the gorge. **Bird Palace**, an aviary, is located beside a park. Across the dam, about one kilometer up the road is the **Observation Platform**. From here you can take a ferry to **Chiayi Farm** (15 minutes) and **Tapu Village** (45 minutes). Three ferry runs go in each direction every day. The farm produces lichees, mangoes, and honey and has a guest house for overnight stays, as well as a camping and picnic area, Alpine-style farm buildings, a tourist orchard, wooded pathways and pony rides for children.

Tapu, situated near the head of the reservoir, is a rustic farming village that produces fruit, sugar cane and, its specialty, bamboo shoots. There are two docks, one old, one new, with a suspension bridge and a park running between them. On the outskirts of the settlement is the government-run Tapu Villa hostel.

The ferries around the reservoir are slow and the schedules inconvenient. However, small work boats with outboard motors can be hired by individuals and small groups. The cost for a half-hour tour of the lake is about NT$500. Transportation between other locations can be arranged, but you must negotiate the price. Ask at the dock at Tapu or Chiayi Farm to find one of the boatmen.

GETTING THERE

Tsengwen Reservoir and Tapu can be reached by taking buses from the Hsingnan Bus Co station on Chungshan Rd in Tainan City; the Chiayi Bus Co in Chiayi City has three buses a day to Chiayi Farm and Tapu.

■ CORAL LAKE

Coral Lake, originally known as the Wushantou Reservoir, got its name from the numerous narrow inlets that jut into the surrounding hills, giving it the appearance of coral from the air. More than 30 mountain streams flow into this 30-meter-deep lake that covers an area of 6,000 hectares. The inlets and more than 100 islets dotting the surface make the lake a maze in which inexperienced boatmen can easily get lost. Coral Lake is filled from the Tsengwen Reservoir, and supplies nearby areas with water for household use, irrigation and industry. Boats can be rented for fishing and sailing, but swimming is not permitted. A network of trails leads all around the lake. Though attractive, Coral Lake is not worth visiting unless you have time to spare.

GETTING THERE

Buses for Coral Lake depart from the Hsingnan Bus Co station on Chungshan Rd, in Tainan.

Southern Cross Island Highway

The Southern Cross Island Highway is a narrow, winding highway that twists its way east for 182 kilometers from Yuching in Tainan County over the mountains of southern Taiwan, to the village of Haituan in the Hualien–Taitung Valley. The bus takes about eight hours to complete the trip. There is little traffic on this highway of unending natural scenery, and it is thus a more suitable route for walking than the Central Cross Island Highway. The route passes hot spring resorts, aboriginal settlements, forested mountains, cliffs and waterfalls. The highway was completed in 1972.

Many people take the bus part of the way and then walk the highway's central section—a three-day hike. This should be done from the gently rising western side of the highway.

Paolai, about 46 kilometers east of Yuching has a large number of bath houses and hotels with hot spring water piped in. Travelers are required to stop here at the police station for a Class B mountain pass if they have not already obtained one. You must pay NT$20 and will need a passport, alien resident certificate or local identification card (if you start on the east coast you will obtain your mountain pass at Haituan). You can have a meal and spend the night at Paolai.

At **Meishan** (860 meters) is the first of three hostels on the highway, the Meishan Mountain Hostel, surrounded by aboriginal houses. **Tienchih** is the midway point of the highway, a bus stop where public buses rest, exchange passengers and then reverse course for the return home. Many people begin walking from here. The **Evergreen Shrine** here is dedicated to the 100 people who lost their lives building the highway.

After completing the first five kilometers of the four-hour walk to **Yakou**, at 2,728 meters the highest point on the highway, pass **Cypress Valley**, densely covered with cypress trees and often shrouded in mist. Next pass through the **Takuanshan Tunnel**, a 615-meter-long tunnel without lighting. Be sure to bring a flashlight. After emerging, continue walking to some buildings on the right. This is the Yakou Hostel, perched on a steep mountain slope, with rocky ridges above and green valleys below. On the road just below the hostel is a small bridge with a waterfall behind it.

From here the highway descends for about 30 kilometers to **Litao** (1,070 meters), by far the most interesting village along the road, situated on a tableland beneath the highway. Litao is a simple Bunun aborigine village.

From Litao it is a three-hour walk to **Wulu Gorge**, formed by the Hsinwu River. This area is often compared to the Tunnel of Nine Turns at Taroko Gorge. Buses for Kuanshan leave here at 8:20 am and once in the afternoon. From Kuanshan you can make rail connections north or south.

Bring warm clothing for the walk at higher altitudes, and a good flashlight. Make reservations in advance if you plan to stay at any of the three mountain hostels and bring your own food because some hostels do not cook for guests on weekdays. Simple food can be purchased at stalls in Meishan and Litao. A class B mountain pass is necessary.

Flowers blossom along the Southern Cross Island Highway

One bus a day leaves from the Tainan Hsingnan Bus Co on Chungshan Rd at 7:30 am. Buses leave the east coast not from Taitung, but from Kuanshan, a short train ride north of Taitung, every day at 8 am. Neither bus goes the entire way. They meet in the middle and passengers switch buses for the remainder of the journey. People have lunch and a rest before boarding the buses again at around 2 pm.

An easier but less scenic way of getting to the east coast is to take the bus from Kaohsiung southward along the shimmering waters of the west coast, turn east and then come up the east coast to Chihpen, a popular hot springs resort, and on to Taitung (see page 238).

Kaohsiung

Kaohsiung, Taiwan's second largest city, lies on the southwest coast fronting the Taiwan Strait. It has a population of 1.5 million and is the site of the island's biggest harbor, the world's third largest container shipping port and the second largest dry dock after Nagasaki. The city is also the island's busiest industrial center, encompassing a sprawling export-processing zone, aluminum-processing plants, oil and sugar refineries, the China Shipbuilding Corp and the China Steel Corp. Economic development has brought problems along with prosperity, evident in traffic jams, air and water pollution, and the array of other problems that plague fast-industrializing Asian cities. That said, Kaohsiung is less crowded and hectic than Taipei in the north. It has few interesting sites for tourists, but is a jumping off place for visits to nearby destinations, such as Kenting National Park and the Penghu Islands.

City Sights

■ LONGEVITY MOUNTAIN PARK (WANSHOUSHAN PARK)
A good place to view this sprawling city and its busy harbor day or night is Longevity Mountain Park, just 20 minutes by foot from the Kingdom Hotel. The park has a small zoo, a temple and a martyr's shrine.

■ HSITZU BAY
Just past Longevity Mountain Park is Hsitzu Bay. A beach here is popular with locals, but the water is not very clean. Sun Yat-sen University is also in this area, as is the former British Consulate, built during the Qing Dynasty. The consulate now exhibits artifacts.

■ **THREE PHOENIX PALACE**
134 HOPEI RD, SECTION 2

Three Phoenix Palace, the largest temple in Kaohsiung, is devoted to Li Na-cha, a demon suppressor. Stone lions stand at the temple's entranceway that leads up to a carved stone facade. In the main hall are the three major icons and gilt altar tables. In the rear hall, up and behind the main hall, is a smaller shrine with three altars, including three gilt Buddhas and numerous guards and deities.

■ **WEN WU SHRINE**
114 FUYEH ST

This three-story Taoist temple is dedicated to Kuankung, the deified warrior, and the scholar Confucius. The ground floor is devoted to martial deities, the second floor to Confucius and the third to the Jade Emperor.

■ **TEMPLE TO THE KINGS OF THE THREE MOUNTAINS**
54 YENHUANG ST

This temple was built in the 1600s and is dedicated to three brothers, teachers of a man credited with saving the life of a Chinese emperor. The emperor rewarded the three by making them kings of three mountainous regions of Fujian Province.

■ **CHENG CHING LAKE**

Cheng Ching Lake is a 90-hectare, man-made reservoir northeast of Kaohsiung, surrounded by a well-landscaped park and a seven-kilometer road. The park includes several pavilions, tree-lined walks, a lotus pond, an orchard, boating, horseback riding and a golf course. The reservoir supplies water to Kaohsiung's industries and households.

Two large aquariums stand just inside the gate. West of here, on a hill overlooking the lake, is the Kaohsiung Grand Hotel, patterned after its parent hotel in Taipei. The Grand Hotel, far from Kaohsiung's hustle and bustle, is near the park entrance. Nine-Turns Bridge, a trademark of the park, is a popular sight for shooting wedding photos.

The path from here leads to a campground with camping equipment for rent. It then climbs to the Chunghsing Pagoda. A panoramic view of the lake and nearby area is revealed from the pagoda's top floor. A long distance from here, across the lake, is the Youth Activity Center, a youth hostel. In the middle of the lake is Fukuo Islet, named in memory of nationalist soldiers who died fighting the Chinese communists on Fukuo Island off Vietnam during the civil war. Also adjoining the lake is the

Tsoying, Kaohsiung

18-hole Kaohsiung Golf and Country Club, which is open to the public.

A public bus travels along the main road, stopping at all the tourist sights in the park. The park entrance fee is NT$20.

The trip to Cheng Ching Lake by taxi from downtown Kaohsiung takes about 15 minutes. The No. 60 bus leaves from in front of the Kaohsiung train station for Cheng Ching Lake about every 30 minutes.

■ CHICHIN ISLAND

This inconsequential island offers some respite from the pressures of city life in Kaohsiung. Swimmers can go to Chichin Beach, a black-sand beach located on the seaward side of the island, away from the murky waters of Kaohsiung harbor. There are facilities here for changing and showering. A small Taoist temple near the beach is dedicated to the God of Medicine. Reach the island via a new tunnel, or by ferry from the harbor near Sun Yat-sen University. The ferry ride takes just five minutes.

SHOPPING & ENTERTAINMENT
■ UNDERGROUND MARKET

Kaohsiung's Underground Market burned down several years ago, but reportedly will reopen. The market had three levels, including shops, food stalls, a bowling alley, roller skating rink, video arcade, an amusement area for children and a movie theater. The arcade is opposite the City Government Building, near the Love River.

■ PUBS

There are numerous pubs in the city, although they open and close so fast it is difficult to recommend any one place. Most are located around Wufu 2nd Rd near the King's Hotel. Stormy Weather, Snows, and Sam's feature beer, darts and simple Western food.

■ CINEMA

The China Cinema, 60 Tzuchang 3rd Rd, has five theaters in one building. Also look for the ubiquitous MTV (Movie Television) centers in which you can choose a movie and watch it in your own private room. A free drink is included in the price of a ticket. These centers are marked by brightly colored MTV neon lights.

■ CHUNGCHENG CULTURAL CENTER

The Chungcheng Cultural Center offers opera performances, art exhibits and other programs. It is located near the intersection of Wufu 1st Rd and Hoping 1st Rd.

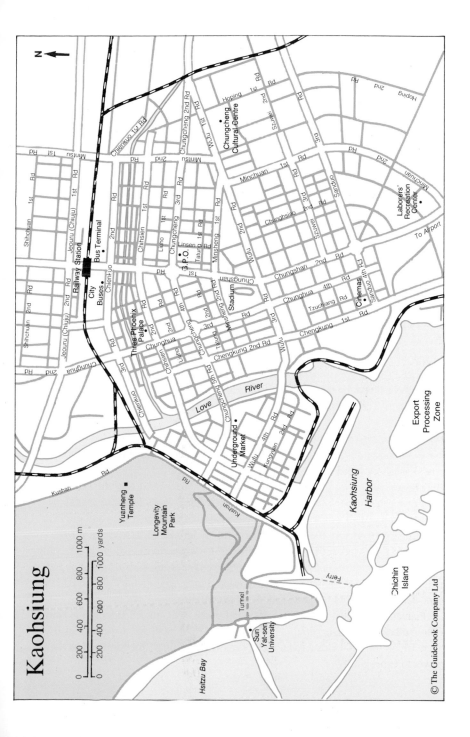

Kaohsiung

0   200   400   600   800   1000 m
0   200   400   600   800   1000 yards

N

Hsitzu Bay

Longevity Mountain Park

Yuanheng Temple

Kushan Rd

Kushan Rd

Sun Yat-sen University

Tunnel

Ferry

Chichin Island

Kaohsiung Harbor

Export Processing Zone

Love River

Underground Market

Wutu 4th Rd

Kungyuan 2nd Rd

Chungcheng 5th Rd

Chengkung 2nd Rd

Chienkuo

Chungcheng 4th Rd

Chunghua

Chihsien 3rd

Luho

Tatung 2nd

Minsheng 2nd Rd

Chungcheng 2nd

3rd

Thien Phoenix Palace

Chihsien 2nd

Chienkuo 2nd Rd

Chungchua 2nd Rd

Shihchuan 2nd Rd

Jeouru (Chiuju) 2nd Rd

Shihchuan 2nd Rd

Jeouru (Chiuju) 1st Rd

Shihchuan 1st Rd

Minsu 1st Rd

Chienkuo 1st Rd

Railway Station

City Buses

Bus Terminal

Chien-Fuo

Chihsien 2nd

Chihsien 1st Rd

Luho 1st Rd

Chungcheng 1st Rd

Linsen 1st Rd

Tatun 1st Rd

P.O.

Chungshan 1st

Stadium

Chungshan

Minsu 2nd Rd

Chungcheng 3rd Rd

Chungching 2nd Rd

Hoping 1st Rd

2nd Rd

Chungcheng Cultural Centre

Wutu

Szuwei

Minchuan 1st Rd

Chunghsiao 3rd

2nd

1st

Minsheng 1st Rd

Chungshan 2nd Rd

Sanduo

Szuwei

Sanduo 3rd Rd

Chunghua 4th Rd

Tzuchiang

Cinemas

Sanduo 4th Rd

Chengkung 1st Rd

To Airport

Laborers' Recreation Center

Minchuan 2nd Rd

Hoping 2nd Rd

© The Guidebook Company Ltd

Around Kaohsiung

■ TSOYING

Tsoying, 20 minutes north of the city, has several attractions, including Lotus Lake, formerly a reservoir used for irrigation purposes, with its Spring and Autumn Pavilion. The pavilion is in the middle of the lake, connected to land by a bridge with nine curves. To the north of the lake is Kaohsiung's new Confucius Temple. Other sites include the twin seven-tiered Dragon and Tiger Pagodas and the South and North Gates built during the Qing Dynasty, with vivid carvings of door gods on their outer walls.

The **Fengshan Old City Wall**, an Historical Site of the First Rank, dates back to 1722, when the magistrate of Fengshan built a four-meter-tall earthen enclosure. Gates stood at the four compass points, and a 2.5-meter-deep moat was dug around the wall. A bamboo fence was ordered erected in 1734, giving the town three lines of defense, and in 1769 cannons were emplaced at the gates.

In 1786, during the Lin Shuang-wen rebellion, the wall was occupied by a rebel leader. After order returned to Taiwan, officials decided that the wall's layout, which followed the mountains' contours, made it vulnerable to attack and difficult to defend. An order was given for a new wall, which later became known as the Old City Wall.

In 1825–6 the government extended the original foundations; the wall measured 3.7 meters tall and 4.6 meters thick. Parapets were built on top of the wall and a moat dug beneath. The four gates of the original wall remained, with cannons placed at each.

This plan represents the layout of the Old City Wall as it is today. No record exists of renovations or repairs after 1850, but the area continued to be a military post throughout Japan's occupation and even after 1945.

The wall and moat gradually deteriorated, and now only parts of the east, south and north gates remain, along with traces of the wall. Today a little over 1,000 meters of the Old City Wall remain, with the sections around the North Gate and the East Gate the best preserved, classic examples of the traditional Chinese city wall. The West Gate, destroyed during the early years of the Japanese occupation, retains only the tablet that once stood over the inner entrance. The South Gate now serves as a traffic circle, but the original structures collapsed long ago, leaving only the entrance core. The gate's restoration was carried out after 1945.

Painted plaster effigies of door gods stand to the right and left sides of the North Gate. Yu Lei, on the right, holds a jade ring in his right hand and a spear in his left. Shen Tu, on the left, holds a spear and a hammer; in Chinese tradition he has the power to expel ghosts.

■ MAOLIN

Maolin, home to the 1,500 members of the Rukai aborigine tribe, is a township just inside the mountains, 45 kilometers north of Kaohsiung. The Rukai are one of the island's smaller tribes. The majority live in the southwestern part of the island and most of their villages are in restricted areas that require a difficult to obtain Class A mountain pass to visit. To enter Maolin you need a Class B pass, which is easily obtained at the entrance gate by producing a passport, alien resident certificate or local identification card.

The town is still relatively unknown to travelers outside of southern Taiwan and remains unspoiled. There are no hotels here, only facilities for camping.

The first and main village of Maolin is three kilometers up the road from the entrance. The village has no traditional structures, as the Rukai live in the same concrete buildings found all over the island. Some 500 meters down the mountainside from Maolin are Lover's Valley, a suspension bridge and areas along the river for camping and picnicking. About 1.5 kilometers up the road from Maolin Village is a much more interesting area, where the Kaohsiung County Government is building recreation facilities. The area, called **Maolin Valley**, has its own suspension bridge and places for camping and picnicking. Across the bridge is a stream that flows over a low precipice into a clear pool and on into the river. A path leading up the left side of the stream crosses a concrete bridge. Follow it for 40 minutes to reach **Maolin Valley Waterfall**. This path, high up on the steep mountainsides, is not dangerous because the slopes are thick with trees and bamboo, though it does entail some serious exertion. The trip is well worth the effort, however. The waterfall falls over a sheer rock into which it has worn a deep groove, and at the bottom forms a pool that drains into the rocky stream bed. A pavilion overlooking the pool is an ideal place for a picnic.

Back on the road, a five-minute walk leads to **Wanshan Village** and other hiking trails. One kilometer on is **Eagle Valley**, where the river makes a horseshoe turn, and where one can actually see eagles in the sky. There is a little store and a pavilion atop a steep hill beside the river.

Several kilometers from here, across the river, up a mountainside, then down a long, gentle incline, is the village of **Tona**, the most interesting place in the Maolin area. Many of the Rukai here live in traditional thick-walled slate houses, although most have modern amenities such as televisions and refrigerators. The main industry is turning out slate goods. Occasionally, Tona women wear colorful festival clothing.

The road stretches for another five kilometers to the **Tona Hot Springs**. The mineral baths were buried by a landslide in early 1991, but residents say they will restore the springs and build a hotel. Some food is available here, but plan to bring your own. There is a road to Tona, but no public transportation covers the 18-kilometer route.

PIGEON RACING

Pigeon racing in Taiwan is not for the chicken-hearted. The sport, a form of gambling, has been popular since around 1900, but the island's economic boom has increased the stakes and made it an increasingly risky proposition.

Some 35,000 people in Taiwan are active pigeon racers, most attracted by the thrill of the sport and the chance for big winnings. As much as US$7.5 million may change hands at a club of 100 members over a five-week season. One racer confided that he had won US$650,000 in a recently concluded season.

'It's very popular in Taiwan because the Taiwanese are gamblers and this is the biggest type of gambling here,' said one foreign businessman who actively follows the sport. 'The Taiwanese feel anxious and excited every time they race, but they only see the money. They are afraid, but they like this feeling and emotion.'

Although the winnings can be great, the cost of playing is high. Though a Taiwanese-bred pigeon costs only US$190, imports from Belgium, where the best racers are bred and trained, can cost as much as US$77,000 each.

Then there are registration fees, which can range from US$380 to US$1,900 per pigeon per season, depending on the club, with each member racing any-where from five to 60 birds. There is also the cost of food, vitamins and other medicines, and veterinary charges.

With only 10–15 racers winning in any one season, most enthusiasts end up in debt. Many have been forced to sell their homes.

The real victims, however, may be the pigeons. They must race in rain or shine with only a few day's rest in between competitions.

The 90-kilometer cross-island races require the birds to cross the north–south mountain range; strong pigeons, eager to stretch their wings, take the longer southern route, while weaker pigeons opt for the shorter northern route. As a result, some owners reduce feedings a few days before the race to weaken their pigeons and assure they take the shorter flight line.

The huge amounts of money involved have led to some deviant practices. To assure races are fair, officials put a secret numbered band on the ankle of each pigeon the night before a race.

In the case of Taipei clubs, the pigeons are trucked to Oluanpi, the southern-most tip of the island, where they are released at daybreak for the 380-kilometer race back to their home lofts in Taipei. When a pigeon arrives at its loft, the owner takes off the secret band and punches it with an official clock that records the bird's arrival time. The owner then heads off to the association for verification and official recording of the time.

The major form of cheating involves building a second loft not far from the release point. An owner in Taipei, for example, may train his pigeon to recognise a second home in Kaohsiung, just north of Oluanpi.

After being released at Oluanpi, the bird will fly to the loft in Kaohsiung where it is picked up and flown back to Taipei, although this time the pigeon is an airplane passenger. This takes about 30 minutes, much faster than the pigeon's average flying time of about five hours. Once in Taipei, the bird is released and returns to his Taipei loft in 'record time.'

A bigger problem, however, is pigeon-napping in the mountains. Pigeons fly a fairly set pattern up and down the island, following the twists and turns of the mountains and flying low when the wind is strong. Poachers stand ready on the mountain tops with long, high nets that snare the birds, cutting short their race.

'Pigeons are smart,' says Liu Wan-lai, a pigeon racer, 'but people are smarter.'

After the pigeon is trapped, the captor uses the owner's telephone number, attached to the bird's ankle, and demands a ransom or part of the winnings, promising to rush the bird to Taipei and release it well in advance of the other racing pigeons. The owners often agree, either out of greed or fear of the extortionists, who are usually members of Taiwan's underground gangs.

Pigeon-napping, rapid urbanization, the stock market and real estate boom, underground investment houses and illegal lotteries have all taken their toll on the sport. As disgruntled pigeon fanciers have found easier ways to make money, it seems the sport will never regain its past fanaticism.

'The nets are a big headache' said the head of one Taipei club, 'and now you can earn money faster in the stock market and illegal lotteries.'

GETTING THERE

To reach Maolin from Kaohsiung take a bus to Pingtung, and from there transfer to one of six daily buses operated by the Pingtung Bus Co to Maolin Village.

■ LIUKUEI (SIX TURTLES)

Not far from Maolin is Liukuei, a quiet village located in a valley northeast of Kaohsiung. There are infrequent buses to Liukuei from Kaohsiung. It is also possible to reach the village by bus from Pingtung City.

■ MEINUNG

Meinung is a very old village, an extremely pleasant place where Hakka culture is diligently maintained.

The Hakkas, literally 'guest people,' originally lived along the Yellow River several thousand years ago, but were forced southward by invasions from northern tribes in the 5th century. They were the first Chinese to come to Taiwan, arriving via the Pescadores Islands.

The town's main part is uninteresting, but if you venture down side streets you will see fascinating old houses. For a better look at the area, hire a taxi for about NT$200 for a long ride through farm areas. Meinung is surrounded on three sides by mountains. The rows of betel nut trees lining the roads and ridges between paddy fields give it a tropical flavor. Meinung is Taiwan's leading tobacco producing area, and from November to February the air is full of the leafy aroma.

Meinung has about 500 small temples devoted to the Earth God, and many traditional *sanheyuan*, U-shaped homes with ancestral shrines. These dwellings, many of which are more than 100 years old, can be found along old streets such as Chungshan Rd, Chungcheng Rd, and Yungan Rd.

Beside the East Gate Bridge that crosses the Meinung River, is **East Gate**, built in 1756 to provide protection from attack. The original gate was destroyed by Japanese artillery in 1895 when they took over Taiwan, and was rebuilt in 1937. The structure's upper room houses Qing-dynasty stone sculptures. Not far from the main town is **Butterfly Valley**, where the air is thick with fluttering butterflies on sunny days between March and June.

Meinung is best known as a producer of oiled-paper umbrellas, an old Hakka craft. Meinung residents say umbrellas are auspicious since their round shape symbolizes completeness and fullness. Take time to visit one of the five family factories where you can watch craftsmen make the umbrellas by hand, an art passed down for generations.

Making a traditional umbrella is a slow process that requires much skill. The first step is to saw special species of bamboo for the buttresses. The bamboo is soaked in water for a month to leech out the sap, which attracts bugs. After soaking the ribs, a head and handle must be formed. A special borer is used to pierce holes at critical spots along the ribs. Then the ribs are tied in place with cotton thread. Mien paper (similar to that used in calligraphy) is immersed in a vat of persimmon juice adhesive for half an hour. The paper is pressed between boards to squeeze out excess moisture and then glued to the ribs. After drying in the sun, the umbrella is given a coat of wood oil.

The umbrellas come in various sizes, sell for NT$450–2000, and are valued more for their beauty than utility; they are often used for interior decoration.

The umbrellas should not be kept locked away. They require airing and occasional sunning to keep them from cracking. Kuo Fu-hsin, who traces his skill back to masters on the mainland, has a factory at 100 Minsheng Rd, Taian Li, Meinung, where you can watch umbrellas being made by hand. Hakka umbrellas can also be bought at a few craft shops in Taipei at slightly higher prices.

The Meinung Kiln, No. 6, Lane 496, Fumei Rd, just off the main road leading into Meinung, sells a unique style of porcelain and pottery designed in-house. Take a walk through the factory and watch pieces being produced. The company has a showroom adjoining the factory where items are on sale.

The earthy Hakka cuisine, a fad in Taipei in recent years, remains almost unknown outside of Asia. It is authentic and cheap in Meinung. Popular Hakka dishes include pig's feet, tripe, *kourou* (fatty pork served with dried vegetable), salted cabbage and pickled vegetables. A delicious snack sold at most shops in the main town is *bantiao,* thick rice noodles cooked in soup and served with thin slices of pork.

GETTING THERE
Frequent direct buses leave Kaohsiung for the one-hour ride to Meinung. You can also take a bus from Tainan and switch for the bus to Meinung at Chishan. The trip takes about 1 1/2 hours.

■ FOKUANG SHAN
Fokuang Shan is a sizeable Buddhist temple that attracts visitors from all over Taiwan and Asia. Run by the flamboyant Master Hsing Yun (Star Cloud), a monk from mainland China, it is one of the wealthiest temples on the island. Crowning the temple's summit is a 25-meter-tall gold statue of Buddha standing on a 12-meter-high pedestal and flanked by 480 other Buddhist images, each 1.8 meters tall. There are several other halls and shrines within the temple, including 'Buddhaland,' a Disneyland-like artificial cave with mechanical Buddhas and numerous other religious exhibits, many of which border on the sacrilegious.

ENVIRONMENT

Several years ago a leading newspaper told the story of a young woman who tried to commit suicide by jumping into the murky Tamsui River. She had second thoughts after hitting the water, however, and quickly swam ashore. After climbing to safety, she reportedly complained that the murky water was 'a fate worse than death.'

When classes opened at the Ta Wen elementry school in the southern city of Tainan, all 200 students sported the latest addition to the school uniform—surgical masks. Like many other residents of Taiwan, the students and faculty of the school were bothered by pollution from nearby factories.

Taiwan's economic miracle has turned the island into a capitalist showcase, but not without serious side effects. Many of the island's major river systems are seriously polluted, the level of metal contamination of farmland exceeds goverment safety limits, cancer is the leading birth defect and lung diseases are on the rise.

While little was said about environmental problems until recent years, economic prosperity and political liberalization have both helped to foster a grassroots concern for the quality of life. As a result, a growing environmental movement is increasingly challenging industries, forcing polluters to clean up or close down and move out.

Industrialists, who say they cannot change overnight, do not try to hide their distaste for environmentalists and the government's failure to control what they see as a reckless movement. 'One should tackle the environmental problem in an orderly manner, with knowledge and priorities,' says a leading industrialist.

Environmentalists, however, say that companies have been unwilling to take measures to correct serious environmental problems on their own and that the government has failed to enforce regulations.

'Over the last 40 years, Taiwanese industry has failed to implement pollution control measures,' says Lin Jun-yi, professor of biology at Tunghai University.

The Environmental Protection Agency is caught between industrialists pushing for moderation and environmentalists complaining that the government has been inefficient and too slow to act.

EPA officials point out that although the government has increased its budget and its staff has more than doubled, it is faced with an enormous task.

According to EPA statistics, Taiwan has the second highest population density in the world, with 553 people per square kilometer. The statistics point to other problems as well. There are 80,000 registered manufacturers around the island—and maybe an equal number that are unregistered—many of them small factories which cannot afford pollution control equipment.

More than two million automobiles and seven million motorcycles ply the island's streets and highways, giving Taiwan the highest vehicle density in the world. The pig population of seven million turns out waste equivalent to that of 42 million human beings. Furthermore, less than 4 per cent of households around Taiwan are connected to sewer systems.

Some companies have been reluctant to make the effort to control pollution, at times prompting the EPA to adopt a get-tough policy. One method that proved successful was Operation Rambo, with the director-general himself leading surprise late-night inspections of major manufacturers known to be shutting off pollution control equipment at night to save money.

A more serious—and potentially explosive—problem concerns plans for construction of the island's fourth nuclear power plant, held up since 1985 in the Legislative Yuan. Taiwan Power Company (Taipower) officials say the island is facing an energy crisis and they will have to ration electricity usage to avoid temporary losses of power. However, environmentalists and scholars say that Taipower has not satisfactorily proved the need for a new plant and has failed to find ways to reduce energy consumption and develop new sources of energy. The government has given Taipower permission to begin construction in 1992, with completion set for the year 2000. The decision led to demonstrations in late 1991, in which one policeman was killed and 17 others injured when police clashed with anti-nuclear demonstrators.

While it appears that some manufacturers and industries will not be able to survive in an age of environmental awareness, the situation is encouraging the government and manufacturers on the island to quicken the pace of industrial restructuring with emphasis on high-tech industries turning out higher quality products with less pollution.

The temple has an international department—it has branches in the United States—with lay volunteers who speak excellent English and who can explain Buddhism and the temple.

Guests are welcome to stay at the temple. The accommodation varies from simple dormitories to hotel-style rooms with air-conditioning, color TVs and other amenities. Guests can enjoy vegetarian meals at the temple's huge dining hall. As in other temples around the island that offer meals, there is no menu. You get what they serve that day. There is no fixed charge, but guests must leave a donation for food and lodging.

GETTING THERE

Fokuang Shan is about an hour northeast of Kaohsiung. Buses leave the eastern terminal in Kaohsiung regularly.

Pingtung County

■ SANTIMEN

Santimen is a small Paiwan aboriginal town located at the juncture of plains and mountains, set in peaceful surroundings with a rushing river. The area has three parts: Santimen, an authentic aboriginal village, Shuimen, the main market town, and the commercial Machia Aborigine Culture Park. The park is open from 9 am–5 pm with morning and afternoon aboriginal performances. Admission is NT$80.

Take a bus from Pingtung City to Santimen. Here you can get buses to Shuimen, from where you can walk to Machia Aborigine Culture Park 15 minutes away. During weekends and holidays there are direct buses to Machia.

■ HENGCHUN

The name Hengchun, Eternal Spring, has evolved over the centuries from a series of transliterations of Langchiao, which means Taiwan's Tail. This name was coined by the aborigines, the area's original inhabitants. This 'tail' was a neglected frontier until 1874 owing to its remoteness. At that time the Qing inspector general Shen Pao-chen, came to survey the Hengchun Peninsula. Shen, a reformist, decided that Hengchun would be a good defensive position against any Japanese invasion. Over the next few years a powerful rampart of brick and lime was erected. This wall was 20 meters high, 8 meters thick, and ran 900 meters from east to west and 700 meters from north to south, with a gate and tall tower on each of the four corners. The walls and towers had either collapsed or been removed by 1945 when the Japanese returned the island to Chinese rule, but the gates remain standing.

There are frequent buses from Kaohsiung.

Kenting National Park

Kenting, nine kilometers south of Hengchun, is the site of Kenting National Park, one of Taiwan's most popular recreation spots. It opened in 1984 and was the island's first national park. Kenting means 'plowmen,' a reference to the early farmers from mainland China who settled the Hengchun Peninsula.

The sea is an attraction here, and there are many good beaches dotting the coast. Since the weather is usually warm, swimming is possible throughout the year, although rough weather and strong currents sometimes make it inadvisable. The beautiful waters and coral reefs off the west coast are home to a multitude of colorful and exotic sealife, making snorkeling and scuba diving popular sports.

The best time to come to Kenting is during the week when there are few visitors. Weekends and holidays are very crowded; be sure to make a hotel reservation.

GEOGRAPHY

Kenting Park is on the Hengchun Peninsula, the southernmost tip of the island, and is bounded by the Pacific Ocean on the east, the Taiwan Strait to the west and the Bashi Channel to the south. Not far to the south lie the northernmost islands of the Philippines; it is likely that many plants and possibly some of the island's aborigines came here from the Philippines.

The park's land area totals 17,731 hectares, and marine areas cover 14,900 hectares. The Hengchun Peninsula is the southern end of the Central Mountain Range.

The park was established to protect the natural scenery, ecosystems and historical heritage of the area. The highly diverse features of the Hengchun Peninsula reveal a living record of the earth's tectonic movement through millions of years.

The long, narrow Hengchun Valley divides the park into western and eastern sections. The western section is mainly made up of the Hengchun Plateau, with its coastal cliffs and coral reefs below. The eastern section includes sandstone peaks, uplifted cliffs, lowlying coral reefs, limestone caves, shell sands, estuaries and lakes.

The climate here is tropical, unlike the rest of subtropical Taiwan, with hot rainy summers and warm dry winters. Rainfall is plentiful in the summer and typhoons hit this region frequently between July and September. During the winter, from October to March, Siberian cold fronts move south down the Taiwan Strait. They gather momentum as they squeeze between the mountain chains on both sides of the narrow sea. As they move further south through the gorge of Shihmen (Stone Gate), the valleys of the Tawu Mountain and the Manchou Terrace, they descend in a swoop on Hengchun. The natives have aptly dubbed this northeastern gust 'loshanfeng', or 'the winds that fall from the mountains.'

FLORA AND FAUNA

The area's variable weather conditions and terrain support an extraordinary variety of plant species. The shore maintains a high complexity of coastal coral reef plants and tropical forests. The mountains preserve low-altitude natural forest communities and coral reef bushes, together with grassland, coast bushes and marsh plants. Land and sea work together to create a fascinating botanical landscape.

This varied topography and flora provide an excellent environment for animal habitats. The diversity of fauna includes 184 species of birds, 190 kinds of butterflies, 27 types of reptiles, 20 kinds of freshwater fish, and all kinds of insects.

Many migratory birds stop over here during different parts of the year, including brown shrikes, gray-faced buzzards, and Chinese sparrowhawks. In the fall, migrating birds stop over from Siberia, northeast China, Korea and Japan on their way to the warmer climes of the Philippines. In the past, the hunting of these migratory birds was a major annual event for the inhabitants of the Hengchun Peninsula, but this tradition can no longer be justified and is no longer allowed. Wild geese and ducks can be seen in the lakes and ponds, while small mammals roam through the uncut forests of Nanjenshan. The 60-kilometer coastline includes both the east and west coasts of the Hengchun Peninsula, and the waters contain a treasure-trove teeming with coral, shell life and tropical fish.

The Kenting Youth Activity Center

SIGHTS

■ KENTING BEACH

Kenting Beach is a white sand beach situated in the resort town of Kenting, where most visitors stay. The town has a variety of small hotels, bungalows, hostels, shops and seafood restaurants. Shops rent bicycles for one, two and three riders, motorscooters and jeeps. The beach across the road from the Caesar Park Hotel is a good place for swimming.

■ KENTING FOREST RECREATION AREA

Situated on a hill above Kenting Beach is the Kenting Forest Recreation Area, frequently mistaken for the national park. The area was formerly known as the Kenting Tropical Botanical Garden, a name given when the Japanese opened it 1906. The Japanese spared no efforts in obtaining plants from all over the world. There are now some 1,280 exotic plants here. The trees—including some which are quite rare—are all identified in Chinese, English and Latin. There is a tropical rain forest and a coral tableland, with limestone stalagmite and stalactite caves. The area is known for its coral formations. An observation tower overlooks the entire Oluanpi Peninsula.

Tachienshih Shan, a gigantic rock just north of the arched gate of the Kenting Forest Recreation Area, towers over the local scenery and has thus become the park's landmark. The rock was caught in a matrix during an underwater earthquake and, owing to its tough material composition, which is harder than the surrounding mudstone, it has with-

Crab, Chichin Island

Lush vegetation

Wildlife

The clouded leopard once freely roamed the mountains of Taiwan. It has not been seen for years, and no one knows how many, if any, still exist. Also conspicuous by its near absence is the Formosan black bear, Taiwan's largest beast. Scientists reckon it crossed over to Taiwan a million years ago when the island was still linked to mainland China. Both species are now classified as endangered. Dozens of other native animals, many of them rare sub-species, are on the verge of extinction, too. They, and endangered wildlife from other parts of the globe, are victims of Taiwan's rapid growth—of industrialization, pollution, indiscriminate hunting, logging, and greed.

'The idea that Chinese live in harmony with nature is just an illusion,' says Liu Hsiao-ju, a researcher with the Institute of Zoology at the Academia Sinica. 'The Chinese use whatever resources they have without considering whether it's good for the environment or not.' Taiwan's newfound wealth is also posing a threat to wildlife. 'With more money, many people want to try different things,' she says. 'They keep a rare bird in a cage or serve a guest an endangered salamander for dinner.'

The government is taking steps to stop the trade in endangered species and protect Taiwan's wildlife. After international observers pointed out that Beijing had enacted a conservation law and was farther ahead than Taipei in protecting endangered fauna, the Taiwan government finally pushed through its Wildlife Conservation Law.

Trade in rhinoceros products has been banned since 1985, and in 1989 the government moved against the sale of rhino horn, asking doctors to register and phase out their stocks. That same year the government announced a ban on the import of all raw and finished ivory products. About two dozen animals were designated 'national treasures' and brought under the protection of the Cultural Assets Preservations Act. Nine nature reserves and five national parks have been established to protect rare animals such as the clouded leopard.

But with pollution, indiscriminate hunting, logging and farming pushing back the odds of survivial for many local species, conservationists say far more commitment is needed from the government and the public if wildlife is to be protected. The government has only ten field zoologists actively involved in wildlife conservation. 'That,' says Liu, 'is like a country doctor serving a population of 200,000 people.'

stood the effects of erosion. Tachienshih Shan stands 318 meters tall and is supported by steep cliffs, looking like a massive slab of stone from one angle. From Oluanpi it resembles a pointed stone, hence its name, 'Big Point Stone Mountain.'

Two routes lead to the top of Tachienshih Shan. Shortly after entering the front gate, look for a dirt road on the left. Walk to the front of the mountain, where you will see cow pastures and a gate. Pass through the gate and walk uphill along the fence until you find the path up to the top. Another route takes you back down the mountain. Both walks are difficult.

■ LIVESTOCK RESEARCH STATION
The Livestock Research Station, located in front of Kenting Beach, is open to the public. The area has more than 1,000 hectares and is the largest ranch in Taiwan, with cattle, sheep and goats.

■ SAIL ROCK
Sail Rock is a huge coral rock 18 meters tall standing in the sea between Kenting and Oluanpi.

■ NANJENSHAN ECOLOGICAL PROTECTION AREA
The rolling terrain of the Nanjenshan Ecological Protection Area, the last remaining virgin lowland forest on the island, is interspersed with mountains and dense colonies of plants. In the back valley, sheltered from the wind, is a tropical rain forest. On the windward side a monsoon forest has been created. Humidity differences and topographical variation have created areas where wetlands and aquatic plants flourish. There are more than 1,000 species of vascular plants in the forest area, some of which are rare and endemic.

According to an old legend, there once stood on the south side of Lofo Mountain some 200 houses, 1.36 meters in length and depth, all built from stone slabs, with deep holes inside. These houses belonged to a tribe called Lofo, whose tribesmen were no taller than the houses, but who were feared by other aborigines for their remarkable strength and savagery. A tribe called the Chulao later trapped and killed the Lofo, but a small number managed to survive and fled to Painan. The stone slabs were removed by the natives, taken away for their own use, and only a few remain.

This aboriginal legend, enhanced by the discovery of stone remains in the forests of Nanjenshan by mountaineers, has stirred up great interest among anthropologists and archaeologists, who have studied the area and found graves and artifacts. The tribe has been identified as the Paiwan, related to people living today in the mountains near Pingtung, and the stone houses are said to date back some 700 years.

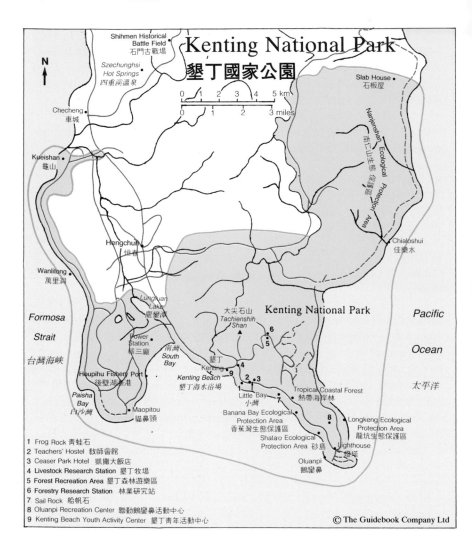

1 Frog Rock 青蛙石
2 Teachers' Hostel 教師會館
3 Ceaser Park Hotel 凱撒大飯店
4 Livestock Research Station 墾丁牧場
5 Forest Recreation Area 墾丁森林遊樂區
6 Forestry Research Station 林業研究站
7 Sail Rock 船帆石
8 Oluanpi Recreation Center 聯勤鵝鑾鼻活動中心
9 Kenting Beach Youth Activity Center 墾丁青年活動中心

© The Guidebook Company Ltd

■ BANANA BAY ECOLOGICAL PROTECTION AREA

The 12-kilometer tropical coastal forest stretching from South Bay to Oluanpi was declared a national monument during the Japanese occupation. Population pressure and destruction of the forest through logging and agriculture after World War II, have reduced it to a small stretch just 1.5 kilometers long. It is now protected from further devastation after being designated a special ecological zone. The remaining forest, though small, is highly complex in its variety of species, dominated by the fruits and seeds which drifted here from the Philippines and the Indo-Malay region.

■ SHATAO ECOLOGICAL PROTECTION AREA

At **Shatao Village** is a section of beach about 150 meters long, paved with minute shells. These shiny, smooth shells are actually a fine blend of shell, coral and quartz all ground by the waves and then washed ashore. They are commonly called shell sand or pearl sand.

■ LUNGLUAN LAKE

Lungluan Lake, three kilometers southwest of Hengchun and just north of a nuclear power plant, is a popular spot for bird watching. Every fall many migrant birds from Siberia, Japan, Korea and Northeast China rest here on their southward flight to the Philippines.

■ MAOPITOU

Maopitou, or Cat's Nose Tip, is located on the southernmost tip of the peninsula's west arm. It is a good place to view Tachienshih Shan, the Oluanpi lighthouse and South Bay. To get to Maopitou, take a bus to Hengchun and change for Maopitou.

■ LONGKENG

Longkeng, or Dragon Cave, is the east coast's point of termination at the southern tip of the island. Currents from the Pacific Ocean collide here, throwing massive breakers against the jagged rocks. Over millions of years the combined force of wind and waves has created coral limestone fractures, deep caves and other interesting formations.

■ CHIALOSHUI

Chialoshui, facing the Pacific Ocean 14 kilometers east of Hengchun, is one of the most popular scenic spots on the Hengchun Peninsula. The area is known for its coral limestone formations, spewed from the bed of the ocean by a huge upheaval long before recorded history.

■ OLUANPI

Oluanpi, eight kilometers south of Kenting on the southernmost tip of the island, is marked by a lighthouse built in 1882. The beam from the lighthouse, said to reach 20 nautical miles, has saved many ships from destruction on the coral shoals.

On a clear day you can see across the Bashi Channel to the Philippines. There are

18 scenic points in Oluanpi, linked by a maze of paved paths leading past ancient and interestingly shaped coral heads that rose from the sea eons ago and became covered with dense vegetation. Along many of the paths are pavilions that provide places of rest and spectacular views. Recent archaeological digs have uncovered pottery and stone utensils, indicating that Oluanpi was inhabited millenniums ago.

The area has several white sand beaches good for swimming, snorkeling, scuba diving and collecting shells.

■ HISTORICAL SITES

The park's many historical sites fall into three categories: prehistoric sites, the Taiya Village sites, and old mountain trails.

More than 60 prehistoric sites have already been identified, including the slab house at Nanjenshan, and a slab coffin, dating back some 4,000 years, at Oluanpi.

The 79 Taiya villages belonged to the Taiya aborigine tribe. Its members practiced facial tattooing and teeth filing. Theirs was a fairly sophisticated culture, with highly developed weaving skills.

The 100-year-old **Hohuan Old Trail** traverses the Liwu River Valley. Many sections of this trail are still in good condition.

GETTING THERE

First go to Kaohsiung by bus or train, a minimum of four hours from Taipei, or by airplane, a 40-minute flight from the Sungshan Domestic Airport in Taipei. There is an infrequent direct bus from Kaohsiung to Kenting; if you miss the direct bus, take a bus to Hengchun, nine kilometers north of Kenting, and switch there for a local bus. The bus from Kaohsiung to Hengchun passes the Kaohsiung Airport so if you fly you can catch that bus directly.

Buses leave Hengchun for Kenting about once every 40 minutes. The ride from Kaohsiung to Kenting takes about two and a half hours, the ride from Hengchun about 20 minutes. Taxis are also available between Hengchun and Kenting. Guests staying at the Caesar Park Hotel can take the hotel's shuttle bus from the Kaohsiung Airport.

Taiwan is home to a wide variety of exotic butterflies

Offshore Islands

Several small islands of interest surround the main island of Taiwan. You must bring your passport when visiting these islands.

Penghu (Pescadores)

Penghu, formerly known as the Pescadores (Fishermen's Isles), a name bestowed by 16th-century Portuguese mariners, is an archipelago of 64 islands that dot a surface area of 1,555 square kilometers in the Taiwan Strait. The total land area is 127 square kilometers and the population numbers about 120,000, with more than half living in the Penghu Island area, mainly in Makung, the only town of any size in the group. Only 20 of the islands are inhabited; Penghu, Hsiyu, and Paisha are the main islands, connected to each other by bridges.

Fishing is the main activity, with farming less so because of the strong winds that sweep across the islands. Vegetable plots are protected from the winds by stone walls. Kaoliang, a type of sorghum used to make a potent liquor, sweet potatoes and peanuts are the main crops.

With the exception of Makung, Penghu remains relatively unspoiled by Taiwan's modernization. Old China persists here in rustic stone walls, farm women with faces covered to protect them from the harsh wind, carts loaded with farm produce, quaint fishing boats and nets hanging on walls.

Because of its location, Penghu has played a pivotal role in the history of Taiwan and China. It was made an administrative territory of China in 1281 and served as a bridge for immigrants making their way to Taiwan 400 years later. Throughout modern history, the islands have been a base for pirates and a staging area for attacks launched against Taiwan proper. At different times Penghu has been occupied by the Dutch, French and Japanese, and in the past numerous Asian and European ships ran aground on the island's treacherous coral shoals. Sites of shipwrecks are marked by memorials along the coast. Its proximity to mainland China makes Penghu strategically important in the defense of Taiwan, as shown by the large military presence.

Penghu Island

Makung is located on the main island of Penghu and is the only city in Taiwan with major portions of its city wall and gate still intact. The white sand beach at Lintou Park and the beach at Shihli, 14 kilometers south of Makung, are good for swimming.

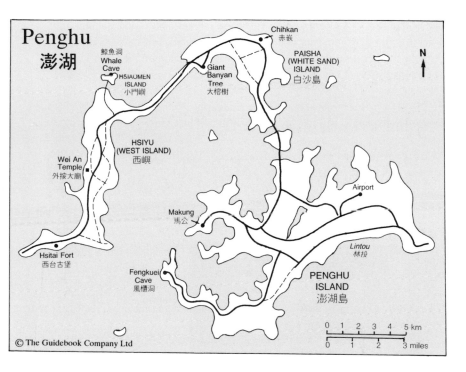

■ MATSU (TIENHOU) TEMPLE

More than 140 temples dot the Penghu islands, but the most important is the Matsu, or Tienhou Temple, one of 18 historical sites of the first rank on the island. The temple was founded in honor of the Goddess of the Sea during the early Ming Dynasty (1368–1644), making it the oldest temple in Taiwan. It was first enlarged to commemorate Yu Ta-yu's defeat of the Japanese in 1563. It was further enlarged and renovated in 1592, when Ming armies won another victory over the Japanese. The temple was renovated again in 1624 when the Dutch left Penghu, and once again in 1923 during the Japanese occupation.

The roof has a wide curve with unusually high, swallow-tailed eaves. Observed from the side, one can see the clustering rooftops of the various halls and chambers. Some of the stone for the walls came from the seaside. The walls are plastered with white stucco.

The front hall, known as the **Hall of the Three Gates**, is marked by superbly carved beams and rafters. The **Pu Kou Colonnade** has pots carved to look like flower pots suspended from the eaves. The border decoration on the colonnade's base depicts episodes from the classical novel, *The Investiture of the Gods*, also the source of operas for temple festivals. The wood carving shows great attention to detail in expression, garments and surroundings. The bracket-sets perpendicular to the right and left of the door are carved with representations of the Eight Immortals and a variety of floral motifs. Note the masterfully carved stone lion above the colonnade.

The door panels of the **Main Hall** are embellished with intricately carved, lifelike bird and floral motifs, with the ground layer carved in a pattern of interlocking swastikas, symbols of never-ending good fortune. The inscription over the altar of the Main Hall is embossed with characters written by Emperor Chien-lung with black characters on a gold background. Also notable here are the gold powder paintings on both sides of the altar, portraying traditional literary motifs common in Chinese religious art. The paint, made from gold powder, must be carefully applied to a black surface, maintaining strict control over the temper and consistency of the paint. One of these paintings shows Meng Hao-jan, a Tang-dynasty poet, searching for plum blossoms in the snow. The paintings, by Chu Hsi-kan and his brother, Chu Shu, (two craftsmen), date from the 1920's.

Chinese New Year door decorations, Penghu

In the **Posterior Hall** is a tablet commemorating the victory of General Shen Yujung over the Dutch in 1604, Taiwan's oldest stelae.

PAISHA (WHITE SAND) ISLAND

Paisha Island is connected to Penghu Island by a bridge. A major point of interest on Paisha is a 300-year-old banyan tree, whose luxuriant foliage is supported by a latticed roof covering an area of 700 square feet. It is situated in front of the Paoan Temple, and faces the five-

Fishing boats, Penghu

kilometer-long Penghu Bay Bridge, which leads to Hsiyu Island. This is one of two bridges that connect the island group.

Hsiyu Island
■ **HSITAI FORT**

On Hsiyu's southern tip is Hsitai Fort, built in 1886 by Liu Ming-chuan, the official who implemented the extensive modernization of Taiwan in the 1880s. War broke out between China and France in 1884, and in 1885 the French seized Penghu under Admiral Courbet. Taiwan itself was in danger of collapsing, but was saved by Liu's valiant defense. After Taiwan became a province of China in 1886, Liu was appointed governor. He set out to strengthen Taiwan's defenses, and built a network of ten forts, including four in Penghu.

The fort is situated on a hill, giving it a vast view of Makung's port below. An extensive network of tunnels runs throughout the fort's walls, with ventilation and light provided by skylights. The overall layout is rectangular, though the passages within follow the pattern of the tridentate Chinese character *shan* (mountain). A small circular platform was designed for cannons, and holes in the wall stored ammunition. The red brick walls, more than three feet thick, were plastered with stucco, and the fort was built to hold more than 5,000 troops. The front gate of the enclosure wall is marked by a massive stone arch, upon which are written the words 'Hsi Tai of the Western Isles,' on a tablet. The inscription was made by the famous Qing diplomat Li Hung-chang (1823–1901). The fort is a Historical Site of the First Rank.

A narrow bridge just off Hsiyu's northern tip links the island to **Hsiaomen**, another small island.

■ SHOPPING

Penghu is known for its coral products, gathered by fisherman and fashioned by local craftsmen. However, Taipei dealers regularly snatch up the best coral so Taipei may be a better place to make your purchase. Penghu peanuts are used to make tasty candies and cookies, and in summer you can buy especially sweet and juicy cantaloupes.

GETTING THERE

Regular flights link Taiwan with Makung. The flight from Taipei takes 35 minutes, and from Kaohsiung 25 minutes. China Airlines, Far Eastern Transport, Formosa Airlines, Fohsing Airlines and Great China Airlines all fly to Penghu. City buses go to the airport about once every hour. Taxis are also available.

A regular ferry service between Kaohsiung and Makung departs Pier No. 1 every morning at 9 am and arrives in Makung at 12:30 pm. Boats leave Makung at 3 pm and arrive back in Kaohsiung at 6:30 pm. Tickets for the boat can be purchased at Southeast Travel Service, 106 Chungcheng 4th Rd, Kaohsiung, Tel (07)231-2181. If you fly to Penghu and want to take the boat back, you can buy a ticket at the Southeast Travel office in Makung, 26 Chungshan Rd, Tel (06)926-1210.

Do not travel to Penghu from October to March. During this winter monsoon season the wind speeds are so high and the seas so rough that fishermen do not allow their boats to leave the harbor, and the passenger ferries from Makung to Chimei do not run, nor are charter boats available to visit the surrounding islands.

OUTER ISLANDS
■ CHIMEI

Chimei, the Island of the Seven Beauties, is 29 kilometers south of Makung. It is only four kilometers wide at its widest point and is no more than ten square kilometres in area. Swimming is possible, but there are no sand beaches.

The island is so named because during the Ming Dynasty (1368–1644) seven virgins drowned themselves in a well to escape being defiled by marauding pirates. People were so moved by the womens' virtue they erected a tomb of honor, known today as the Tomb of the Seven Beauties.

Some 10 minutes south of Nanhu Harbor is a walled cove called Big Harbor, a popular place for fishing and watching the tides. To the west are spectacular views of a cliff made of vertical black basalt columns. Beside the cove along the coastline are a series of conical stone structures topped with small figures such as dragons, birds and unicorns, creatures that repel evil forces.

A short distance down the road from here is the Tomb of the Seven Beauties, and a colorful temple. Further on at the tip of the island is a white lighthouse and a pavilion for looking at the 'stone woman,' a rock formation that resembles a pregnant woman lying down. According to local lore, the wife of a fisherman lost at sea sat here waiting for his return until she turned into stone.

The road here heads north up the east coast past small villages, harbors and basalt cliffs. Not far from the north shore are two modern windmills. At the island's northeastern tip is a harbor made of piled stone. The road along the north shore is unpaved and uninteresting. It winds southward past the airport, then heads back into populated areas. A new tourist attraction here is the newly reconstructed town wall, originally built in the mid-1700s.

GETTING AROUND CHIMEI

You can rent motor scooters to get around the island; there are also a handful of taxis, private cars and minibuses. A public bus runs two or three times a day, mainly as a schoolbus. Taxi drivers, who ferry visitors to and from the airport, are also available for tours around the island, which take about 1 1/2 hours. A good way to see the island is to walk its perimeter. A leisurely walk takes half a day and enables you to visit all the scenic places.

The village has a few basic inns and simple restaurants.

GETTING THERE

Boats operating between Chimei and Makung take about two hours, depending on the sea's roughness. Two light aircraft serve Chimei, one with eight seats and the other with 16 seats. The flight from Makung takes just 15 minutes, and the one from Kaohsiung, 40 minutes.

■ CHIPEI ISLAND

Visiting Chipei Island is like stepping back in time. The main part of this rustic town has only a few shops and restaurants. There are no vehicles on the island, so walking and bicycling are the main forms of transportation. The beach here is made of tiny coral and not sand, so it is slightly rough on the feet. The Chipei Spa Paradise, located on the beach, has dormitory rooms for NT$200 and twin rooms for NT$1,000. There is also an area for camping if you bring a tent. Beach bicycles with large round tires for riding on the water are available for rent, as well as other equipment for water sports. In the village there are some guest houses.

GETTING THERE
No airplanes fly to Chipei, but several companies in Chihkan, on the north coast of Paisha Island, operate a boat service: Hawaii Boat Co, Tel (06) 993-2237; Paisha Boat Center, Tel (06)993-1917; Aimin Boat Co, Tel (06)993-2232.

Hsiao Liuchiu

Hsiao Liuchiu is a small island in the Taiwan Strait about 20 kilometers off the southwest coast of Taiwan. The island is less than seven square kilometers in area and the main industry here is fishing. Tourist sites are few and they can be covered in just a few hours by renting a motor scooter or taxi; about NT$300. A walking tour takes four hours and is more enjoyable. If you start at the ferry, walk through the village of **Matou** and proceed along the shore road heading southeast. You will soon leave the village and find yourself on a paved road that twists along the shoreline, punctuated by the occasional house, temple or tomb.

Moving south along the east coast of the island you will pass through several small villages. At the island's southern tip is a fork in the road; one road continues along the coast, and the other turns inland. Follow the coastal road until you reach a stretch of coral beach. If you swim, be careful of the strong undercurrents and wear rubber shoes to protect your feet.

Here at the southern tip is **Haikou**, a small harbor village, where you can rest and buy something to eat and drink. After you pass through Haikou continue to the west coast and in about a quarter of an hour arrive at **Black Ghost Cave**, with its natural freshwater spring and coral formations. People say this spring was once the campsite of the remnants of a Dutch naval force attempting to escape from Koxinga. When the Dutch withdrew from the cave they left their sick black galley slaves behind. The men later recovered but dared only come out at night to search for food. One year later some British seamen stopped here to get water. The frightened galley slaves killed the seamen and threw their bodies into the sea. The British retaliated by blocking the mouth of the cave with driftwood and setting it on fire. According to local legend, ghosts haunt the area, and are reportedly seen during Ghost Month (the seventh lunar month).

After leaving the cave continue north, and in about ten minutes you will see two beaches. After rounding the island's northern tip you reach **Beautiful People Cave**.

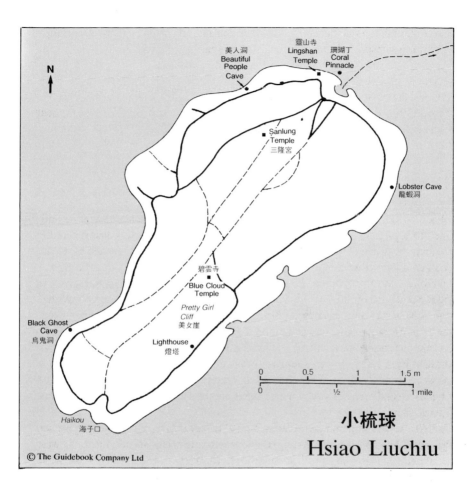

美人洞
Beautiful
People
Cave

靈山寺
Lingshan
Temple

珊瑚丁
Coral
Pinnacle

N

Sanlung
Temple
三隆宮

Lobster Cave
龍蝦洞

碧雲寺
Blue Cloud
Temple

Pretty Girl Cliff
美女崖

Black Ghost
Cave
烏鬼洞

Lighthouse
燈塔

0   0.5   1   1.5 m
0   ½   1 mile

Haikou
海子口

小梳球

Hsiao Liuchiu

© The Guidebook Company Ltd

Despite the name, this cave is supposedly the place where unwanted female infants were left to die. A shrine here is for offerings to appease the souls of the poor infants. After you walk around a bluff you will see statues of Chiang Kai-shek and Sun Yat-sen, completing your circular trip which begins and ends in Matou.

GETTING THERE
Take a bus from the Kaohsiung suburban bus terminal to Tungkang fishing harbor. Ferries leave from Tungkang frequently for the 40-minute trip to Matou, the largest village in Hsiao Liuchiu. The Chan'an Boat Co, Tel (07)211-2123, offers a package ticket for NT$260 including transportation to the ferry and the round trip ferry ride.

Its boat leaves from Linyuan, a small harbor north of Tungkang, with the departure at 7:30 am and the last boat back to Tungkang at 4 pm. You may be asked to show your passport or alien resident certificate before boarding the ferry.

There are several hostels on the island. The Hsiao Liuchiu Hotel, Tel (08)861-116, costs NT$150 a night for a dormitory bed and NT$550 for a single room, (NT$800 on weekends). The Pailungkung Lushe, Tel (08)861-2536, charges NT$200 for a double and NT$350 and up for a single with a private bath.

Lanyu (Orchid Island)

Lanyu, 76 kilometers off Taiwan's southeast coast, is the home of the Yami tribe, Taiwan's smallest and most primitive aborigine tribe. The name of the island comes from the profusion of wild orchards that grow on its steep hills.

During the occupation, the Japanese closely studied the tribe and treated the island like a living anthropological museum. It was only after Taiwan was returned to Chinese rule that the people began to have free contact again with the outside world. The Yami, not to be confused with the Ami, Taiwan's largest tribe, now number less than 3,000. They depend on fishing, and flying fish are a vital part of their diet. The Yami strictly follow ancient rules and taboos regarding the catching and preparing of the fish. Their main crops are taro, sweet potatoes and millet. They are ecologically-minded, planting only as much as they need, and gathering only what they can eat.

The origin of the Yami is obscure, though they are known to be closely related to a people living in Batan, an island lying in the Bashi Channel, halfway between Taiwan and the Philippine island of Luzon. The Yami say they sailed to Lanyu from Batan and this is likely since they speak the language of the people of Batan.

They live in six compact villages on the coast. Since the Yami for the most part continue to live their traditional life, few of them have much cash. Yet, with the exception of two villages that have been declared cultural preserves, most of the traditional dwellings are gone, and the Yami now live in nondescript concrete houses.

The main part of the traditional Yami house, called the winter house, is built in a stone-walled hole in the ground, leaving only the top of the roof exposed to the typhoons that sweep through here between May and November. The second part of the Yami dwelling is the work house, or summer house, which is built beside and at a right angle to the winter house, half above and half below the ground. The third section is the cool house, a simple thatch roof built over a platform with no walls that sits on stilts. This is the family room where members relax, smoke, and chew betel nut. Each house has a fish rack where the popular flying fish and other meats are hung out to dry.

Unlike other aboriginal tribes in Taiwan that have adopted western clothes, the older Yami men still wear loincloths and other traditional garb, and on special occasions wear ceremonial helmets made of silver rectangles beaten thin and tied together.

The Yami are known for the beauty of their small, graceful, high-prowed canoes, their most prized possession. A boy is accepted as a man when he builds his first boat, a job that takes months of work. The boats are made of planks of virgin timber joined by pegs. Despite the fact that no modern tools are used, the boats produced by the Yami are of perfect symmetry and flawless lines.

The island attracted a great deal of outside attention in recent years following the government's decision to locate a nuclear waste dump site there. The move led to

strong protests, which have not yet completely died down. The island is expected to be designated Taiwan's fifth national park soon.

Lanyu's beautiful coast deserves to be seen. Its perimeter of 37 kilometers can be walked in one long day or driven easily. Lanyu is very hot so be sure to wear a hat, carry water and bring suntan lotion. The only beach suitable for swimming is near the Lanyu Hotel, one of two hotels on the island offering basic accommodation; rooms can be booked by the airlines.

■ GETTING AROUND LANYU

Buses from the hotels travel around the island and stop at all the tourist sites, mainly stone formations on the coast and the cultural preserves at Yehyin and Langtao villages. The cost is NT$300 per person. A sedan with driver can be hired for NT$1,500 for the same tour. Motor scooters are available for hire at the hotels and cost about NT$100 an hour, or NT$500 per day.

■ SHOPPING

The Yami make clay figures, wooden boxes and carved replicas of their colorful boats. Though friendly, they do not like to be photographed and will object if you try to do so without asking first. Some may even ask for cigarettes or money. Photographers with a professional interest can obtain assistance from the Council for Cultural Planning and Development in Taipei; 4th Fl, 102 Aikuo East Rd, Tel 351-8030.

GETTING THERE

Formosa Airlines and Taiwan Airlines (Taiwan Aviation Co) operate about a dozen flights a day between Taitung and Lanyu. Small propeller aircraft are used for the trip which takes about 25 minutes. The round-trip ticket costs NT$1800. There are also three flights a day from Kaohsiung, 50 minutes away. Formosa Airlines plans to start a direct service from Taipei (check with the airline). The round-trip ticket is NT$2800. During off-peak periods, tickets can be purchased on the day you intend to fly. During the peak season in the summer and on weekends, make a reservation at least one day in advance. In bad weather air service is suspended. Both airlines have ticket offices in major cities around Taiwan.

The Lanyu Shipping Agency, a cargo shipper, takes passengers to Lanyu via Green Island, but in rough seas the trip is uncomfortable and the schedule uncertain. The ship usually departs from Fukang port on Tuesdays and Saturdays at around 5 am, which means spending the night at Fukang or taking a taxi from Taitung, 25 minutes away. The sea trip takes 4–5 hours and costs NT$300. The ship stops at Green Island to drop off cargo, allowing time for a quick swing around the island by taxi. Taxis are available for hire at the Green Island pier.

Coral wall, Feng Kuei, Penghu Island

Green Island (Lutao)

Green Island, known for its coastal scenery, is part of the East Coast National Scenic Area. The island remains essentially unspoiled and its reefs, clear water and beaches are good places for fishing, snorkeling and scuba diving.

The island, 42 nautical miles north of Lanyu and just 18 nautical miles off the east coast of Taitung County, has a population of just 4,500 people. It is home to a prison that once housed hard core criminals and political prisoners. Green Island is less interesting than Lanyu or Penghu and has remained off the tourist track; only travel there if you have extra time to spare.

The island, perhaps settled by the Yami several centuries ago, now has no aborigines and is entirely inhabited by Chinese. It was discovered by accident in 1804 when a small group of Chinese sailing from Hsiao Liuchiu was blown off course in a storm on its way to Hengchun. Chen Pi-hsien, one of the shipwrecked, returned the next year and settled on the island's north coast with several dozen other Chinese, at the site of present-day Kungkuan. The island was known as Fire Island prior to 1949 because of the fires lit to guide fishing boats safely home.

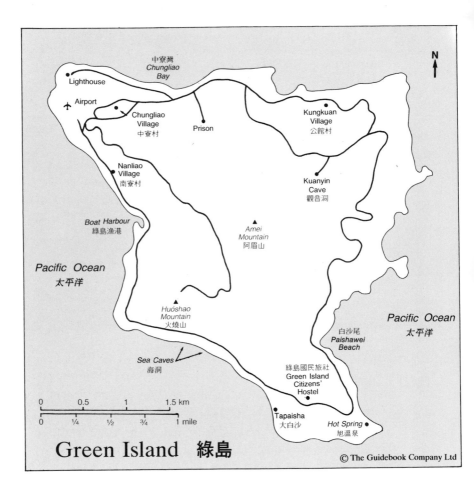

Green Island 綠島

© The Guidebook Company Ltd

Fishing is the main industry here, but some rice and other crops are grown. The main livestock here is deer, popular for its meat and the medicinal properties of its horns and other by-products.

The mountainous, volcanic island has remnants of craters on its forested peaks. The highest peak is Fireburn Mountain (261 meters). A road, mostly paved in concrete, runs along the shoreline around the island for 17 kilometers; it can be covered in about six hours on foot. Many people take a taxi from Kungliao halfway around to the hot spring on the island's southern tip and then walk back the other half to Chungliao Village on the northwest side of the island, close to the airport. Taxis charge about NT$600 for the entire trip, but make sure to agree on the price beforehand and be certain the driver will stop at the main points you wish to see.

A good place to start your tour is the colorful village of **Kungkuan** on the north coast. From here you can walk up the hill to Kuanyin Cave, a cool grotto with a small stream and a Goddess of Mercy shrine. According to one story, a fisherman lost at sea saw a fireball in the sky that led him to this cave. Inside the cave he found a rock that resembled Kuanyin and regarding this as a divine sign, prostrated himself in gratitude for his safe return. The stalagmite is now covered with a cape, and the shrine attracts numerous visitors from Taiwan who come here to burn incense.

Next head down the rugged, beautiful eastern coastline, with mountains dropping sharply into the sea and interesting rock formations on the shore and beyond.

The most popular attraction on the island is a **saltwater hot spring** at its southern end, said to be the only one in the world outside of Italy. The spring bubbles up through the rock that forms the southeastern shore, filling a series of holes just the right size for people to soak in. The water gets as hot as 55°C (130°F).

On the southwest coast is **Tapaisha**, or Big White Sand, noted for its long coral reefs. The coral comes right up to the shore so this is not a good place to swim. However, the colorful coral makes it an excellent place for snorkeling. A glass-bottomed boat is available for those who do not want to swim. From here, head up the west coast and pass three caves, a small port and several small villages before ending at the village of Chungliao.

The island's tallest lighthouse (35 meters) stands near Chungliao on the north coast. In 1937, the American steamer President Hoover was heading for Singapore on its maiden voyage when it ran aground here in thick fog. The natives of the island braved the rough night seas to save passengers and the crew, and later the foreigners donated money for the construction of this lighthouse.

■ GETTING AROUND GREEN ISLAND

Taxis are available and groups can rent small buses. The Green Island Hotel has two vans. Motor scooters can be rented at the airport for NT$300.

GETTING THERE

Far Eastern Air Transport offers two flights and Formosa Airlines offers four flights daily from Taipei. From Taitung, Formosa Airlines and Taiwan Airlines together offer about 13 flights daily in light, twin-engine aircraft. The flight takes just 15 minutes. Two ferries also travel to Green Island infrequently, and the trip takes 1 1/2 hours. A cargo boat run by the Lanyu Shipping Agency also visits the island twice a week on its way to Lanyu (see page 302). Remember to bring your passport or alien resident certificate.

Quemoy (Kinmen)

When the nationalist troops retreated in defeat from mainland China in 1949 they hung on to Quemoy and Matsu, two islands close to mainland China's Fujian Province. The military controlled the administration of the islands and established a significant troop presence. Military rule and martial law only came to an end in September 1991. There has been speculation for several years that Quemoy would open to tourism, but the island continues to be off limits for most people, open only to local residents, journalists and VIPs.

Quemoy, known as Kinmen, or Golden Gate in Chinese, is an island fortress 150 nautical miles from Taiwan, but just one kilometer from the nearest communist-controlled island, and just a few kilometers from the Chinese city of Xiamen (Amoy). Quemoy proper is the largest in an archipelago made up of 12 islands and covering an area of 148 square kilometers.

Chinese migrants first settled here in the early years of the Jin Dynasty (AD 265–316). In 803, a Tang-dynasty commissioner was appointed to develop the island, and his activities brought waves of new migrants from China. In 1387 the Ming government put up defensive walls, towers and earthworks. Ancient ruins and artifacts dot the island.

The island is a strategic defensive point blocking any possible attacks from the mainland against Taiwan. The Chinese communists have attempted on several occasions to take over the island. On October 24, 1949, after the communists had seized control of the mainland, some 28,000 Red Army troops sailed to the island on 3,000 boats in the Battle of Kuningtou. With their backs to the sea, the nationalist soldiers struck back fiercely, completely destroying the communist advance 56 hours later, leaving thousands dead on both sides.

In August, 1958 the well entrenched forces on the island were the target of a massive communist artillery barrage that saw half a million shells rain down over the next 44 days, killing 800 civilians and 600 soldiers. Taiwan struck back with 75,000 shells, destroying 279 artillery pieces, 97 artillery positions and numerous other military facilities on the mainland, while its air force knocked 31 communist planes out of the sky. Beijing announced a cease-fire on October 5 and on October 12 put into effect the even day cease-fire program, under which the two sides traded shells on odd days and observed a cease-fire on even days until 1978, when the United States officially recognized Beijing. Now the only sound comes from four microphones, 200 loudspeakers and a compact disc bombarding the mainland with rock songs and anti-communist messages. China stopped its propaganda broadcasts in mid-1991 to reduce tensions. The island remains in a state of military preparedness, with an estimated 60,000 soldiers stationed there.

Quemoy's terrain is rugged, and the sandy soil is suitable for only a few crops, such as peanuts, sweet potatoes, corn, wheat and barley. There are 43,000 civilians on the island, each of whom becomes a member of the Self-Defense Garrison upon reaching the age of 16.

Despite being a military fortress, Quemoy has a lot to offer the potential tourist.

■ MONUMENTAL STONE GATE
  TUNG-MEN ST, HOU-PU

In Kincheng, a Qing-dynasty stone gate honors Madame Hsu, the virtuous wife of General Chiu Chih-jen. Widowed one month after giving birth to their son, she endured great hardship to raise him while refusing to re-marry. The son, Liang-kung, went on to become a military governor of Zhejiang Province, and later requested permission from the emperor to raise this gate in memory of his mother. Madame Hsu was posthumously raised to the order of Grand Dowager of the first rank and worshipped with special rites to honor her virtue. This gate was constructed during the Chia-ching reign (1796–1821), and has four pillars and three bays beneath five tiers. The excellent stone used is both *qing cao* (green grass) stone from Fuzhou and white stone from Quanzhou. The workmanship is a beautiful example of the stone-masons' art of old China. The main horizontal beam is embellished with a pair of dragons fighting for a pearl. Above this are figures representing the imaginary return of General Chiu, coming home after achieving great fame for his rectitude. The inscription on the main cross beam reads: 'Imperially manifesting filial virtue.' The insignia in the center at the very top proclaims: 'By imperial mandate', signifying imperial permission had been granted for the gate. This imposing structure has been designated a Historical Site of the First Rank.

■ TOMB OF PRINCE LU

The Prince of Lu and Koxinga established a base on Kinmen for military campaigns to oust the Dutch from Taiwan and to restore the Ming emperor. Lu is now buried here.

■ HAIYIN TEMPLE

This Song-dynasty temple was established during the reign of Emperor Tu Tzung (1265–74).

■ KINMEN FOLK VILLAGE

The Kinmen Folk Village was originally a Fujian-style residential compound built for the Wang clan in 1900. The area includes 16 family homes, a schoolhouse and a family shrine. The compound fell into disrepair and was reconstructed as a tourist attraction in 1980, and walls and a garden were added. Inside the buildings are antiques and an exhibit of furnishings and items from the past.

■ SHOPPING

Kinmen is famous for four products: *kaoliang*, a fiery liquor similar to the mainland's *maotai*, kitchen knives made of scrap from the steel shells shot from the mainland, *kungtang*, a peanut candy cake once used as an offering by the royal family in Beijing, and ceramics. Originally set up to make bottles for the kaoliang distillery, the Kinmen Ceramic Factory now makes artistic ceramics in cooperation with the National Palace Museum.

A brightly painted Chinese-style door at the Kenting Youth Activity Center

Facts for the Traveller

Tourist Information

The Tourism Bureau's Tourist Information Hot Line (02) 717-3737, provides a wide range of information in English regarding travel in Taiwan. The service operates daily from 8 am–8 pm. Calls can be made from anywhere in Taiwan or around the world. The hot line's computers contain a wealth of information on scenic areas, transportation, timetables, hotels, restaurants, folk arts and cultural activities. This service also handles emergency assistance, lost and found, language problems and complaints.

Customs

A written declaration is required when bringing dutiable articles, such as new electrical appliances or televisions, into the country. Duties are charged on gold in excess of 62.5 grams and no more than NT$40,000 in cash may be brought into the country by each passenger. Any excess amount will be confiscated if not declared. Incoming visitors who want to bring in more than NT$40,000 in cash should apply, prior to entry, for a permit from the Ministry of Finance. Departing passengers may not take more than US$5,000 in cash or the equivalent in any other foreign currency from the country unless the amount was brought in within the preceding six months and declared on arrival. Traveler's checks, personal checks, and bank orders are not restricted.

One bottle of alcoholic beverage, 25 cigars, 200 cigarettes and one pound of other tobacco products per person may be brought in duty-free.

The following articles are prohibited from entry: counterfeit coins, security notes, bank notes, gambling apparatus, lottery tickets and other similar prize tickets unused in foreign countries; obscene and indecent books, publications, films and pictures; and films, publications and articles propagating communism.

Articles that may not be taken out of Taiwan include unauthorized reprints or copies of books, records and videotapes, antiques, ancient coins and paintings.

Visas

Visitors to Taiwan must have visas. Citizens of countries maintaining diplomatic or friendly relations with Taiwan should apply for them at official or unofficial Taiwan representative offices. Tourist visa applicants may be asked to show evidence of confirmed onward transport.

Citizens of countries which do not maintain ties with Taipei may be given special temporary permits after application to a Taiwan office. These applications may require a reference in Taiwan. European travellers may be given letters of introduction by the Taiwan offices; these letters are exchanged for visas at a consular window before the immigration lines at the Taipei and Kaohsiung airports.

The government recently changed the number and types of visas it issues to foreigners. A single tourist visa now replaces the old Transit, Commercial, Tourist A and Tourist B visas.

Tourist visa holders may stay in Taiwan for two weeks to 60 days. Unless restricted to two weeks, visa holders may apply for a maximum of two extensions of 60 days each, for a total of six months. The visa may be single or multiple-entry, valid for up to one year for stays of up to six months. Holders of the tourist visa are not permitted to accept employment without authorization.

Visa extensions can be obtained at the Foreign Affairs Dept, National Police Administration, 96 Yenping South Rd, Taipei. Tel (02) 381-8341.

Visa renewals can be processed at the Ministry of Foreign Affairs, 1 Kueiyang St, Section 1, Taipei. Tel (02) 389-7711.

Public Holidays

January 1	Founding day of the Republic of China
January 2	Bank Holiday
March 29	Youth Day
April 5	Qing Ming (Grave Sweeping Day)
June	Dragon Boat Festival (lunar holiday)
September 28	Confucius' Birthday
September–October	Mid-Autumn Festival (lunar holiday)
October 10	National Day of the Republic of China (Double Ten; tenth day of the tenth month)
October 25	Retrocession Day (return of Taiwan by the Japanese in 1945)
October 31	Chiang Kai-shek's birthday
November 12	Sun Yat-sen's birthday
December 25	Constitution Day

Clothing

Casual clothing is *de rigueur* for travelers to Taiwan. Lightweight clothing is best from April to October and humid weather may require frequent changes.

Air-conditioning in restaurants is often turned up high, so a light sweater in summer is useful when dining out. Handbags, shoes and clothing not used constantly during the winter may get moldy. Umbrellas are necessary all year round.

Cooler months call for medium-weight clothing, including sweaters and light coats. Mountain areas are cool throughout the year and warm clothes are necessary during the winter.

Money

The New Taiwan Dollar (NT$) is the legal currency, pegged loosely to the US dollar at a ratio of approximately 25:1; the rate fluctuates slightly. The smallest denomination is the NT$1 coin and the largest is the NT$1,000 bill.

Major foreign currencies may be exchanged at banks and at most hotels in Taipei. Many rural areas will not accept foreign currency, so make sure you take enough NT dollars with you when traveling to out of the way places.

If you want to change NT dollars back to foreign currency before departure, be sure to retain the original conversion receipt. If you have lost the receipt and the amount you are changing is not significant, you can still convert your money.

Major credit cards are accepted and traveler's checks can be cashed at some tourist businesses and most international tourist hotels. American Express traveler's checks can be cashed at the American Express office, 214 Tunhua N Rd, Taipei. Tel (02) 715-1581.

■ BARGAINING

Department stores and most large stores usually have set prices, but bargaining is possible at markets, streetside stalls and in smaller shops.

■ TIPPING

Tipping is generally not necessary in Taiwan. Hotels and most restaurants add a 10 per cent service charge to bills, so tip only if special service has been given. Taxi drivers do not expect tips. NT$50 per piece of luggage is standard for baggage carries at airports and harbors.

Telecommunications

Local telephone calls are NT$1 for three minutes. Calls are automatically cut off after three minutes so you must redial. Long distance calls may be made at any office of the International Telecommunications Administration (ITA). Dial 100 for the international operator. For directory assistance in English, call (02) 311-6796.

International cables, faxes and telexes may be sent from hotels and ITA offices. The main ITA office, 28 Hangchow South Rd, Section 1, Taipei, is open 24 hours. Ring the bell beside the door if it is locked.

Business Hours

Government and private offices are open from 8:30 am or 9 am–noon and from 1:30 pm–5:30 pm on weekdays. Saturday hours are from 8:30 or 9 am–noon; Sunday is a day of rest.

In the heart of Taipei, the Central Post Office (on Chunghsiao West Rd, near the old North Gate, is open daily from 8 am–6 pm and maintains a 24-

hour telephone and telegram service. Branch offices keep the same hours as the central office, but are closed after 1 pm on Saturdays. Banks are open from 9 am–3:30 pm on weekdays and from 9 am–12 noon or 1 pm on Saturdays.

Shops have variable hours but generally open from 9 am–9 pm. Big department stores are usually open from 10 am–10 pm. Most shops and department stores are open on Saturdays and Sundays. Restaurants are open from about 11 am–9 pm, but it is wise to begin dinner before 8 pm at larger restaurants. Smaller places open earlier.

Buses normally start operation at 6 am and stop around 11:30 pm. Taxis have no set hours.

Electricity

Electric current is 110 volts, 60 cycles, AC.

Media

■ NEWSPAPERS AND MAGAZINES
Two English language dailies, the *China Post* and *China News*, cost NT$12. An important source of general information are the numerous free tourist guides in hotels, restaurants, shops and bars, including *Travel in Taiwan, This Month in Taiwan, CKS Airport and Taiwan Guide*, and the *Taiwan Hotel Guide*.

■ TELEVISION AND RADIO
ICRT, the island's only English-language radio station, broadcasts news, plays and music on FM 100 and AM 576, 24 hours daily. For an interesting discussion on controversial topics in the news listen to 'Issues and Opinions' Monday nights at 8:30 on ICRT FM 100.

The island's three television stations broadcast primarily in Chinese, but a number of foreign programs are aired in English each week.

Health

■ VACCINATIONS
A smallpox vaccination certificate is no longer required. Travelers coming from areas with cholera must have cholera inoculations more than seven days but less than six months before arrival.

■ HEPATITIS
If you plan to spend any length of time in Taiwan, it is highly recommended that you get immunized against Hepatitis B. Hepatitis B can cause liver damage that can lead to liver cancer. Perhaps 20 per cent of people in Taiwan are carriers of Hepatitis B. A series of 3 or 4 injections are given over a six month or one year period, depending on the vaccine. Vaccines are available in Taiwan.

■ WATER
Water must be boiled before drinking. Water served in hotels and restaurants is either boiled, distilled or bottled mineral water.

■ TOILETS
Toilets in public places and smaller restaurants and stores are frequently the

Rock garden, Tien Hu (Matsu) Temple

squat type, so it is best to use restrooms in hotels and fast food restaurants. Always bring some toilet paper with you.

Hospitals

TAIPEI
Adventist Hospital (Taiwan)
424 Pateh Rd, Section 2.
Tel (02) 771-8151
台安醫院 八德路二段424號

Mackay Memorial Hospital
92 Chungshan North Rd, Section 2.
Tel (02) 543-3535
馬偕醫院 中山北路二段92號

National Taiwan University Hospital
7 Chungshan South Rd,
Tel (02) 397-0800
台大醫院 中山南路7號

Taipei Municipal Yangming Hospital
105 Yusheng St.
Tel (02) 835-3456
陽明醫院 雨聲街105號

Veterans General Hospital
201 Shih Pai Rd, Section 2.
Tel (02) 871-2121
榮總醫院 石牌路二段201號

TAICHUNG
Taichung Veterans General Hospital
160 Chungkang Rd, Section 3.
Tel (04) 359-2525
台中榮民總醫院 中港路三段160號

CHIAYI
Taiwan Provincial Chiayi Hospital
228 Wenhua Rd.
Tel (05) 223-3128
省立嘉義醫院 文化路228號

TAINAN
Father Fox Memorial Hospital
901 Chunghua Rd.
Tel (06) 252-1176
逢甲醫院 中華路901號

National Cheng Kung University
Hospital
138 Shengli Rd.
Tel (06) 235-3535
成功大學附設醫院 勝利路138號

KAOHSIUNG
Kaohsiung Veterans General Hospital
386 Tachung 1st Rd, Tsoying.
Tel (07) 342-2121
高雄榮總醫院 高雄市、大中一路386號

TAITUNG
Taiwan Provincial Taitung Hospital
1 Wuchuan St.
Tel (089) 32-4112
省立台東醫院 五權街1號

Getting to Taiwan

■ AIR

Taiwan has two international airports
and is served by some 20 airlines. The
main airport is Chiang Kai-shek International Airport, 40 kilometers from Taipei. The smaller Kaohsiung International
Airport is in the south, seven kilometers
from downtown Kaohsiung. The airport
departure tax is NT$300 for all passen-
gers over two years old. The tax must be
paid before checking in.

Airlines serving Taiwan include Eva
Airways, China Airlines, Cathay Pacific,
Delta Air Lines, Japan Asia Airways,
Garuda, Korean Air, Malaysian Airline
System, Singapore Airlines, Northwest
Airlines, Asiana Airlines, Philippines
Airlines, Thai Airways, and South Afri-
can Airways.

CHIANG KAI-SHEK INTERNATIONAL AIRPORT

Inexpensive and convenient airport
shuttle buses leave every 20 minutes for
Taipei. Two lines serve different parts of
the city and stop at several hotels. A sign
in front of the bus stop lists the destinations in English. One line ends at the
Taipei train station, and the other at the
Sungshan Domestic Airport. The fare is
NT$72, and tickets can be purchased in
the arrival area, or outside near the
boarding area.

Buses to the airport can be boarded
at the West Bus Station, just west of the
Taipei Train Station, or at the Sungshan
Domestic Airport Bus Station. Taxis are
available outside the arrivals terminal; a
50 per cent surcharge above the fare
shown on the meter is added for trips
from the airport. The average fare to
Taipei, including surcharges, is about
NT$1000. A taxi from Taipei to the
airport should only charge what is on the
meter. Any problems with taxi drivers
should be reported to the airport police
at (03) 383-2242. The trip by bus or car
takes 45–60 minutes, depending on the
time of day. Buses also go from the airport to Taichung and Kaohsiung. Money
can be changed in the arrival area and on
both levels of the departure area.

There are no porters at the airport, but baggage carts are available. A hotel reservation center stands immediately outside the customs area.

KAOHSIUNG INTERNATIONAL AIRPORT
Kaohsiung Airport is close to town and is served by city buses. These are inconvenient if you have a lot of baggage. A taxi to downtown Kaohsiung costs less than NT$200. An information counter at the airport makes hotel bookings.

■ SHIP
The Japanese Arimura Line sails weekly between Taiwan and Okinawa, with connections to and from Japan. The trip costs NT$3,216 one-way (no returns available). For more information, contact Yung An Maritime Co, 11 Renai Rd, Section 3, Taipei. Tel (02) 771-5911.
永安船務代理顧問有限公司 仁愛路三段11號
Ships also travel between Kaohsiung and Macau, leaving Macau on Tuesday and returning on Wednesday; economy class costs NT$2,800, and first class is NT$3,400—both one way. For more information contact Kuohua Travel, 11th Fl, 82 Sungkiang Rd. Tel (02) 531-0000.
國華旅行社 松江路82號

Domestic Travel

The language barrier is the biggest obstacle to travel in Taiwan. Still, transport facilities are excellent and, with a little planning and use of the English-speaking staff of tourist establishments (hotels, travel agencies, railway and bus information services), you can easily get around. Your hotel can arrange train and bus tickets for you for a small service charge.

The key to traveling in Taiwan is preparing enough material—transport bookings, directions written in Chinese—at one English-speaking center to get you through to the next.

■ TAXIS
Taxis are metered and cost NT$40 for the first 1.5 kilometers and NT$5 for each additional 400 meters, plus an additional NT$5 for every five minutes the cab is standing still or moving below five kilometers an hour. A 20 per cent surcharge is imposed between 11 pm–5 am and during rush hours.

Taxis in Taipei, Taichung, Tainan, and Kaohsiung must have meters. In smaller towns and cities you must agree on the price before getting into the taxi, usually NT$50 to NT$70 for any destination within that town or city. If going out of the town, negotiate the price before you set off.

Since few taxi drivers understand English, ask your hotel clerk or a Chinese friend to write destinations or instructions in Chinese. Bilingual business cards are also helpful for finding well-known locations. It is difficult to get a taxi during rush hour and so it is best not to arrange any important appointments at this time.

Taxis can be hired for country trips. Some, known as 'wild chicken' taxis, specialize in certain runs—Taichung to Sun Moon Lake, for example—and

TSAI CHIH-CHUNG

When Taiwan cartoonist Tsai Chi-chung appeared at the Xinhua Bookstore on Beijing's Wangfujing St to autograph mainland editions of his comic books, his fans patiently stood outside in line for up to two hours, snapping up 2,400 copies. But the masses, who bought 6,000 copies over the next three days, are not the only ones who enjoy reading Mr Tsai's comics.

Deng Lin, the artist daughter of China's strongman Deng Xiaoping, admitted in a private meeting with Tsai that her whole family has read his works.

Tsai, the first local to break into the international comic book market, is fast becoming one of Asia's most popular cartoonists.

In addition to the mainland editions of his works, which are printed in the simplified characters used in the People's Republic, translations are available in Japan, Korea, Hong Kong, Singapore and the United States.

In the late 1980s, Tsai sold hundreds of thousands of copies a year in Taiwan alone, making him the best selling author on the island. His success is based on a relatively simple formula.

He has summarized 26 erudite Chinese classics in a way that appeals to everyone, from elementary school students to senior citizens. Despite a typical student aversion for the classics, which can be extremely dry and stuffy, Tsai has succeeded in breathing life into the works of ancient scholars. While old masters such as Confucius, Chuang Tzu (Zhuang Zi) and Lao Tzu (Lao Zi) are depicted in a likeable and comical way with interesting facial expressions, Tsai does not let the vernacular dialogue of his colorful characters drift from the essence of the original meaning. He supplies the original classical text on the side of the page for reference.

The Taiwanese cartoonist describes his comic books as a kind of intellectual fast-food: 'My works are like McDonald's hamburgers—easy to digest and time-saving.'

However, he says that his readers like his works mainly because of what's inside.

'I emphasize taste and content,' says Tsai. 'I don't want the reader to finish the book and just forget about it. I want my books to provide a lot of nourishment.'

And he modestly declines to take all the credit for his success: 'My success is not the result of my effort alone, but because the ideas in my books have value and thousands of years of history.'

The soft-spoken Tsai grew up in a village in Changhua County, in central Taiwan. His father was a clerk in a government office, one of the village's few intellectuals and a man respected for his skill in calligraphy. In the evening after work, the elder Tsai tended to his own farmstead.

Tsai loved comic books as a child, and his addiction led him to drop out of junior high school at the age of 15—with his father's approval—to strike out for Taipei with just US$6 in his pocket, to work for a local publisher.

Although his first company originally promised to pay him US$7.50 a month, his boss immediately took a liking to him and doubled his salary. Within three months the talented Tsai jumped to a bigger publishing company and was pulling in an impressive US$75 a month, considerably more than his father earned at his local government job.

After a stint in the military and work in TV and animation production, he returned to writing comics in 1985. That same year he was named one of the Ten Outstanding Youths of the Year, and thanked his father for allowing him to follow his dream.

Despite his wealth, which has enabled him to buy five houses and apartments around the island, and a house in Canada, Tsai, a Catholic, remains a Taoist at heart.

He has shoulder-length hair, wears faded blue jeans and lunches on simple noodle dishes, boasting that he spends no more than a few dollars a day.

In an interview with one Singapore journalist, Mr. Tsai, who goes barefoot in his Taipei office, said, 'Keeping long hair is one of the ways in which I show my disregard for other people's opinions. You see, I refuse to be good from head to toe.'

Sadly for his fans, Tsai retired from the world of comic books in 1990 when he finished the 26th and final volume in the Chinese classics series.

'I understand my ability and when I do something until my ability can no longer advance any more, I change to a new art,' says Tsai. 'Otherwise the fire in me will go out.'

Chapter 4, paragraph 17,

To Live Among the Benevolent

见贤思齐焉，见不贤而
内自省也。
里仁第四——十七

1. When I meet a virtuous man I try to be his equal.

2. When I meet a man who is not virtuous,

3. I engage in self-examination,

4. To see if I share any of his undesirable traits.

lower the individual traveler's cost by loading up with four passengers. These specialized taxis usually start near the train or bus stations and the drivers will openly solicit passengers by calling out the name of the destination. Determine the price before beginning the journey.

Women should avoid taking taxis alone late at night.

■ BUSES

Taiwan's comprehensive bus network utilizes round-island, cross-island, coastal, internal and connecting highway systems. An air-conditioned, non-stop bus service—the Kuokuang—operates between Taipei and points south on the super highway. Reserved tickets may be purchased two days in advance. Another air-conditioned express bus—the Chunghsin—operates from Taipei to major cities in central and southern Taiwan, is cheaper than the Kuokuang, but does not have a toilet. The Chunghsin line also operates on the super highway. Seats may be reserved on highway buses up to 24 hours before departure. This is best done through your hotel or travel agent, however, since advance tickets are sometimes sold in places other than the highway bus station. In towns served by the railway, the bus stations are invariably within walking distance of the train station.

Coaches out of Taipei leave from the bus stations near the central railway station: southbound from the west station and northbound from the east station. The two main bus routes from Taipei extend to Kaohsiung in the south via the cities of Taichung, Chiayi and Tainan, and to Hualien on the east coast via Lotung on the island's northeast coast.

Highway buses operate from the central city of Taichung to the famous Sun Moon Lake resort and via the East–West Cross Island Highway to Lishan, Tienhsiang, Taroko Gorge and Hualien. From Hualien, highway buses maneuver the spectacular east coast road that winds precariously along the cliff face to the fishing town of Suao. Farther south, buses make the trip around the island's extremity, connecting Taitung and Kaohsiung, and include a side spur to Oluanpi on the southernmost tip.

In Taipei, books in English lay out the numerous bus routes that criss-cross the city. Bus fares in Taipei are NT$8 for regular buses and NT$10 for air-conditioned buses. No change is given on buses, so make sure you have the exact fare. You can buy a 10-ticket multiple journey punch card for the regular buses at newspaper kiosks and shops near most bus stops. The buses display designating route numbers. Stop signs are all in Chinese characters, so try to find someone who speaks English to tell you where your stop is.

■ TRAINS

A trunk line with sea and mountain branches runs the length of the island through the low country of the western plain, linking Keelung in the north with Kaohsiung in the south via Taipei, Taichung and Tainan. From Taipei another line runs around the island's northeast corner through Fulung, Ilan and Suao to the city of Hualien. Another line links Hualien with Taitung in the south.

The main west coast line has several express classes, though each train is a single class. Categories include: the high-speed, air-conditioned Tzuchiang, the luxury Chukuang, also air-conditioned but slower, Fuhsing, air-conditioned, but slower and less comfortable than the Chukuang, the Pingkuai, a cheap train with no reserved seats and no air-conditioning that stops in smaller towns, and the Putongche, the slowest local train, without air-conditioning.

The Tzuchiang runs from Taipei to Kaohsiung in just over four hours. All express trains are excellent, varying only in service, speed and plushness. Hostesses provide tea, magazines and newspapers. The Chukuang sometimes has a dining car. Snacks and rice lunchboxes are sold on most trains.

Advance tickets for express trains can be bought one or two days in advance at the train station (8 am–10 pm). Tickets for same-day express trains can be bought up to departure time but are often sold out. You can always buy a standing ticket. Be sure to hold on to your ticket. You will need to turn it in when you exit the station at your destination. Otherwise you will have to pay a heavy fine.

The Taipei train station contains a post office, telecommunications office and restaurant.

■ DRIVING

An international driver's license is required. A local license may be obtained without taking the driving test if you have a valid license from your home country or an international driver's license. You will need to take a physical exam at a public hospital and an eye examination to apply for a Taiwan license. For applications and information call the Office of Motor Vehicles. Tel (02) 763-0155. If you are involved in an accident call the Foreign Affairs Police. Tel (02) 537-3852.

CAR RENTALS

Avis Corp, 10, Lane 76, Anho Rd. Tel (02) 500-6633.
艾維士租車 安和路76巷10號

Central Auto Service, 1098 Chengteh Rd. Tel (02) 881-9545; day and long-term rentals.
易昇小客車 承德路1098號

■ AIR

Domestic flights operated by China Air Lines, Far Eastern Air Transport, Formosa Airlines, Great China Airlines, Makung Airlines, Taiwan Airlines, and Fohsing Airlines link Taipei with other cities, including Tainan, Kaohsiung, Hualien and Taitung. Domestic airlines also serve the offshore islands. Foreigners must show a passport for all domestic flights.

■ SEA

Travel agencies can arrange sea bookings between Kaohsiung and Makung in the

Pescadores islands and between Taitung and Lanyu (Orchid Island).

■ LOCAL TOURS

A number of tour companies arrange tours of Taipei and the island. Orthodox tours range from a half-day whiz through the capital's major sights (NT$500) to a three-day excursion to Taroko Gorge and Sun Moon Lake (NT$6,600); this price includes shared accommodation, but not meals. Popular tours in the Taipei vicinity include a night tour of Taipei (NT$850) which includes a Mongolian barbecue dinner, visits to the Lungshan Temple, night markets and the Chinese opera; a half-day tour of the Wulai aboriginal village (NT$750); and a half-day north coast tour of Yehliu Park and Chinshan Beach (NT$650).

A one-day tour of Taroko Gorge costs NT$2,900 (including airfare and lunch) and involves flying to Hualien and driving by air-conditioned coach through the gorge. A two-day tour of Sun Moon Lake by bus costs NT$3,500; the price includes shared accommodation, but not meals; a three-day tour of Sun Moon Lake and Alishan costs NT$7,000, including shared accommodation, but not meals, and a four-day round-the-island tour, excluding meals, costs NT$8,500. Single accommodations for the above overnight trips are priced slightly higher.

Special interest tours can also be arranged.

Tea Tour: A visit to an experimental tea station in Yangmei, a tea art demonstration, and lunch at a teahouse.

Ladies Tour: Visit Taipei's tourist sites, a tea art demonstration, Chinese cooking classes, seafood dinner, lunch at a teahouse, full-body massage and sauna, and a complete Manchu banquet.

Chinese Cuisine Tour: Taipei tourist sites, full-day study of Chinese cuisine, and a sampling of several types of cuisines at local restaurants.

Other special tours include the Hot Spring Tour, Golf Tour, Nature Tour, and Butterfly Collecting Tour.

Taipei is overflowing with tour and travel agencies, so stick to the ones recommended by your hotel or by the Taiwan Visitors' Association. Some suggested tour operators are:

South East Travel Service, 60 Chungshan North Rd, Section 2. Tel 551-7111
中山北路二段60號

China Express Transportation Co, 70 Chungshan North Rd, Section 2. Tel 541-6466
中山北路二段70號

Pinho Travel Service Co, 3rd Fl, 142-1 Chilin Rd. Tel 551-4136
吉林路142-1號3樓

Taiwan Coach Tours, Rm 802, 27 Chungshan North Rd, Section 3. Tel 595-5321
中山北路三段27號802室

Leisure Activities

■ DIVING

The coastal waters of Taiwan offer snorkelers and scuba divers a chance to

explore a fascinating underwater world of strange coral formations and bioluminescent tropical fish.

The north shore, from Tamsui to Suao, is one of Taiwan's most popular summertime diving areas. In winter, divers move to Kenting National Park in southern Taiwan, the island's best diving area. The water between Maopitou and Oluanpi is sparklingly clear and is home to a variety of tropical coral and fish. Diving is also popular around Green and Orchid islands, off Taiwan's southeast coast.

A day of scuba diving, including an experienced guide and rental equipment, costs about NT$6,800. Certification from a major national or international diving organization is also required; many local diving companies have certified diving courses which last from one to three weeks. For information and equipment rentals, call the ROC Diving Association in Taipei. Tel (02) 567-0256.

■ HIKING AND MOUNTAIN CLIMBING
Special permits are required for climbs to many of the high mountains. The Class A Mountain Pass (for highly restricted areas) can be obtained only through the ROC Alpine Association in Taipei, which can arrange trips with accredited English-speaking guides for groups of four or more. The Alpine Association is at 10 Fl, 185 Chungshan North Rd, Section 2, Taipei. Tel (02) 594-2108.
中山北路二段185號10樓

Class B passes (for less restricted areas) can be easily obtained for a small fee from police stations bordering restricted areas or at the National Police Administration, Chunghsiao East Rd, Section 1, opposite the Lai Lai Sheraton Hotel.
警政署 忠孝西路一段7號

A passport is necessary to obtain a mountain pass.

■ GOLF
Taiwan has 25 golf courses open to visitors and 12 are within easy reach of Taipei. Major hotels can make arrangements for regular members to sponsor visitors; all of the courses rent equipment and caddies.

Three clubs in Taoyuan, near Taipei, have special 'golf days' for non-members (rates are NT$800–1,200). They are the Taoyuan Golf Club. Tel (03) 470-1616, Taipei Golf Club. Tel (03) 324-1311, and Marshall Golf & Country Club. Tel (03) 322-1786.

Hotels

Taiwan has comfortable hotels to fit everyone's budget.

After the nationalist government was defeated by the Chinese communists on the mainland it attempted to wipe out all traces of its foe. As a result, the hotel rating system utilizes plum blossoms instead of stars, which are a prominent symbol in the People's Republic of China. Thus you will find five plum blossom hotels in Taiwan, but no five star hotels.

Hotels have been divided into three categories: **International class hotels** costing from US$100 and up a night for a single; **Moderate hotels** costing between US$50–100 for a single; and **Budget hotels and hostels** costing under US$50. Hostels often cost no more than US$5–10 a night.

The majority of hostels in Taiwan are operated by the China Youth Corps (CYC). The CYC is not affiliated with the International Youth Hostel Association (IYHA), and so an IYHA membership card is not required. Another type of hostel is the Laborers' Recreation Centers in Kaohsiung and Tainan. Many hostels also have private accommodations. It is advisable to make reservations at hostels, which are often fully booked on weekends and holidays. This is especially true with hostels that are off the beaten track, such as along the Central East–West Highway, where visitors seldom venture during the weekdays.

The hotels and hostels appear under their respective town/city headings, which have been ordered alphabetically. Some are listed under their respective highway headings (as in the main text).

ALISHAN
■ MODERATE

Alishan House: The best hotel on the mountain. Doubles start at NT$1200. Near the old train station; 2 West Alishan, Hsianglin Village.
Tel (05) 267-9811
阿里山賓館　西阿里山2號

Alishan Train Hotel: Also operated by Alishan House. Features restored old railway cars. Doubles cost NT$800 and twins are NT$1200. Near the old train station. Tel (05) 267-9811
車廂旅館

Alishango Hotel: Past the old train station; group rooms available from NT$1500, doubles for NT$700 and up. Tel (05) 267-9611
阿里山閣國民旅社

■ BUDGET

Alishan Hostel: 1 Alishan, Hsianglin Village. Tel (05) 267-9611

Alishan Mountain Hostel: Dormitory NT$150. Tel (05) 277-0482-3
阿里山山莊

Kaofeng Hotel: Tatami rooms from NT$200 and up, doubles for NT$400–800.
高峰飯店

Catholic Hostel: NT$200 for a dormitory bed. At the lower end of Alishan Village, near the entrance gate.
天主教堂

It is also possible to rent a room with a local family. Ask the vendors in the square.

CHANGHUA
■ MODERATE

Taiwan Hotel: 48 Chungcheng Rd,
Section 2. Tel (04) 722-4681
台灣大飯店　中正路二段48號

■ BUDGET

Hongye Hotel: NT$300. 5, Lane 100,
Changan St. Tel (047) 222667
紅葉大飯店　長安街100巷5號

Lees Hotel: Rooms start at NT$500.
566 Chungcheng Rd, Section 1.
Tel (047) 236164
雲河大飯店　中正路一段566號

CHIAOHSI
■ MODERATE

Jei I Hotel: 16 Tehyang Rd.
Tel (039) 881211
嘉一大飯店　德陽路16號

The following hotels are located near the
Wufengchi Waterfall:

Wufengchi Hotel: Doubles NT$700.
Tel (039) 885211-5
五鳳旗大飯店　五鳳路69號

Happy Hotel: Doubles NT$1000 and up.
Fax (039) 882108

A wide variety of seafood displayed at a night market stall

CHIAYI

■ MODERATE

Gallant Hotel: 257 Wenhua Rd.
Tel (05) 2235366
嘉南大飯店 文化路257號

■ BUDGET

Penglai Hotel: 534 Jenai Rd.
Tel (05) 227-2366
蓬萊旅社 仁愛路534號

Hotel Shin Kao: 581 Chungshan Rd.
Tel 227-2252
中山路581號

Chiayi Hostel: No. 3, Community 4,
Hsihsing Village. Tel (05) 252-1710
嘉義農場國民賓館 西興村七之八號

Luscious peaches

CHIHPEN

Hotels in Chihpen offer a 20–40 per cent discount during weekdays. Ask for a discount when you check in.

■ MODERATE

Jyhbeen Hotel: Two outdoor springs, one hot and one cool; once the main hotel here, but now a bit run-down. Doubles are NT$1300–1600. 5 Lung-chuan. Tel (089) 512220
知本大飯店 龍泉5號

Rainbow Hotel: Near the Chihpen Forest Recreation Area; clean rooms and outdoor hot spring pools. NT$1300 for a single, NT$1800 and up for a twin. 78 Lungchuan. Tel (089) 513181
汚泉大飯店 溫泉村龍泉路139巷1號

Dongtai Hotel: Also near the forest recreation area with an outdoor hot spring pool; doubles are NT$1600. 83 Lung Chuan. Tel (089) 512290, 512918
東台大飯店 龍泉83號

Lung Chuan Mountain Hostel: One of the cheapest places to stay; doubles from NT$900–1600; Japanese-style tatami rooms for up to eight people for NT$2000–2400; 20 per cent discount offered on weekdays. 86–23 Lungchuan. Tel (089) 513930
龍泉山莊 龍泉86-23號

Mingchuan Hotel: Just past the suspension bridge; doubles for NT$800. Cottages also available. Tel (089) 513996
名泉旅遊山莊

CHINGCHING FARM
■ BUDGET
Youshi Mountain Hostel: Dorm NT$150, doubles NT$400. Tel (049) 802533.
清境農場

Chingching Citizens' Hostel: Dormitory NT$300, doubles NT$700 and up. Tel (049) 802748
清境國民賓館 定遠巷25號

CHINGSHAN
■ BUDGET
Chingshan Mountain Hostel: NT$150 for a dormitory room. Tel (045) 244103
中國青年反共救國團

CHINSHAN
■ BUDGET
Chinshan Youth Activity Center: At the beach, with dormitories for NT$100, doubles for NT$400 and bungalows for NT$1200. Make reservations in the hot summer months. Tel (032) 981191
金山活動中心

CORAL LAKE
■ MODERATE
Wushantou Hostel: 92 Chianan Village, Kuantien Hsiang. Tel (06) 698-3121
烏山頭國民旅社 嘉南村92號關田鄉

FENCHIHU
■ BUDGET
Catholic Hostel: Dormitory rooms for

NT$120. Tel (05) 256-1035
天主教堂

Chinri Mountain Hostel: Dormitory rooms for NT$180, doubles for NT$850 and up. The hotel has a restaurant. Tel (05) 256-1034
今日山莊

Chongshan Mountain Hostel: Dormitory rooms for NT$200, doubles starting at NT$850. Tel (05) 256-1052
中山山莊

FENGSHAN
■ BUDGET
Fengji Mountain Hostel: Nice dormitory rooms for NT$150, doubles starting at NT$500. Tel (05) 266-1363
豐吉山莊

FULUNG BEACH
■ BUDGET
Fulung Hostel: Situated on the beach; cabins for NT$500–700; camping area costs NT$40. 40 Fulung St, Fulung Village, Kungliao Hsiang. Tel (02) 499-1211
福隆國民旅社 福隆街40號

GREEN ISLAND
■ BUDGET
Zhongguang Hotel: NT$300 for a double; located in Chungliao Village. Tel (089) 672516
中光旅社

Lutao Hostel: In Kungkuan Village; rooms for NT$1000. Tel (089) 672314
綠島國民旅社

Songlong Hotel: Near Nanliao Harbor; doubles for NT$1200. Tel (089) 672515
松榮大旅社

HOHUANSHAN
■ BUDGET
Sung Hsueh Lou (Pine Snow Hotel): The only lodging here. A tatami dormitory is NT$150, doubles are NT$1200. Tel (049) 802732
松雪樓

HSIAO LIUCHIU
■ BUDGET
Bailonggong Hotel: Tel (08) 861-2536
白龍宮

Hsiao Liuchiu Hotel: Tel (08) 861-1133
小琉球大飯店

HSITOU
■ MODERATE
Mingshan Hotel: The only hotel outside the gate, with a wide variety of accommodation; dormitories are NT$150, and other rooms start at NT$500. Tel (049) 612121
明山別館

Hsitou Restaurant Hotel: On the left as you enter the park. You can book rooms here for the Hsitou Youth Hostel, which is several kilometers inside the park, or make a reservation for the Fenghuan Guest House, the Kuomin Hotel, and the Hanguang Hotel. Rooms range from NT$750–1500. 10 Scnlin Lane. Tel (049) 612345
溪頭餐廳旅社 森林巷10號

HUALIEN
■ INTERNATIONAL CLASS
CITC Hualien: 2 Yunghsing Rd. Tel (038) 221171
中信大飯店 永興路2號

■ MODERATE
Marshal Hotel: 36 Kungyuan Rd. Tel (038) 326123
統帥大飯店 公園路36號

Astar Hotel: 6-1 Minchuan Rd. Tel (038) 326111
亞士都大飯店 民權路6之1號

■ BUDGET
Teachers' Hostel: Located near the bus station; a good place to stay, though doors close at 11pm and there are no wake-up calls for the early morning bus up the Suao-Hualien Highway. A dormitory room is NT$150. 10 Kungcheng St. Tel (038) 325880
教師會館 公正路10號

Hualien Student Hostel: NT$150 for a dormitory bed. 40-11 Kungyuan Rd. Tel (038) 324124
花蓮學苑 公園路40之11號

Lienwu, or wax apple; plum blossoms and star fruit are common in Taiwan

Youth Hostel: Actually a privately run hotel; rooms from NT$160–350; a few blocks from the bus station; 84 Chungshan Rd. Tel (038) 324132
五州旅社 中山路84號

HUISUN (HWEISUN)
■ BUDGET
Huisun Forest Hostel: 1 Shanlin Lane, Hsinsheng Village, Jenai Hsiang. Tel (049) 941041
惠蓀林場國民旅社 新生村山林巷1號

ILAN CITY
■ BUDGET
Hill Garden Hotel: 6 Tehyang Rd, Chiao Hsi. Tel (039) 882011
礁溪飯店 德陽路6號

JUILI
■ BUDGET
Chingye Mountain Hostel: Dormitory rooms for NT$130, doubles for NT$650. Tel (05) 250-1031
青葉山莊

Jolan Mountain Hostel: Dormitories run from NT$130-150, doubles cost NT$850 and up. This is not on the main road. Ask the bus driver to let you off in front of the Chingye Mountain Hostel then walk a very short distance down a path to the hotel. Tel (05) 250-1210
若蘭山莊

Meihua Mountain Hostel: Dormitories for NT$130, doubles for NT$800 and up. Tel (05) 250-1522
梅花山莊

Rey Lee Hotel: Largest hotel in Juili, about a 45 minute walk from the town center. Doubles cost NT$900, twins NT$1200 and up, dormitory rooms NT$250. Tel (05) 250-1310
瑞里大飯店

KAOHSIUNG
■ INTERNATIONAL CLASS
Ambassador: 202 Minsheng Second Rd. Tel (07) 211-5211
國賓大飯店 民生二路202號

Grand Hotel: Cheng Ching Lake. Tel (07) 383-5911
圓山大飯店 澄清湖畔

Holiday Garden: 279 Liuho Second Rd. Tel (07) 241-0121
華園大飯店 六合二路279號

Hotel Kingdom: 42 Wufu Fourth Rd. Tel (07) 551-8211
華王大飯店 五福四路42號

Hotel Major: 7 Tajen Rd. Tel (07) 521-2266
名人大飯店 大仁路7號

Summit Hotel: 426 Chiuju First Rd. Tel (07) 384-5526
皇統大飯店 九如一路426號

■ MODERATE
Buckingham: 394 Chihsian Second Rd. Tel (07) 282-2151
白金漢大飯店 七賢二路394號

A Dangerous Drug

Of all the products of Formosa none is of such interest as Camphor. The fact that it is snatched from the jungle over which the wild savage roams, and that it is not produced to any extent in any other part of the world, save Japan, accounts for this. It would be an inviting subject for the statistician, whose hobby is to study problems such as how many days' consumption of matches placed end to end it would require to encircle the world, to figure out how many drops of human blood are represented in the few ounces of Camphor which the humane young lady purchases to keep her dainty garments free of moths, or how many lives are lost that some decrepit old gentleman may be cured of his rheumatic pains. The trees which produce this valuable article are unfortunately within the country of the aborigines or upon the immediate border of it. The methods of obtaining the drug adopted by the Chinese necessitates the destruction of the trees, which are never replaced; and while temporary permission is sometimes granted by individual savages or their village headmen to work certain border districts, the aboriginal population as a whole naturally views with deep concern the gradual encroachment on their native soil; and, as a consequence the border districts have, since the earliest days, been in a chronic state of disturbance. Every opportunity has been seized for the perpetration of outrages, and, sad to say, these outrages have not been on the part of the savages alone, for the Chinese, on their side, seem never to have let slip any chance which presented itself of wreaking their vengeance on the unfortunate aborigines. The lives that during the last twenty-five years have been lost directly in consequence of this would sum up a very large number; while indirectly, for instance among soldiers sent into the savage districts to avenge the murder of some Camphor worker, and vice versa, among aborigines making a raid on Chinese peasants living near the border, there must have been a deplorable addition to the above mentioned loss of life.

James W Davidson, Consul of the United States for Formosa, *The Island of Formosa* (1903)

Grand China: 289 Chungshan First Rd.
Tel (07) 221-9941
中華飯店 中山一路289號

■ BUDGET
Hungpin Hotel: Rooms start at NT$400.
40 Chienkuo 3rd Rd.
Tel (07) 291-3173
皇賓旅社 建國三路40號

Duke Hotel: Inexpensive rooms for
NT$400–650. 233 Linsen First Rd.
Tel (07) 231-2111
公爵大飯店 林森一路233號

Chengching Youth Activity Center: By
Chengching Lake, an inexpensive, clean
place, with two swimming pools and a
restaurant.
Tel (07) 371-7181
澄清湖活動中心

Kaohsiung Laborers' Recreation Center:
NT$200–400. 132 Chungshan Third Rd.
Tel (07) 332-8110
高雄勞功娛樂中心 中山三路132號

KEELUNG
■ MODERATE
Kodak Hotel: 7 Yee First Rd.
Tel (02) 423-0111
柯達飯店 義一路7號

KENTING
■ INTERNATIONAL CLASS
Caesar Park Hotel: A plush international
resort hotel with swimming pool, tennis

court, sauna and fitness room; singles
start at NT$4200. 6 Kenting Rd, Heng-
chun Township.
Tel (08) 886-1888
凱撒大飯店 墾丁路6號

■ MODERATE
Kenting House, Kenting Park: The area's
oldest major hotel, located within the Kenting Forest Recreation Area; twins cost
NT$1600, a cottage for four costs
NT$3200. Kenting House also has a slightly
more expensive hotel on the beach.
Tel (088) 886-1301
墾丁賓館 墾丁公園

■ BUDGET
Kenting Youth Activity Center: A complex of buildings built in traditional
Fujian style, with red brick walls, pale
red roof tiles and horseback roofs. These
buildings were designed by Han Pao-teh,
an expert on Chinese traditional architecture. The center has 98 rooms, designed for groups of three and six, and
can accommodate a total of 400 guests. It
is usually booked in advance by groups
on weekends.
Tel (08) 886-1221-4
墾丁活動中心

Teachers' Hostel: Dormitory rooms for
NT$150, doubles for NT$300. The hostel is almost always full.
Tel (08) 886-1241
教師會館

Catholic Hostel: Dormitory rooms for

NT$150.
Tel (08) 886-1540
天主教墾丁活動中心

Hongbin Hotel: In the center of town;
rooms start at NT$400.
Tel (08) 886-1003
鴻賓旅社

Kenting Unno Hotel: A comfortable
small hotel run by a friendly family. 52
Kenting Rd, between the main road and
the beach.
Tel (08) 886-1426
墾丁海野別館 墾丁路52號

There are numerous other small
hotels along the main street of the village; just look for the signs. During the
weekends, when the area becomes
crowded, room rates can double.

KUKUAN
■ MODERATE
Dragon Valley Hotel: 136 Tongkuan Rd,
Section 1.
Tel (045) 951325
龍谷大飯店 東關路136號

Utopia Holiday Inn: 7 Wenchuan Lane,
Tongkuan Rd.
Tel (045) 951511
假期大飯店 東關路

LANYU (ORCHID ISLAND)
■ MODERATE
Lanyu Hotel: Faces the island's best
beach; dormitory rooms for NT$250,
singles start at NT$1000, doubles are

NT$3000. 7 Red Head Village.
Tel (089) 326111.
蘭嶼別館 紅頭村7號

Orchid Hotel: NT$250 for a dormitory
room, NT$1,760 for a single, NT$3,000
for a double. 14 Kaiyuan Village.
Tel (089) 320033
蘭嶼大飯店 開元村14號

LISHAN
■ MODERATE
Lishan Guest House: Tel (045) 989501
梨山賓館

■ BUDGET
Fuchung Hotel: 61 Chungcheng Rd.
Tel (045) 989506
福忠大飯店 中正路61號

Lishan Hostel: 94 Chungcheng Rd.
Tel (045) 981331
梨山國民旅社 中正路94號

Litu: Tel (045) 989256
梨都大旅社 民族路22號

Fairyland Hotel: Tel (045) 989256
好望角大飯店 民族路52號

Try also hotels on Mintsu Rd, which
runs parallel to Chungcheng Rd.

LOSHAO
■ BUDGET
Loshao Mountain Hostel: Dormitory
NT$150, double NT$400. Tel (038)
691111.
洛韶山莊

Winding Taroko Gorge

LUSHAN HOT SPRING
■ BUDGET
Skyline Hotel: Tel (049) 802675
天蘆大飯店

Honeymoon Hotel: Tel (049) 802355
密月館大飯店

Policemen's Hostel: For police officers, but anyone is welcome to stay here as long as there is room; doubles NT$200–400. The hostel has its own hot spring baths.
Tel (049) 802529
警光山莊

NORTH CROSS ISLAND HIGHWAY
■ BUDGET
Fuhsing Mountain Hostel:
Tel (03) 382-2276
復興山莊

Paling Mountain Hostel:
Tel (03) 333-2153
巴陵山莊

OLUANPI
■ MODERATE
Oluanpi Inn: Doubles for NT$1400; 20 per cent discount on weekdays.
Tel (08) 885-1261
鵝鑾鼻休假別墅

Nan Yang Hotel: NT$2100–3000.
Tel (08) 885-1088
南洋大飯店

■ BUDGET
CSF Oluanpi Recreation Center: Located just above the village of Oluanpi; excellent view of the region, beautiful sunrises, Western restaurant. 16 Oluan Rd. Tel (08) 885-1191
聯勤鵝鑾鼻活動中心

PEITOU
■ MODERATE
Communications Palace Hotel: 25 Yuya Rd.
Tel (02) 891-3031
交通大飯店　幽雅路25號

I-Tsun Hotel: 140 Wenchuan Rd.
Tel (02) 891-2121
逸邨溫泉旅社　溫泉路140號

PENGHU
■ MODERATE
Pao Hwa Hotel: 2 Chungcheng Rd, Makung.
Tel (06) 927-4881
寶華大飯店　中正路2號

Hotel Chang Chun: 8 Chungcheng Rd, Makung.
Tel (06) 927-3336
長春大飯店　中正路8號

Four Seas Hotel: 3 Chienkuo Rd.
Tel (06) 927-2960
四海大飯店　建國路3號

■ BUDGET

Penghu Youth Activity Center: Dormitories from NT$150–250. 11 Chiehshou Rd, Makung.
Tel (06) 927-1124
澎湖活動中心 介壽路11號

Teachers' Hostel: Dormitory rooms for NT$150. 38 Shuteh Rd, Makung.
Tel (06) 927-3692
澎湖教師會館 馬公市樹德路38號

SOUTHERN CROSS ISLAND HIGHWAY

■ BUDGET

Each of the following hostels costs NT$100 per night.
Meishan Mountain Hostel:
Tel (07) 747-0134-5
梅山山莊

Yakou Mountain Hostel:
Tel (089) 329891
啞口山莊

Litao Mountain Hostel:
Tel (089) 329891
利稻山莊

SUAO

■ BUDGET

Suao Hotel: Best and cleanest in town; doubles NT$700. 7 Sutung Chung Rd.
Tel (039) 965181
蘇澳飯店 蘇東中路7號

King Ein Hotel: Basic accommodation; doubles NT$300. 49 Chungshan Rd.

Tel (039) 962-372
金燕大旅社 中山路49號

Haitien Hotel: NT$400 for a double. 96 Chungshan Rd.
Tel (039) 962576
海天大旅社 中山路96號

SUN MOON LAKE

■ INTERNATIONAL CLASS

China Trust Sun Moon Lake Hotel:
23 Chungcheng Rd, Section 2.
Tel (049) 855911
日月潭中信大飯店 中正路二段23號

■ MODERATE

Sun Moon Lake Tourist Hotel: Near the Wenwu Temple; has rooms for NT$1900–2100. 23 Chungcheng Rd.
Tel (049) 855911
日月潭大飯店 中正路23號

■ BUDGET

Evergreen Hotel: Doubles and twins start at NT$900. 142 Chunghsing Rd.
Tel (049) 855311
涵碧樓 中興路142號

Sun Moon Lake Youth Activity Center: On the southeast side of the lake, just northeast of the Aborigine Village.
Tel (049) 850070
日月潭青年活動中心

Numerous other hotels are available around the village.

TAICHUNG
■ INTERNATIONAL CLASS
Hotel National: 257 Taichung Kang Rd, Section 1. Tel (04) 321-3111
全國大飯店　台中港路一段257號

Plaza International Hotel: 431 Taya Rd. Tel (04) 295-6789
通豪大飯店　大雅路431號

■ MODERATE
Taichung Hotel: 152 Tzuyu Rd, Section 1. Tel (04) 224-2121
台中大飯店　自由路一段152號

Park Hotel Taichung: 17 Kungyuan Rd. Tel (04) 220-5181
敬華大飯店　公園路17號

Twinstar Hotel: 158 Fuhsing Rd, Section 4. Tel (04) 226-1811
雙星大飯店　復興路四段158號

■ BUDGET
First Hotel: 51 Chikuang St. Tel (04) 222-2205
第一旅社　繼光街51號

There are no hostels in Taichung but you can find several cheap hotels near the train station.

TAIHO
■ BUDGET
Taiho Mountain Hostel: Tatami rooms for NT$100, doubles for NT$1200.

Tel (05) 266-1222
太和山莊

TAINAN
■ MODERATE
Hotel Tainan: 1 Chengkung Rd. Tel (06) 2289101
台南大飯店　成功路1號

Redhill Hotel: 46 Chengkung Rd. Tel (06) 22508121
赤嶺大飯店　成功路46號

Oriental Hotel: 143 Mintsu Rd. Tel (06) 222-1131
華光大飯店　民族路143號

■ BUDGET
Tainan Student Hostel: A bit far from the downtown area, but clean and inexpensive; dormitory rooms NT$150. Lane 300, Funung St, Section 1. Tel (06) 267-0526-8
台南學苑

Tainan Laborers' Recreation Center: Dormitory rooms NT$150, doubles NT$430. 261 Nanmen Rd. Tel (06) 263-0174
台南勞功休假中心　南門路261號

TAIPEI
■ INTERNATIONAL CLASS
The following international hotels in Taipei have swimming pools, fitness clubs, international direct dialing, busi-

Sugar harvesters depicted by a Manchu painter, 1743

ness centers and other amenities.

Grand Hyatt: This is one of Taipei's newest and most grandiose hotels, located in the far eastern part of the city, next to the Taipei World Trade Center, 2 Sungshou Rd. Tel (02) 720-1234

凱悅大飯店 松壽路2號

Sherwood Hotel: This graceful hotel opened in December 1990 and is the only international class hotel located in the financial district. 637 Min Sheng East Rd. Tel (02) 718-1188

西華大飯店 民生東路637號

Regent: Voted the Best New Hotel of 1991 in Executive Travel Magazine's annual reader survey of hotels, the Regent is located in one of the city's most important business and shopping districts. 41 Chungshan North Rd, Section 2. Tel (02) 523-8000

麗晶酒店 中山北路2段41號

Grand Hotel: The Grand does not come up to the standards of other international hotels in Taipei. However, its distinctive and imposing red palace-style architecture with traditional Chinese designs make it a popular place to stay. The hotel, built under the direction of Madame Chiang Kai-shek, has an interior of paneled teak ceilings, tasseled Chinese lanterns, red lacquered columns, thick-piled rugs woven in traditional Chinese patterns and hand-carved furniture. Sitting in the north of the city on a ridge below Yangmingshan, the Grand Hotel commands the best view of the city and

the winding Keelung and Tamsui Rivers below. The site is isolated and inconvenient, though, and taxis can be difficult to find at times. Tel (02) 596-5565

圓山大飯店

■ **MODERATE**

China Hotel: This convenient hotel is located close to the train and bus stations. 14 Kuanchien Rd. Tel (02) 331-9521

中國大飯店 館前路14號

Flowers Hotel: Also close to bus and train stations. 19 & 36 Hankou St, Section 1. Tel (02) 312-3811

華華大飯店 漢口街一段19-36號

Leofoo Hotel: 168 Changchun Rd. Tel (02) 507-3211

六福客棧 長春路168號

■ **BUDGET**

Miramar Hotel: 3 Nanking East Rd, Section 2. Tel (02) 511-1241

文華大飯店 南京東路二段3號

Phoenix Palace Hotel: Near train and bus stations but accepts only those staying one month or more. 4 Hankou St, Section 1. Tel (02) 371-3151

鳳宮大飯店 漢口街一段4號

Paradise Hotel: Near train and bus stations. 7 Huaining St. Tel (02) 331-3311

南國大飯店 懷寧街7號

■ HOSTELS

Taipei Internatonal Youth Activity Center: 30 Hsinhai Rd, Section 3. Tel (02) 709-1770
國際活動中心 辛亥路三段30號

ABC Hostel: 14th Fl-3, 266 Fu Hsing North Rd. Tel (02) 507-3397
復興北路266號

Amigo Hostel: Friendly and clean. NT$160 for a dormitory room. 4th Fl, 286 Chilin Rd. Tel (02) 542-0292
吉林路286號4樓

The Formosa Hostel: NT$150 for a dormitory room; has kitchen and washing machine facilities. 3rd Fl, 16, Lane 20, Chungshan North Rd, Section 2. Tel (02) 562-2035
中山北路二段20巷16號3樓

Friendly House: 10th Fl, 50 Poai Rd. Tel (02) 381-8804
博愛路50號10樓

Happy Family Hostel: Clean and conveniently located near the train and bus stations. Call before you go because it is frequently full. NT$160 a night. 4/F, 16-1 Peiping West Rd. Tel (02) 375-3443
北平西路1號

Roosevelt Hostel: 4th Fl, 96-5 Hsin-sheng South Rd, Section 3. Tel (02) 363-8943
新生南路三段96之5號4樓

Taipei Hostel: A popular place located near the Lai Lai Sheraton, it has laundry service, but is not as clean as the other hostels mentioned above. NT$160 for a dormitory room. 6th Fl, 11 Lane 5, Linsen North Rd. Tel (02) 395-2950
林森北路11巷5號6樓

TAIPINGSHAN
■ BUDGET
Taipingshan Hostel: Taiping Village, Taiping Road. Tel (039) 891692
太平山莊 太平村太平路

Jentse Mountain Hostel: Near the foot of the mountain and Jentse Hot Springs. Dormitory NT$300, doubles NT$1400. Tel (039) 809603
仁澤山莊

TAITUNG
■ MODERATE
Lion Hotel: 572 Chunghua Rd, Section 1. Tel (089) 328878
獅子王旅社 中華路一段572號

■ BUDGET
Ren Ai Hotel: Just behind the bus station; singles for NT$200. Tel (089) 322423
仁愛大飯店

Hsin Hsin Hotel: NT$500 for a single. 429 Chungshan Rd. Tel (089) 324185
欣欣大旅社 中山路429號

Dense vegetation thrives in the wet mountain areas

Dongpin Hotel: Rooms for NT$300.
536 Chunghua Rd, Section 1.
Tel (089) 322222
東賓旅社　中華路一段536號

Teachers' Hostel: A clean, affable place;
singles are NT$450, doubles NT$600.
19 Nanching Rd.
Tel (089) 310142
教師會館

TAOYUAN
■ INTERNATIONAL CLASS
CKS Airport Hotel, CKS Airport:
Tel (03) 383-3666
國際機場旅館

■ MODERATE
Taoyuan Plaza: 151 Fuhsing Rd.
Tel (03) 337-9222
南華大飯店　復興路151號

TAYULING
■ BUDGET
Tayuling Mountain Hostel: Dormitory
NT$150.
Tel (038) 691111
大禹嶺山莊

TEHCHI
■ BUDGET
The Tehchi Mountain Hostel: Overlooks

the Tehchi Dam. Dormitories NT$150.
Tel (045) 981-1592.
德基山莊

TIENHSIANG
■ MODERATE
Tienhsiang Lodge: The only standard
hotel in this scenic tourist area, often
filled with tour groups, even during the
middle of the week. Tel (038) 691155-8.
In Taipei reservations may be made by
calling (02) 551-5933
天祥招待所

■ BUDGET
Catholic Hostel: This clean, friendly
place has been a favorite with foreign
travellers for decades. A dormitory room
costs NT$80, doubles are NT$500. Located on a hill overlooking a parking lot.
Tel (038) 691122
天主堂

Tienhsiang Youth Activity Center: Just
behind the Catholic Hostel; A dormitory
bed is NT$150, and doubles are NT$500.
Reservations are a must.
Tel (038) 691111
天祥青年活動中心

TSAOLING
■ MODERATE
Green Mountain Hotel: Best and most
expensive hotel in Tsaoling; rooms start
from NT$2000. Tel (055) 831208
高山青大飯店

■ BUDGET
Tsao Lien Hotel: Dormitory rooms for
NT$180, singles for NT$800, doubles
for NT$1000–1500. 36 Tasoling, Kuke-
ng Hsiang. Tel (055) 831228
草嶺大飯店

Yunglih Hotel: Dorms for NT$200,
doubles starting at NT$1000.
Tel (055) 831012
永利賓館

Tsaoling Guest House:
Tel (055) 831121
草嶺山莊賓館

Sing Ming Hsiu Hotel: Tel (055) 831116
新明休大飯店

TSENGWEN RESERVOIR
■ MODERATE
Chiayi Farm Guest House: Has a fruit
farm, camping and picnicking facilities,
shops and restaurants.
Tel (05) 252-1710
嘉義農場國民賓館

Tapu Villa: Government-owned hostel
surrounded by sugar cane fields and
palm trees; said to be the best-run hotel
at the reservoir. Tel (05) 252-1610
大埔山莊

■ BUDGET
Tsengwen Youth Activity Center:
Camping, swimming, badminton, roller

skating and picnicking, with equipment for rent; bungalows are available.
Tel (06) 575-2775
曾文活動中心

TUNGPU
■ BUDGET
Ti Lun Hotel: Best hotel here, near the bus stop; doubles are NT$1000, twins are NT$1200. Tel (049) 701616
帝綸大飯店

Tungpu Mountain Hostel: Doubles for NT$1000 and up. Tel (049) 701090
東埔山莊

Aboriginal Youth Activity Center: Hot spring water is piped into the bathrooms. NT$150 for dormitories, NT$500 and up for doubles. Tel (049) 701515
山地活動中心

Shenghua Hotel: Next to the Aborigine Youth Activity Center; doubles for NT$600. Tel (049) 701511
勝華大飯店

Hongling Hotel: Below the Shenghua Hotel; doubles for NT$550, small group rooms for NT$800. Tel (049) 701569
鴻林別館

TZUEN
■ BUDGET
Tzuen Mountain Hostel: Dormitory NT$150. Tel (038) 691111
慈恩山莊

WULING FARM
■ MODERATE
Wuling Guest House: 3-1 Wuling Rd, Pingteng Village, Hoping Hsiang. Tel (04) 590-1183
武陵國民旅社

WUSHE
■ BUDGET
Wuying Hotel: 59 Jenho Rd. Tel (049) 802360
霧櫻大旅社

Wushe Mountain Hostel: Tel (049) 802611
霧社山莊

YANGMINGSHAN
■ MODERATE
Hotel China Yangmingshan: Swimming pool and a basic fitness room; close to Yangmingshan National Park. 237 Kochih Rd. Tel (02) 861-6661
中國大飯店　格致路237號

Yang Ming Shan Hostel: 12 Yangming Rd, Section 1. Tel (02) 861-6601
聯勤陽明山招待所　陽明路一段12號

Restaurants

As with the hotels, these are listed under their respective town/city headings, which are themselves ordered alphabetically.

ALISHAN

Restaurants are located in the square near the bus terminal. Cold Alishan is an ideal place to warm up over a fire pot, or hot pot, a popular winter dish in which you cook your own vegetables and meat in a boiling pot of water at your table.

CHIAYI

Laotang Niurou Mian: specializes in beef noodles and dumplings. 504 Chungshan Rd. Tel 223-2662
老唐牛肉麵　中山路504號

Ni Jia Wo Jia: Hot Sichuan dishes. 441 Chiuyang Rd.
你家我家　垂楊街441號

Ba Ba Ba: for seafood. 457 Chuiyang Rd.
八八八海鮮　垂楊街457號

There are numerous other restaurants and noodle shops along Chungshan Rd.

HSITOU

Food is available at the hotels and at small restaurants just outside the main gate. These serve local specialties. Try dishes using locally grown bamboo shoots.

KAOHSIUNG

Wu's Chao Shou: famous for wonton served in a fiery mixture of sesame oil, hot pepper oil, and peppery hot sauce, fish with hot bean sauce, diced chicken with hot pepper, and broiled shrimp. 148 Chihsien 3rd Rd. Tel 561-2276
吳抄手　七賢三路148號

Chin Hsi Lou: this Zhejiang restaurant serves smoked yellow fish, steamed green crabs and roast duck.
Tel 333-1145
金喜樓

Chuan Wei Sichuan: specialties are smoked duck, spiced potatoes and 'two-flavored' shrimp. 226 Tatung 1st Rd.
川味四川　大同路226號

Hai Pa Wang (Sea King): a Taiwanese seafood restaurant with several branches around the island. Try baked mullet roe, fried clams, spicy clams and corn soup with seafood. 2, Hsingchung 2nd Rd. Tel 333-4486
海霸王　光中二路 2 號

Liu Jia Xiao Guan: offers reasonably priced Sichuan dishes. 52 Minsheng 1st Rd.
劉家小館　民生一路52號

KENTING

Numerous restaurants are on the main street. Good, but expensive, food is available at Ceasar's Park Hotel.

PULI

Try the numerous simple restaurants near the Taiwan Bus Co terminal.

SUN MOON LAKE

Most people eat at their hotels or at the restaurants near the bus terminal. Food is expensive here.

TAICHUNG

Shanghai Restaurant: serves specialties from Wuhsi, Jiangsu Province, including 'three-flavored' shrimp and spare ribs with brown sauce. 71 Chungcheng Rd. Tel 224141, 200735
上海餐廳　中正路71號

King Jade Restaurant: serves Cantonese food. 27 Kuanchien Rd. Tel 228-7777
金碧園　關權路27號

TAINAN

Beiping Yimu Yuan: north China dishes. 135 Tungning Rd. Tel 238-8720
北平一畝園　東寧路135號

Ronghsing: for spicy Sichuan food. 56 Chungcheng Rd. Tel 221-3134.
榮欣　中正路56號

Lao You (Old Friend): acclaimed for its excellent dumplings and other low-priced dishes. 268 Shengli Rd. Tel 234-7057.
老友　勝利路268號

Vegetarian Restaurant: simple and cheap; serves Buddhist vegetarian dishes. Next door to McDonald's on Tahsueh Rd.
天然素食館

Tian Xin Yan: an upmarket vegetarian restaurant, with moderate prices. 31 Minsheng Rd, Section 1. Tel 220-1206.
天心岩素食餐廳　民生路一段31號

There are dozens of inexpensive restau-

rants near Chengkung University, mainly on Tahsueh Rd and Shengli Rd.

TAIPEI

Taipei is a gourmet's paradise; long-time residents argue that the city has the best and most varied Chinese cuisine on the planet. In 1949, when the communists forced the nationalists off the mainland, some two million Chinese, hailing from every corner of the nation, came here. Many soon began earning a living by cooking their native specialties. Eating is one good reason to come to Taiwan.

■ BEIJING

Tao Jan Ting: Peking duck, cold plate, and other Beijing specialties. 16, Alley 9, Lane 49, Chunghsiao East Rd, Section 4, near Ding Hao.
忠孝東路四段49巷9弄16號

Celestial Kitchen: Peking duck and other north China specialties in bright, pleasant surroundings. 3rd Fl, 1 Nanking West Rd. Tel 563-2171
天廚　南京西路1號3樓

Genuine Peiping: One of the oldest Beijing restaurants in Taipei, with excellent Peking duck at reasonable prices. The restaurant is located in the run-down Chunghwa Market, but the great food still attracts old Beijing residents living in Taiwan. Chunghwa Market, Block 7, 2nd Fl. Tel 312-1001
眞北平　中華商場第七座二樓

Ching Chao I: An old Taipei favorite;

specializes in Beijing-style snacks, some of which date back to the Yuan and Tang dynasties. The restaurant serves delicate noodle dishes, such as *zha jiang mian*, served with soybean paste, ground pork, and cucumbers. Another good noodle dish is *lan rou mian*, noodles with stewed meat. Try the excellent sweet snacks: walnut and sesame pastes, lotus seeds with crystal sugar, violet rice cake, and fresh milk with fermented rice and sugar. There are two restaurants:
2, Lane 16, Lishui St. Tel 392-8833; and 21–2, Lane 107, Fuhsing South Rd, Section 1. Tel 721-8653
京兆尹　麗水街16巷2號
　　　　復興南路一段107巷21之2號

Tu I Chu: A fantastic Beijing restaurant, opposite Sun Yat-sen Memorial Hall. 506 Jenai Rd, Section 4. Tel 729-7853
都一處　仁愛路四段506號

■ JIANGZHE

Hsiulan: One of Taipei's oldest restaurants, a favorite of the island's mainland community; government officials often eat here. The Hsinyi branch, older of the two branches, was recently renovated, taking away its old charm. A bit expensive. 5–4, Lane 198, Hsinyi Rd, Section 2. Tel 394-3905; 118 Minsheng East Rd, Section 3. Tel 712-5775
秀蘭　信義路二段198巷5-4號
　　　民生東路三段118號

Ding Tai Feng: A very popular restaurant. Special dishes include: *xiao lung tang pao* (steamed buns stuffed with

Wufengchi Waterfall, Chaochi

crabmeat and pork); *luo mi xiao mai* (a delicious steamed dumpling stuffed with glutinous rice and topped with a dried shrimp); *cai rou zhen jiao* (steamed vegetable dumpling); *xia ren xiao mai* (shrimp wonton); and *hong xiao niu rou mian* (beef-stewed noodles with soup). Ding Tai Feng also serves a gingery beef broth and a delicate chicken broth. For dessert try *dou sha xiao bao* (tiny red bean paste buns) or *ba bao fan* ('eight treasures' rice—glutinous rice covered with eight types of candied preserved fruits). Avoid Sundays when there is a long waiting line. No English menu, but owners are friendly and helpful.
194 Hsinyi Rd, Section 2. Tel 321-8927
鼎泰豐　信義路二段194號

■ HUNAN

Pengyuan: Excellent spicy Hunan dishes. This busy restaurant is rather large and noisy. Private rooms are available for groups up to around 12. A banquet menu can be worked out in advance with the manager. 63 Nanking E Rd, Section 4. Tel 541-9102

澎園 南京東路四段63號

■ SICHUAN

Ronghsing: A Sichuan version of Pengyuan (above). 45 Chilin Rd. Tel 521-5340

榮欣川菜館 吉林路45號

■ TAIWANESE

Chi Chia Chuang: specialties include 'three-flavored' chicken, pig's heart, and *kou rou* (fatty pork cooked with salted dried vegetable). Just off Chungshan North Rd, at 45 Changchun Rd. Tel 581-4360

雞家莊 長春路45號

Hsing Yeh: 34–1 Shuangcheng St. Tel 596-3255

欣葉 雙城街34之1號

Tainan Tantzumian: Well-known for its seafood dishes and the most expensive noodles in Taiwan. The small restaurant has crystal chandeliers and Corinthian columns and serves its food on Wedgewood china; valet parking. 31 Hwahsi St. Tel 308-1123

台南担子麵 華西街31號

Papa's Lover: The clock has been turned back to the 1950's on the ground floor of this trendy Taiwanese restaurant, decorated with a mock barbershop, bicycle shop, pharmacy, nightclub and theatreticket window stand; all part of the owner's attempt to bring back the flavor of old Taiwan. 71 Hsinyi Rd, Section 3.

信義路三段71號

■ CANTONESE

An Lo Yuan: One of Taipei's best Cantonese restaurants. Try the roast pork, stir-fried garoupa and shrimp balls. 232 Tunhua North Rd. Tel 715-4929

安東園 敦化北路232號

■ YUNNAN

Jen Ho Yuan: 2nd Fl, 16 Nanking East Rd, Section 4. Tel 751-7236

南京東路四段16號2樓

■ VEGETARIAN

Fa Hua: 132 Minchuan East Rd, Section 3. Tel 717-5305

法華 民權東路三段132號

Mei Lin: 14 Peiping East Rd. Tel 391-0833

梅林 北平東路14號

■ MONGOLIAN BARBECUE

Ploughman's Inn: The downstairs of this English pub is probably the best Mongolian Barbecue restaurant in the city. About NT$300 per person. 8, Lane 460, Tunhua South Rd. Tel 773-3268

敦化南路460巷8號

■ MISCELLANEOUS

Xiao Jin Hua: A small restaurant with interesting dishes. Try the *niu rou da bing* (thinly sliced beef topped with a sauce and wrapped in thick pancakes), *dao xiao mian* (a thick doughy-type noodle sliced into boiling water and served with vegetables and meat), *xian bing* (a small fried beef pie), *mao er duo* ('cat's ears', small pasta triangles boiled and then fried with egg, tree fungus and vegetables), *rao bing*, a crispy layered bread eaten in place of rice. Two locations: 4, Lane 198, Hsinyi Rd, Section 2. Tel 396-7951; and 6, Hsinsheng South Rd, Section 3. Tel 366-0694

小金華 信義路二段198巷4號
京華園 新生南路三段6號

Shih Tou Chi: This restaurant is named after one of China's most famous novels, the Dream of the Red Chamber, and serves elaborate dishes described in the novel. It has a Chinese garden, and the furniture in the dining room is suggestive of the Tang Dynasty. Try *chieh-hsiang* (diced chicken with eggplant, mushrooms, bamboo shoots, dried tofu and assorted nuts), *lin-chung yu-tai* ('jade girdle in the forest': scallops and broccoli) or *chin-tsan wo-hsueh* ('golden hairpin lying on snow-clad ground': fried cuttlefish chips layered with white noodles). An à la carte meal for one costs around NT$400. The restaurant, known in English as Jane's Bungalow, also plans to stage afternoon folk art shows and musical performances. 87 Juian St. Tel (02) 702-5465

石頭記 瑞安街87號

Tangshan Chayan: A pleasant and beautifully decorated teahouse-restaurant specializing in noodles, a variety of steamed dumplings and snacks, and tea. The restaurant's small garden provides a relaxing atmosphere in the heart of Taipei. 4, Lane 11, Linsen South Rd, near the Lai Lai Sheraton.

唐山茶園 林森南路11巷4號

■ SWISS-GERMAN

Chalet Swiss: managed by Swiss restaurateur Horst Trummer, serves authentic Swiss-German cuisine. Reservations are a must. 47 Nanking East Rd, Section 4. Tel 715-2051

南京東路四段47號

■ ITALIAN

Casa Mia: 628 Linsen North Rd. Tel 596-4636

林森北路628號

■ INDONESIAN

Pulau Kelapa: an inexpensive Indonesian restaurant near National Taiwan University. 86 Tingchou Rd, Section 3. Tel 368-4717

椰島 丁州路三段86號

■ SRI LANKAN

Lanka: a small, family-run Sri Lankan restaurant in the city's northern part. 48 Chungyi St, Shihlin. Tel 832-0153

忠義街48號士林

■ THAI

Royal: 49 Jenai Rd, Section 2. Tel 351-0960

仁愛路二段49號

TAITUNG

There are numerous restaurants along Chunghua Rd. Take your pick.

TIENHSIANG

Tienhsiang Lodge: the only decent restaurant in town; closes at 7:30 pm.
天祥招待所

A cluster of small restaurants stand near the bus station. Food is also available at the Youth Activity Center. Tickets must be purchased 30 minutes before meals: breakfast begins at 7 am, lunch at noon and dinner at 6 pm.

TSAOLING

The choice in Tsaoling is limited to hotel restaurants and a few noodle stands and rice shops on the main road.

Useful Telephone Numbers

Board of Foreign Trade
Tel (02) 351-0271

China External Trade Development Council (CETRA)
Tel (02) 725-5200

CKS International Airport Tourist Service Center
Tel (03) 383-3666

Directory Assistance in English
Tel (02) 311-6769

Fire
Tel 119

The Foreign Affairs Police is the division of the National Police Administration that deals exclusively with foreigners. Most police officers in the division speak English. Taipei: Tel 311-9940; Taichung: Tel 241141; Kaohsiung: Tel 221-5796

Government Information Office
Tel (02) 322-8888

International Phone Assistance
Tel 100

Ministry of Foreign Affairs
Tel (02) 311-9292

Police
Tel 110

Taiwan Visitors Association
Tel (02) 594-3261

Tourism Bureau
Tel (02) 721-8541

Tourist Information Hot Line
Tel (02) 717-3737

Trader's Hot Line
Tel (02) 725-5960

Travel Information Service Center, Sungshan Domestic Airport
Tel (02) 514-2688

Recommended Reading

History

Davidson, James. *The Island of Formosa, Past and Present* (Taipei: Southern Materials Center, 1988). The author served as a war correspondent with the Japanese Army during the 1895 takeover of Taiwan. He was later appointed US Consul for Taiwan, during which he devoted eight years to writing this book, first published in 1903.

Goddard, W G *Formosa: A Study in Chinese History* (London: Macmillian, 1966)

Crozier, Ralph. *Koxinga and Chinese Nationalism: History, Myth, and the Hero* (Cambridge: Harvard University Press, 1977)

Kerr, George. *Formosa Betrayed* (Boston: Houghton Mifflin, 1965). An account of the February 28th Incident.

Campbell, William. *Formosa under the Dutch* (Taipei: Chengwen, 1967)

Meskill, Johanna. *A Chinese Pioneer Family: The Lins of Wufeng 1729–1895* (Princeton: Princeton University Press, 1979)

Politics

Copper, John. *Taiwan: Nation State or Province ?* (Boulder: Westview Press, 1990)

Fiction

Sneider, Vern *A Pale of Oysters* (London: Harborough Publishing, 1958)

Guides to Living in Taiwan

Cole, Dorothy Orr . *Quest for the Best in Taiwan* (Taipei: China Commercial Service, 1991)

Community Services Center. *Taipei Living* (Taipei: Community Services Center, 1991)

Travel

Mooney, Paul. *Taipei* (Singapore: Times Editions, 1988)

Reid, Daniel. Insight Guides: *Taiwan* (Hong Kong: APA Publications, 1989)

Storey, Robert. *Travel Survival Kit: Taiwan* (Hawthorn: Lonely Planet Publications, 1990)

General

Bo, Yang. *The Ugly Chinamen and the Crisis of Chinese Culture.* Translated and edited by Don J Cohn. (Sydney: Allen & Unwin, 1992)

Index